# IN THE FOOTSTEPS
# OF THE LINCOLNS

FIREPLACE IN HISTORICAL MUSEUM OF HINGHAM, MASS., FIRST AMERICAN HOME OF THE LINCOLNS. THE LINCOLNS LANDED ABOUT 1637

By such a fireplace seven successive generations of Lincolns plied their industries, read their books, and knelt in prayer

# IN THE FOOTSTEPS OF THE LINCOLNS

*By*

## IDA M. TARBELL

AUTHOR OF "HE KNEW LINCOLN," "LIFE OF ABRAHAM LINCOLN,"
"IN LINCOLN'S CHAIR"

*Illustrated*

PUBLISHERS

HARPER & BROTHERS

NEW YORK AND LONDON

MCMXXIV

# CONTENTS

[v]

# CONTENTS

# LIST OF ILLUSTRATIONS

[vii]

# LIST OF ILLUSTRATIONS

# PREFACE

This book reports a pilgrimage undertaken to refresh and enlarge the author's previous studies of the life of Abraham Lincoln. The pilgrimage began in Hingham, Massachusetts, where two hundred eighty-six years ago the first of the family line, Samuel Lincoln, a boy of seventeen, came as a pioneer; it passed from there to New Jersey, Pennsylvania, the Shenandoah Valley of Virginia, into Kentucky, Indiana, Illinois.

I found it an inspiring thing to trace the roads these seven successive generations of Lincoln pioneers traveled, to look upon the remains of their homes, reconstruct from documents and legends their activities, judge what manner of men and women they were, the place they held among their fellows. In these wanderings the whole history of the United States seemed to unroll before me. In this Lincoln migration we have the family history of millions of our contemporaries.

And this story of their vigorous, independent pioneering, their passion for self-help and self-rule, goes far to account for Abraham Lincoln. He was not an accident. These Lincolns were behind him, preparing for the miracle.

Not only has this pilgrimage given me at least a partial explanation of Abraham Lincoln, it has broken down more than one accepted tradition of his youth and his immediate forebears. There is the old notion that Thomas Lincoln, his father, was a shiftless vagrant, poor in mind and spirit. There is abundant evidence to show the tradition a libel. Thomas Lincoln was the child of an advancing pioneer army.

[ix]

PREFACE

His father fell in that advance, shot by Indians. The boy,
orphaned, made himself a place in a new country, acquired
land, became a good craftsman, held various local offices,
was a trustee of his church—its moderator and committeeman
again and again—a trusted, respected man. In the end he
fell a victim to disease—attacked at fifty, he never rallied.
We do not despise the soldier who in a front line of battle
is wounded, gassed, shocked beyond action. We pity and
honor him. Thomas Lincoln was a pioneer soldier, a victim
of the conditions under which the advance was made.

Again there is the tradition that Abraham Lincoln's childhood and youth were passed in hopeless and sordid poverty
and hardship. There were poverty and hardship, but they
were never hopeless, therefore never sordid. They were regarded as a necessary stage in the great undertaking of opening, taming, and developing a new land. These men knew
what they sought. To treat them as vagrants is to fail to
understand the spirit of the pioneer. Abraham Lincoln's
youth was passed in one of the most daring and promising
struggles to which American men have ever put their hands.
He weathered it, expanded under it, saw the meaning of it
—and flung himself into the struggle to realize literally the
great creed of Liberty for which his forebears had made their
sacrifices.

As the attempt to trace the footsteps of these forebears
has broken down for me the "poor white" tradition, so the
attempt to follow anew Lincoln's footsteps through his Illinois life has intensified my feeling that his rise to power was
one of the most logical in our history. It was the natural
triumph of an active, ambitious imagination, of a stern purpose
to develop both mind and character and to drive them in the

[x]

# PREFACE

same harness, of a passion for fair play and free opportunity.
Great mental and moral qualities, rigorously trained and kept
steadily at work, brought Abraham Lincoln naturally into the
Presidency of the United States, where this book leaves him.

I. M. T.

# IN THE FOOTSTEPS
# OF THE LINCOLNS

# LINCOLN

*In him distilled and potent the choice essence of a race!*
*Far back the Puritans—stern and manful visionaries,*
*Repressed poets, flushed with dreams of glowing theologies!*
*Each new succession, out of border hardship,*
*Refined to human use the initial rigor of the breed,*
*Passing to the next the unconscious possession of a perfecting soul!*
*Each forest clearing gave something of neighborly grace,*
*The rude play of cabin-bred natural people something of humor,*
*Each mountain home something of inner daring,*
*Each long-wandering life something of patience and of hope!*
*In the open, far-seen nature gradually chiseled*
*The deepening wistful eyes.*
*Each axman and each plowman added*
*Another filament of ruggedness;*
*Unknowing minds dumbly cried for liberty;*
*Mute hearts strove against injustice. . . .*

*At last was ready the alembic, where Nature stored and set apart*
*Each generation's finest residue,*
*Waiting for the hour of perfect mixture—*
*And then the Miracle!*

JOHN S. PHILLIPS.

1908

# IN THE FOOTSTEPS OF THE LINCOLNS

## I

### THE FIRST LINCOLNS IN AMERICA

THE story of Abraham Lincoln begins in Hingham, Massachusetts, in the year 1637, when the first of his family line came to the Puritan colony of Boston Bay. This was his great-great-great-great-grandfather, Samuel by name, a boy of but seventeen or eighteen at the time—such a boy as we would send to high school or college in these days.

Young as Samuel Lincoln was, he was not without some experience of life. He had sat on a backless bench in a seventeenth-century schoolroom in Hingham, England, and received his share of its narrow but thorough teaching. And, because he was to earn his living, and weaving was the natural trade for a boy in Norfolk County, England, at that time, he had been apprenticed—apprenticed to a man by the name of Francis Lawes, living in Norwich, not many miles from Hingham.

When you were apprenticed in those days, you left your family and became a member of your master's family. You had more to do than to learn to weave. In fact, you were what was called an indentured servant. Mr. Lawes was under contract to teach Samuel the trade and to give him his keep and a small—probably a very small—weekly or monthly sum. Samuel in turn was obliged to obey Mr. Lawes, and that meant not only that he must learn to weave, but he must wait on the family. If the family was ungenerous and domineering, it is easy to see that the apprentices had a bad time. Indeed, they had so bad a time that only a few years after Samuel left England there was what was called the "Apprentices' Revolt"—strike, we should probably say to-day. It produced the state of things which led Daniel Defoe to complain that while once apprentices cleaned their masters' shoes and brought in water and waited at the table, now their masters were obliged to keep porters, or "fetch men," as he calls them, to wait upon the apprentices.

Samuel did not profit by the apprentices' strike, for, in 1637, Francis Lawes decided to go to America and to take him along. It was in April that they "passed into foreign parts," as the record has it—a long voyage, over two months —and in June arrived in Salem, Massachusetts. Samuel did not stay in Salem. Before many weeks he took ship for a town twenty miles or thereabouts to the south, called Hingham, or New Hingham, after his old home in Norfolk County, England.

I say "took ship," and that is sure, for in those days he could not have gone overland. Safe trails had not yet been established, and there was no way to cross so wide a river as the Charles; but of fishing and trading boats there were already not a few plying along the coast. And it was in one of those that Samuel sailed out one day from Salem.

What a sail—that from Salem into Hingham Bay—to take before man had slashed the great timber that came down to the very water's edge of many a promontory and island, before he had seized the rocks and bluffs of Boston Harbor for his lights and marks, his guns and forts, his factories and chimneys!

The bay into which Samuel came is one of rare interest

and beauty. You make it coming from the north by turning around the tip of that curved finger of land we know as Hull. Across its water to the south lies a cove, Bare Cove, the first settlers called it, and it was into this that the vessel on which Samuel was a passenger made its way.

Bare Cove ran up between two high bluffs in those days, a snug and sheltered water where now are asphalted streets, railroad tracks, rows of houses and shops. Indeed, one of the most puzzling things for a sightseer in Hingham to-day is to read on a tablet, high and dry, above a street along which automobiles run, and a block and more away from the present wharf, the fact that Peter Hobart, about whom we are to hear later, debarked on that spot in September, 1635.

Samuel hardly stopped, however, to look about him in his first moment. It had been months now since he left Old Hingham, and in that time he had seen few old friends; but here, awaiting him on the wharf, were many, among them two of his brothers, Thomas, the oldest of the family, a weaver, his brother Daniel, only two or three years older than himself, and with them a cousin, Nicholas Jacob. All three of these men had been in Massachusetts nearly four years, and already were householders and landholders in New Hingham.

Why were they here—these brothers of his—this cousin? Why was this tiny New Hingham made up of people from Old Hingham? We have been taught to say that it was because they sought a place in which they could worship God according to the dictates of their own consciences. It is an incomplete explanation.

True, these people that Samuel had joined and their forbears for generations had been struggling in England to escape the tyranny of priests and prelates, to secure the right to own and read the Bible, to interpret it in their own way,

[3]

to make and say their own prayers, and to do away with the complicated ceremonial that, in their judgment, the Church had substituted for righteousness of heart.

They had been struggling, too, for a government in which they could have a full representation, for the right to run their own local affairs, to hold meetings, improve their schools, own their land. Their struggle had had its ups and downs, and from the point of view of many of them was at this time almost hopeless. When Samuel left England it had been eight years since there had been a meeting of Parliament, Charles I having shut the doors on its members in 1629.

All these things go into the explanation of their migration, and it was these things, fought over year after year, that had broken down old institutions, destroyed industries, driven out much of the skilled management that heretofore had directed affairs, until finally the agricultural and industrial machine, particularly of the eastern part of England, had been thrown into such confusion that self-support was almost impossible. The group that Samuel joined in New Hingham left Old Hingham largely because they were no longer able to earn a decent living there.

But there was much more with Samuel, and probably most of the young. There was adventure. What more royal adventure has the world ever offered than this of crossing a mysterious ocean to a continent only a fragment of whose shore line had been charted—a continent inhabited by a strange people—a continent where, so it was believed, there was fabulous wealth for the taking?

At the time of Samuel's coming the Hingham "Plantation," as the settlements were called, numbered perhaps fifty people—there were only about 14,000 in all the New England colonies. Every month this number increased, and what was of interest to Samuel was that he knew so many of the people that came.  Most important of all these early arrivals was that of Robert Peck, the minister who is supposed to have baptized him in 1622 in England, and to have brought him up in the strictest Puritan way.  Robert Peck had been one of the most uncompromising of his faith—one who could be counted on boldly to disobey any order of a bishop of which he did not approve.  He would not preach in a surplice.  He would not read the "Book of Sports" which the Church authorities thought would be good for the Puritans—a seventeenth-century attempt to introduce the continental Sunday into England.  Particularly he would not consent that the communion table be removed from the nave of the church, where everybody could reach it, to its former place of honor at the end of the chancel.  And when, in 1634, the archbishop thought himself strong enough politically and ecclesiastically to force the table back into its old place, and the order was carried out in the Old Hingham church, Robert Peck rose in holy indignation and called his parishioners together.  There is little doubt that Samuel was in the group, or on its outskirts, that dragged the altar from its new place, stripped it of its gilding and candles, and actually lowered the floor of the chancel several inches below that of the nave.

Robert Peck had to pay the price of his continued revolting.  He was stripped of his living—ex-communicated.  There was nothing for him to do, so he thought, but to follow the Puritans to the New World.

And this he did in 1638, landing only a few months after Samuel.

His going was a dreadful loss to Old Hingham.  But what was a tragedy to Old Hingham was a blessing to New, for Robert Peck became their first teacher, and to see him going in and out among the little houses of New Hingham must have done much to make life more natural for young Samuel.

Another early arrival that meant much to him was that of Daniel Cushing, a young man near his own age, with whom he had no doubt gone to school and to church and played whatever proper games Robert Peck had tolerated in Old Hingham. He was a young man of ambition and energy —a very human person, too. He ran a general store, became town clerk, grew prosperous and influential in New Hingham. The most satisfactory record of what went on in the town that we have is Daniel Cushing's account book, in which he not only set down his daily transactions, but many of the doings of his neighbors—the time that Israel Leavett abused Mr. Norton and his wife with "base speeches"; the time his boy got drunk at Enoch Hobart's; the case set down in a numerical alphabet he sometimes used of a hasty marriage, a premature birth, the kind of thing that proves to us that the Puritans, with all their severity, never succeeded in suppressing drunkenness or immorality—makes us suspicious, indeed, that their very severity may have stimulated what they sought to root out.

It humanizes one's ideas of Hingham no little to know that there were men of Daniel Cushing's journalistic bent in the community. Samuel Lincoln and he must have talked over things in the town many a day, much in the fashion, I fancy, that a couple of hundred years later, a great-great-great-great-grandson of Samuel's was to gossip and discuss in a country store of southwestern Indiana, a country store over which he presided in New Salem, Illinois, and, later still, in a drug store on the square in Springfield, Illinois. Daniel Cushing was just about the same kind of a man to talk with that Abraham Lincoln found in all of these towns.

When Samuel Lincoln arrived in Hingham it was little more than a collection of log houses, strung along a brook which flowed into the head of Bare Cove—one of those clear,

[6]

musical, New England brooks, bounding down over the rocks, through narrow meadows of high lush grass—a brook which to-day, unhappily, one would not know was in existence, so thoroughly has it been boxed in for the convenience of the town.

The valley in which the little settlement lay was narrow, steep hills rising on each side, clothed with timber—primeval timber—oak, hemlock, walnut, shagbark, ash, beech, cedar, elm, wonderful woods to work with. Across from the main group of houses, to the south of the brook, "on an eminence," stood the church, of logs, thatched, and, soon after Samuel's arrival, to be surrounded by a palisade.

One of the first things Samuel had to learn was why it was necessary to have a citadel in this little settlement, and why military service was required of every one that had reached his age and strength. The settlers then—and indeed through all his life—had to keep the Indian constantly in mind. Samuel was not allowed to go a mile from his home without his musket. When he went to church or to a town meeting, he must go armed. There was a compensating convenience, for bullets were legal tender, passing freely for farthings. He took his turn at the guard that was set at sunset. He learned, too, the Indian method of warfare, fighting behind trees. To perfect her militia in this, Hingham early forbade the cutting of the big timber in certain sections in the town—it was kept for training purposes. One part of the furnishing of Hingham church was a barrel of powder, always kept full. So at the very start of Samuel's life in the new world, there was the thrill of danger and the responsibility of doing his part to meet it.

Samuel's first problem was to find work. There was no chance for him at his trade. A man could not be spared at that moment for weaving. The settlers' looms, what there

[7]

were of them, had been turned over to the women. But if there was no work at his trade, there was plenty of other kinds. It was nip and tuck to raise corn enough for the winter, to catch and salt enough fish, to cut wood for the fire, to build the new houses that the rapidly increasing population demanded. New Hingham was growing, and a strong young man was in demand.

There was work in near-by settlements, too, when the town consented that one go. There was Scituate, only about ten miles to the southeast, several years older than Hingham. There were Braintree and Hull, near neighbors. There was Boston, rapidly growing, and demanding timbers, planks, boards. There were young shipyards at various points, ready to take masts. Then, too, a lively exchange of commodities was soon going on with the English settlements to the south in Virginia and the West Indies. We often forget, in reckoning the chances that the New England settlers had for trade, the excellent market provided by their own people in the Barbadoes, Bermuda, St. Kitts, Old and New Providence. As a matter of fact, when Samuel Lincoln began his business career in New Hingham, there were four times as many English people in the South and the West Indian colonies as in all of New England.

In 1644 Samuel Lincoln's brother, Daniel, a bachelor, died and left everything he had to Samuel. It helped him to buy a five-acre tract of land in one of the best locations along the brook, as one can see, going into Hingham to-day. As you come in on the train from Boston you cannot miss, looking out at the right, a glittering white statute of Daniel Webster, standing in a beautifully kept flower garden. These are the fields once owned by Samuel Lincoln, and up the street a little farther stands an old house on the site of the one that he built—or bought—in 1649. Nothing of the original is left except some of the timbers.

Into this house Samuel took a wife. All that we know of her is that her name was Martha. A nice problem for ambitious young genealogists is to solve the family name of the woman that Samuel Lincoln married. She must have been a vigorous woman, for she was splendidly equal to the chief duty the settlement of a new country lays on women, the bearing of many healthy children. Her first son was born in 1650 and baptized Samuel. In twenty-three years Martha brought into the world eleven children. Advocates of birth control may raise their hands in horror and expect to find records of death accompanying those of birth. Three of Martha's children did not grow up, but eight lived for seventy years or thereabouts. And as for Martha herself, she outlived Samuel, dying in 1693.

Though there is nothing but a few old timbers left of the home in which Samuel and Martha reared their family, it is not difficult to reconstruct it. A house of stout timbers, the very heart of which was the great fireplace, with its wide hearth and deep oven, its shelf for dishes and cranes for pots, its curved settees at either side, a candle shelf in the middle of each high back, making cozy ingle nooks for the children and their elders. Before this fireplace food was prepared and eaten. Before it the family gathered to carry on a score of simple industries. Before it they talked, popped their corn, and melted their maple sugar. Before it, too, they knelt morning and night for prayer.

No doubt among the iron and pewter and wooden utensils preserved to-day so carefully in New England by descendants of the settlers, there are articles that Samuel and Martha used; but, so far as I have been able to find, there are only two in existence which we can say with any certainty were once

[9]

in their hands. These are a big and a little wooden mortar, with their pestles, owned, as is proper, by descendants of one of the early Hingham Lincolns. But if we cannot put our hands on the chairs, the tables, the bedsteads and coverlets, the Dutch oven and toasting fork, the wooden porringer, the plates and saucers that they used, we can to-day with certainty see what they were like in the town's excellent museum.

In Hingham, as in all of the Massachusetts colonies of that day, the minister was the ruling spirit. The character, the intelligence, the tolerance or intolerance of the community depended largely upon him. When a man was a member of the church—and he had no standing in the community if he was not a member, not even being allowed to vote in civil affairs—his thinking and actions were largely shaped by the minister. Luckily for Samuel, and I think for his descendants, the minister under whom he sat was far and away from being the worst of the Puritans. The Reverend Peter Hobart had an independent spirit and a more liberal mind than the men at the head of the government and many of the ministers of the Colonies.

He was devoted to his parish. Much of the little documentary evidence of what went on in the town in Samuel's day comes from Peter Hobart's habit of setting down what happened from day to day. His diary, carefully done up in red morocco, has found a safe place in the files of the Massachusetts Historical Society.

It is a book well worth looking at—bound in wizened leather, a homemade binding, I take it, from the way the leather is folded over the pasteboard cover and from the narrow leather thongs that bind it—a wonderful thing to get your hands on if you care for ink and paper and the way they stand up under time. I have seen two manuscript copies of Peter Hobart's diary, the one made perhaps forty, the other fifty, years ago, and in both of them the ink and paper are faded and old, compared with the original, the first entry of which was made at least 287 years ago, with the introductory remark: "I with my wife and four chyldren Came safely to New England June ye 8: 1635: for ever praysed be the god of Heaven, my god and king."

On almost every page of the book one finds a Lincoln— born, married, died—a populous, growing line. These were not all kin to Samuel, by any means, for to Hingham there had come just before or after he did other Lincolns, distantly, if at all, related. Indeed, there were at least eight settlers of the name—sturdy people. To-day, as in Samuel's day, the most frequent name in the town records of Hingham— including the telephone book—is Lincoln.

The fact that Samuel Lincoln was and remained a church member throughout his life is proof enough that he walked a straight and narrow path. Life was a serious matter under Peter Hobart—a matter of strictest rules, that the church authorities saw to it that you obeyed or knew the reason why. There was no escape from church going, for every Sunday morning a church officer went from house to house, running in idlers. There was no sleeping in church, for at every service a hawk-eyed watchman sat in the rear of the great bare room, knocking the head of any man who dozed with a pole, tickling the ear of any woman with a feather. You must at least appear to listen to Peter Hobart's two-hour sermons on fallen man, an angry God, election, damnation, eternal fire.

Severe and forbidding as it all sounds, life must have been, in the main, healthy and full of interest. Theological discussions exercise the mind if they do not entertain it. There is a curious kind of pleasure in horrors, and no doubt the orgies of terror in which the early Puritans indulged had their fascination.

Their religion, too, was not of a kind which made men inexpressive or servile. Under Peter Hobart's leadership, indeed, it was just the opposite. Samuel has been but a few years in Hingham when the town was enlivened by a quarrel with the General Court, a sort of colonial council at Boston, which set them all by the ears: a test—most necessary at the moment—of how far central authority was to interfere with local liberty.

The trouble arose over the captaincy of Hingham's company of militia. The majority of the town fell out with the man who had held the position for some time and elected a successor. The General Court refused to ratify. Peter Hobart led in a revolt against this decision, and signed a petition asking reconsideration. Governor Winthrop and the magistrates resented this questioning of their authority. There was a trial—a trial which went against Hingham and led to the fining of a number of the citizens, Peter Hobart among them. Hobart was loud in contempt; there was no reason for the fine, he said, except that he had signed a petition, and he hinted that the General Court was going beyond the powers of its charter, not only in this case, but others.

All of this, of course, only stiffened the backs of the authorities. Hobart was a marked man. On a later occasion, when the ministers of the colony had been summoned to consultation, he was ordered out of the meeting. And again, when a great marriage of a former Hingham resident was to be solemnized at Boston, and Hobart was asked to come and preach, the magistrate sent him home. The reason they gave was that he was a "bold man and would speak his mind."

The quarrel was a long time in subsiding. The minority

which backed up the central authorities claimed that the development of Hingham was seriously injured by its spirit of revolt. However, what they may have lost in numbers was balanced by a vigorous spirit which continued unafraid to challenge even ecclesiastical authority if their rights were invaded.

Just as Samuel Lincoln was obliged to consider where local authority should end and central authority begin, so he was early obliged to consider that standing question of the relative rights of rich and poor. Almost immediately the unenfranchised settlers—and they made up four-fifths of the people—had lined themselves up against the ruling few. Again and again the struggle shows itself in the records of the doings of the magistrates.

A classical case is that of Mrs. Sherman, who had lost a sow. Runaway animals, particularly pigs, were one of the chief annoyances of the early settlers, and it is not to be wondered that a stray was often captured and confined by the husbandman prosperous enough to provide himself with pens. Mrs. Sherman had no pen, and she brought suit against a neighbor who, she believed, had captured the animal she had lost. The documents in the case seemed to show that the lady did not have satisfactory evidence that the sow she claimed was hers, and yet, in spite of this, the deputies stood by her—she was poor, the man she sued was rich.

Indians, damnation, infant baptism, the rich against the poor, the tyranny of the General Court—these were the questions that Samuel Lincoln was forced to consider and decide—questions that kept his and his neighbors' minds active—not altogether peaceful subjects, but stout ones, fit for men, bound to develop grit, character.

Unhappily, not all of the Hingham discussions in which Samuel Lincoln must have taken part were as worthy in substance as these. In the later years of his life, Hingham was rent in twain by a row over the site of a new church—a common enough happening among the Puritans. Indeed, Cotton Mather complains that in the Colonies "the rebuilding and removing of meeting houses unfitted neighbors for lifting up pure hands without wrath in those houses." It certainly did so in Hingham.

A new meeting house had become necessary. It was estimated that it would cost £450, besides what could be gotten for the old building. In 1680 a subscription was taken up to which 143 members put their names. Samuel and his sons did very well, putting in, between them, something like £5. Then came the question of the site. It was to be changed, and there was sharp division of opinion. In 1681 the constable took a vote "for another place to get ye new meeting house on." The majority ruled, but the feud has never quite died out. "If they had not put the meeting house there," I once heard a Hinghamite say!

However, that meeting house, built in 1681 with the money that Samuel and his sons and his neighbors subscribed, still stands; its splendid timbers, sound and seasoned, are to be seen in its loft. It has been enlarged, to be sure, ceiled, made comfortable in many ways unknown to Samuel's day, but its bones and sinews are the same. And it has the distinction of being the oldest meeting house in this country, to have been in continuous use for as long as 240 years.

Samuel Lincoln worshiped in it to the end of his life. That end came on May 26, 1690. Under that date, Daniel Cushing put down in his account book: "old Sam Linkoln dyed of the smallpox." Dread disease—the only disease one finds mentioned in Peter Hobart's diary or Daniel Cushing's account book.

Samuel undoubtedly was buried in the family lot in the

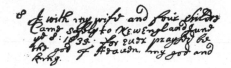

OPENING ENTRY OF THE DIARY OF REV. PETER HOBART

RECORD OF SAMUEL LINCOLN'S DEATH FOUND IN DANIEL CUSHING'S ACCOUNT BOOK

"OLD SHIP CHURCH" OF HINGHAM, MASS., BUILT IN 1681 AND IN CONTINUOUS USE FOR
MORE THAN 240 YEARS

old cemetery, but no mark of his grave nor of that of Martha, his wife, nor of the three babies she lost, exists to-day. Hingham seems to have gone through a period of vandalism in the latter part of the eighteenth and early part of the nineteenth centuries, when its chief idea was to rid itself as completely and as rapidly as possible of the old graveyard and all that was in it, above and below the ground. I do not know that I have ever come across any more ruthless treatment than this that Hingham gave to the graves of the men and women who had broken the first ground and put up the first houses and built the first church, as well as the church of which they are so proud to-day. They wanted the land, wanted it for shops and an easier approach to the bluffs beyond, so they hacked down the hill, dumping bones and headstones into something like a garbage heap as they went. Hingham's boys and girls of the early nineteenth century remembered the old burial ground as a cow pasture, with heaps of broken coffins, fragments of shrouds and decaying bones scattered about. They played push ball on the flat tombstones and fought Indian battles among the graves of their fathers.

The old slate headstones, one of which undoubtedly belonged to Samuel, were many of them sold. There are at least two chimneys to be seen in Hingham to-day into which it is known that headstones went, and I was told on a visit to the town in 1922 that only a short time before, when repairs were making on the old dye house, the great doorstep —a fine piece of stone—was turned over, only to discover that it was the headstone of one of the Rev. Peter Hobart's family.

But Samuel Lincoln, though dead and his bones unhonored, did not pass out of the life of New Hingham. He left behind four sons, grown, and four daughters. These

[15]

children he had seen married into the best of Hingham's families. In the old home in which he died his oldest son, his namesake, was living, and there, sitting at the fireside, was his grandson, Samuel. He was not to know it, but it was to be true, that out of the line of this oldest son were to come some of the most distinguished of New England's citizens, among them three governors of commonwealths. He was not to know, but it is true, that from another of his sons, the one whose acquaintance we shall now make, was to come the man who was to contribute, as much as any man which this or any other country has produced, to the solution of those tangled problems of liberty and authority, of the rich and the poor, of tolerance and intolerance, with which he had been forced to grapple in those early days.

## II

WHEN Samuel Lincoln came to New Hingham in 1637, the settlements of the Massachusetts Colony and its neighbor, Plymouth, to the south, were but little more than scraps of human fringe along the Atlantic coast. The problem of the newcomers was to strengthen the footholds which they made and to widen, stretch, and unite them. This meant for their children that some should stay at home, that others should go north or west or south. Of Samuel and Martha Lincoln's four sons it fell to the oldest, the father's namesake, to stay in the old homestead in Hingham, to ply his trade, which was that of a carpenter, and to Daniel, the second, to cultivate the lands there which had come into the family by purchase, allotment, or inheritance.

It fell to the other three sons to go out from their home town and extend the work of settlement. It is with the third, Mordecai, we are concerned, because he was to carry down the line to Abraham Lincoln.

In 1655, Martha had given birth to a baby boy that had lived only about three weeks. She called the child Mordecai. Two years later she bore another boy, and him, too, she called Mordecai. It was a practice common enough in those days, this carrying on of a name. Indeed, back in England, it had not been uncommon for two living children to be called by the same name, senior and junior being used to distinguish them.

Little Mordecai had the training that Hingham was giving to all its boys and girls—eleven months and two weeks steady

[17]

of school. The teacher, whose pay, so the records show, was twenty-four bushels of grain, paid quarterly, taught the children not only their three R's, but a little of Latin and Greek. It was severe teaching. No modern ideas softened it, and the only appeal that was made to the imagination was the appeal of terror. In all New England at this date there was scarcely a book—and certainly none within the reach of boys and girls—lighter in weight than the *Doomsday Book*.

Mordecai went to church as well as to school, and sat through two-hour sermons. He listened to them, too, for he knew well enough that both at home and at school he would be catechised on their content.

It takes more than a scowling church and a stern schoolmaster to kill joy in well-fed youth. Mordecai Lincoln's home overran with youth, brothers and sisters tumbling over one another. The town was full of youth, and there was the wonderful out-of-doors. The Puritan fathers probably did not approve of the beauty of the New England spring, the warmth of its summer, the glory and languor of its autumn, nor the warm tingling of blood that the cold of winter brought; but they could not destroy them, nor prevent the stir and the happiness they brought to the heart of the young.

Mordecai Lincoln grew up a husky boy, full of energy—the kind that is eager to move on, to strike out for himself. He must have a trade, and he chose that of blacksmithing. Why he should have left Hingham and gone across the bay to Hull to learn blacksmithing, I do not know. Possibly there was a better chance there, but I like to think it was a girl who was drawing him. At least, if it was not before he went to Hull that he met Sarah Jones and found that she was the one for him of all the daughters of the coast, he discovered it soon after, and married her.

# MORDECAI LINCOLN, IRONMASTER

The Jones family to which Sarah belonged had come to New Hingham about the same time that Samuel Lincoln did, and later established themselves at Hull, where Sarah had 'been born and reared. She and Mordecai remained in Hull some years, and there, or possibly across the bay at Martha Lincoln's, her first two children were born. The elder, who came in 1686, Sarah named after his father, Mordecai; the second, two years younger, she called after her father, Abraham—the first Abraham in the Lincoln family.

There is every reason to suppose that Mordecai Lincoln prospered in Hull, but he was not the kind of a man to remain at a forge which was not his own. Why should he not have a forge of his own? Why should he not become an ironmaster? He began to look about for a site, with power, somewhere outside of Hull. And, naturally enough, he looked toward a new Hingham development, Cohasset, where already his older brother, Daniel, was settled, and where there was every prospect of a thriving independent town.

What a human story is the settlement of Cohasset! The township that we now know under that name lay next to the sea on the southern border of the Plantation of Hingham. Just to its south was the northernmost settlement of Plymouth Colony, Scituate. Between the two a natural boundary lay, a bay and a long salt inlet with great marshes covered with rich salt grass. The boundary between this part of Hingham (Cohasset) and Scituate had not been fixed at the start, and there was, naturally enough, much contention over the fine uplands and these rich marshes. The very year that Samuel landed in the new world the two colonies had appointed a commission—so far as I know the first intercolonial commission appointed in what was to be New England—to fix this boundary.

There were great names on that commission—John Endicott, Governor Bradford, Edward Winslow. They fixed a brook, flowing into the salt inlet—Bound Brook, it is called —as the dividing line. Scituate was never satisfied with the decision and frequently pulled up the stakes that the Hinghamites had set and cut grass that they claimed. There was bickering for years over this boundary. As a matter of fact, it took two hundred years to settle it finally, and it is easy enough among old settlers in those parts to-day to get up a heated discussion over the settlement finally made.

The Hinghamites not only quarreled with Scituate over the Cohasset hills and meadows, they quarreled with one another about the use of them. As soon as the hay was cut it was customary to send their dry cattle, many hogs and goats, there to pasture; and, although the town kept a herdsman to look after these animals, they were constantly mixing, and disputes over the ownership of a sow, a heifer, a goat disturbed the peace of the community.

The value of these common lands and the trouble that grew out of a general use of them caused strong pressure, of course, for their division. It took a long time to hit upon a plan to which every one would agree. Finally the tract was cut up into seven hundred shares, and then there was a drawing by lot. Samuel Lincoln and his family came off well in this drawing, as any one can see that examines the original plot. Mordecai's older brother, Daniel, took advantage of the new property. He was one of the first persons to build a house in Cohasset. This was in 1685.

It was natural enough, then, with the family holdings that lay in Cohasset, and with Daniel in a fair way to become one of the settlement's leading citizens, that Mordecai should look about in that vicinity for a site for his proposed water power.

A couple of miles from his brother Daniel's place he

found what he wanted—a little fall where Bound Brook leaps into an arm of the salt inlet, called the Gulf. Here was power to be had by building a dam. A half interest in this fall, in enough of the brook for a pond and enough land on which to put a mill, Mordecai bought in 1691 for $35. And here he soon had a sawmill.

On the rising land above the marshes on the Cohasset side he built a house—a hip-roofed house with long sloping rear, burned only a few years ago. The new home looked out over the marshes and to the mouth of Bound Brook, where Mordecai had made his pond and built his mill. To this house he brought Sarah and his two boys.

But this mill did not satisfy Mordecai. He followed up the stream to a second dip in the water, and there he built a dam and a grist mill; and then still farther up to a place where a little island rises in Bound Brook, and here he built a third dam, this time for a forge.

There are times in the year when Bound Brook has no great flow of water, and it became Mordecai's problem to so utilize what did come that he could run each one of his three plants at least two days of a week. The scheme he worked out won him fame through all the Hingham and Scituate settlements.

On Saturday night he closed his upper dam in such a way as to save all the water that came down. By Monday morning there was enough to run his upper mill for two days. By closing the second dam, he could hold this water so that he could run mill number two for two days. He repeated the process at the lowest dam, at the mouth of the brook. That is, during all the dry season, so the story runs, Mordecai Lincoln had water to run his three mills a part of each week.

His best title to fame, however, is not this ingenious manner of handling water. It was the fact—and a fact to

[21]

be noticed in the industrial history of the United States—
that this great-great-great-grandfather of Abraham Lincoln
was one of the first ironmasters in the country; that is, one
of the first men who actually made iron.

At his upper dam he and a group of neighbors started a
furnace. The ore that he used he brought from the bogs to
the south in the township of Pembroke, some ten miles away.
It was what is known as bog iron—moor iron, the English
call it. It lay in lumps of moderate size—lumps full of
holes, much of it so soft that it could be crushed between
the fingers.

Down in this Pembroke district, where Mordecai Lincoln
went for his iron ore, lived a man whose name arouses speculation to-day—Benjamin Hanks. Were he and Mordecai
friends? Hanks was one of the leading Pembroke citizens,
and he must have been a man of imagination, a lover of
the sea and exposed sites, for a few years later it was he
who bought Saquish Head, looking northwest across Duxbury
Bay to Captain's Hill, where the Standish monument stands,
southwest to Plymouth. Benjamin Hanks took his family
here and built a home, which still stands. It is believed by
many, though they are unable to give convincing documentary
evidence of their belief, that this man was the first American
ancestor of Nancy Hanks, the mother of Abraham Lincoln.

For smelting the Pembroke ore, Mordecai, of course, had
to have charcoal—not a difficult thing to get, with an
abundance of the best woods for that purpose all about him.
Those of Cohasset to-day who explore the hills around, looking for tilting rocks, big bowlders, pot holes, striations, kelms,
and the numerous other interesting glacier evidences in which
this neighborhood is so rich, are sure, sooner or later, to
stumble upon the remains of one of Mordecai Lincoln's charcoal pits.

# MORDECAI LINCOLN, IRONMASTER

Mordecai not only made iron in his smelter; he set up a forge with a trip hammer, and here made the articles most needed in the community—nails, bolts, hinges—witch hinges, perhaps—pots, skillets, andirons, tongs, shovels, pokers—kind of things that you could not well get along without, either within or without doors. Pity is it that he did not put his mark upon these articles. Who can say what of the primitive iron utensils that are treasured in museums and households up and down the south shore were or were not made by Mordecai Lincoln?

His busy, successful life was saddened toward the end of the century by the death of Sarah, his wife. She left him with four children, the oldest, his namesake, probably about fourteen, the youngest a little girl of five or six. He was not slow, however, in remarrying. His choice was a widow of Braintree, Mary Chapin—six years his junior.

For this new wife he built a spacious home in one of the loveliest sites of all Scituate—a little promontory running into the Gulf at the mouth of Bound Brook. Here, looking out over the marshes on one side, on to falls, mill pond, and mill on the other, the house still stands. You reach it from the Cohasset station by following South Main Street for perhaps two miles. As you approach the mouth of the brook, there rises to your right a height known as Lincoln Hill.

A little farther on the road turns across the stream and one comes suddenly on to the mill and the house. The original mill has been replaced again and again, I take it, for almost without cessation some kind of activity has gone on there. The house was one of the most attractive of the satisfactory New England designs—two stories, with a square entry, a winding stair in the center, a tremendous chimney. To the left of the entry was the kitchen, with its oaken rafters, ceiled walls, and noble fireplace. For over two hundred years this

[23]

home that Mordecai Lincoln built for the Widow Chapin has stood. And to-day one has the solid satisfaction of knowing that it is in the hands of those who appreciate both its fine, simple architecture and its historical significance. If modified by sun porches and conveniences and coats of paint, it has been, luckily, not ruined. The present owner treats it with both love and reverence. "Think of having come from the West," he says, "and to have stumbled upon a thing of this kind. How did it escape from all those Easterners who come out from the cities for summer homes and build nothing so good? And as for the site, look at it. What a joy it is!"

Absorbed as Mordecai Lincoln was in his business, there were town affairs, church affairs to which he must give attention. There was the heated agitation as to whether or not Cohasset should have its own church and school, now that the settlement was growing so large. Here they were, residents of Hingham, of course, but forced to travel four or five miles to church and school. For most of the elders and probably all of the children, it meant walking—walking many months of the year in snow and cold. Where there was a horse in a family it was used, generously used, too, for the Cohasset settlers frequently practiced what was known as "riding and tying"—a couple riding a mile and tying their horse and walking ahead. The first couple of walkers behind took the horse and rode until they overtook the owners. In this gracious way the Cohasset settlers, many of them, made their way to the old church in Hingham.

As for the school, the children could not go, at least regularly. It was not only the distance, the exposure in bad weather, but it was the danger, the hills of Hingham at certain seasons of the year being beset with wolves. The pits in which they were captured can still be seen. There began to be

House Built in Scituate, Mass., Early in the 18th Century by Mordecai Lincoln, Son of Samuel Lincoln

(From photograph made in 1922)

Restored Tap Room of the Old Ordinary—Now the Historical Museum—of Hingham, Mass.

frequent petitions that Hingham would allow them a school of their own. That meant, however, that they should be relieved of the taxes that they were paying for the Hingham school. This could not go on indefinitely. They urged and urged upon Hingham to let them build their own meeting house, hire their own schoolmaster. It was not until 1713 that the hard-headed inhabitants of the mother settlement granted that the "inhabitants of Cohasset shall have liberty to get up and erect a meeting house there on that land called the plain."

In this long contention Mordecai Lincoln's brother Daniel took a rather more prominent part than Mordecai did. As a matter of fact, Mordecai, having his residence just over the line in Scituate, was not so nearly concerned. Daniel, however, was a leader in the movement. Indeed, to his death, he was distinctly a first citizen, a prosperous farmer, so prosperous that he was one of the handful of people in Cohasset who owned a slave.

Mordecai and Daniel were obliged to consider matters of more serious import than their local independence. It was in their time that the magistrates of Massachusetts waged their frenzied war against witchcraft in the colony. The blackest page in that warfare was the strange and hysterical persecutions in Salem, where scores of people were imprisoned or hurried to the gallows.

This terrible outbreak produced a reaction against intolerance all up and down the shore. Men like Mordecai Lincoln, men of healthy living, wholesome common sense, even though brought up in the stern Puritan tradition, dealt with all kinds of men. They instinctively revolted against the Salem madness. It was people like them, the plain people outside of ecclesiastical circles, that set their faces—slowly, cautiously, to be sure, but increasingly—against the intoler-

[25]

ance of the Puritan church. The Puritan fathers did not realize it, but they had put into the hands of the colonists whom they were trying to beat into submission, the tools for the ultimate overthrow of their ecclesiastical dictatorship. When they made the colonists landholders, when they insisted that every child should learn to read and that he should read the New Testament as well as the Old, they created weapons sure one day to act as boomerangs. Mordecai and Daniel Lincoln were landholders, with all the independence of spirit that controlling a bit of land gives. They were enterprising business men, pushing ahead the material interests of their family, their towns, their churches. They had been taught to think by the hard Puritan discussions. The very training of their stern old leaders led them slowly to desert those leaders.

Their instinct to revolt was fed constantly through growing communication with the outside world. The harbors of Hingham and Cohasset were busier and busier with ships coming and going. Men from the West Indies, Virginia, New York, from across the seas, were constantly arriving. Land travel was opening up. The Indian trails were now followed by travelers on foot or horseback; and there were not many nights when the "Old Ordinary" at Hingham did not put up travelers that had come in overland as well as those that had come in by sea. Its taproom buzzed with news, and often, too, with sounds of revelry.

It was from those that gathered in the taproom, that came to do business with them at the forge, to buy corn or lumber, that Mordecai and Daniel had news of what was going on in Rhode Island, in New York, in the new settlement called Jersey, where it was said men could believe and practice whatever religion they wished, where even Quakers were tolerated. Under the impact and challenge of the young spirit of independence and of tolerance springing up in the Colonies along the Atlantic coast and brought to them now constantly, strict interpretation of the Puritan tradition was not long possible for men of affairs like Mordecai Lincoln.

A few years after the death of Sarah, his wife, and his marriage to the Widow Chapin, a second break came in the family of Mordecai Lincoln: his oldest two sons, Mordecai and Abraham, the one born in 1686, the other in 1688, left him. One can only speculate why. So far as I have been able to find, there is no scrap of paper in Scituate, Cohasset, or Hingham to indicate why, when, or where they had gone. Was it the stepmother? One asks the question with interest. She had given her husband a son. Did young Mordecai and Abraham reckon that possibly there would be other sons coming, and that their chance to carry on their father's activities would be slimmer than they had hoped? These are speculations. All we know is that Mordecai's older two sons left him, that their brother Isaac, nearly twenty now, remained, and that when, in 1716, he married, his father built him a house across the inlet.

The Widow Chapin added a daughter to the son she had given. The house filled up. Mordecai saw grandchildren coming. He saw his family among the most populous and prosperous in Hingham and Cohasset. Indeed, if one reads the early records of Hingham and Cohasset to-day he finds scarcely any other name more frequently mentioned. Many families, afterward to be distinguished in the country, were his neighbors there in Cohasset—Beals, Pecks, Bateses—but as numerous, prosperous and as useful as any was his own.

Such was Mordecai Lincoln, such his position in the community, such his surroundings, when suddenly, in 1727, a fit of apoplexy carried him off. He had lived out his three-score years and ten, and, so far as worldly things were concerned, was prepared for death, for his will was made.

He left behind a big estate for those times—£3,099 14s 8d.—carefully divided. The biggest part of the estate went to the Widow Chapin's son Jacob—the house he had built for her at Scituate, with its contents and with the lands and mills. To his son Isaac, the house on the heights, across the brook.

That there had been no serious differences between the father and the sons, Mordecai and Abraham, whose disappearance from Cohasset I have mentioned, the will shows, for to the older son he gave £110 in bills of credit, and to the younger £60, "besides what he hath," which means, of course, that he had already done something for Abraham. That he knew where his sons were and that they were already fathers of children is true, because he makes bequests to their older children. An interesting provision in his will is that for contributing to the "learning" of three of his grandchildren, should their parents bring them up to "liberal education." Whether any one of them ever availed himself of the chance I have been unable to find out.

Upon visiting Mordecai Lincoln's home to-day, one should, on leaving it, drive south past the railroad station of North Scituate, a half mile or so ahead, and inquire for the Groveland Cemetery.

They send you over a pleasant road, up a hill, and there you find it—an old, old yard, still in use and in good condition. A little hunting brings you to the old slate headstones. And there, looking as fresh as the day they were put up, you find, side by side, the stones of Mordecai and his second wife, who had outlived him by eighteen years.

To those who love to reconstruct the lives of the sturdy people who have made this country, there is a curious consolation in sitting beside a well-kept, clearly marked grave of a man who left behind him more blades of grass than he found, a clean memory, a better chance for his sons and daughters. A headstone and a grave seem strangely to round out the earthly span. It seems a man's right. At all events, after vainly hunting through Hingham graveyards to find the resting place of Samuel Lincoln and discovering that in the necessary extension of the town its first graveyard had been destroyed, there is satisfaction in knowing that Mordecai Lincoln, his son, the great-great-great-grandfather of Abraham Lincoln, has a peaceful resting place on a quiet hillside, not far from the home he built and loved.

# III

THE same reasons that brought the first American ancestor of Abraham Lincoln to the Massachusetts coast
drove his successors deeper and deeper into the new world.
Samuel Lincoln came to America in 1637 because of the dis-
content of his family and friends with religious, civil, and
economic conditions. He came, too, because he was young
and a wide ocean and a mysterious land invited him. In
every American generation he fathered there were one or more
men who, like him, pushed ahead into unbroken territory,
allured by the hope of larger wealth, of greater freedom of
action and thought, of more congenial companionship, and
always by the mystery of the unknown, the certainty of adventure.

This pioneer spirit was particularly strong in two of
Samuel Lincoln's many grandsons—Mordecai and Abraham
—the former the great-great-grandfather of Abraham Lincoln, the latter a great-great-grand-uncle. Mordecai Lincoln
must have been at least twenty-one, his brother between
eighteen and twenty, when they left New England. The
first spot in which they took root was Monmouth County,
New Jersey.

And why New Jersey at the beginning of the eighteenth
century? There were all the reasons for going there that call
men to new lands. After many years of struggle with the
Dutch, England had possession of the territory for good and
all, it seemed. She was anxious to settle it. She advertised

it broadly in Europe as a refuge for the oppressed, promising
"free liberty of conscience without molestation or disturbance
in the way of their worship." The oppressed—and Europe
had no lack of them—came in droves—Germans from the
Palatinate who had suffered from the persecution of Louis
XIV, French Huguenots, English Quakers and Baptists.

Go up and down New Jersey to-day. Study the names
of its towns, hunt up the history of many a deserted or semi-
deserted church, read the inscriptions on the tombstones, and
you get some sense of the variety of peoples that sought the
country when the word went abroad that here was a land
where there was to be complete freedom of thought.

The appeal drew not only people from the other side of
the ocean, but many from New England who had found the
Puritan domination hard. New-Englanders began early to
settle in the New Jersey territory; thus Newark was settled
by malcontents from Connecticut. Not only was New Jersey
advertised as a land of liberty, but it was pictured in a way
that would have done credit to the promoter of a modern
colonizing scheme, as a land of fertility, of mines—a place
where all of the women were beautiful; and, as one entertaining chronicler declared, "every one carried a beautiful and
healthy child on her knee." It was to this land of freedom and
of promise that Mordecai and Abraham Lincoln made their
way.

It was probably in Middletown that the young men made
the acquaintances which were to decide where they were to
settle in New Jersey. A number of men had gone out from
Middletown some years before the Lincolns arrived, taking up
adjoining tracts of land in Freehold Township, Monmouth
County. The Burlington path, one of the most important of
the early New Jersey roads, formed the southern border of
these tracts. To the north of the "Middletown men's lots,"

[31]

as they are called in the old deeds, lay a tract of some 2,100 acres, known as the Buckhorn Manor, owned by one of the leading men in the province, Richard Saltar.

There was a stream and pond within the Buckhorn Manor —a good place for a forge, and the Middletown men needed a forge. What more natural than that the young Lincolns, fresh from their father's ironworks in Massachusetts, should have seen the opportunity and arranged to set up a forge on Richard Saltar's land, or perhaps to carry on one already there. Whichever it was, tradition still connects their name, not Saltar's, with the old forge, though neither of them ever owned land here.

Not long after Mordecai reached Freehold, he married— married "well," one would say, for it was to no less a lady than Hannah Saltar, the only daughter of Richard Saltar, owner of Buckhorn Manor and other New Jersey lands. Their marriage brought young Lincoln into a circle of people of influence in the colony—Lawrences, Bordens, Holmeses. The most important of his new relations was his wife's uncle, Captain John Bowne, a rich merchant of Middletown.

How do we know this? One of the curious features in a hunt for ancestors is the help one gets out of ancient quarrels, usually quarrels over property. Genealogists and biographers would be sadly hampered if it were not for the inability of men to settle disputes out of court. It is because of a dispute over property that we have the necessary documentary proof that Mordecai Lincoln married Hannah Saltar.

As I have already said, Hannah had a prosperous uncle, Captain John Bowne. He was a fine, friendly man, but, particularly in the latter part of his life, seems to have been much worried over what was to become of his estate, for his wife, though by all accounts an elegant and charming lady,.

was a spendthrift. Never had he had so much trouble in the
world, he said, as with her. And finally, to prevent her
squandering his estate after his death, he made a will, limiting
her power and carefully dividing his property among relatives, appointing as executors his son Obadiah and his nephew,
Richard Saltar. Among the bequests in this will, which was
made in 1714, was £250 to a niece, "Hannah Lincon."

Now, Obadiah Browne, though able and active, was of
hasty and pugnacious temperament. On his father's death
he wanted the estate settled, and settled at once. He claimed
that several members of the family owed money, and he
pushed them hard for immediate payment. Richard Saltar
did not like this harsh hastiness, nor did Richard's son, John,
for he wrote a long conciliatory letter to "Hon'r Uncle
Obadiah," pleading for courtesy, particularly to "brother
lincoln." Obadiah remained obdurate, however, and when
"brother lincon" failed to pay what he demanded, evidently
on the ground that he did not owe it, brought suit. And it
is throught this suit, brought before the New Jersey court six
different times in four years, and finally withdrawn by consent of Obadiah's attorney, that we know that the Lincoln
named both in Captain John Bowne's will and in John Saltar's letter was Mordecai.

Between the lines of the scant court record of these proceedings, one reads various things—the persistent character
of Obadiah and the equally persistent character of Mordecai.
We also find there what one finds everywhere that the Lincolns settled the trouble that county officials had in the spelling of their name. In these brief entries there are four different spellings—Lincoln, Lincorn, Linckorn, Lincon.

Whatever may have been Obadiah's rights, one cannot but
be grateful for his tenacity. If he had been as "courteous"
in money matters as his nephew John Saltar had asked him

to be, it is quite possible that Captain John Bowne's will would never have been recorded, and that we would never have known whom Mordecai Lincoln married.

True to the Lincoln tradition, that with a trade should go ownership of land, both Mordecai and his brother Abraham soon began to acquire property in New Jersey, Mordecai buying of his father-in-law, in 1723, 400 acres in Middlesex County, and Abraham what amounted to at least 440 acres by 1730. Abraham's land lay about a mile and a half to the east of the forge.

Although Mordecai Lincoln lived in Monmouth County for many years, adding to his land, and although probably it was here that Hannah Saltar bore all of their six children, and although when he died in 1735—then a resident of Pennsylvania—he still held something like 600 acres of land in New Jersey, there are to-day only meagre evidences of his passing. Indeed, in but one other place where the Lincolns halted in their migration from Massachusetts to Illinois— a journey some 200 years long—have I found so little material evidence of their life and labors. No timber of the house in which Mordecai and Hannah lived seems to be left. And as for the forge with which tradition links his name, I once spent a day driving from point to point in Monmouth County, consulting the best local authorities, and yet I could find no reason for believing that it was in one place rather than in another.

His name has persisted, however, or at least it did up to the Revolutionary War—Mordecai's Gap and Lincoln Gap are spots named in the orders given to the commander of the militia of Monmouth County, in 1779, as localities for beacon fires in case of danger.

One touching evidence of the passing of the Lincolns through this part of the world is found in a little hillside

cemetery, just beyond the boundaries of Buckhorn Manor—
an ancient ground, first a family plot. On an uncut, red
sandstone block is an inscription which reads: "Deborah
Lincon aged 3 years 4 months May 15 1720" Standing
in this little yard, looking across a lovely valley to the low
hills of Monmouth County, one can picture the pathetic little
procession which moved through the not too well worn paths
of the forests and valleys on that May day. There was no
church nor churchyard near them. The nearest place of
burial was this little family plot, and here, through neighborly
kindness, Mordecai and Hannah brought their little girl.

In spite of their holdings in New Jersey, Mordecai and
his brother Abraham were not satisfied. The transportation
facilities were much more difficult here than they had been
accustomed to in Massachusetts. Again, the settlement
around them was not growing with anything like the health
and rapidity that they had seen in the home from which they
had come.

Not far away, however, there was a thriving city—Philadelphia. No doubt they carried there many of the products
of their Monmouth County forge. No doubt they went there
for supplies. It was clear that there was a great future for
the iron industry along the Schuylkill River. Mines had
been opened in the mountains, there was transportation and
water power, furnaces and forges were beginning to spring
up, and it was natural enough that when Mordecai made the
acquaintance of two ironmasters, whose names are familiar
in the manufacturing history of that period—Samuel Nutt
and William Branson—and was invited into a partnership
with them, he should have taken advantage of the opening.
This he did in 1722, joining the two men in building iron
works at a place called Coventry, near where the French Creek
flows into the Schuylkill River.

The three acquired over 600 acres of land and built a "forge with engines," besides dwelling houses and "other Buildings and Erections."

It was a beautiful spot on which they built their iron works. Indeed a fairer land can hardly be imagined than this Schuylkill River country, with its river, hills, valleys, growing in delight the higher you ascend. But what man has done to this land into which Mordecai Lincoln came! Following the Schuylkill out from Philadelphia, up past Coventry—acres and acres of furnaces, and miles and miles of junk! One understands as he passes there to-day why there must be saloons and dance halls and riotous amusement for men and women who work and live in these reeking places. They must have something to make them forget. But when Mordecai Lincoln had his forge in this land, the day's work done, he did not have to run away from his thoughts. He had the beauty of things, the quiet of things all about him. His home was not like the homes in this tormented, dirty, dust-ridden place. It is certainly a far cry from the conditions under which Mordecai Lincoln made iron to those under which most iron is made to-day.

Beautiful as the land was, and successful as the iron works were, Mordecai did not long continue in the partnership. In 1725 he sold, for £500 of "Current lawful Money of America," his one-third interest in the undertaking. There is nothing in the papers recording the transaction that indicates why he withdrew. It may be that he had too much on his hands, for evidently he was still carrying on his Monmouth County business. Indeed, soon after this sale we find him buying, in 1726, one hundred acres more of land of his father-in-law, Richard Saltar.

But 500 acres in New Jersey does not seem to have been enough for him. His eyes had rested too long on the Schuylkill country, for whose extraordinary beauty he appears to have shared William Penn's enthusiasm. There was a general belief, too, that up the river, in the mountains, were rich mineral deposits. Mordecai, naturally land hungry and naturally adventurous, and having money at his command (his father died in 1727 and left him £110), bought in 1730 a tract of some 300 acres. Three years later he built a home on his new estate, and into it he moved his family.

The house still stands. In August of 1922 I started out from Reading, Pennsylvania, to find this home of Mordecai Lincoln. I had studied my records to bad purpose. They told me that when he first went to this part of the Schuylkill country, Berks County, he had settled in the town of Oley. Later they said he lived in the town of Amity. Carelessly neglecting to do what every student of American localities should do at the start, that is, study the changes in county and township boundaries made through the years, and also never failing to remember that when the record talks of the town of Oley or of Amity, it probably means a township, I wandered about Berks County for twenty-four hours, seeking sites that do not exist. Finally I discovered that Mordecai Lincoln's land had first lain in the township of Oley, that a re-division of the county had put it in the township of Amity, and that a second re-division had put it in the township of Exeter. With the three sites simmered down to one, it was an easy enough matter to find the home.

You must leave the highway to do it, but if it is in summer or fall, with solid country roads, you have a delightful drive, winding in and out country ways, with always new glimpses of mountain and river. You come to the house as a surprise —a turn in a descending road and there it is—steep-roofed, deep basement, plastered walls—snuggled into the side of a

[37]

hill, above a brook which rushes down a mile or less to join the Schuylkill. Beyond rises a blue mountain.

Nestled there on the hillside, with its terrace of old red sandstone, its vines, its tiny servants' quarters, it has a look of something foreign, something like that which one often comes across in Brittany. Although the house has been enlarged, so that the date stone "M L 1733," unfortunately, has been covered, nothing of its original charm has been destroyed. They even insist—those who hold it now—that the gnarled old apple trees were planted by Mordecai Lincoln. It is pretty certain that the hand-wrought hinges and bolts came from his forge.

It was a pleasant place in which to live, and we know from the inventory of his personal estate that it was well furnished, for the time. Moreover, we know from this same inventory that in the servants' quarters, which still stand practically unchanged, Mordecai housed at least two slaves to help him in his work!

To this pleasant place Mordecai Lincoln took a large family. Not Hannah Saltar—she had died probably about 1727, leaving behind her five living children—her oldest a son, John, and four daughters, all of whom were later to marry into well-known families of Pennsylvania—Millard, Yarnall, Tallman, Boone. Mordecai, like his father before him, seems to have remarried promptly enough. There is doubt about the family name of Mary, his new wife, though probably it was Robeson—early settlers in this part of the world.

The Lincoln's were not without neighbors. The most important of these were the Boones. There was George Boone, about Mordecai's age, with Deborah Howell, his wife, living with their ten children not far away. There was Squire Boone, the father of Daniel, with his big family. Any one visiting Mordecai Lincoln's home in Exeter to-day should

HOUSE BUILT IN 1733 IN BERKS CO., PENNSYLVANIA, BY MORDECAI LINCOLN, GREAT-
GREAT-GRANDFATHER OF ABRAHAM LINCOLN

(From photograph made in 1909)

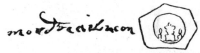

FACSIMILE OF SIGNATURE OF MORDECAI
LINCOLN, SR., FROM HIS WILL,
DATED MAY 3, 1727

(Courtesy of Houghton, Mifflin Co.)

HEADSTONE OF A GRAVE IN COVELL'S
HILL CEMETERY, MONMOUTH CO.,
NEW JERSEY

Deborah is believed to have been the
child of Mordecai and Hannah
Lincoln

certainly not fail to go across field if he loves walking or drive around to the home of Squire Boone. It was a fine house that he had built over the hill from Mordecai Lincoln's. It is a fine house to-day, though vacant. In the summer of 1922 its doors were wide open, there was no caretaker on the place, its only protection the fact that it is reached by a little-traveled cross-field road.

The Lincoln and Boone children grew up together. One can see them racing back and forth over the fields, and naturally enough, although Mordecai was not to live to see it, as they grew older, falling in love. Mordecai's daughter Sarah was to marry a Boone, and his youngest son, Abraham, a daughter of that house.

The Boones were Quakers, as indeed were many of Mordecai's friends. His association and the subsequent intermarriage of his children with Quakers, as also the children of his brother Abraham, who by this time had left New Jersey and settled near Philadelphia, show how far this branch of Samuel Lincoln's family had gone away from Puritan intolerance. They were living in neighborly, friendly fashion beside a sect that only a few years before had been brutally treated in the Puritan Plantation which their father and grandfather, their uncles and granduncles had helped to found and to whose ecclesiastical dictatorship they had been loyal.

As a matter of fact, at this point of the association of the Lincoln's with the Quakers, the intolerance is shown on the other foot. When Mordecai's youngest son, Abraham, came to marry Ann Boone, as he did in 1760, she was disciplined for her "disorderly act."

There is every reason to believe that Mordecai Lincoln at once stepped into a good position in the country to which he had come. We find him a justice of the peace, and an inspector of highways. If he could have lived to the good old

[39]

age of his father and grandfather, there is little doubt that he would have been prominent in the affairs of the colony, but only two years after he built his new house he was stricken. In February, 1735, when he was only forty-nine years of age, we find him making his will, evidently in a great hurry, "being sick and weak in body," as he says.

The estate which Mordecai Lincoln had accumulated in the forty-nine years of his life, and now divided, was a substantial one. There were at least 1,000 acres of land, combining what he held in New Jersey and in Pennsylvania; and it is interesting to note that he gave all of his New Jersey lands to Hannah Saltar's children, his Pennsylvania holdings to the children of his second wife.

Mordecai Lincoln took care, too, that his going should not break up the home in Exeter, for in giving all his "goods and chattels, Quick (slaves!) and dead" to his "beloved wife Mary," he enjoined her to remain on his "plantation" until his children were all of age, "the better," as he puts it, "to bring up all of my children without wasting or embezzling what I have left them." Mary Lincoln carried out his wish, staying on with her four step-daughters and her two little boys, Mordecai, now six, and Thomas, four. Five months after her husband's death, in 1736, she bore a third son, and to this son she gave the name of Abraham.

It was her sons, not Hannah Saltar's, that carried on the name of Lincoln in Berks County—and carried it on with honor. When the struggle for independence came, one of her boys, Mordecai, served as a quarter-master in the Revolutionary army. Later the boy Abraham—the boy born after his father's death—became a prominent man in the state, representing Berks County in Pennsylvania's most important deliberations. It was this Abraham that married Ann Boone, and his descendants are still counted among the useful and respected citizens of this part of Pennsylvania.

How can one, following this outline of Mordecai Lincoln's struggle with the wilderness, and taking a glimpse at what he left behind him, say that he had not played the part of a man in the world, a man not afraid to give himself to daring enterprises, not afraid to throw aside the prejudices of his early surroundings and live in tolerance and friendliness with those of different religion and tradition—a man, too, who left behind him noble sons and daughters to carry on noble lives? How untrue and unjust are those biographers who, even today, speak of Mordecai Lincoln and his descendants as "wanderers of the forest" who "sank to the bottom of the social scale"?

## IV

### "VIRGINIA JOHN"

IT was Mordecai Lincoln's intention—one gathers from his will—that 300 acres of the land he owned in New Jersey should be carried on by his oldest son, John, the child of his first wife; and, had John been content to settle in New Jersey and prove himself an industrious and conservative citizen, he might have gone far because of his excellent family connections. He had an uncle—his mother's brother—a member of the New Jersey Council and later chief justice of the Supreme Court of the state. He had hosts of cousins—first, second and third—among the Saltars and Holmeses, and Lawrences and Bownes. But John Lincoln was too much like his father to retrace steps that he had taken westward; and, instead of going back to New Jersey after his father died in 1737, he remained in Pennsylvania.

He acquired property in Berks County. He made connections in Lancaster County to the south. He married a wife, who began to bear him sons and daughters; Rebecca her given name; and that was all that was known of her until Waldo Lincoln, President of the American Antiquarian Society, published recently his account of the descendants of Samuel Lincoln—over 3100 of them! There we learn that Rebecca was a widow with one son when John Lincoln married her in 1743—Mrs. Rebecca (Flowers) Morris, probably of Berks County.

All we know of John Lincoln comes from assessment rolls, deeds, the dry words by which men keep track of taxes and

[42]

property, words which so rarely give you a gleam of anything personal with which to build up the character and the activities of the man in whom you are interested. What can we gather of the kind of man John Lincoln, the great-grandfather of Abraham Lincoln, must have been from the fact that in 1746 he bought some fifty acres of land on Union Street in Berks County, or that two years later he sold the New Jersey land his father had left him—300 acres—for "200 pounds current money of N. J. at 8 shillings p. ounce"? Very little. What can we learn of his activities in Lancaster County from the fact that in 1748 he wrote into the deed by which he conveyed his New Jersey property that he was a weaver and of the "Township of Carnarvin (Caenarvon), county of Lancaster and province of Penselvania." It is so little that, in the fall of 1922, I went to Lancaster County to see for myself just what remnants of his doings there he had left behind.

So far as I was able to find, there is no stone or record to show that he was ever in that county, except his own statement in the deed I have referred to, dated 1748. And yet, in this corner of Lancaster the name Lincoln is common enough. Mordecai's Thomases and Abrahams lie in the graveyards. One of the finest old places in the vicinity of Churchtown, Lancaster County, "Whitehall," was long the property of an Abraham Lincoln, described by those who knew him as the "very image of the President."

One thing we can be sure of is that John Lincoln was an active business man. He had written himself down as a weaver, but what amount of weaving he did or where he did it there is no indication. When it came to dealings in land, however, it is another matter. His transactions were numerous and profitable. Indeed, on two parcels in Berks County he made some £534 in two years.

The rapid rise of land values in the Schuylkill country

[43]

was due to many things—the fertility of the soil, its mineral riches, its varied industries, and particularly the highways. Two of the most important roads in the country ran through Lancaster County—one westward to Pittsburg and the other —which interests us particularly—southward from the borders of Canada, through the Shenandoah Valley of Virginia to the Yadkin River in North Carolina. They were a tremendous asset to Berks and Lancaster counties.

Then, too, the variety of industries carried on by the settlers had its influence on values. It was not only farming and mining that they were developing. Beautiful printing was done at the Ephrata Cloister—a settlement of Seven-Day Baptists, neighbors of John Lincoln when he lived in Caenarvon township. Glassware, ironware and pottery also were made, the pieces of which are treasured to-day for the quality of their workmanship, the quaintness and originality of their designs. It was in this part of the world that was developed that wonderful carryall which has taken such a large part in the opening of the country, the Conestoga wagon.

Not only was John Lincoln living among a people who were pushing forward an unusual industrial development, but a people of varied religious and social points of view. Nowhere had there settled so many different sects, and nowhere did they, on the whole, live side by side with so little contempt and persecution of one another. There had early come into this land Moravians, Dunkards, Amish people, and these lived undisturbed side by side with Quakers, Catholics, Jews, as well as descendants of Puritans. They are there to-day, wearing the same cut of hat and coat and bonnet and gown that they did in John Lincoln's day, following the same simple forms of worship, living as frugally and accumulating as steadily. They give a sense of stability which is usually lacking in even the best of purely American towns,

They give Lancaster County a picturesque quality unlike anything else that I know in the country. Moreover, they are a
continual call to peaceful living.

But, prosperous and interesting as the country was, it was
not holding John Lincoln. He had begun to feel the pull of
a new migration, a pull to which many about him were yielding, that of the Shenandoah Valley, the land through which
the great southward highway ran.

It was early in the century that stories of this new land
began to come back. They came from those daring explorers,
who, frequently alone, gun in hand, made their way deeper
and deeper into the wilderness, led sometimes by hope of
founding an empire for themselves, sometimes through pure
love of adventure, and not unfrequently by the desire to carry
some favorite form of religion to the Indians. Many of
these early visitors into the Shenandoah Valley were Germans
from Lancaster County. Indeed, the first real settler, one
Adam Miller, came from Lancaster.

Virginia was liberal in grants of land and of trade mo-
nopolies to those who promised a bona fide settlement beyond
the Blue Ridge, and one of the first of these early grants went
to a member of a family that John Lincoln and his father
must have known well back in New Jersey, Benjamin Borden.
John's uncle Abraham had been a neighbor of these Bordens,
their lands adjoining. The Virginia Borden advertised his
land briskly in Pennsylvania, and what more natural that, in
carrying on this advertising, he should look for those with
whose names he was familiar. And that meant, of course,
he would look up the Lincolns.

As early as 1735 a neighbor of John's father, George
Boone, bought a large tract in the Valley. There must have
been much talk about the Lincoln fireside of this purchase,
as well as of what Borden was offering. Every day John

Lincoln saw the "Northern men," as the Virginians called the Pennsylvanians, migrating south in increasing numbers—Germans, Scotch-Irish, now and then a Hollander, as well as representatives of all of the varieties of religious sects which surrounded him. What was happening really was that the Shenandoah Valley was becoming an extension of Pennsylvania.

The settlers naturally enough made Lancaster their chief trading point, so that there came back continually reports of what was going on in the new country; stories, too, of its fertility as well as of its beauty. One strong recommendation was the cheapness of the land. You could get it from six to seven pounds cheaper per hundred acres than in Pennsylvania.

Just when John Lincoln began to yield to the call of Virginia, we do not know. All we know is that in June of 1768 he bought 600 acres of land a few miles north of the present town of Harrisonburg, in Rockingham County, then Augusta. He is set down in this deed as a citizen of the County of Augusta and the Colony of Virginia, which must mean that he had been on the ground some time before he made the actual purchase of the farm.

The deed says, too, that he bought houses and orchards and what it calls "commodities, hereditaments and appurtenances"—whatever they may be. That is, John Lincoln had a house into which to move his family when he reached the Shenandoah Valley.

In the fall of 1922, Dr. J. W. Wayland of Harrisonburg, the chief authority on the history of the Shenandoah Valley, conducted me over the land. It lies perhaps twelve miles from Harrisonburg, along a well-known tributary of the Shenandoah, Linville Creek. It gives one a high respect for John Lincoln that he should have selected such a noble tract of land. It rolls up from the creek valley, wide and high, looks westward to the Alleghenies, eastward to the Blue Ridge. The value to-day, without buildings, is probably $120,000.

At the time that he bought this property there were probably three to four thousand persons in what is now Rockingham County, of whom possibly eight hundred were taxable. Among them were a few negroes. Dr. Wayland, who has studied the records of the county to better effect than anybody else, claims that probably few of the taxpayers had slaves. I know of no evidence that John Lincoln owned negroes, though there is a persistent tradition in the Valley that he was a slave holder.

Whether John Lincoln had slaves or not, it is certain that he could have used them with profit. He had 600 acres of land, much of which he had to clear. Then, too, undoubtedly his chief crop, and his legal tender, was tobacco, for prices were nearly all at this time reckoned in pounds of tobacco. Tithes were paid in tobacco. Merchandise was exchanged for tobacco. The salary of the clerk of the court was paid in tobacco. In 1779 the jailer of the county was paid "2790 pounds of tobacco at £5 a 100 wt. for committing and releasing of the tories"—a little item that shows that sentiment in the Valley was not all going one way!

When the Lincolns arrived in the Valley there was already a good beginning for orderly living—a court of justice, a few churches, an occasional school. As important as anything to the social and political life, as well as the industrial, was Felix Gilbert's general store, some twelve miles from where John had settled. The general store in those days was a real community center. You bought few luxuries at Felix Gilbert's— saws, augurs, nails, gimlets were the chief purchases of the men; knitting needles, flannel, linen, thread (by weight) of the women. You paid for what you bought by trade chiefly, oftenest of course tobacco—sometimes by labor, reaping, sewing, weaving; if you owned a slave, by his labor.

While buying and selling was the excuse for Felix Gilbert's store, its real importance was the fact that it was the social and political headquarters of the neighborhood.

Thus, life in the Shenandoah Valley when John and Rebecca Lincoln settled there was not the isolated affair that many imagine. Living in closely congested districts as we do to-day, able to reach in hours points that took the Lincolns days—able to talk on a minute's notice with friends often a thousand miles away—it takes both imagination and information to judge of their life. The nearest of their neighbors may have been a dozen miles off, and the roads at certain seasons almost impassable; but that did not mean that John and Rebecca did not see many people. Colonial agents, agents of the great land schemes of the time, came and went. Men of science came and went. Peddlers with wares, and, most frequently, missionaries. Whole families arrived for visits—often came unheralded, staying for days, and always welcome.

With these visitors the settlers discussed many and serious things. The women told one another their housekeeping devices, exchanged recipes and remedies, talked in lowered tones of childbearing in the wilderness, of accidents and death. The men discussed their needs—schools, roads, and always—men and women—wrangled over the interpretation of the scriptures, and the creeds and practices of the curious sects that surrounded them.

As the months went on, local and religious discussion gave way more and more to political. Not long after John Lincoln settled in the Shenandoah Valley, the community was knit—and also divided—by the experiences of the Colonies with England. More and more, indignation was stirred by the tales that reached them of interference with what they conceived to be their rights. They were not men to be tampered with; they were deeply conscious of what they had done. It was they who had opened the land, stood off the Indians, and who had never—men or women—shown themselves afraid of any danger—wild beasts, Red Men, incredible hardships. They had been forerunners, breakers-away. Their experiences had made them free speaking, resolute, tenacious of what they conceived to be justice. They had none of the traditions, none of the loyalties of men of conventional association. England must show herself fair—let them have a voice in what concerned them, or they would not tolerate her government. They would submit to no taxes about which they had not been consulted, and so when Boston revolted and held her famous Tea Party, the settlers down John Lincoln's way took up a collection at the general store—a collection of wheat. I do not find John's name in the list of those who contributed, though no doubt he did his share, for we do know that when the time came Rockingham County was quick to organize its militia and that one of John's sons —the one who interests us most—was a leader in that organization. But that story belongs to our next chapter.

It is probable that we would know more of John Lincoln's activities in the Revolutionary period if it had not been for the Civil War. In the summer of 1864, when the Federal army, advancing up the Valley, approached Harrisonburg, the county seat, certain of the citizens, fearful lest the court records be destroyed, loaded a great quantity of them into a wagon and started for the mountains. A detachment of Federal troops, meeting them, seized the wagon and set fire to its contents. Later, when it was discovered that it was nothing but records that were being carried off, the fire was stifled with green hay, and the partly burned papers collected and sent back to the county seat. Great damage had been done, however. Many of the papers were entirely destroyed, and others so badly scorched that it has been only by years of patient and tedious effort that they have been restored.

What information about John Lincoln and his family went up in smoke in that panic—quite understandable, but, as it turned out, foolish—we shall never know. If it had not been for a quarrel between two of his children over the administration of the property he left, we would not have even the date of his death—November, 1788, for although the family burying ground in which he undoubtedly lies is carefully protected on the slope of one of his fine fields, looking out on the Alleghenies, no headstone was ever put to his or Rebecca's grave. His son Jacob lies there with other of his descendants, their graves well marked, but there is nothing to show where John lies.

John Lincoln's will, saved to us by the quarrels of his children, proves him a devout man. "Principally and first of all," its opening clause reads, "I give and recommend my soul into the hands of God that gave it." The will shows him a careful man, doing his best to provide for his "dearly beloved wife Rebecca" and to recognize all his nine children in the division of what he calls "such worldly estate wherewith it has pleased God to bless me in this life."

It was no great thing by this time, for he had been using both his land and his money to help his children start in life. Four hundred acres of his original 600 had gone in 1773 to his sons Abraham and Isaac—evidently sums of money had been distributed to others, but what remained he divided meticulously. The legacies of money are particularly interesting: "To my son Abraham the sum of five shillings" (Abraham was now in Kentucky and unhappily never to know of the bequest, since he was killed by Indians before his father's death) ; two shillings and 14 pence each to "my daughters Hanna and Lydia and my sons Isaac and Jacob." A careful and unequal will which requires more "inside information" to explain than we shall ever have.

Of the children recognized by John Lincoln the one to become most prosperous was Jacob. To Jacob the homestead finally went and here, about 1800, he built a large and dignified house, from bricks made on the place. A little later Jacob's son Abraham enlarged this house and had made for it some fine old mahogany pieces, which are still owned by descendants in the Valley. The homestead itself passed out of the Lincoln family only a few years ago.

What we have then from a study of the records concerning John Lincoln, the great-grandfather of President Lincoln, records scattered through three states—New Jersey, Pennsylvania and Virginia—crabbed, ill-spelled, dry, and, in the case of Virginia, scorched, proves that this great-grandfather of Abraham Lincoln was a man of courage, energy, fidelity. He must have been a tolerant and a level-headed man, too, to have lived on peaceful terms with so many varieties of insistent sectarians. To live among the freakish without becoming freakish or contemptuous takes both character and brains.

A man is also judged by the children he leaves behind him. John Lincoln founded a line in the Shenandoah Valley that has carried on to this day, as his father did in Pennsylvania and his grandfather and great-grandfather in Massachusetts. It makes one catch his breath to go 150 years after John and Rebecca settled on Linville Creek into a pleasant home, twelve miles away, and be introduced to a three-year-old Abraham Lincoln, to look into the faces of Lincoln men with the pronounced features made so dear and so familiar to us by our acquaintance with the face of Abraham Lincoln; but that is the experience that one has to-day in the Shenandoah Valley. John Lincoln stamped himself into that country and lives there through those that have come after him.

PORTRAITS OF ABRAHAM LINCOLN AND HIS SECOND COUSIN, DAVID LINCOLN, OF THE
VIRGINIA BRANCH OF THE FAMILY, SHOWING STRIKING RESEMBLANCE IN FEATURES

HOUSE BUILT ON LINVILLE CREEK OF THE SHENANDOAH VALLEY, VA., IN 1800 BY JACOB
LINCOLN, GREAT-UNCLE OF ABRAHAM LINCOLN, ON LAND BOUGHT IN
1768 BY "VIRGINIA JOHN" LINCOLN, JACOB'S FATHER

### V

### THE CALL OF KENTUCKY

IT is unusual to start the story of a man's life with his marriage license, but, as things have stood in the genealogy of Abraham Lincoln's family, the first certain date that we have had concerning his grandfather was that on which he took out a license to be married. Waldo Lincoln's "History of the Lincoln Family" published this year—1923—gives us an earlier start—the date of his birth. In the extensive researches for his book Mr. Lincoln found in Ohio an undoubtedly authentic "Memorandum of the Births of the sons & daughters of John Lincoln & Rebecca his wife." This tells us that the first child, a boy named Abraham, was born May 13, 1744 "(old stile)." In the next 23 years Rebecca bore eight more children, four boys and four girls, but it is with her first born that we are concerned.

We can say with certainty that his birthplace was either Lancaster or Berks County, Pennsylvania, where his father John had lived from the time he left New Jersey until he settled in the Shenandoah Valley. It meant much to be born in that part of the world, around the middle of the eighteenth century, for it was a land teeming with people of different nations—English, Scotch, Irish, Germans, Dutch. It was highway for north and south and east and west travel—a home in which industries and arts were taking root, and in which all sorts of ideas, political and religious, sound and freakish, were seething. Schools were rapidly building up, and it is certain that young Abraham Lincoln had a better chance of schooling than his father had had.

When John Lincoln yielded to the migratory spirit and pulled up stakes in Pennsylvania and moved southward into the Shenandoah Valley, Abraham was 24 years old—old enough to take a full part in that serious—and dangerous—task. The Indians, allied with the French in their war on the English, had for several years made life risky for the scattered settlers and travelers in Pennsylvania. The air was filled with rumors, true and false. Refugees continually sought safety in the large towns like Reading and Lancaster and defense parties went out to help those who stayed at home get in their crops. Those who followed the great route south in 1768 kept a watchful eye against surprise by marauding bands.

When the Shenandoah Valley was reached and the family settled in the new home, there was plenty of opportunity for work for him. He no doubt knew something of all the trades. Probably, like his father and great-great-grandfather, he could handle a loom; like his grandfather and great-grand-father he was something of a blacksmith. The settler had to be a little of everything, and undoubtedly young Abraham Lincoln could turn his hand to any one of a multitude of tasks that arise in a family situated as was theirs.

A marriage license that he took out in 1770 argues that he immediately improved the social opportunities of the Valley, for his bride was, it is now believed though not proved, Bathsheba Herring, the daughter of one of the first families of Rockingham County.

There is a possibility, though I have come to the conclusion that it is not a probability, that Bathsheba was his second wife. Until some fourteen years ago her name was unknown to Lincoln genealogists; the grandmother of President Lincoln, the wife of his grandfather Abraham, was supposed to have been a North Carolina girl, Mary Shipley, whom he had found on a visit to the Yadkin region, where his friends and relatives, the Boones, lived. J. Henry Lea, one of the most important to date of Lincoln genealogists, believed that Mary Shipley was a first wife, though it was he who proved that, whether this was true or not, he certainly did marry a Bathsheba, believed to be a Herring.

According to the members of the Herring family still living in the Shenandoah Valley, as reported by one of them to Mr. Lea, in 1908, "Abraham Lincoln, who married Bathsheba Herring was a poor and rather plain man. Her aristocratic father looked with scorn on the alliance and gave his daughter the choice of giving up her lover or being disinherited. The high-spirited young woman did not hesitate. She married the man she loved and went with him to the savage wilds of Kentucky in 1782. Her husband was afterwards killed by an Indian, and one of her sons, a lad of 12 years, killed the Indian, avenging his father's death. Bathsheba Herring was a woman of fine intelligence and strong character. She was greatly loved and respected by all who knew her."

"Poor and plain" though Abraham Lincoln may have been, he seems to have been able promptly to establish himself in the Valley. Three years after the license was taken out his father, John Lincoln, deeded to him 210 acres of the 600 he bought when he first came into the country. Five shillings and "one peppercorn on Lady Day next if the same shall be lawfully demanded" was the price he paid. To this land, six years later, he added fifty-two acres adjoining, paying for the same the sum of £500 in the depreciated currency of the colony equal to about $60.

But he was doing more than growing in property in the Valley. The dangers from the Indians made a strong militia

[55]

necessary in a remote region like that of the Shenandoah and when the Lincolns arrived they found the Augusta County militia a well organized body. Abraham Lincoln soon became a member of this militia, and as early as 1776 was a captain. At least a part of his company in the summer of that year took part in an expedition against the Cherokee Indians. Whether Captain Abraham Lincoln himself commanded his troops we do not know, though we do know that in the year 1776, 1777 and 1778 he served as a judge advocate of the court.

The court was composed of the colonel, lieutenant-colonel, major and a captain of the county militia. Charles Kemper, the present leading authority on the Augusta County records, tells me that they represented the best element of citizenship of the county. Among the captains were many whose names are still well known. That Abraham Lincoln was chosen from this group to serve on the court shows that he must have been, if "poor and plain," a man of as good or better education than most of the others, and a man, too, that had won the respect of his fellows. No document that we have concerning him is a better indication of the standing of the President's grandfather than this from the court militia records of Augusta County.

Whether he saw service in the field in the Revolution, I do not know, but he was doing his part, just as many of his relations in Massachusetts and in Pennsylvania were doing  A first cousin of his, Hananiah Lincoln by name, living back in Berks County, near Abraham's early home, had been in the Reading company of Rifles which reported from the "camp at Cambridge, Mass.," in 1775. Hananiah became a lieutenant in the Twelfth Pennsylvania Regiment, but, disgusted because he was not promoted after the battle of Brandywine, he resigned. He was back again the next year, however, and promoted to a captaincy. Up in Massachusetts, Amos Lincoln, like Abraham a great-great-grandson of Samuel Lincoln, the first of the family to come to the United States, had been a member of the Boston Tea Party and afterwards a captain of artillery.

That there was opportunity for Abraham Lincoln in Rockingham County, the history of the Lincolns who stayed behind proves. With 260 acres of rich land, and a creditable record of local service, he might have gone far. His brother Jacob, who remained in the Valley, certainly did so. But Abraham Lincoln was like his father John, his grandfather Mordecai. He had the imagination, the independent and restless spirit and the daring of the pioneer. He lived, too, in one of the most irresistible migratory currents that ever ran across this country, something that had more of the dash and the pull of California in '49 than anything that we have ever seen. It was Kentucky that pulled Abraham Lincoln.

Reading the records to-day of the years of suffering, disappointment and murder that the pioneers of that state went through, it is hard to understand how any man with a young family and a fair chance would risk everything in a venture which had cost so many lives, over so long a term of years. A bloody ground, indeed, it had been, and nobody knew better than Abraham Lincoln what it had cost, for the most indefatigable explorer of that territory was his friend and relative, Daniel Boone.

Abraham Lincoln knew how again and again Boone had gone into the Kentucky region and returned without the furs he had taken and on which he was depending to support his family, and, moreover, without the companions that he had induced to follow him. But always, whatever his misfortune, he came with wonderful tales of the promise of this Kentucky land. Boone and others like him had finally worn the trail

[57]

through the Cumberland Gap, northwestward into Kentucky, into something like a road—the Wilderness Road. They had carried on their dangerous work until they actually finally had won over the Southern Indians, who claimed the central Kentucky country and considered it their fairest hunting grounds, to give them an enormous tract between the Kentucky and the Cumberland rivers.

It was a vicious contract they made with the Indians—a cabin full of paltry English goods for thousands upon thousands of acres of the best of Kentucky's lands. To handle this great tract they formed a company known as the Transylvania, and hastened to establish settlements there, in the meantime advertising their undertaking far and wide.

The Transylvania Company had no sanction from any Colonial government. Indeed North Carolina and Virginia called them a band of land pirates, pointing out that they were violating the king's express orders to let the Western lands alone. It did not disturb the promoters, nor did it deter settlers. It was a great chance. You could go to Transylvania and with a compass and chain lay off as much or as little land as you chose. All you needed to do was to pay the land office fees that were required by the company. That the adventurers who came to obtain lands paid no attention to one another's surveys, that they lapped and over-lapped seems at the moment to have gone unnoticed. Transylvania was one of the first of those magnificent land schemes that even to-day fascinate American speculators and are the easiest of baits for American investors.

This undertaking was short-lived. The Revolution had led the British to attempt a backfire against the Colonies. They officered the Indian tribes and set them on brutal raids, into Pennsylvania, the Shenandoah Valley, and particularly into Kentucky. Again and again the settlements which had been formed in Kentucky were raided. No man, woman or child was safe; yet, in spite of the dangers, the settlers increased. Finally, in 1780, Virginia took the matter in hand, establishing her own land offices. She began about this year also to improve the Wilderness Road, the only half-safe entrance at that time into the country, the Ohio River being practically in the hands of the Indians and the British.

It looks as if it may have been the action of Virginia that suddenly decided Abraham Lincoln to try his fortunes there, for although late in 1779 he had added to his Virginia farm, he sold out his entire holdings of 250 acres early in 1780, and in May of that year entered 400 acres of land in Jefferson County, about twelve miles east of the present city of Louisville on a fork of what is known as Floyd's Creek. A few days later, June 7, he entered 800 acres, just below the Green River.

It is probable that before he went back to the Shenandoah Valley he began to clear one or the other of these tracts in preparation for a home for his family.

The next year, 1781, Abraham Lincoln was back in Virginia settling up affairs. Bathsheba, his wife, had been ill, so that the deed for the farm he had sold before he went to Kentucky had not been properly recorded. Indeed it was necessary for the Rockingham court to send "gentlemen" to examine Bathsheba as to whether she was willing to relinquish her right of dower to the land. As the records show they went and came back to declare "the 24th day of September 1781" that "she freely & voluntarily relinquished the same without the Force threats or Compulsion of her said husband."

It was in 1782, if the best tradition is to be believed, that Abraham Lincoln set out for Kentucky with his wife and little family of probably four children—Mordecai, Josiah, Mary, and Thomas.

[59]

Of course, they did not start over the Wilderness Road alone. No family ventured on that dangerous trip without many companions. There is a tradition among the Herrings of the Shenandoah Valley that one of Bathsheba's brothers, with a large family, "went West" in 1782. It is not improbable then that they were with her. It is fairly certain, too, that one of the party was Captain Hananiah Lincoln, a cousin of Abraham. In 1776 when he resigned from the army after the battle of Brandywine, he visited Daniel Boone in North Carolina, and I am inclined to think that he was the Lincoln for whom Boone entered land in that year. At all events, his name begins to appear in Kentucky records soon after 1782.

It was not difficult for the Lincoln party to make its way to the beginning of the Wilderness Road, a point known as the Block House, in the northeastern corner of Tennessee. Here the custom was for the travelers to wait until enough guns were gathered—a gun in their parlance being an armed man—to make a fair guard. They waited, too, until word came back from the settlements along the way that the Indians were comparatively quiet. They knew well enough—these hardy people—that whatever the reports, there would never be an hour that there would not be danger of attack. Without this fear, the journey was hard enough, particularly with women and children to protect. There were numberless rivers to be crossed—easy enough if the water was low, but difficult indeed if there was a freshet. There were mountains to be climbed, long marshes to be traversed.

But, endless as the difficulties were, the extraordinary beauty and interest of the country—its great forests, the thrill of adventure, the promise of future wealth and comfort, the realization that they, who were taking their lives in their hands, were doing something for the future, some-

[60]

thing big and important—all of this carried them through whatever they may have had to encounter from day to day. Then, too, to cope with danger and hardship was the habit of their lives. They were schooled to it. If they knew its terrors and sorrows, they knew also its joys and its hopes.

What happened to the Lincoln party in its journey of something over 200 miles from the Block House to the central Kentucky stations, we do not know. We do not even know what time of year they made their journey, nor when they arrived. Were the Lincolns at Bryan's Station in August of 1782 when a great number of Indians from the North suddenly surrounded the little group? And was Bathsheba one of that courageous body of women, who, knowing that they had not water in the stockade sufficient to stand a siege, boldly went out with pails on their heads, laughing and talking as if there were not an Indian within miles, filled their pails and came back before the watching eyes of the savages in the forest? Or had they reached Harrodsburg? And were Abraham and Hananiah Lincoln in the company of Captain John Todd who, when the rumors of what had happened at Bryan's Station reached him, quickly collected 150 or more "guns" and attacked the besieging Indians, with terrible results to both sides? These things we do not know; but we can be certain that all the facts of these horrors and many others of the terrible year of 1782 were familiar enough to the Lincolns, and that little Mordecai, Josiah and even Thomas then began to learn something of what Indian warfare meant. We can be sure, too, that Bathsheba Lincoln, living in the midst of constant alarms and threats, must many a time have gathered a child to her bosom, ready to fly; many a time have loaded her husband's rifle as he shot through loop holes at prowling Indians; possibly even herself aimed the rifle.

[61]

At least four years, and possibly six, after he led his family over the Wilderness Road, Abraham Lincoln fought to protect wife and children and labored to make them a home. We have only the meagerest details of what he did. We do know that he continued buying land on treasury warrants, principally along the Green River. The Rev. Lewis A. Warren of Kentucky, who has followed the Lincolns through the state with more intelligent patience than any other recent investigator, says that he has found evidence that Abraham Lincoln took up over 2,000 acres on the Green River. All this doubtless meant frequent trips away from his family. We do know that in the fall of 1784 the tract of 800 acres he bought on his first trip into Kentucky in 1780 was surveyed for him, and that in May of 1785 the 400 acres near Louisville were surveyed, he acting as marker and his cousin Hananiah and his son Josiah as chain carriers. The probability is that in the summer of that year he took his family to a stockade called Hughes Station, known to have been near his tract. Few people in Kentucky at that time lived outside of the stockades, and those that did were usually within easy reach of some kind of garrison.

Desperate things had happened in the neighborhood of Abraham Lincoln's land, but he, like so many of the settlers, was impatient of danger. It was hard to keep the restless pioneer inside the stockade whatever the possible danger without. He could not resist the desire, as well as the necessity, of opening up his tract, and thus it was that one day, while he was working on his clearing, an Indian dashed from the woods and killed him.

His three little boys, Mordecai, now about 14, John, 12, and Thomas, 8, were with him at the time. The two older escaped to the stockade. Mordecai seized a gun and shot the Indian, who was carrying off their little brother. The exact

spot of this tragedy has never been satisfactorily settled. In
the last two years, however, there has been an investigation
carried on by members of the Filson Club of Louisville to fix
by documentary evidence the exact boundaries of Abraham
Lincoln's tract and its relation to Hughes Station. The tract
has been laid off and its history since it was entered by Abraham Lincoln worked out. Personally, I am inclined to believe that these careful investigators will soon be able to
prove that Hughes Station was close to the line of the Lincoln
tract and close to the cabin which Abraham Lincoln was
building. The site of a cabin long known in the neighborhood
as the "Lincoln Cabin" and of a spring known as "Lincoln's
Spring" have been determined. There are unmistakable remains of the chimney on the cabin site, and if one will dig
a bit, as I did recently, in the ground about he will turn up
bits of yellow crockery with the well-known lines of yellow,
brown and blue. There is little doubt that here Abraham
Lincoln was building his home.

But even a more interesting deduction from the investigations of the Filson Club is that not over 400 feet away, and
just beyond the Lincoln spring, are the unmistakable ruins,
if we may use the word of chink and chimney stones, of a
structure fully 100 feet square, with an open court within.
It seems reasonable to believe that here was the Hughes
Station in which Abraham Lincoln and his family were living
at the time of his death.

But what became of Abraham's body? Perhaps a quarter
of a mile away from the site of the Lincoln cabin and the
possible site of the stockade, at the end of a high tongue of
land, lying between two tributaries of Long Run Creek and
overlooking the valley of that stream and on to the hills beyond, stands a famous old church, surrounded by an ancient
graveyard, the Long Run Baptist meeting house, dating back

[63]

to 1797. The land of the church and the burial ground occupies a corner of Abraham Lincoln's 400 acres.

Was he the first, or one of the first, to lie in the ancient ground? So far as I know, it was not until two or three years ago that the question of where he was buried was ever raised. Close to the stockade—they would not have dared to take his body further—men have said, and they let it go at that. But two or three years ago the Filson Club was questioned and an investigation was started with the result that a local tradition to the effect that Lincoln's grandfather was buried in the old graveyard was unearthed.

Old people of the locality told of hearing their grandparents say of this or that early settler that he was "keeping company with old man Linkorn in the Long Run burying ground." A tradition so widespread and persistent could not be disregarded, and the more one studies the old yard and its head stones and its relation to the Lincoln home, the more probable it seems that the tradition is correct and that in one of the long sunken graves, marked, if at all, by rude pieces of uncut native red sandstone, Abraham Lincoln's body was laid away.

"Why not open these old unmarked graves?" was my instant question, as I went about the yard. But a wise old trapper and explorer of the region scoffed at the query. "They wrapped him up in a deer skin or a blanket—he had no coffin; his remains are long ago turned to dust. You would find nothing." That may be true. And yet one cannot but wonder if Bathsheba or young Mordecai or one of their friends might not have buried with Abraham Lincoln some mark of identification—a stone, a bit of metal, even a weapon on which his name was scratched? It was the ·practice of the times to put rude markers everywhere. I can scarcely believe that there would not have been put with the body of this man something to identify it. At least the possibility is sufficient to justify a thorough search. But, whether identified or not, the probability is that this ancient graveyard of the Long Run Baptist Church in Jefferson County, Kentucky, is the resting place of the grandfather of Abraham Lincoln, sixteenth President of the United States.

# VI

## THE YOUTH OF THOMAS LINCOLN

FOR a hundred and fifty years the Lincoln family had been in the vanguard which was opening the new continent. Their migration from New England to New Jersey, New Jersey to Pennsylvania, Pennsylvania to Virginia, Virginia to Kentucky, marked as it had been by hardship and perils, had been made without tragedy. But when Abraham, the grandfather of the President, while at work on his clearing, near Louisville, was killed by an Indian, the irreparable pioneer tragedy took place—the death of the head of a family where the children were still young.

Bathsheba Lincoln must have asked herself, again and again as she bent over the dead body of her husband, what was to become of her and of her children. There were five of them now—three boys and two girls—the oldest, Mordecai, not over fourteen. True, she had upwards of 3,000 acres of land, but, even if the Indians had not been so threatening, her boys were too young to finish the cabin that Abraham Lincoln was building when he was killed, and to carry on the clearing and cultivation of the 400-acre tract which they had chosen for their home.

Fortunately for Bathsheba Lincoln, she had friends, not a few of them, about forty miles to the south in what is now Washington County—families that had come into Kentucky either with her or near the time that she did. Most important to her no doubt at this sorrowful moment was her husband's cousin, Capt. Hananiah Lincoln. He had become a man of considerable importance in the country by this time. There is an entry in the Washington County records of one tract of between eight and nine thousand acres in Hananiah's name. He bought and sold tracts, too, in other parts of the country, and he had sufficiently established himself in the respect of the community for the court to appoint him a captain of militia in the First Battalion. In the record of this appointment, to be seen in the Bardstown Court House, he is recognized as "gent." That is, Bathsheba had a man of parts, related to her husband, to befriend her. Then, too, we must remember that the pioneers turned, as a matter of course, to help those in trouble. The orphan was "passed around," as the phrase was, and the labor on the widow's land was divided among the kindly disposed. Bathsheba found many friendly hands stretched out to her when she reached Washington County; and from that time to her death she continued to live there, her name appearing regularly on the tax lists up to 1793.

This fact and the fact that the inventory and appraisal of Abraham Lincoln's personal property are in the Court House of Bardstown, Kentucky (then the county seat of Washington County), have convinced many people that the Lincoln family had always lived there and that Abraham, Sr., was killed there. More than one of the first families in that region has in the later years made affidavit that this has always been the tradition of their people. One interesting affidavit even goes so far as to describe with great particularity Abraham's powder horn!

In my judgment, there must be better evidence than we yet have to upset the belief that Abraham Lincoln met his death in Jefferson, not Washington County, and that, after this loss, his widow came with her children to the little group of friends and acquaintances near Springfield. Certain it is that it was in the first, not the second, place that he owned land.

Washington County has a fine group of Lincoln traditions to develop without this, much as she wants it and feels it is rightfully hers, for here certainly Bathsheba and her family came to live. And what did she have to live on? The inventory referred to above shows that she had two horses, three cows—two yearlings and three calves. She had a few farm implements—a plow, hoes, some tools, guns and rifles. More interesting is what she had for the inside of her house. It is comforting to know that she had "three feather beds and furniture," which certainly meant bedsteads, and, let us hope, dressers. She had a dozen pewter plates and two pewter dishes, a candlestick, a Dutch oven, a small kettle and two big cales or tubs. And, most important, she had her flax wheel. Enough, you see, to set up housekeeping with, in a one-room log cabin, which was all that she or many other people in Kentucky, even in good-sized towns, had at that moment. Bardstown, where this inventory was filed, was then but a log stockade, though since that day it has become one of the most finished small towns in the United States.

In this cabin Bathsheba must bring up her children. What was the life of little Thomas, now eight years old—the one of her children in whom we are particularly interested? It has been common to speak of his life after his father was killed by the Indians as that of a wandering orphan boy—his son once thus described it; but it seems to me certain that up to 1793 at least, possibly longer, Thomas had the care of a mother, a well-born woman, more or less attention from his father's cousin, a man of parts, set down in the records as a "gentleman," and at least kindly interest from a group of families that were to figure in his future history—the Berrys, the Thompsons, the Hanks. That would include a little schooling. People of the training and antecedents of his mother and of Hananiah Lincoln, of the Berrys and the Thompsons, always saw to it in those days that after food and protection were granted to children, they be taught to read and to work. It was part of their creed.

There has long been a tradition that Thomas Lincoln could neither read nor write. We have the documents to prove that he did sign his name—"bunglingly," to be sure, as his son has said; but if one will examine the records of Kentucky at this period, he will find that many a man of eminent name could do little more than to sign his name "bunglingly." The writing and spelling of the aristocrats of those days, if judged by present-day standards, or by the standards which Abraham Lincoln evidently applied when a grown man, would prove them almost illiterate. People had something to do in settling a new country, overrun with wild beasts and Indians, besides practicing in copy books.

I take it, then, as certain as any deduction that Bathsheba Lincoln and her friends were giving to the little Lincolns, the little Berrys and the little Thompsons as good instruction as they could. Certain it is, too, that they were familiarizing them with the Bible and the stiff moral code of the day. We must not forget that most of these people accepted very definite religious and ethical principles. Puritan, Quaker, Methodist, Baptist traditions of creed and of conduct regulated the lives of the people among whom Thomas Lincoln was reared.

Moreover, it was a time of the most earnest discussion about the future of the country which they were settling. What should it be? Should Kentucky be, as the great Transylvania Land Company had planned, a state by itself? Should it yield to England? Should it join Spain? Should it be a state in the Atlantic Colonies, newly joined in the

United States? Not on the terms which many in Virginia were trying to enforce, that is, a dependency, a colony. If they went with the United States, they must have independent statehood. It was a vigorous struggle, and these woodsmen were prepared to back it, by force if necessary. This was the kind of strong political meat that young Thomas Lincoln was hearing on every side.

Just when his mother died and he was thrown out of a home we do not know, but probably it was around 1793. We do know, however, that soon after this he went on what must have been an exciting journey for him, a trip of some 200 miles into the beautiful Wautauga Valley of Tennessee.

To this country his uncle Isaac had migrated with his family about 1780. Isaac was a well-to-do man when he left Virginia, and he had married a well-to-do woman of an important family, Mary Ward by name. He had prospered on the Wautauga, acquired lands in various parts of the country, was a flax grower, a slave holder; a careful man, and "close," they say. When his widow died in 1834, she left two finely equipped plantations and forty-two slaves; that is, when young Thomas went to visit his uncle Isaac he found a comfortable pioneer home. He found his uncle's family, too, connected with the best of the countryside.

Isaac Lincoln might very well have adopted Thomas, for his only son had recently died. However, he is said to have found his nephew lazy. I am inclined to think that this explanation has grown out of later-day insistence that laziness was Thomas Lincoln's leading characteristic—an insistence that documents greatly modify—and that the real reason that he did not take the boy permanently into his home was that his wife wanted to adopt children from her own family. At least, that is what she did, leaving to them when she died the greater part of the estate Isaac had left her. No one of the Lincoln nephews or nieces was remembered by her.

Just how long Thomas stayed in Tennessee I do not know —probably about a year; but down in the Wautauga Valley there are people who still claim that it was here he found his future wife, Nancy Hanks, and lived with her as a common-law wife, and that it was here that Abraham was born. The site of a cabin upon the hills above the Wautauga is still pointed out as that of the Lincoln cabin. But this is one of the traditions that documents riddle. There are records to show that Thomas Lincoln was back in Washington County by 1797. Moreover, there are many to prove that from that time on he remained in Kentucky until he left the state for Indiana in 1816.

When he returned, it was no doubt at first to the home of his older brother, Mordecai. In 1797 Mordecai sold the 400 acres near Louisville, where his father had been killed, and for £100 bought of Sarah Thompson, one of the neighbors with whom the family had always been associated, a tract of 300 acres on Beech Fork, Washington County, near the newly formed town of Springfield. A few years later his brother Josiah bought an adjoining farm.

The farms of the Lincoln boys, Mordecai and Josiah, bordered on that of Richard Berry, a man whose name is of importance in the Lincoln story. I think we may set it down that here on the Beech Fork was the first permanent Lincoln settlement in Kentucky. It was here that a little later a cousin of theirs from the Shenandoah Valley, David Lincoln, a boy then about twenty years of age, found them, and years later, in 1848, wrote to Abraham Lincoln, then a member of Congress, telling him of his trip. David no doubt came to Kentucky to see what the chances were for him there, and we can take it that he found them less than at home, for he went back and later built up a prosperous business on the turnpike north of Harrisonburg, Virginia, at a place called Lacey's Springs, where his descendants are still living.

A visit to this first place in which the young Lincolns established themselves in Kentucky is worth while if we want to visualize the spot where Thomas Lincoln, father of the President, probably spent much time after he was seventeen.

The land lies some eight miles from Springfield, the county seat. It is a rough and even dangerous ride, ending in a fording of the Beech Fork, something which, I imagine, could only be done in the dry season. Along the bank of the stream comfortable white cottages are strung—Poortown, they call it. Poortown turns out when a car approaches. They know the value of the Lincoln connection and eagerly point you out the site of Mordecai Lincoln's cabin. It was a pleasant site, looking down a long valley. There is nothing left now of the cabin, though a fine old mill stone marks the spot on which it stood. They tell you there, with every proof of conviction, that here Abraham Lincoln was born; and all Poortown feels naturally enough that it is wrong indeed that the noble marble monument that stands in Hardin County, near Hodgenville, should not be theirs, that they should not have enjoyed the increase in land values that Hodgenville has had, and that they should not have the roads that the Lincoln Memorial has brought to Hardin County.

It was a pleasant and easy path over the hillside from Mordecai Lincoln's cabin to that of his neighbor, Richard Berry; and if it is true, as I myself believe, that in this household of Richard Berry there was living at that time a young orphan girl called Nancy Hanks, it is easy to see how young Thomas Lincoln, when making his home with his brother, might have walked back and forth from the Berry home many an evening for a sight of her, to take her to church, to camp meetings, to corn huskings, "bees," house raisings. There were many things to bring the pioneers together. It is only ignorance that makes us picture the life of the time in this part of Kentucky as devoid of social and religious opportunities. It was full of them. The pioneers were building up a community. They had brought with them from Virginia and Pennsylvania a fine body of traditions. They were trying to work them out, and in every way the school, the church, the neighborly gathering was fostered.

How much of his time Thomas Lincoln spent in Washington County with his brother Mordecai is uncertain. He was young and strong; it was necessary for him to earn his living. Workers were in great demand. The year round there was something for every pair of hands in the community. But Thomas did not want to be a jack-of-all-trades. He wanted to be a carpenter, a cabinet-maker, and accordingly apprenticed himself, probably, though not certainly, by 1800 to one Joseph Hanks of Elizabethtown, some 35 miles in a direct line west of Mordecai's home.

This Joseph Hanks, in whose shop he now went to learn a trade, was the son of a Joseph Hanks whose will, properly probated, shows that he died in 1793, leaving eight children. Joseph seems to have been a particularly respectable citizen, hard working, carrying out the pioneer tradition of combining a trade with a farm. It was a good place for young Thomas Lincoln to be.

But Thomas had the family thirst for land strongly in his blood. A trade was not enough for the Lincolns. Run back over the line that we have been following from Hingham, Massachusetts, in 1637, down, and you will find them always adding land to their trades—Samuel a weaver as well as a landholder—Mordecai I and II blacksmiths and landholders —John a weaver like his great-grandfather, and a landholder.

[73]

If John's son Abraham had a special trade we do not know. Soldiering and pioneering played so large a part in his career that he never was able to specialize, but that he was a jack-of-all-trades, we can be sure. Thomas, true to form, now specializes as a carpenter. But in 1803, when he was 23 years old, he bought 238 acres of land. He had to pay for it before its transfer £118.

Where did he get the money to buy this land? Possibly he had earned it. Certain, he could have done so if he had been as diligent as he might. Again, his uncle Isaac might have helped him a little, though that gentleman's reputation does not give much foundation to the idea. It is more probable that by this time his father's estate had been settled, and that he had received something toward the sum necessary to pay for the property.

The fact that Mordecai had a few years before bought the farm in Washington County, of which we have already spoken, and Josiah was a little later to buy a piece of property adjoining Mordecai's, seems to show there had been some division of whatever was realized on the 2,000 and more acres of land which Abraham Lincoln, Sr., had bought in Kentucky in the early 1780's.

The location of the land which Thomas Lincoln bought in 1803 has only recently been settled. That indefatigable Lincoln student, the Rev. William E. Barton, started the search which finally located the tract some twelve miles north of Elizabethtown on a tributary of Salt River, called Mill Creek. Possibly the fact that both of his sisters, now married, lived near here brought Thomas into the neighborhood. Whether he ever built and lived in a house on his farm, cleared and sowed and reaped fields, I do not know. It is probable most of his time was spent in carpentry work in Elizabethtown.

[74]

# THE YOUTH OF THOMAS LINCOLN

Of course carpentering in Elizabethtown does not mean that he was confining himself to that settlement. In those days men traveled far for a job, and it is probable that Thomas Lincoln was working in more than one county at his trade. Of what he was making out of it, however, we have no record—enough to marry on, certainly, since on the 10th day of June, 1806, he and one of his brother Mordecai's neighbors, Richard Berry, put their names to a bond for the "full sum of £50 current money," the condition of which was that Thomas should "shortly" marry Nancy Hanks, of whom Thomas' fellow bondsman, Richard Berry, claims in the document to be the guardian—and he spells it "garden."

We know that this marriage took place two days later— the 12th of June, 1806, at Richard Berry's home, a place called Beechland, near which, as we have already seen, Mordecai was living and near which, too, Bathsheba Lincoln had undoubtedly spent her remaining years after the murder of her husband. We have the best of proof of this in the return of the minister who performed the ceremony.

Those whose minds have been confused by the contradictory tales that for years have been told about the father and mother of Abraham Lincoln, would do well to make a pilgrimage to Springfield, Washington County, and see there for themselves the records proving this marriage. You will find them, not in the court house, but in an office across the street. You will not have any difficulty finding this marriage bond and the return by the officiating clergyman, Jesse Head, for both are now carefully preserved under glass, and when a carload of sightseers turns up in Springfield, one of the first things that the clerk in his depository of records does is to bring out these two framed documents. Would that he had as strong a sense of the value of other documents!

Careful searchers for exact documentary material about

[75]

the Lincolns in Washington County, have, within recent years, turned up tax lists which show, among other things, that in 1811 Thomas Lincoln was taxed in this county on "one horse mare."

There is always a satisfaction in looking on such a record, although it may have been printed and you may have the utmost confidence in this printed source, so I asked to see the tax list. Nobody knew where it was. I think it must have taken half an hour for the clerk to discover in an upper room what looked to me like an old lard can, into which had been thrust a quantity of yellowed papers, printed and written, among them the crisp old assessment list of which I was in search—carelessly folded and stuck into this receptacle. If the papers had ever had a binding it had disappeared, and naturally, so old are they—at least 111 years—it is almost impossible to handle them without tearing.

Samuel Haycraft, who at this time was clerk of the court in Elizabethtown, says in his Memoirs that, in the early days of Hardin County, the records were kept in a big wooden bread basket. It was a much better receptacle than that in which Washington County is to-day allowing some of its precious historical records to lie. Springfield and Washington Counties are eager to prove their claim to the birthplace of Abraham Lincoln, but they are making poor progress when they handle any record touching the Lincoln family carelessly.

But Springfield is by no means the only delinquent in these matters. In Frankfort, Kentucky, recently, the very tax lists by which the Rev. William E. Barton has been able to prove that Bathsheba Lincoln was alive as late as 1793, were, I have been told, all but burned as waste paper. They had lain so long untouched that the order had gone out to destroy them, but a vigilant woman official gave the order that they were to be examined. To be examined it was necessary to take them into the open and to sweep them in the direction of the wind, so heavy was the accumulation of dust. But to those who look over old records this is an old story. Only a few days before this experience in Springfield, I had a similar one in Virginia—dust so thick on old records that after three hours' work, nothing but a vacuum cleaner and a Turkish bath would have made me really dustless.

Carelessly kept records have been one of the difficulties that Lincoln students have had from the start in untangling the story of Thomas Lincoln and Nancy Hanks and their life in Kentucky. The statement, spread so diligently after Mr. Lincoln's death, that his father and mother had never been married took root because not only no indices of the records in Washington County had ever been made but because those records had been treated as "old papers" and stuffed into out-of-the-way places.

Resentment at the scandal which he believed to be false led Squire R. M. Thompson of Springfield, whose mother claimed to be an own cousin of Nancy Hanks, to undertake a search for the marriage bond and return which the law required. The clerk of the court discouraged him, but Squire Thompson persisted, and finally the papers were found, scotching forever, for people of decent mind, the tale which had been repeated with such relish not only by Mr. Lincoln's political enemies, but as well by envious friends.

It is by patient research like this, carried on persistently ever since the death of Abraham Lincoln in 1865, that has gradually brought together so many scraps of indisputable evidence concerning his father—now a will, now an inventory of personal property—a tax receipt, an appointment to some small post, a deed—that we are able at last to make out of him a much more decent, industrious and respectable man than early and more ignorant tradition painted him.

[77]

### VII

### THE MOTHER OF ABRAHAM LINCOLN

WHO was Nancy Hanks, the mother of Abraham Lincoln? That she was the true and lawful wife of Thomas Lincoln we have seen. But who was she? Do we know her antecedents as we do those of Thomas Lincoln? Is it possible to trace the Hanks family, step by step, from its coming into America as we can the Lincoln family? Unfortunately, not with the same completeness and definiteness. We do know, however, that side by side with the Lincoln family from the time that they settled in Pennsylvania there always had been a Hanks. One of Mordecai Lincoln's nearest neighbors in Berks County, Pennsylvania, was a John Hanks.

John Hanks was a Quaker, and we have interesting records in the minutes of the Philadelphia Monthly Meeting of his difficulty in bringing himself to what he regarded as "necessary clearness in relation to marriage." His struggle brings to mind that which his possible, though not proved, descendant Abraham Lincoln was having about one hundred years later "in relation to marriage" !

We are fairly certain that John Hanks and his family joined the migration into the Shenandoah Valley and southward about the time that John Lincoln did. We do know that in various counties of Virginia—Amelia, Bedford, Lunenburg—there are in the records traces of Hankses. We find traces of them, too, in North Carolina and South Carolina. An Abraham Hanks was a member of one of the first parties that went over the trail called the Wilderness Road—not a man who carried on to the end, however, for the entertaining journalist of the trip, after telling of the various troubles that Abraham had had with his dog and his horse, recounts that he became frightened at the stories of hostile Indians ahead, and went back. Later, however, members of the Hanks family went into Kentucky, but, so far, the documentary evidence of what they did between their arrival and the time of Nancy Hanks' marriage is very meager. So far as we know they were all, like the Lincolns, of small means. More than one biographer, not having discovered any members of the family that owned lordly acres or built big houses, has dismissed them as "poor whites" just as more than one biographer has dismissed the Lincolns as belonging to that class.

But what is a "poor white"? Poor whites are the back-wash, not the vanguard of the pioneer army. In every onward movement into the wilderness there were those who, through bodily weakness, fear, discouragement, misfortune, dropped by the way. They were like soldiers, wounded or gassed in the front line trench beyond any future hope of active service. Without them the pioneer army could not have advanced as it did. They were part of the sacrifice that opening the new continent demanded.

To those who through weakness or misfortune fell back, there were joined, particularly in the mountain regions of Tennessee and Kentucky, a group of convicts and pirates, chased from the south Atlantic settlements—people who went to the mountains for a reason, and stayed.

Now, the Lincolns and Hankses were of neither class. They moved ahead into the very heart of the Kentucky battle ground, and there planted themselves and withstood the perils and hardships of the early period. Moreover, as we shall see, the Hankses, like the Lincolns, kept the pioneer spirit.

[79]

They pushed ahead with the vanguard which went later into Indiana and Illinois. They were never laggards behind, that is, they never were of the "poor white" class.

But where does Nancy Hanks belong in the group of Hanks families that certainly came into Kentucky about the same time as the Lincolns? Is there anything in the records of the counties where they settled that places them beyond dispute as the Lincolns we are following from Massachusetts westward are placed? Until twenty-five years ago there was nothing. Then a document of first order was found —a will, drawn in 1793 by one Joseph Hanks, who at that time owned property and was living with his family in Nelson County. This will had been signed, sealed and delivered in the presence of men whose names are familiar in the development of that part of the state, friends and neighbors of Joseph.

This discovery, so surprising to Lincoln students, was made by Mrs. Caroline Hanks Hitchcock, now of Cambridge, Massachusetts. Mrs. Hitchcock had undertaken some time before this to collect material for a genealogy of her family in America. In her search through the records of different states where branches were known to have settled, she came of course to Kentucky, and in the court house at Bardstown found this important paper—the first time, so far as I know, that any student had looked upon it. Visitors to Bardstown to-day, interested in Lincoln genealogy, will do well to look it up, and at the same time to ask for that other interesting document of which I have already spoken, the inventory of the personal estate of Abraham Lincoln, Sr.

Joseph Hanks, in this will that Mrs. Hitchcock found, recognized eight children, by leaving each a legacy—a horse to each of the five boys, a "Heifer Yearling" to each of the three daughters. To one of his sons, Joseph, he left the farm of 150 acres in Nelson County on which he was living at the time of his death, which leads us to suppose that he may already have given land to his older sons, as was the practice in well regulated families of that day. The estate, however, was not to be disturbed as long as his wife, whom he affectionately calls Nannie, lived.

As soon as Mrs. Hitchcock found a Nancy Hanks recognized in this will—the "Heifer Yearling" Joseph left her was called "Peidy"!—her natural question was: May it not be that this is the Nancy Hanks who in 1806 married Thomas Lincoln and became the mother of Abraham Lincoln? She might very well have been old enough at the time. Was there another Nancy Hanks recognized anywhere in Kentucky records? She could find none of a proper age, nor has any one else found one of proper age. Then the question which Mrs. Hitchcock naturally asked herself was whether the descendants of any of the men or women that Joseph mentioned in the will ever had any association with Nancy Hanks Lincoln, whether there were any of these descendants that claimed her as sister or aunt or great-aunt.

By following the family of Joseph Hanks, the son to whom the father had left a hundred and fifty acres when the mother should be through with it, Mrs. Hitchcock secured considerable convincing testimony of the relationship she was trying to establish. This Joseph Hanks we have already met in an earlier chapter, for he was the carpenter and cabinetmaker of Elizabethtown with whom Thomas Lincoln is believed to have learned his trade. These two men lived side by side for several years, both working at carpentry and cabinetmaking in the same district and doubtless often on the same jobs. Joseph married in Elizabethtown, so the marriage records say, a Mary Young, and several of his children were born there. About 1826 he took his family to

[81]

Illinois, settling in Adams County, near Quincy, on the Mississippi River; and here his children grew up, married, and scattered, in the way of families, into various parts of the country.

Mrs. Hitchcock had no trouble in locating these descendants of Joseph Hanks, and from them she was able to secure a number of letters giving their reminiscences of their father or grandfather as the case might be. All of these letters claim definitely that Joseph and Nancy Hanks were brother and sister. One of them tells of hearing Joseph Hanks talk of Nancy herself, of her sweetness and gentleness; another recalls things that he told of Thomas Lincoln and the life of the two together in Elizabethtown. Fragments from these letters Mrs. Hitchcock published in 1899 with a facsimile of the will she had found.

An interesting confirmation of the truth of Mrs. Hitchcock's theory that the Nancy of Joseph Hanks' will was the Nancy who married Thomas Lincoln, came to me unsolicited over twenty-five years ago, from a daughter-in-law of Joseph Hanks, Mrs. Jacob V. Hanks, and her son, J. M. Hanks, at that time superintendent of the public schools of Fremont County, Colorado. Both Mr. Hanks and his mother (an Adams—her father a cousin of John Quincy Adams, President of the United States) were people of education and character. Mr. Hanks helped Mrs. Hitchcock in collecting data for her proposed genealogy. I have before me a letter of his, written after Mrs. Hitchcock's book had come out, in which he rejoices that she has "cleared up and set right," as he puts it, the story of his kinswoman, the mother of Abraham Lincoln.

Did President Lincoln know anything about the relationship of his mother to Joseph Hanks and his sons and daughters? He certainly did, for in the first brief notes which in 1858 his friends were able to wrest from him for a campaign biography, he made this statement: "My mother, who died in my tenth year, was of a family of the name of Hanks, some of whom now reside in Adams, some others in Macon Counties, Illinois." As we have seen, the Hankses in Adams County were Joseph Hanks and his family. Mr. Lincoln, whenever he was in Quincy, went out to see "Uncle Joe," as he called him, and one can be sure, as his grand-children have reported, that the two men often talked to-gether not only of early days in Elizabethtown when his father was starting out in the world, but still more of Nancy, his mother, who had left him in his tenth year, but whose memory seems always to have remained with him—something tender and precious.

As to Macon County, the Hankses there were none other than the family of William, the oldest of the sons, the executor of Joseph Hanks' will. William Hanks came into Illinois about the time that his brother Joseph did, settling near the present town of Decatur. Although his son John is better known to Lincoln biographers than William, the records show him to have been an important man in the new settle-ment. As a matter of fact, William Hanks and Jesse Fell once owned a part of the land on which the town of Decatur stands. That Mr. Lincoln had familiar relations with the Macon County Hanks family is well known.

Now here is a natural, simple chain of evidence; but reasonable as it is it must go if a stronger and completer chain is produced. I have seen none so far, though that tire-less Lincoln investigator, the Reverend William E. Barton, has recently announced that he has found in a remote section of Kentucky evidence completely shattering the conclusion that Mrs. Hitchcock drew from the Joseph Hanks will and the corroborating testimony. If I understand Mr. Barton's claim it upholds a theory of Mr. Lincoln's mother's origin which was broadcasted after his death by a man who had been associated with him as a friend and a law partner for twenty years, Mr. William H. Herndon.

Almost immediately after the tragedy of the President's assassination, Mr. Herndon began gathering material for a life of his old friend. Among other things he set down, and begin to repeat as early as 1866, his recollections of a conversation which he said he had had with Mr. Lincoln in the early fifties.

It was an affecting tale that Mr. Herndon told, of how, in a moment of deep depression, Mr. Lincoln had confided to him that his mother was the illegitimate daughter of a Virginia planter by a woman called Lucy Hanks. It was from this Virginia planter, Mr. Herndon said, that Mr. Lincoln believed that he had inherited his "power of analysis, his mental activity, his ambition." Of course at the time of the reputed conversation neither of the two men knew that it was unnecessary for Mr. Lincoln to seek an explanation of his superiority so far afield, that, as a matter of fact, he had it in his father's family, members of which at that date were filling important positions in the public and professional life of the East.

Mr. Herndon seems to have realized that if his version of a confidence, given fifteen years before and long before he could have had any idea of writing Mr. Lincoln's life, was to be accepted, he must have some kind of backing. He sought it from one Dennis Hanks, then living in Coles County, Illinois.

This Dennis Hanks called himself a cousin of Nancy, and he was, by his own statement, "base born." Dennis always talked as if he and Nancy had been children together, in spite of the fact that she was some sixteen years older

[84]

and that he was only seven when she was married. However, he had been associated long with the Lincolns, for he followed them after Thomas Lincoln moved into Indiana in 1816, and remained with them until they moved on into Illinois fourteen years later.

A more picturesque and entertaining story-teller could not have been found than Dennis Hanks, and his satisfaction in having a fresh audience in Mr. Herndon is evident in all the testimony of which we have notes, either in his or in Mr. Herndon's hand. He delighted in remembering things as long as anybody would listen to him, and his own opinion of the value of his recollections was magnificent.

"William," he wrote in one of his communications, "let in, don't keep anything back, for I am in for the whole hog sure; for I know nobody can do any for you much, for all they know is from me at last. Everything you see is from my notes—this you can tell yourself."

Unhappily for the picturesqueness of my page, the spelling of this note was revised before publication. Dennis's spelling, as I will show a little later, was of the earliest pioneer type.

Dennis Hanks seems to have agreed with Mr. Herndon that Lincoln's mother was a Lucy Hanks. Whether he ever said definitely or not that Nancy was born out of wedlock I cannot make out from the notes that have been published. If he did, he was quick to take it back, for as early as February, 1866, he wrote Mr. Herndon:

"Hir Name was Nancy Sparrow; hir fathers Name was Henry Sparrow, hir Mother was Lucy Sparrow, hir Madin name was Hanks, sister to my Mother. 2nd. You say why was she called Hanks?

"All I can say is this She was Deep in Stalk of the Hanks family. Calling hir Hanks probily is My falt. I allways

told hir She Looked More Like the Hankes than Sparrow."
(Remember, Dennis was but seven when Nancy was married!)
"I think this is the way; if you call hir Hanks you Make
hir a Base born Child which not trew."

This statement, so flatly contradicting Mr. Herndon's
theory of illegitimacy, naturally irritated him.  He besieged
Dennis with written questions, but received in return answers
which only still more confused the issue.  Little wonder that
when Ward Lamon came to use Mr. Herndon's notes for a
Life of Lincoln, which he published in 1872, he said of
Dennis that he was "painfully weak on cross-examination."

One other witness that Mr. Herndon called in was John
Hanks of Macon County—a solid citizen, John Hanks, and
of much soberer mind than Dennis.  He backed up Dennis,
however.  "Nancy Sparrow," he wrote Mr. Herndon in 1865,
"was the mother of Abraham Lincoln, her mother's name was
Lucy Hanks, was born in Virginia."  It is interesting to note
that sons of Dennis and of John later worked out the
genealogy and made Nancy Hanks a sister of William Hanks,
as Mrs. Hitchcock makes her.

Mr. Herndon rested his case on his belated recollections
and on the testimony of Dennis and John Hanks; and when
his own Life of Lincoln was finally published in 1890 he
repeated, in a more detailed form of course, the above theory
of Nancy Hanks' origin.

Personally, I have never believed that Mr. Herndon would
have accepted and insisted on the story if it had not been
that at the time he set it down, and for long after, his
mind was confused and weakened by alcoholism.  A brilliant,
lovable, undisciplined person, with all the defects, as well
as the qualities of a radical mind and temperament, excessive
drinking injured his powers.  When he gave up his practice
finally in Springfield, it was with the despairing cry:  "I can't

see—I can't hear—I'm going to quit." If it had not been for the faithful and intelligent coöperation of Jesse W. Weik, we would not have the valuable Herndon life of Abraham Lincoln.

Familiar as I have been for years with Mr. Herndon's theory of the origin of Nancy Hanks, I have never been more convinced of the flimsiness of the testimony on which it is based than I have been in reviewing it in the pilgrimage which I have been making for these chapters. One cannot do much historical and biographical work without learning that the memory of man, when it comes to exact details, is painfully unreliable. A conversation is rarely repeated twice alike. With no malice, with no intent to deceive, men distort the thing which has been told them twenty-four hours before, and with every day and month that passes, if they repeat the tale, this distortion grows and changes. I do not believe that Mr. Herndon knew exactly what Lincoln told him in the conversation which he describes. As for Dennis Hanks, I do not understand how he can be taken as a serious witness in matters of genealogy. Let any one of us try to set down without documents the names of families into which relatives have married, the dates of births and deaths, and we quickly find, unless we have a taste for genealogy which we have steadily cultivated, that we fall into all sorts of errors.

However grateful we may be to Dennis for the color and liveliness which he has contributed to an important segment of the Lincoln story, a segment of which he knew much, he cannot be taken seriously as a genealogist. If he and Mr. Herndon are right we must have documents to prove it. If I understand Mr. Barton's announcement he believes that he has them. We owe much to Mr. Barton—how much I had not realized fully until I began to follow again the Lincoln trail, seeking what had been added to our knowledge in the twenty-five years since I first took it. If now, Mr. Barton can establish beyond dispute the place of Nancy Hanks in her family he will have relieved future Lincoln biographers of much bewilderment and disgust—but his chain must be faultless.

What is needed to settle finally this unpleasant discussion is a thorough and complete genealogy of the Hanks family. The records of Virginia, North and South Carolina, through which they certainly passed, have never been thoroughly ransacked. No more have the records of Kentucky, of Indiana and Illinois. You establish a family line, not by word of mouth, but by piecing together a multitude of items, hidden away in the records of the counties through which branches of the family have passed. It is in tax lists, deeds, wills, returns of marriages and deaths, the testimony brought out in lawsuits, church records, tombstones—all of the minute facts which men have agreed to save in order to fix definitely who and what we are, what we did, where we came from, and when we left it all. These are the things which must be found and fitted together before we can finally answer with absolute sureness the question: Who was Nancy Hanks, mother of Abraham Lincoln?

We have the trail. It lies close beside that of the Lincolns from the Atlantic coast; but, while we can put our feet into the Lincoln tracks, from Massachusetts to Illinois, we must guess those tracks in the case of the Hanks family. That finally they will be found, I firmly believe. These things come slowly. In 1858 Abraham Lincoln wrote in regard to the Pennsylvania Lincolns that the effort to connect them with the New England family of the same name had been a failure; yet about twenty-five years later, through the efforts of a patient student, the connection was made. One after another unsettled points in the genealogy of the Lincoln family have been cleared up. Not a decade passes that something is not added; and there is no reason why a persistent, intelligent, scientific effort to establish the Hanks genealogy should not be as successful as it has been in the case of the Lincolns.

One thing is certain, no such discussion as this disturbed the peace of the marriage of Nancy Hanks and Thomas Lincoln. That marriage on June 12, 1806, at Beechland, Washington County, Kentucky, was a gay affair, with a great dinner and friends and neighbors from far and wide. The ceremony was performed by one of the best known clergymen of that part of Kentucky in that day, Jesse Head, whose marriage returns, to be seen in the Springfield court house, report the wedding he had celebrated.

Traditions of Nancy Hanks have come down in many a family represented at that wedding—in the family of Richard Berry, who sets himself down on the bond as her guardian—in the family of the Thompsons, the Mitchells, the Shipleys. Nowhere do you find more indignant denial of a reflection on the character and origin of the girl than in these, for years leading families of Washington County.

They picture her as vivacious, spirited, beautiful; they tell of her skill in handicraft—spinning, weaving, all the household arts of the day. She was an orphan, for her mother died soon after her father, and she was obliged to pay her way in the families where she lived as in the Berry family, but she was a welcome guest wherever she went, industrious, cheerful, competent. Such, we have every reason to believe, was the woman that Thomas Lincoln had taken to be his wife.

# VIII

## ABRAHAM LINCOLN'S BIRTHPLACE

SOON after this wedding and the jolly infare or celebration which followed it, attended by the whole countryside, the young couple set up housekeeping in Elizabethtown, twenty-five miles to the west, where Thomas Lincoln had his carpenter shop, and some twelve miles from which lay the 238 acres of land he had bought—and paid for—in 1803.

A recent Lincoln biographer describes Elizabethtown when Thomas took his wife there as a "poor new village, made up of groups of log cabins, huddled along a few neglected lanes, with muddy streams instead of streets during rains, a stench of pig styes at the back"; its inhabitants, he intimates, were "a shiftless, unstable class."

I should like to hear what Major Benjamin Helm would say about that. Four years before Thomas brought Nancy to Elizabethtown, Major Helm had built there a two story brick house, 50 by 25 feet, its walls 18 inches thick, its lower rooms wainscoted in black walnut, its mantelpieces of walnut. In the gable was a huge date mark:

## BEN HELM
### 1802.

It would be entertaining, too, to hear what the people of Elizabethtown at that day would say about this description, for at that moment all Elizabethtown was excited over their new court house, just finished—this, too, of brick, made in the local brick yard. Great things went on in that court house, for here were growing up some of the most important of Kentucky's lawyers, men like Ben Hardin, William P. Duvall, John Pope.

Besides, Elizabethtown had already begun to set up the machinery of an intelligent, accomplished society. She not only had her churches and schools, held wherever they could get a roof, but she had a debating society and a dancing master—who was also the town tailor!

It is true, of course, that the majority of the people like Thomas and Nancy lived in log cabins, but log cabins which were rapidly being enlarged and improved. That is E-town, as it is often called, an energetic, growing pioneer settlement, not a backwash as the writer above quoted would have us believe. Tom and Nancy fitted into the life of the town, poor people, to be sure, but honest working people. There is no doubt that Thomas Lincoln was having his share of the carpentry and cabinet making that the rapidly growing town furnished.

He had need to work for, in February of 1807, Nancy gave him a daughter—Sarah, she was called—a name frequently appearing in past generations of the Lincoln family. A wonderful event, the birth of a child in a pioneer home!

When little Sarah was about eighteen months old, Thomas decided to move to Hodgens' Mill, or Hodgenville, as it is now called, twelve miles away, an energetic settlement and a rival of Elizabethtown. Good families had settled about —the Brownfields, the Creals, the Enlows.

This move of Thomas Lincoln's from Elizabethtown has often been cited as a proof of shiftlessness. It does not necessarily mean anything of the kind. A working man in those days went—as he does now—to the point where he thought he could get the steadiest and best paying job, and then, as now, he took his family with him; and in these changes, made to better his situation, it was no sign of shiftlessness that he rented a home, as Thomas did, at the start. By the fall of 1808 he had settled two and a half miles south of Hodgenville on a small farm furnished with the typical cabin of the period.

In this cabin on the twelfth of February the year after he moved, 1809, a boy was born to Nancy—a glad hour for her. But what a solemn and amazing hour it would have been if she could have known that a hundred years later thousands of mothers looking at new-born sons would pray that they might grow up to be such a man as this son of hers was to be. They do it—do it in Kentucky to-day.

One day a year ago while on a pilgrimage through the Lincoln country of Kentucky I stopped in a little town thirty-five miles from the cabin where Abraham Lincoln was born. It was one of those little towns that disputes with Hodgenville the honor of being Lincoln's birthplace. Like Homer in Greece, Lincoln in Kentucky is claimed by, if not seven, at least several different places. Seeking information, I knocked at an open door, and when there was no answer entered, and there on a big bed in a darkened room lay a woman. Alarmed lest I had startled her, I hastened to apologize. "Look!" she said, and threw back the covers. There lay the round red head of a two days' old baby! And then, like all the people in this part of the world, she began to question me. "Where do you come from?" "What are you doing here?" I told her I was following the traces of the Lincolns. "Oh!" she said, "prove he was born here. I want my son to have been born near him. Maybe then he would grow to be like him."

No doubt Nancy Lincoln dreamed as all mothers do of

a great future for her son. But she could not have dreamed anything so wonderful as this.

Childbirth for the pioneer man, as well as the pioneer woman, was an anxious event. There were few doctors. The woman must depend upon what the French call the "wise woman," we the midwife. And usually the wise woman was not called until the last moment. Thus it was that we find Thomas Lincoln one morning early in February hurrying down the road, and meeting one of his neighbors, Abraham Enlow by name, telling him of his difficulty, and Enlow answering, as any kind neighbor would then or now, "You go back and stay with Mrs. Lincoln and I will get the granny woman." (Several versions of this incident have been reported; I simply paraphrase what they all amount to.)

There was no lack of friendly help when the neighbors learned what was about to happen in the Lincoln cabin. More than one of the descendants of the families then living near-by has set down what he had been told by father or grandfather, and more than one has boasted that his aunt or his grandmother hastened to Mrs. Lincoln's side; and in the days after, when she was convalescing, went back again and again to take care of the cabin, cook food for Thomas, wash the baby, and comfort the mother. Everybody lends a hand when a new baby comes in a pioneer community, as they do indeed whenever there is unusual trouble or unusual joy.

Abraham Enlow, who had befriended Thomas at the start, used to boast years later that it was because of his neighborliness at this time that Thomas's new son was called Abraham. But here, as we know, Mr. Enlow was mistaken. Thomas Lincoln named his son after his father, whom he, a boy of eight, had seen killed by an Indian. As a matter of fact, there had not been a generation of Lincolns without an Abraham since Mordecai Lincoln, late in the seventeenth century, married Sarah Jones, daughter of Abraham Jones, of Hull, Massachusetts, and brought the good old Biblical name into the Lincoln family.

Unhappily, nearly sixty years after the birth of little Abraham, this story of Abraham Enlow's relation to his birth was falsely and maliciously distorted. Men came to the neighborhood asking, "Who was Lincoln? What do you know of his family?" And embittered political opponents answered with a leer, "Abraham Enlow must know something about him. He was named after him." And thus, by a process with which every one is familiar, slowly, but surely, a natural, neighborly act in a time of trouble was twisted into a hateful scandal. Abraham Lincoln's father, so the tale ran, was not Thomas Lincoln, but Abraham Enlow. This distortion was so evident and so malicious that only the fact that it is widespread would justify even this slight reference.

There are few more precious birthplaces on this earth than this where Abraham Lincoln first saw the light. Certainly in all our United States but one other is equally sacred. It is a deep satisfaction to know that at last the spot is honored as it should be. For many years men talked of its sacredness, but they were less energetic than men who realized that the cabin particularly might be made a money-maker. It was the money-makers who first laid hands on the Lincoln cabin. It was torn down, dragged about the country, and shown in settings so vulgar and inappropriate that it was made to seem almost a ridiculous thing. Finally, when the exploitation was no longer profitable, the cabin was stored in a cellar on Long Island, New York.

The very land on which the cabin had stood finally came into the market, and it was then that a group of men, led by Richard Lloyd Jones, the present editor-in-chief and publisher of the Perry-Lloyd-Jones Newspapers, who had long dreamed of a monument at Lincoln's birthplace, formed the Lincoln Farm Association, and undertook to collect from the people of the United States the money to acquire the property and to rear upon it a suitable monument. That it be a popular undertaking, they asked that no sum greater than twenty-five dollars be contributed, and welcomed even more gladly a subscription of twenty-five cents. Eighty-one thousand people enrolled themselves in the Lincoln Farm Association. Three hundred thousand dollars was collected, over $200,000 of which came in twenty-five-cent pieces. The finest talent of the country was secured to plan the memorial and its setting, and on September 4, 1916, the work was done and a great concourse of people gathered at the dedication of what Mark Twain once called "The little model farm that raised a man."

It was not until October of 1922 that I saw the completed work. I dreaded to see it, for when I learned that it had been decided to build upon the farm a Greek temple, I shrank from the idea of the connection. I did not know what should be done, but in my ignorance it seemed to me that they were doing what should not be done.

You approach the monument by a winding driveway, on each side of which the natural growth of the land has been left, all the beautiful and varied growths of this part of Kentucky. A place of gorgeous color in the clear sunlight of a perfect October morning. My first visit was on one of the loveliest of October days.

The little temple stands on a rising slope of ground—exquisitely white, small, serene—approached by a long, broad, generous stairway of marble. It is a triumph of perfection. Its proportions are right, its size is right. The landscape gardening simply protects the drive, the staircase, the temple

[95]

itself from the encroachment of the woods, leaving the natural setting undisturbed. It is a joyful thing to see.

But in the exultation of finding it so beautiful, I dreaded an entrance. Would not the little cabin seem mean? Would not its placing inside this perfect thing make it ridiculous by contrast?

The beauty and the wonder of it is that it is not so. It somehow belongs. Why, I do not know; but it stands there so simply what it is—a thing without pretension, but of an extraordinary dignity in its simplicity. You have only the native log structure, the clay chimney; but every stone of the chimney, every timber of the cabin is there because it was needed. Never have I been so impressed with the dignity of the thing which fits the need.

In these surroundings, one visualizes with wonderful sympathy and clearness the little Lincoln family in their one room home. This cabin sat on a rising slope, with the same lovely surroundings that you may see to-day—trees of every kind, vines underbrush, fruit. Nancy and her children on the doorstep at eventime looked out on as beautiful a place as heart could wish.

The life that Nancy Hanks with her children led in this cabin was in all its details the same life that she was to lead up to her death. Here on her hillside farm there were none even of the simple excitements that she may have enjoyed in E-town. She was more alone here, though she had neighbors at no great distance. But her life was like that of them all, and in many of its details like the life of the Lincolns who first came to this country, Samuel and his wife Martha in Hingham, Massachusetts, in the middle of the seventeenth century.

Here, as there, the fireplace of the cabin was the very heart of the place. Nancy's fireplace, as we see it to-day,

MEMORIAL AT ABRAHAM LINCOLN'S BIRTHPLACE NEAR HODGENSVILLE, KY., DEDICATED IN 1916
The original cabin stands within the Temple

was deep and wide, with a long stone mantel and big hearthstone. The chimney was outside—a cat-and-clay chimney, as it was called, made by mixing cut straw or grass with stiff clay and laying it in alternate layers with split lathes of hard wood. Within, hooks were fitted and the long crane from which to suspend pots.

The feeding of the fireplace was one of the essential tasks of a pioneer home. And it was one of the tasks that later was to fall to the baby that now lay in Nancy's arms. He was to learn that a wood pile was only one degree less important to the life of the home than the cupboard. He was to learn to gather for the fireplace for months before winter set in, as Nancy did for her larder. There must be logs as long as the opening, of a half dozen different sizes; they must be green and dry, hard and soft, and there must be chips to kindle a low fire, brush to make a blaze. He was to learn that a fire must never go out after cold sets in. And he was to master all the ceremonials of the fireplace—putting on the back log, packing the coals at night, stirring them in the morning, and choosing just the right wood for quick heat. The baby Abraham was to learn all this, and to learn—who ever better?—the joys of the fireside, and how it might light one on the way to knowledge.

Nancy was not troubled at her fireplace with a multiplicity of cooking utensils like a housewife of to-day. Her chief reliance was the Dutch oven, a big iron pot with a cover, standing on long legs and kept continuously on the coals. After the Dutch oven, the most important article was her long-handled frying pan. On this she roasted the game with which the larder of her home was always filled, both in Kentucky and later in Indiana. Here, too, she fried the salt pork and bacon which the pioneer always preferred to venison, rabbit or wild turkey, and, of course, it was on this frying

[97]

pan that she made the hot bread and cakes which went with the meats. One of the proudest accomplishments of house-wives at that date was the ability to turn a cake high in the air at the precise moment it should be turned. It was like the feat of which skilled cooks so boast—turning an omelet at the critical instant.

Her bread baking she did in a clay oven—not so good an oven as that which Thomas's mother had used back in Virginia, for that was brick, but it was an oven of the same kind. Nancy had an outside fireplace, too, where in summer she kept her Dutch oven going, and in the fall tried out lard, and made soap and prepared the tallow for the candles. All through the summer, like every pioneer housewife, she gathered wild berries and dried them. All through the fall she cut and strung apples and pumpkins to dry. It was a time of dehydration, as we used to say so importantly during the war, but there was nothing that we tried to teach then that Nancy Lincoln did not know and practice. In the fall, too, she wrapped up in dry leaves or bits of paper apples and pears to keep for her children's Christmas. I found a little Kentucky housekeeper of Nancy's type doing this very thing a year ago.

She was skilled in spinning and weaving, and there were few days that did not find her at her loom or wheel, or cutting up and making into garments for Thomas, little Sarah, the baby Abraham, the linsey woolsey she had spun. From her loom, too, came woolen blankets in the fine and simple designs of her time. When she collected by long patience enough pieces of cotton for a quilt she patched it in some famous pattern, and as she worked she rocked her baby in the simple cradle we can well believe Tom Lincoln had made for her. Every household had one, and probably Nancy's was a better piece of craftsmanship than many, for, as we shall later see, her husband was no mean cabinetmaker, given his time and chance.

We can be sure that Nancy Lincoln's working day was systematic. These early housekeepers followed a strict schedule, washing on Monday, ironing on Tuesday, baking on Saturday, church-going on Sunday. She made the best of her time, and like every self-respecting woman of that day rarely failed to find time "to rest a spell."

It is rather a shame that the Lincolns did not live long enough in the cabin on the hillside for little Abraham to have really tasted its joys, to have discovered the wonderful Cave Spring, to have explored the tunnel, to have played under the big oak. He knew nothing, however, of his birthplace except what his father and mother may have told him. For before he was four years old, Tom Lincoln had decided to move. He had found a farm in a near-by valley, not over eleven miles if you follow the road to Hodgenville and descend Muldraugh's Hill, though there's a shorter way— down a hollow, along a creek bottom. No less a person than Mr. John Barry, the editor of the Rolling Fork Echo of New Haven, the town that is nearest to the site of Tom Lincoln's new farm, believes that it was down this creek bottom that the Lincolns moved. It would be easier, he claims, than to have descended Muldraugh's Hill, which in those days—as it certainly is now—was what Mr. Barry characterizes as a "tough proposition." It is a long and dangerous winding descent, interesting to us not because of its difficulties but because at one time Thomas Lincoln was appointed surveyor of a portion of it. In the document which is still preserved in Elizabethtown recording this appointment Muldraugh's is called the Bigg Hill, and it deserves the name.

Perhaps a mile beyond the foot of the Bigg Hill the road crosses a valley, the valley of Knob Creek, which a few miles to the northeast flows into the Rolling Fork River. It was here where the road crosses the creek in a wide and fertile field running back between high limestone bluffs that the new home cabin of the Lincolns stood.

# IX

## THE FIRST HOME LINCOLN REMEMBERED

THE place Knob Creek I remember well—but I was not born there. . . . I was born in Nolin, nearer to Hodgenville than the Knob Creek place is. My earliest recollection, however, is of the Knob Creek place." So wrote Abraham Lincoln in 1860 to a Kentuckian who had invited him to visit "the place of his nativity."

What was it like—this farm that Abraham Lincoln remembered—the place where his childhood experiences began to sink in deeply enough to be held, where consciousness was born? I never saw the place until October, 1922, and although I had read many descriptions, examined many photographs and thought I had visualized it, I found when on the ground that it was very different from what I had imagined, and—to my joy—richer in resources, closer to the tide of the life of the day.

One should go to the Knob Creek farm from Lincoln's birthplace, three miles to Hodgenville, then eight miles northeast, descending into Knob Creek Valley by the long and somewhat perilous Muldraugh's Hill, of which I spoke in the last chapter. Here you find wide fields, long tongues of level land, excellent land. One cannot but applaud the wisdom of Thomas Lincoln in moving from the rough and only partially cleared farm where his son was born to these broad and open fields—the best alfalfa fields in the county, the neighborhood claims.

The cabin into which the Lincolns moved—a cabin of

[101]

the same type as that in which Abraham was born—stood not far from the bank of the creek, looking down the valley. Steep limestone bluffs, heavily wooded, rise on every side, and from them in times of heavy rains pour down streams of water to swell the creek and its tributaries. Knob Creek is as temperamental as the weather, and in the spring the freshets cover the land—an exciting place for children, if trying for their elders.

In front of the Lincolns' door ran the highway from Louisville to Nashville—the most important turnpike in that part of the world and one freely traveled. That is, young Abraham Lincoln came to consciousness in a spot where the world was passing by—a young and eager world, full of adventure—not in a backwash as we used to believe. This must not be forgotten when we attempt to estimate the influences molding the little boy.

Pioneers with heavily laden wagons, driving their live stock, forded the creek close to his doorstep; peddlers came and stopped, spreading their wares on Nancy Lincoln's floor. There were local politicians, soldiers returning from the War of 1812, promoters of alluring land schemes. John Filson, the first historian of Kentucky, may have found his way along the road and stopped at the Lincoln cabin. There were missionaries of every sect, and now and then a scientist. One of these latter, who knew Thomas Lincoln's cabin on Knob Creek and never failed to stop when near, was Christopher Columbus Graham, a man who for years traveled the highways and byways of this part of the world, gathering specimens of the flora and fauna and strata of Kentucky.

Graham had been at Nancy Hanks' wedding in 1806, and in his hundredth year set down an account of the affair along with much picturesque description of the life of the early Kentucky settlers, centering it all around the Lincolns.

# THE FIRST HOME LINCOLN REMEMBERED

He knew them, that is sure; often sat at their table, and though his recollections are those of an old, old man, who prides himself on his memory, they are the record of a trained observer whose mind remained alert and active to his death at the age of 101.

What did the child remember of this life? What do any of us remember of our first seven years? A few definite things which we tell and retell; one or two definite things of which we never speak; much that is vague, and often painful —the beginnings of understanding that life is more complex and mysterious than our elders would have us believe.

In Lincoln's definite recollections of Knob Creek, the one that has played the biggest part in the stories of his life there has been that of an exciting adventure which he and a schoolmate a few years older had one day when the creek was running high. Lincoln fell in. His playmate, Austin Gollaher by name, by his courage and quick wit saved his life. Lincoln never forgot it, and as for Austin it became years later his chief claim to a place in history. It was a real adventure, the kind of thing that links you with grown-up story-tellers and forever lifts life a little above the commonplace. He had almost drowned! He had been saved!

But Abraham and his sister Sarah and Austin had many more adventures along Knob Creek, for a more varied playground one cannot imagine. Particularly tempting is a deep pool a little way down the stream where it makes a sharp bend and is joined by a fork from the hills. The rushing waters have cut into the deep soil of the fields and through the limestone rock until you have here banks five or six feet high. Over them hang old sycamores and elms, and along the slopes are heavy fringes of willow. The pool is some twenty feet in diameter, and when the streams were in flood it must have eddied and boiled in a way to stir children to the very bottom. And a dangerous place it would be, too, and one to which Nancy Lincoln would forbid the youngsters to go unattended. But when it was low, when you could go wading without danger or float in your homemade boat—and I am sure Thomas Lincoln had one tied to one of the over-hanging sycamores—it must have been a favorite playground of the children. One resource of the creek is an abundance of beautifully tinted mussel shells, and one need not doubt that Abraham and Sarah carried home many a pocketful.

The surrounding bluffs offered as much excitement to the children as Knob Creek. Lincoln laid the foundation here of his exceptional fund of wood lore. Trails ran up the steep sides of the bluffs—you can see one to-day zig-zagging up-ward from a point near the site of the cabin—which the boy must often have followed, as it led to his friend Austin's home. Across this path numbers of small animals ran, and Lincoln's first knowledge of their tracks, their habits came here. Here, too, he began to learn the birds, distinguish their notes, know the ways of snakes, watch for fox and deer. He was beginning to observe. It may be that Christopher Columbus Graham, with his talk of stones and flowers and animals, stirred the boy to attention. If a "great man" like Dr. Graham noticed such things they must be worth while.

Here on Knob Creek the boy began to learn to work as well as to play. Certain easy "chores" fell to him as soon as he was strong enough to do them: filling the woodbox, bringing in the water, weeding the garden, calling his father from the field, running errands, picking wild berries, quanti-ties of which grew on the surrounding bluffs, helping gather the grapes for the wine and jelly which everybody made, pick-ing up persimmons for beer—a long list of little tasks to which the pioneer mother trained her child from the start, much to his future advantage, let it be said.

# THE FIRST HOME LINCOLN REMEMBERED

From what we know of the boy's later life, we can set it down that Nancy Lincoln had no hard task in training young Abraham. He was naturally willing, affectionate, helpful. In Indiana, when his father was hiring him out to farmers and neighbors in and around Gentryville, one thing that the women of the household always noticed was that when he came in at noon or at night for his meals he of his own accord filled the water pail, brought in the wood—a kindly, thoughtful, well-trained boy they set him down to be. Nancy Hanks must be given her share of credit.

The most exciting and definite incident of Lincoln's labor life in these years on Knob Creek, he told a group of visitors once in the White House. I heard the story many years ago from a man who was present, Dr. J. J. Wright of Emporia, Kansas. They were talking of the President's life in Kentucky. "I remember the old home very well," he said. "Our farm was composed of three fields, which lay in the valley surrounded by high hills and deep gorges. Sometimes when there came a big rain in the hills the water would come down the gorges and spread over the farm. The last thing I remember of doing there was one Saturday afternoon; the other boys planted the corn in what we called the 'big field'— it contained seven acres—and I dropped the pumpkin seed. I dropped two seeds every other hill and every other row. The next Sunday morning there came a big rain in the hills; it did not rain a drop in the valley, but the water, coming down through the gorges, washed ground, corn, pumpkin seeds and all clear off the field."

It was here in this Knob Creek that Lincoln made his first acquaintance with schools. In his own brief records of his experience, he has not much to say for them, only that before leaving Kentucky he and his sister "were sent for short periods, to A, B, C schools, the first kept by Zachariah Riney

[105]

and the second by Caleb Hazel." According to Mr. Barry, the schoolhouse was two miles up the road — a little log room about fifteen feet square, with a fireplace at one side. It was later made the starting point of a comfortable white frame house. The owners show you the room to-day proudly, but you would never dream it had once been a log schoolhouse, so completely has it been clapboarded without, ceiled and plastered within. It is a good example of the use many people made of the log buildings they acquired with a piece of land.

For lack of any particular knowledge of the two schoolmasters Lincoln names, it has been the habit of biographers to treat them as men of little account, men of scant education and scant contacts with life; I am convinced, however, from the information concerning the pioneers of this part of the world which is gradually accumulating, that both Caleb Hazel and Zachariah Riney were better teachers than they have been painted. Caleb Hazel, for instance, was by no means a wanderer. He was a man interested in the development of the country, buying and selling land freely. Looking over the records of Hardin County recently I found his name repeatedly. Mr. L. A. Warren, who with Mr. Barton has done so much research in the Kentucky records, says in his little book on the Lincoln Louisville Loop, a book which Kentucky tourists should not neglect to take with them, that Caleb Hazel owned a farm adjoining the Lincolns' and was evidently a friend of the family.

As for Zachariah Riney, Mr. John J. Barry, the editor of the Rolling Fork (New Haven) Echo, is sure that he was a man of considerable cultivation, "a gentleman"—teaching manners as well as morals. Riney was a Catholic, and there were many of the Church in that part of the country. The institutions they had already founded have grown to be among the show places of this section. One of these early Catholic settlements, now the famous monastery of Gethsemane, was only eight miles from the Lincolns, near New Haven, their nearest town; another eighteen miles away at Bardstown. The presence in the neighborhood of these devoted and frequently cultivated people, passing back and forth as they must have done constantly before the Lincoln cabin, and a man affiliated with them, Zachariah Riney, as one of Abraham's teachers, had its unconscious effect on the lad. At all events, it is something to be glad of that the more we know of his two early teachers, the more respectable they become.

Nancy Lincoln's part in the education the boy was getting in this period has always been dwelt upon, and rightly. It was she who, in the winter time by the big fireplace, told the children Bible stories and helped them with their lessons. It was she who, in the summer evenings, sat on the doorstep and talked over the day—its incidents, the passers-by, what the peddler said, what the man who gathered flowers and stones and snake skins said. I think, however, we have been inclined to underestimate Thomas Lincoln's part in this education.

Largely from lack of knowledge, Tom Lincoln has been set down as a shiftless, rather no-account person; but the more information we have about him, the better man we find him to have been. That he was a man of varied pioneer experience we know; also his reputation as a great story-teller is firmly established. What a fund of stories he must have had! He had seen his own father killed by an Indian. How often he must have rehearsed the scene. Abraham Lincoln, in one of the few records that he made of his childhood, says that the story of his grandfather's death, and of his uncle Mordecai killing one of the Indians, was the legend more strongly than all others imprinted upon his mind and memory.

[107]

Then, too, Thomas Lincoln had many close hand stories of the Revolution. He had been associated from boyhood in Kentucky with his father's cousin, Hananiah, a captain in the war at Lexington and at the Brandywine. And when, as happened often, other Revolutionary soldiers dropped in on Captain Hananiah, there must have been famous hours. Of the Indians and their ways, of wild animals and their ways, of the Spanish, the Mississippi, the great adventurers that had traveled Kentucky, Thomas Lincoln could not but have known a great deal. Here were stories, and he poured them out to his boy.

Moreover, Thomas Lincoln was a more active and respected citizen in those days than we have supposed him to be. This will be soon proved conclusively, I believe, by the publication of documents that have been gathered by the Rev. L. A. Warren. Some five years ago, Mr. Warren, just out of college, found himself the pastor of a church at Hodgenville. Perplexed by the contradictory traditions of Lincoln's birth, and of the character of Tom Lincoln, he undertook a detailed documentary study of the Lincolns, of the related families, and of the environment in which the boy Lincoln grew up. This work Mr. Warren has carried on in some nine different counties. He tells me that he has over a hundred separate items, gathered from court records, all going to prove that Thomas was an active, respected citizen, that he filled more offices than we have known, that he owned more property and of more kinds that we have ever known, and that when he had trouble with his neighbors and it came to suit, he always won out. That is, Abraham Lincoln, at this time, was under the influence of a father who was respected, and at least fairly hard-working.

That he was a religious man, taking his part in the Baptist Church, to which he belonged, loyal to its tenets, there seems

to be every reason to believe. It is certain that he owned a
Bible in a day when Bibles were hard to get, and, according
to Christopher Columbus Graham, cost as much as the
spinning wheel, loom, or rifle. That he did his best to bring
up his children in the way that he conceived the Bible taught
they should go, is sure. Church-going was a regular feature
of Abraham Lincoln's early life. The Baptist Church of that
period insisted on the attendance of members, disciplining
those who without cause were absent from the services, irregular as they probably were around Knob Creek. Nancy and
Thomas would never fail to take their children behind them
on horseback to every service held—any more than Samuel
and Martha Lincoln back in Hingham, Massachusetts, in the
seventeenth century, would have failed to lead their boys and
girls to the Meeting House. They would have been "visited"
had they not done so!

The public matter in which Thomas Lincoln seems to have
been in this period of his life most deeply interested was
slavery. He belonged to a branch of the Baptist Church
which had long been fighting slavery. And he was on friendly
terms with members of that branch of the Methodist Church
that had seceded from the regular church, largely on account
of slavery. To this branch belonged Jesse Head, the man
who had married him to Nancy Hanks, in 1806. Associated
as Jesse Head had been with the Lincoln family, it is quite
believable that he had done his part to influence their opinion
in this matter. Christopher Columbus Graham declares that
they were "just steeped full of notions about the wrongs of
slavery and the rights of man, as explained by Thomas Jefferson and Thomas Paine"—notions which, it should be said,
Mr. Graham himself did not share.

It was not only by the church and such friends as
Jesse Head and the leaders of the Rolling Fork Baptist As-

sociation that Thomas Lincoln had been influenced; there was a big group of citizens of Kentucky that had put up a strong fight when the state constitution was framed to bring the state in free. They had failed, but their agitation had not ceased. In Shelbyville, to the northeast, not very far away from where Thomas Lincoln's father had attempted to build his home, and lost his life in the attempt, there was a strong anti-slavery group publishing a paper. Their agents traveled the highway, scattering their literature, giving their message to groups and to individuals. That is, Abraham Lincoln was, at this period, under direct anti-slavery influence, and that influence centered in his own home. Arguments against the institution were an incessant matter of discussion with the strangers who sat at the fireside, or stopped on the road. The boy listened; asked questions. We have his own word for it, that often as a child he walked the floor with what were to him the dark sayings of his elders, trying to understand. The puzzle of slavery, his father's claim that it contradicted the precepts of both the Bible and the Declaration of Independence, which men held so sacred, began to take root. If we are to understand the Abraham Lincoln of the future, of forty or fifty years hence, we must not overlook what Thomas Lincoln was thinking and saying in these days on Knob Creek. Something of what he heard lay smoldering in the boy's subconsciousness. Not a year, from that time on, but something was added to these first unconscious impressions. He lived in an anti-slavery atmosphere from his earliest years.

But deeper mysteries than that of slavery were touching Abraham Lincoln. Birth and death came into the cabin. What did Thomas Lincoln do with his children when, in 1815, a baby came? Were they hurried off to a neighbor's, and told fables when they came back to see a new brother? One of the child's unforgettable impressions is the first sight of a new-born child. What did little Abraham do—think? Be sure he remembered.

And the baby died. More mystery—more unreason— and a heaviness of heart that he no more understood than he understood the joy of the birth—or why his father should make a box and shut the little one in it—nail down the lid and they all go to a far-away place and put the box in the ground and heap dirt upon it.

Nancy and Thomas Lincoln's grief over the death of their son came at a difficult time, for they were having "land troubles." The recklessness with which patents were granted in the old days, the purchases made by private companies from the Indians in defiance of Colonial claims, the irresponsibility in overlapping surveys, all were coming back to tease the Kentucky settlers. Thomas Lincoln encountered one of these tangled situations when he settled on Knob Creek. Just what his claim to the land in the first place was, by what right he was there, I have not been able to make out. Those who seemed to have the best title to the land he occupied claimed he had no right, and early in 1815 brought a suit for ejectment. The court did not sustain them, however. They declared it a false claim and ordered that they pay Thomas Lincoln the costs.

The experience seems to have been a discouraging one. It looks as if he might have been certain that in the long run he could not have held the land. At all events, in the next year, 1816, he decided, because of his trouble as well as because of his desire to live in a free state, that he would follow a new tide of immigration flowing by his door. that into southwestern Indiana.

He had some money, no doubt, for in 1814 he and Nancy had sold the farm on Mill Creek near Elizabethtown, which he had bought three years before they married. They had received for this land 100 pounds. With this and what he may have accumulated, Tom Lincoln now prepared to do as his father, his grandfather, and their forbears had been doing ever since Samuel Lincoln landed in Massachusetts in 1637 —move on in the vanguard of Western settlement.

Like them, he made a preliminary trip, the preparation for which must have been highly exciting to his children. He began by building a boat. According to Christopher Columbus Graham, Tom had his own ideas of boats. He thought they should be high and narrow, for the sake of speed. His neighbors laughed, but he carried out his notion. Where did he build his boat? I should like to think it was in the big pool down the creek. It was near home—his timber was at hand, and when the water was high he could easily have traveled from there the three or four miles to the junction of Knob Creek with the Rolling Fork, the river he must descend on his way to the Ohio and Indiana. We may be sure the children watched that boat with wonder and delight; watched, too, when Tom Lincoln loaded it with the produce he had accumulated—including, so the legends say, at least two hogshead of whisky! Along with the whisky went skins, no doubt; roots, too, like "gensang," for which there was always a market; honey and beeswax, and cloth from Nancy's loom, and last, his kit of tools—"the best in Washington County," his old friend Dr. Graham asserts. And thus equipped, away he sailed to locate a new home in a new land.

With what anxiety Nancy and Sarah and Abraham must have watched for his return. Wives and children in pioneer days in Kentucky were used to these separations. Men went on long journeys down the Mississippi seeking a market. They were gone for months prospecting—north into Indiana and Michigan, west into Missouri. Thomas was doing now only what his elder brother Josiah had done some years before. Josiah had settled not far east of the present city of Indianapolis. The Boones had, many of them, gone to Missouri. It was only the settler who had been especially fortunate that was not restless. Nancy and the children who waited for Thomas Lincoln did not wonder. He was only following the way of his world.

# X

AFTER Nancy Hanks Lincoln and her children waved
their last farewell to Thomas as he paddled down Knob
Creek on his way to Indiana, they saw no more of him until
weeks later he suddenly walked in. He brought back a fine
story of adventure, thrilling to young Abraham, for he told
them how as he made his way from the mouth of the Salt
River into the Ohio his boat had overturned, and tool chest
and whisky barrels, together with all his produce, had gone
to the bottom. He told them what he had done to rescue
tools and whisky, and how he had then made his way down
the river to a point on the Indiana side, near a little settlement called Troy, where he had stored his goods with an
enterprising settler called Posey. From there he had struck
into the unbroken country and selected, about sixteen miles
northwest of the river, the site of their future home.

I have no doubt that Tom Lincoln painted glowingly the
land he had chosen. He saw it with a pioneer's eyes, cleared,
its fields under cultivation, a home, a shop, stock in comfortable barns—he saw it better than it is even to-day!

The preparations for the removal to the new home were
quickly made. There was probably a sale of whatever possessions they had that it would be unwise to attempt to move.
There would be a little of Tom's homemade furniture, a few
head of stock, and the sale would be a species of farewell to
the neighborhood, for which Nancy Hanks would provide a

dinner assisted by all her near-by friends, Mrs. Caleb Hazel, the wife of Abraham's school teacher, Austin Gollaher's mother, and possibly a few women from near the old home at Hodgenville; such was the way of the pioneer farmer, as indeed it is the way of the farmer to-day when he "moves out."

I can scarcely believe that Nancy and Thomas Lincoln would have left the state without a farewell visit to Washington County, where both of them had spent so much time in their youth and where they had been married. Thomas's brother, Mordecai, still lived on his farm near Springfield. He had become a man of some importance in the county. There is a tradition that he had even been sent to the Kentucky Legislature, though there is no document to prove it; possibly he was a candidate but defeated. At all events he was held high by his relatives, his nephew Abraham claiming that he "had all the brains in the family." Then there were all of Nancy's people, the Berrys, Thompsons and Mitchells. Surely, they would not have left Kentucky without seeing them.

The visits and the sale over, then would come the packing. To know how to pack for migration was as much the business of a pioneer as to know how to build a log cabin or plant a field. The Lincolns had lived too long on a highway over which a continual stream of migration was flowing not to have picked up much of the technique. No doubt their cavalcade was simple, a covered wagon, stout and roomy, horses, not less than three, a cow or two, a few hens "to start with," and, of course, a dog. It was simple, but not mean as those who, for partisan or other reasons, would have us believe. Thomas Lincoln might be a poor man, but he had not been shiftless, and he was not without some means when he left Kentucky. He was a good carpenter, a trader, a farmer; that is, he had the knowledge and experience with which to make a start in a new land.

The parting, of course, was hard for the boy. It was his first experience in breaking off friendships, saying good-by for good and all to a playmate whom he had come to look upon in the way of children as a part of his life. Before he was eight years old, little Abraham Lincoln had his first painful lesson in the transient nature of human relations. It is one of the hard things that youth has to learn.

The route the Lincolns followed from Knob Creek to the Ohio is, I find, in dispute in the neighborhood. There are those like Mr. John Barry, the editor of the Rolling Fork Echo, who think they went by boat, as Thomas Lincoln had gone on his reconnoitering trip. Tradition is against him, however, and so is probability. It would have been more difficult and more uncertain than going overland by wagon.

The point they wanted to reach on the Indiana side was the mouth of what is known as Anderson Creek, near Troy, where Tom had left his possessions when he first landed. In a straight line Troy is about seventy-five miles to the northwest of the Knob Creek home. To get there, they must follow roads and trails to the Kentucky side of the ferry which crossed the Ohio from Anderson's Creek. This northwest route would lead them through Hodgenville, and give them a chance to see their friends there, and then to Elizabethtown, where, of course, they would halt for visits. Here lived Joseph Hanks with his young family, a man dear to both Nancy and Thomas, always their friend and the friend of their boy. The travelers no doubt "put up" with him, and from his home said good-by to those they knew in Elizabethtown. Even young Abraham had his friends there, for he had often gone with his father on his business trips and sat on a nail keg in the grocery and eaten the lumps of sugar the

[116]

clerk gave him. Years later this clerk, the Hon. J. B. Helm, grew to be a man of importance in Missouri, and both he and Mr. Lincoln meeting there in a political campaign recalled the visits and the sugar. Mr. Lincoln remembered something else, that this friendly clerk was the first man he knew that wore "store clothes" all the week!

Leaving Elizabethtown, the Lincolns went no doubt by their old farm on Mill Creek that Tom Lincoln had sold two years before, for near here lived his two sisters, both married, with families. That is, the first period of their journey was made over roads that they knew and their stops were at the homes of relatives and friends; but after that they came into country new to them, and all the more exciting because new. It was a beautiful rolling country, with many streams to be forded, heavily timbered, sparsely settled. The fall was coming on, and the weather at this season in Kentucky is dry and warm, a perfect time for following the road. Every day would be full of exciting incidents for the children, the cap of them being the making of camp for the night. Whatever the day's troubles—difficult fords, straying animals, broken wheels—all is forgotten when the campfire blazes at the close of day and the bacon begins to sizzle.

It took the Lincolns no less than a week to reach the Ohio after leaving Elizabethtown. The river at this point makes a magnificent bend, the water moving as silently and smoothly as if it were the surface of a lake. What a wonder this first big water that he had ever seen must have been to the young traveler. The crossing over landed them at the foot of Anderson's Creek, a point which in the future was to play a big part in Abraham's life. Anderson's Creek flows down to the Ohio between high banks, and there is a long wide flat at its mouth which had been found by the river boats to be an excellent landing place. Here they often tied up for the night,

[117]

and here the settlers of the young town of Troy near-by had already established a trade in pork and other produce. Here, too, they had a big wood yard where the river steamers took on fuel. It was a bustling place when the boats were in, and it was well for the Lincolns to make acquaintance with it, for it was to become their future market place.

Although Thomas Lincoln remained no longer at Anderson's Creek than was necessary to make preparations for the trip through the forest to his new land, there are people living there nowadays who insist that he remained a year, and show you the house he lived in to prove it. Local historians who care more for facts than they do for any possible profit that the community or any individual in it may get from a Lincoln tradition are irate and emphatic in denying this tale. They scoff at one property owner who has advertised for sale in the last year or so the "Anderson Creek home of the Lincolns." This is one of those exploitations against which tourists in the Lincoln country must always be on guard. Many a motor car has stopped in the last two years before this advertised house, kodaks have snapped and plates have been marked, "The home of Thomas Lincoln on the Ohio River."

We can be sure there was no delay in getting on. They had sixteen miles to travel, and the sooner they were at the end of the journey, the more comfortable would be their winter. I think one may rightfully envy them that journey, and will if he has a drop of gypsy blood in his veins, for it was made through a forest which in its autumnal colors was a thing of rarest beauty. The country through which they traveled was not a jungle, as it has often been described. Southwestern Indiana had long been the home of Indian tribes and there were cleared spaces left by them. The forests had been kept largely free of underbrush by occasional prairie fires; that is, it was a fairly open land; there were trails,

[118]

too, and the beginning of roads. Thomas Lincoln was by no means the first settler in this part of Indiana. In the records at Rockport I found entries of land within a few miles of where he settled made in 1811; that is, when the travelers made their way northwest, they passed within reach of more than one settler that had preceded them, and no doubt took pains to call and to pick up whatever information they could about conditions.

The October glory was still on the trees when the little party reached the knoll on the land which Thomas had chosen for them. They could not have known then how really beautiful a site it was. To-day, with the land cleared so that one can look over the great valley, see the line of Pigeon Creek, locate homes of neighbors with whom Abraham was to grow up, identify point after point connected with his life here, you get a very genuine respect for Thomas Lincoln's choice of a site in what was then an unbroken forest. Probably there was nothing to be seen about them but trees, trees of great size, many primeval timber: elms, chinquepin oaks, walnut, maple, birches, sassafras, trees which now were gold and red and yellow; when the sun sifted through them they became things of pure color, almost without substance.

Along the stream there were cleared places covered with crimson sumac and masses of golden rod, wild rose, black-berry vines, an almost impenetrable tangle. Not far away, too, there was what was called a "deer lick," a salty marsh to which wild animals came, a precious neighbor to the settler who must depend upon his gun for his supply of meat.

There was no time now, however, for exploring the country; a shelter must be ready for winter, and Thomas Lincoln and his son fell at once to cutting and clearing and preparing for what was known as a half-face camp. I am pretty sure that they were not unaided in this work, for settlers were already within reach of them, building like Tom Lincoln. Some of them were no doubt in need of a carpenter's skill. That is, from the first Tom had work at his trade, and much of this work would be done in exchange for help in clearing and building.

Many mournful pictures have been drawn of this first shelter of the Lincolns in Indiana, but the half-face camp was like the sod house of the prairie, the shack of the mining town, and quite as good as either. The best description of its making which I have ever seen is the one given by one of Mr. Lincoln's friends on the Circuit, Mr. Henry C. Whitney. It is not improbable that his description was based on talks which he had with Mr. Lincoln, for the two men frequently discussed pioneer life and its makeshifts. According to Mr. Whitney, the first step in establishing a camp was to select a site on a southern slope where two straight trees stood about fourteen feet apart east and west. These trees were trimmed and topped to serve as corner posts for the open front of the structure. Logs were then cut about fourteen feet in length sufficient for three sides; they were fastened with wooden pins to the posts that had been prepared, and laid in log cabin fashion until the walls reached the proper height. A roof of small poles interwoven with branches and thatched with brush and dry grass was built above these three sides. The openings between logs were then filled with mud. The result was a warm and tight structure open to the south.

In front of this open face a fireplace was built of stone; it was big and solid, for the whole comfort of the family through the winter depended on this fireplace. Quantities of fuel must be ready to keep it going, big back logs of hard wood, smaller stuff, branches and boughs for blazes, chips to kindle quickly. After cold weather set in this fire was not allowed to go out. It was not only warmth and a place for cooking that the fireplace gave, it was protection from wild animals. There were many of them; indeed, one of the two things that made an impression deep enough on Abraham Lincoln at this time for him to have remembered when years later he came to record his memories of this first year in Indiana was the number of wild animals!

His second strong impression was of the ax. "This most useful instrument," so he wrote in 1860, was put into his hands on their arriving in Indiana and, as he intimates, was rarely dropped until he was twenty-three!

It was hard work, no doubt, but the boy was young, strong and large for his age, according to his own account, and work done for so fine and obvious a purpose as this work has its compensations. He was helping build a home, and took pride in his part of the undertaking. As a matter of fact, I think the boy Lincoln was just discovering that he might be something of importance, something useful. The boy's natural pride in being allowed to work with men was particularly strong in his case.

It was not only building the camp that occupied him and his father. There was the stern necessity of seeing that there was food in the larder before the winter; also that there was a bit of clearing ready for corn in the spring. The game that was on all sides, big and little, was joyfully followed by Tom Lincoln, always an eager hunter. Deer was killed and hung to dry. There were wild turkeys, duck, quail, and there was an occasional bear. The game meant something more than meat to the Lincolns. It meant skins, and skins meant not only clothes and covering for them, it meant something to trade with. There were few settlers of this time that did not make the trapping and killing of fur-bearing animals a part of their winter business. Young Abraham learned to skin and cure, and the walls of the half-face camp were probably decorated continuously with a variety of valuable furs.

The hardships of this first winter have been long dwelt on, but the compensations have been generally passed by. The woodman's life has its joys. The forest in its winter garb is always a beautiful thing. Every morning brings its enjoyments. The weather itself is a constant interest, shaping as it does the day's work. The devices for meeting the problems of food and shelter kept the wits awake and the fingers busy. The Lincolns' first winter was so filled with tasks necessary to keep themselves alive, that the spring would be upon them before they knew it.

The spring in southwestern Indiana is a wonderful thing. It comes early, usually with great floods of water; with flocks of birds, big and little; with a riot of flowers followed by many small fruits. Life became a busy thing for the boy then. There was probably a calf or two to look after and there was planting, and in the intervals there was work on the new cabin, for which part at least of the logs had been cut in the winter. It was a big cabin for the time, eighteen feet square, with a loft and a huge chimney. It stood near the camp and on the top of the knoll. The location is marked today by a marble slab, and clear as the country is now, one can realize how finely it was placed.

To make this cabin habitable within and attractive without became Nancy Lincoln's business. The settler's wife invariably brought with her some root of a favorite flower, a bulb, a bit of vine to plant by her cabin door, something to remind her of the home she had left. Nancy Lincoln planted her vines and in the clearing near-by fruit trees were soon set out. There are straggling remnants of them still to be seen on the slope. Between house-building, clearing and planting, the boy would be busy enough. Then, too, they were beginning to make some connections in the neighborhood. Pigeon Creek Valley was filling up. A church had been organized, though there was no building yet and only irregular services held in private houses, and there was talk of a school, though not yet a school. I cannot believe but that this first year was one of real interest as well as hard work for the boy.

They were joined in the fall of 1817 by three relatives from Kentucky, Thomas and Betsy Sparrow, and with them a cousin of Nancy, Dennis Hanks by name, a boy about ten years older than Abraham. The coming of these old acquaintances made life more interesting and gave more strong hands to push the development of the farm. In every way then the second winter was easier for the Lincolns than the first. The second summer undoubtedly gave them still further hope, for by this time Tom Lincoln had his hands full of carpentry work. Things would have gone from now on increasingly well, I am convinced, if in the fall of 1818, just about two years after they came into the country, there had not come to Thomas Lincoln that greatest of blows for the pioneer, the death of his wife.

The country in which the Lincolns had settled was a rolling, wooded one, as I have said. The wide valleys, threaded as they were by big and little creeks, were usually deep in matted vegetation, the accumulation of hundreds of years. True, an occasional forest fire swept down the vegetation, but usually its heavy growth simply rotted during the winter. The frequent heavy rainfalls filled the streams to overflowing, soaking the accumulated leaf mold until it was a rank malarious mass. Through the fall heavy fogs frequently lay over the land, so that the poison that rose from the valleys was not taken care of by air and sun. This had its inevitable effect upon the settlers. Chills and fever, ague, was common.

[123]

When the conditions were particularly bad an intensified form of malaria resulted, commonly known in southwestern Indiana as "milk-sick." There was an outbreak of this disease in the fall of 1818. It attacked more than one of Nancy Lincoln's neighbors, and she went from one house to another, helping as she could to take care of the sufferers. Among them was one of her best friends, a Mrs. Brooner, whose children lived to tell of her kindness to their mother. Mrs. Brooner felt sure she was going to die, but Nancy Lincoln reproved her. "Tut, tut!" she said; "you will soon be well and strong again. Woman, keep up your courage." Homely, well-meant comfort, but unavailing. Mrs. Brooner died, but before her death Nancy Lincoln herself was stricken with the epidemic. Death followed quickly, so quickly that to the unprepared family it must have been like the hand of an angry God laid upon them.

This sudden death of his mother came to young Abraham Lincoln as an irreparable tragedy. A boy of nine or ten depends upon his mother in a very special and intimate way. It has never occurred to him that life can go on without her, and then to have her taken almost without warning from the home makes an unforgettable impression. It certainly did on Abraham Lincoln. I am inclined to think that the deep melancholy of his nature was then first stirred into life, that here he began to question, as we know he did later, the rightness and goodness of the world in which he found himself.

Death was a peculiarly intimate thing in a home like that of the Lincolns. The body lay in the cabin where you ate and slept. You must yourself make all the preparations for burial, even to building the coffin in which the dead body was to be laid away. In a hundred ways we protect ourselves from the presence of the dead to-day, but in those days every detail of the preparation for burial was under your eye. Nothing could be covered up, spared you. Thus to young Sarah and Abraham this death of their mother was a more intimate matter than death could be in a more highly developed home.

The burial of the dead in the pioneer community is always a matter of general concern. It is a community event, and it is a part of neighborliness to be present at funeral services and the grave; but here in a country where sickness was in every household, where every household was stricken, where there was no church or minister, all of the usual cere-mony must be dispensed with. Tom Lincoln and his children must go practically alone to the burial of Nancy Hanks.

They laid her in a beautiful spot. Perhaps half a mile from their cabin was a knoll heavily wooded, uncleared, a spot where probably already a grave or two had been dug. It was October and the woods were in full color, red, yellow, brown. Let us hope it was a sunny day, for the heart-broken little family had little or nothing of that which they felt was due to the dead to comfort them, no burial service, no sympathetic neighbors. They were alone and forlorn in a stricken land.

It was many months before the funeral services, which they felt, as all people of their traditions felt, were necessary, were held. It was owing to Abraham's efforts that, months after her burial, a minister held Nancy Lincoln's funeral. But there is nothing surprising about this. It constantly happens in remote communities that funeral services are as long delayed as they were in the case of Nancy Hanks Lincoln.

Tom Lincoln and his children would go often to visit her grave, but they were never able to do more to honor her than to put up what was common in the world at that time, what one sees everywhere still in the old graveyards, an uncut

[125]

fragment of red sandstone, no lettering, no date, only this marker. And so the grave lay for sixty years, when, in 1879, a friend of her son put a fence about the grave, set up a headstone and upon it wrote the inscription:

Nancy Hanks Lincoln,
Mother of President Lincoln,
Died October 5, A. D. 1818,
Aged 35 Years.
Erected by a friend of her
Martyred Son.

I know of no woman's grave in this or any other country which more deeply—and rightfully so—touches the heart than that of this simple pioneer woman, the mother of our greatest American. How worthily and beautifully is the place marked! The hilltop on which she lies with the group of little graves which gradually grew around hers has been turned into a park—not a pretentious park, but a rarely lovely one. Hundreds of beautiful trees cover the knoll. Between them one looks out upon the fertile, well-developed valleys, distant farms—the kind of thing which Thomas and Nancy Lincoln had in mind when they started overland into the new country. I think it must be a regret to many people that generous friends of Nancy Hanks have in recent days insisted on putting before her grave a pretentious marble monument, feeling that the modest gravestone first set up does not sufficiently honor her. They are wrong. It is much more beautiful, more suitable. The park itself, with its outlook over the wide sweeping country which she gave her life to help open to the future, is her true monument. I wish they would take the big stone away!

It was a sad household to which Tom Lincoln and his children returned after Nancy Hanks' burial, a disease-ridden household, too, for there quickly followed the death of both Mr. and Mrs. Sparrow, leaving the home without a woman, only the child Sarah, now but eleven years old. Abraham Lincoln was having at nine his first experience with the deepest of sorrows and with all the perplexing problems that sorrow brings. It was not until a year later that life again took on something of the old order and peace, and that came from Tom Lincoln's bringing into the home a second mother.

## XI

### LINCOLN LEARNS FROM LABOR

IN the meager gallery of Lincoln portraiture there is no picture of stronger appeal than that of the woman who in December, 1819, Thomas Lincoln brought back to Indiana to be a second mother to his children. It is the face of a brave, patient, enduring woman. Her clear eyes—I think they must have been gray—are direct and unwavering with a look of pain in them, a woman who through a long life of labor and poverty had held to those things she believed to be good. Surely Thomas Lincoln must have been more of a man than he has usually been painted to have won and kept two women so worthy of respect as Nancy Hanks and Sarah Bush Johnston, his second wife.

It was a year after Nancy's death that Tom went back to Kentucky undoubtedly with the idea of proposing marriage to Mrs. Johnston, whose husband had been dead for many months. It has always seemed probable to me that he made a reconnoitering trip; that is, I see no reason why he should have gone prepared to bring her back.

Thomas Lincoln had known Sarah Bush as a girl in Elizabethtown; indeed, he is said to have courted her before he did Nancy Hanks, but as she was only eighteen years old when he and Nancy were married it seems a bit doubtful. However, they were friends, and when he came back a widower and found her husbandless and with three children it was natural enough that he should seek her. That she did not hesitate to accept him those nearest to the pair all testify.

[128]

Perhaps the best authority is a nephew of Tom's, Mr. J. L. Nall.

"Uncle Thomas," he says, "came back to Kentucky after the death of his first wife, Nancy Hanks, and proposed marriage to the Widow Johnston. She told him that she would be perfectly willing to marry him as she had known him a long time, and felt that the marriage would be congenial and happy; but it would be impossible for her even to think of marrying and leaving the state as she was considerably in debt. Uncle Thomas told her that need make no difference, as he had plenty of money, and would take care of her financial affairs; and when he had ascertained the amount of her indebtedness and the names of the parties to whom the money was due, he went around and redeemed all her paper and presented it to her, and told her, when she showed so much honor about debts, he was more fully satisfied than ever that she would make him a good wife. She said as he had displayed so much generosity in her behalf she was willing to marry and go with him to Spencer County, Indiana."

I should like to think that Thomas when he had secured her promise went back to Indiana and told the children something of their new mother and then taking his wagon and horses went after her, her children, and her household furniture. Think of the days of eagerness and dread for Sarah and Abraham. Probably the talkative Dennis Hanks did little to quiet their alarms. Dennis, now about nineteen, was at an age when his talk on marital affairs was probably anything but fit for the ears of a boy of ten.

Any misgivings the children may have had about their new mother faded at the sight of her. Sarah Lincoln was a vigorous, blooming woman of thirty-one. All the traditions preserved of her harmonize with the story her portrait taken in her old age tells. She was what is called a good housekeeper, a good neighbor, a kindly, resourceful woman. She came now bringing treasures and comforts such as the Indiana home of the Lincolns had never known. She brought companions, too, for Sarah and Abraham, two girls and a boy about their own age. In a day the little family of four became eight. The cabin was filled to overflowing, but never had life been so comfortable and orderly as now.

To the boy Abraham the new mother's coming was of special importance. Abraham Lincoln had that need of women, natural to all strong masculine natures—need of their companionship, confidence, affection. Without it life for him at every stage would be incomplete. His mother had given completeness to his childhood. His hunger for her must have been pitiful. The healthfulness of the period of adolescence which he was now entering was bound to depend upon the woman his father had brought home. I think he never had a doubt of her from the start. In his autobiography, written in 1860, he speaks of her as "a good and kind mother." As for Mrs. Lincoln, her tribute to her son made to Mr. Herndon after Lincoln's assassination shows something of the relation between them. "He was a good boy, and I can say what scarcely one woman—a mother—can say in a thousand, he never gave me a cross word or look. I never gave him a cross word in all my life; his mind and mine seemed to run together. I think he loved me truly. He was the best boy I ever saw."

It was real friendship between them, mutual understanding and mutual protection. He had the consideration for others that belongs to a big nature, and in a hundred ways no doubt from the start served his stepmother; she in return saw something of his growing ambitions and protected him in his efforts to learn.

For the great service she undoubtedly rendered Abraham

Lincoln in those difficult years when, as one wise educator has said, "every boy is a little mad," Sarah Lincoln has received scant public recognition. So far as I know it was not until the fall of 1922 that there was ever placed anywhere in her honor so much as a single tablet. It is fitting that Elizabethtown, Kentucky, from which Thomas Lincoln took her, should be the first to remember her. In the fall of last year the Woman's Club of the town conducted the ceremony at the placing in position in the court house of a bronze tablet to Sarah Lincoln, presented by a native of the town, Dr. W. A. Pusey of Chicago. In connection with this ceremony the club published a pamphlet giving some details of Mrs. Lincoln's life. This work is in line with other excellent local historical work which the women had already done; the most important of which has been the publication of the diary and notes of Samuel Haycroft, for many years the county clerk—the man whose name appears on the license issued on December 2, 1819, permitting "any authorized minister of the gospel or authorized magistrate to join together in the honorable state of matrimony Mr. Thomas Lincoln and Miss Sarah Johnston."

It now remains for others to mark Sarah Johnston Lincoln's grave, to-day the one unremembered grave among those of the women known to have been dear to Abraham Lincoln.

Outwardly the boy's life from now on until he was a man grown was that of a day laborer; he was a farm hand, a carpenter's assistant, a ferryman, a hired man. These were his jobs. What part did they play in his making? What was their educational content? Considerable, I have always believed. In the first place they clearly proved to him and to others that he was not meant for manual labor. If he had been "born" for the farm here was his chance; with his ambition and intelligence he might have gone far in farming in southwestern Indiana, giving the business the touch of genius in that locality which it seems always to have lacked. There were those of his friends who did take to the farm; it was their natural bent, but not his. Strong, good natured, eager to excel, whatever the task he would go to any exertion to outstrip those beside him. He seemed naturally to have conscience about his work. Self-respect made it necessary for him to keep up his end. These qualities made him a valuable farm laborer, but the laborer never won; he seems never to have had an idea of making farming a permanent occupation.

It was the same with carpentry and cabinetmaking. He was Tom Lincoln's assistant, and Tom Lincoln was good at his trade. How skillful a cabinetmaker he was I never realized until recently I examined a piece of his work exhibited in the relic room of the fine court house in Rockport, county seat of Spencer County, Indiana, the town where the Lincolns used to go to pay taxes and attend to court business. This cabinet is perfectly authenticated, but in addition to the testimony tacked on one of its front panels I had as a guide a man who could tell me truthfully, "It stood in the very room where I was born. Many is the time that as a child I have gone to that cupboard for something to eat."

My guide was Mr. W. F. Adams of Rockport, a grandson of Josiah and Elizabeth Crawford, the neighbors who figure most largely in the Lincolns' lives in Indiana. Josiah Crawford was a wheelwright, making not only wagons, but big and little spinning wheels. Tom Lincoln did all the carpenter work for their comfortable frame house—window frames, doors, cupboards. Abraham had worked with him on this job and had frequently served Josiah Crawford as a hired man, indeed he had so completely won the heart and respect of his employer—not an easy man to win if tradition is to be believed—that, Mr. Adams declares, Lincoln's assassination literally killed him. "He began to go down from the day he heard of it."

Now this cupboard, so well authenticated, is important as a proof of a considerable degree of craftsmanship on the part of Tom Lincoln. It is thoroughly well made and carries a rather elaborate cornice, but what interested me most was an inlaid decoration in white ash running down the door jambs on each side and the inlaid initials E. W. on the left-hand door panel. The design is crude, to be sure, but it shows a sense of decoration and patriotism combined, for the curving streamer falls from a star and at each bend there arises a tiny flag. The inlaying is so well done that in spite of fully ninety years of scrubbing and scouring it remains intact.

What this amounts to is that if Abraham Lincoln had had any strong craft sense here was his chance. Furniture at that day was largely made on the premises. Indeed at this very moment back in the Shenandoah Valley, Tom's own cousin, Abraham Lincoln, son of his uncle Jacob, was having made in the garret over the kitchen of his fine house huge pieces of mahogany furniture—a swelled front corner cabinet, a tall clock, an elaborate desk. The wood, so the tradition goes· in the family, he had brought by ox teams from New York City But cabinetmaking was no more the boy's bent than farming.

It was clear before Abraham was sixteen that the chief interest he found in labor was the opportunity it gave him of meeting men. That was why he liked going to the mill; here were new people, fresh talk, news. He was greedy for men and what they could tell him; that was why the jobs he must take away from home after the summer's work was over interested him. An ideal one came in the fall and winter of 1826, when he was 17; this was running a ferryboat across the Ohio from the mouth of Anderson's Creek where the Lincoln's had landed in 1816.

It was a busy place, this landing, for here a big business in shipping pork and corn and in supplying river steamers with fuel had grown up. Chief of the pioneer merchants was James Taylor, who managed the ferry, and to him Lincoln hired himself out for the season; his pay six dollars a month and board—board in his employer's family, where, luckily for Abraham, there was a boy about his own age—Green Taylor, later to be known as Captain Taylor. Twenty-five years ago I was in correspondence with the captain, whose recollections of Lincoln were definite and kindly. The thing which he said most impressed him was Lincoln's reading often "far into the night." Captain Taylor did not report to me a story current in the neighborhood to-day of a quarrel with Lincoln over a girl. There had been a husking bee and Abraham drew a red ear. It gave him the right to kiss the girl he liked best, and more honest than discreet he kissed his friend Green Taylor's girl! The next day there was a fight and, so goes the story, "Lincoln hit Taylor with an ear of corn, making a scar Green carried as long as he lived!"

It was the ferry which gave him interest and excitement. The stream of travel was constant. Not since he left the Knob Creek home on the Nashville and Louisville Pike had he seen so many people of so many kinds. There were pioneers moving north and eager to know all he could tell them of the country ahead; politicians sounding him out on what people thought; anti-slavery agitators distributing pamphlets and arguments; traders of all kinds; an occasional scientist asking him questions about river life and habits; and every now and then an itinerant preacher or circuit rider concerned for his salvation—the motley life of the advance guard of civilization, a strange blend of adventure and hope, mean-

[134]

ness and courage, selfishness and devotion. He liked it all, and daily soaked in its flavor and its meaning.

The travel down the river contributed no little to the variety of his life, for here at Anderson's Creek the steamers frequently tied up for the night and passengers and "hands" came ashore for talk or fun. William Owen, who with his father, Robert Owen, came down the Ohio on one of these river boats in 1824 on their way to buy New Harmony from the Rappites, tells in his journal of one of these night frolics at an Indiana landing. The passengers going ashore built a great fire and roasted beef for supper. Then, to end their fun, burned down a tree! These were the kind of sights and contacts running a ferryboat brought to the observing and eager boy that winter.

The river itself played upon his awakening nature. We too easily overlook the part the natural world about us has in our development—what the seasons, the stars, the trees, the winds do to us. The Ohio here at Anderson's Creek makes a majestic bend, giving an impression of vastness to the river— the water steals rather than flows. There is so little perceptible movement, so little sound that at night it is mysterious and almost fearsome, but in the mornings, the evenings, under starshine and moonlight is marvelously beautiful. To watch the great stream as he lay at night on its bank must have stirred young Abraham often and deeply. And now and then a lighted steamboat went by—lights from stem to stern, music, song, perhaps something of revelry. What allurement there must have been to the watching boy in such a passing boat, coming from a world of which he knew nothing, going to a world of which he knew less. How it must have pulled at his head and heart and at all the young passions in him!

When spring opened Abraham went back to the farm with

an idea. Why should they not raise enough produce to stock a flatboat and he take it down the river to New Orleans in the fall—go where the steamers went, you see! The produce was raised largely by his efforts; the boat was built by him, but he did not get to New Orleans that year, nor do we know how he disposed of his stock; indeed, the only incident of this venture of which we do know is one he once related to Secretary Seward. It seems to have been the birth in him of the idea that he could earn money—money for himself. His boat had been finished and he was looking it over, wondering if it were fit for the voyage, when a couple of men came down to the bank and asked him to row them out to a steamer which they had hailed and which had stopped to take them aboard. He rowed them out and they threw down to him from the steamer's deck fifty cents apiece—a dollar! "I could scarcely believe my eyes as I picked up the money," Secretary Seward reports Mr. Lincoln as saying. "I, the poor boy, had earned a dollar in less than a day!"

But if Abraham did not get to New Orleans that year he did the next, and in his autobiography, written in 1860, in the third person, he tells the story quaintly and humorously, if briefly:

"When he was nineteen, still residing in Indiana, he made his first trip upon a flatboat to New Orleans. He was a hired hand merely, and he and a son of the owner, without other assistance, made the trip. The nature of part of the 'cargo-load,' as it was called, made it necessary for them to linger and trade along the sugar coast; and one night they were attacked by seven negroes with intent to kill and rob them. They were hurt some in the melee, but succeeded in driving the negroes from the boat, and then cut cable, weighed anchor and left."

There's adventure for you! And what a fight it must have been! And to what good purpose Abraham's great fists and powerful arms must have worked!

# LINCOLN LEARNS FROM LABOR

A life of labor, hard but varied, marked by new scenes, fresh contacts, fresh efforts, a constant call to ingenuity. Lincoln himself was wrong when he said of his life at this period that there was nothing in it to awaken ambition. It was his "inferiority complex" that spoke. This "complex" troubled him all his life, and had it not been for his ambition, his healthy common sense and the well of humor forever bubbling in him it would undoubtedly have been his ruin.

Lincoln learned much in this period of labor important in later life. His very speech took flavor from it. The horse, the dog, the ox, the chin fly, the plow, the hog, these companions of his youth became interpreters of his meaning, solvers of his problems in his great necessity, of making men understand and follow him.

An element in the great strength of his debate with Douglas is the understanding and feeling it shows for labor and the man that labors. He had learned in these days in Indiana the place labor plays in man's progress; how an advancing civilization is built on it. The trees must be cut and the fields cleared before food and shelter were possible. Roads must be opened and wagons built before barter of extra produce could begin. It was by the labor of their hands and brains that he, his father and their neighbors had opened southwestern Indiana to the uses of men. He saw labor as the foundation of all that might come after it, for he had labored himself, starting a community.

This respect for the fundamental worthwhileness of labor permeates the great debates, and gives to them a quality which is found in no other of the many splendid arguments of the period against the extension of slavery.

If Lincoln underestimated the "educational content" of the many tasks to which his hands were turned in these years it is because they were only a necessity, a temporary duty, a

[137]

makeshift for him. His mind was bent on another field. He was after that kind of education which made "great men." How did they become so? What were they like? Along with farming and carpentering, flatboating and bartering went from the first years in Indiana a search for knowledge.

# XII

## LINCOLN'S INTELLECTUAL AWAKENING

PITY for Abraham Lincoln because he had no better opportunities for schooling in the years he spent in southwestern Indiana has come to be a fixed tradition. I think
he always pitied himself a little. "Nothing but A, B, C
schools," kept "by littles," where a teacher who knew Latin
was looked upon as a wizard—"absolutely nothing to excite
ambition for education"—this was the despondent tone in
which he talked of his early chances. One might pity him
if, like most of his fellows, he had found no substitute; but
as it was, he is rather to be congratulated, for his mind wak-
ened up early, eager, greedy for knowledge. He had what
schools exist to give, and so many succeed only in stifling—
curiosity—curiosity about men and life—insatiable curiosity.
His was the kind of mind that found food anywhere—found
it in southwestern Indiana—plenty of it.

He may have had little chance at school, but he made
much of that chance—much of his books—books like "The
Kentucky Preceptor"—a comprehensive, serious, grown-up
book, its reading exercises not expurgated of all high and
serious ideas, written down for young minds, but rather
selected for the purpose of pulling up young minds to solemn
and elevated thinking. They told of great deeds, of sacrifices
for freedom, of hatred of tyrants, of contempt for mean actions. "The Kentucky Preceptor" was calculated propagan-
dism for the ideals of democracy!

The very arithmetic that Abraham Lincoln studied puts

[139]

its problems in terms of American history: "General Washington was born in 1732. What was his age in 1787?"

As only the teacher had a book, the pupils must commit the selections. The whole school room studied out loud, and passers-by dubbed it the "blab school." It was in this "blab school" that Lincoln began the training of his memory, to hold, as it did, page after page of verse and prose, to acquire the habit of going over out loud the speech or document he was preparing. He did it all his life, the sound of the phrase helping him to clarify his thoughts.

He had, too, his first training in debating and declamation in these schools. And there was no question that the community counted him its prize boy, the one that was sure to "stand up" longest at the spelling match, to win the debate, to take the recitation prize. Every one of that considerable group of southwestern Indiana people who remembered him in his youth, and who repeated their reminiscences from the time that reminiscences of him began to be collected to the day of their death, have testified to his superiority over his fellows. All of them had some individual experience to offer to prove that Lincoln was "different" from those about him. He used his time differently, reacted differently to the life of the community, found interest in things that meant nothing to his associates. He was not merely concerned, like those about him, with his job, his meals, his fun, his neighbors. He took his part—a big part—in all these things, but there was something more—something that impressed him on them, and made the elders among them prophesy a future for him.

The intentness of his interest in knowledge, his power of concentrating on books was particularly marked by these serious elders. Josiah Crawford, for whom Lincoln did much work as a hired man, talked of this. Crawford was the only one among his neighbors, so far as I know, that ever remarked Lincoln's habit of sticking out his left lower lip when his mind was concentrated in reading or thinking. This habit, fallen into in his youth, resulted in that protuberance of the lower lip which is a distinguishing characteristic of his face. Crawford used to banter the boy on his "stuck out lip."

In 1844, after fourteen years' absence from southwestern Indiana, Lincoln came back in the Harrison campaign to speak at Rockport, his old county seat, and Josiah Crawford went down to hear him. In those days an Indiana audience measured the importance of a speaker by the number of books and pamphlets he brought with him. Lincoln came without a printed page, and it bothered Mr. Crawford. "Where's your books, Abe?" he asked. "I haven't any. Sticking out my lip is all I need." The old man told this tale with glee to his death. It was their own little joke!

The only institution in the community outside of the "A B C school" was the church. It was regarded by all as the chief formative influence. It set the standard for conduct. It acted as arbiter and frequently as policeman. The church had a first place in the Lincoln family; just how important has only recently been proved. That is, it is only within a few years that the records of the Pigeon Church, which Tom Lincoln and his family attended, have been made public. My attention was first called to them by Mr. W. E. Ellsworth, formerly of The Century Company, whose lecture on Lincoln is so widely and favorably known.

In the fall of 1922 I first had my hands on the ancient book in which the minutes of the church's business meetings were set down from its organization in 1816 on into the thirties. It's a precious document to a book lover, its big sheets, probably 24 x 9 inches in size, being bound in a home-made cowhide cover, from which the hair has been almost entirely worn. Fortunately the Pigeon Church knows its value, and one of the trustees, Mr. Louis Varner, of Booneville, Indiana, guards it jealously. I went over every line of the record last fall, but never for a moment was I out from under a watchful eye, which is the way it should be. There would be many more Lincoln papers in their proper places, particularly in Illinois court houses, if their guardians had exercised anything like the care Mr. Varner does over his trust.

The whole history of the church in the years the Lincoln family lived in the neighborhood is set down in the minutes. Although organized in 1816, it was not until 1822 that there was a building in which to hold services. They had the same trouble in Spencer, Indiana, in the early nineteenth century in deciding on a site for the meeting house, on its size and plan, as they had in Hingham, Massachuseets, in Samuel Lincoln's day.

So far as the records show, Tom Lincoln did not take an active part in the discussions, which stretched on for many months before a decision was finally reached which brought the church within a mile of his home—a short mile across country, a difficult mile with present roads. When the church was finally established in his neighborhood, he joined by letter, as the record shows:

"June 7, 1823, received Brother Thomas Lincoln by letter."

From the start Thomas Lincoln seems to have been active in church affairs. For three years he was a trustee, being finally relieved at his own request. It was the custom for a church to send visitors to neighborhood churches, generally on letters of invitation, and in 1824 Tom Lincoln, with two of his neighbors, was sent to the Gilead Church as a visitor. The conduct of members of the church was strictly watched; the separation of a husband and wife, quarreling brothers and sisters, absence from service, irregularities of every kind, misconduct in meeting, were turned over to committees for investigation and report. Tom Lincoln frequently served on such committees. That is, from the time the Pigeon Church was established, he was one of the five or six most important men in it.

The minute book contains only one record of subscriptions to the support of the church. It is interesting as showing how they did things in those days, also how they spelled:

"We the undersined do asign our names to pay the sevrial somes annexed to our names in produce this fall to be delivered betwixt the first and 20th of December, the produce is as follows corn wheat whiskey pork Linnen wool or any other article or material to do the work with. the produce will Be Dilevered at the meting hoas in good marchanable produce.

"William Barker ere."

Lincoln's name is in the list of the "undersined"—"Thomas Lincoln in corn manufactured pounds 24."

He and his wife Sarah remained in good and regular standing in Pigeon Church up to the time that they left Indiana in 1830, when they were granted a "letter of Dismission." This letter was followed by an unpleasant incident. After it was given, "Sister Nancy Grigsby" informed the church that she was "not satisfied with Brother and Sister Lincoln," and the trustees agreed to call back the letter they had given until satisfaction could be obtained. It was obtained, and a month later, to show the confidence which the church had in Tom Lincoln, it appointed him on a committee of five to settle a difficulty between the same Sister Grigsby and Sister Betsy Crawford!

We can take it as certain that Abraham Lincoln was a regular attendant at this church in which his father took so important a part. There is a tradition that he acted as its

[143]

janitor, but of that there is no proof in existence, so far as I know. The important thing, from the point of view of his development, is what this church taught, what were its articles of faith.

These are set down in the first page of the minute book of Pigeon Church:

"We believe in one God the father the word and the Holy Ghost, who hath created all things that are created by the word of his power for his pleasure.

"We believe the old and new Testaments are the word of God and there are every thing contained therein necessary for our salvation and rule of faith and practice.

"We believe in the fall of man in his public head and that is incapable of recovery unless restored by Christ.

"We believe in election by grace given us in Christ Jesus before the world began and that God calls regenerates and sanctifies who are made meet for glory by his special grace.

"We believe the righteous will persevere through grace to glory, and none of them finally fall away.

"We believe in a general resurrection of the Just and unjust and the joys of the righteous and the punishment of the wicked are eternal.

"We believe that good works are the fruits of Grace and follow after justification.

"We believe that Baptism and the Lords supper are ordinances of Jesus Christ and that true believers are the only proper subjects and the only proper mode of Baptism is immersion.

"We believe the washing of feet is a command to be complied with when opportunity serves.

"We believe it is our duty severally to support the Lords table and that we ought to administer the Lord's supper at least twice a year.

"We believe that no minister ought to preach the gospel, that is not called and sent of God, and they are to be proved by hearing them, and we allow of none to preach amongst us but such as are well recommended and that we ought to contribute to him who faithfully labors among us in word and doctrines according to our several abilities of our temporal things."

The record shows that these articles of faith were faithfully followed. They were careful whom they should invite to speak, no "strange foreigner" being allowed unless he came "well recommended as a preacher of the Gospel." They held their communion service regularly; they baptized by immersion, and foot-washing was practiced regularly, as it is to-day in this same church.

Abraham Lincoln never joined Pigeon Church. Its peculiar ceremonies made little or no impression upon him; but that he pondered deeply the articles of faith, and the interpretation given them by those he heard in the pulpit, and in the constant discussion of them that went on at his own and neighboring firesides, is certain. It is certain, too, that out of this pondering there came a deep reverence for the spirit of Christianity and a code of conduct for his relations with men and women as nearly in accord with the spirit of the Gospels, as high, as noble, as generous as that which has regulated the life of any man in the public life of this or any other country.

It was in books, however, that Lincoln began, probably as early as ten years of age, to find the most satisfying food for his curious, searching mind. We have his own word for it that the first book that stirred his curiosity in regard to this country and how it came into being, as well as awakened his reverence for the ideas behind it, was Weem's "Life of Washington."

In February of 1861, when he was on his way to his inauguration, he told the senate of New Jersey that this book fell into his hands in the earliest days of his being able to read, and that the impressions it made had lasted longer than any others. And they were fine impressions—of men struggling for their liberty—they stirred his imagination and assumed more and more importance in his mind; they meant something more to him than national independence, he said;

[145]

they held out "a 'great promise to all the people of the world, for all time to come.' "

I have always believed that the book which gave body to this aroused interest, which helped him to define and clarify the notions that the "Life of Washington" had aroused in him, was a book which one of his older friends in the neighborhood, Mr. David Turnham, of the town nearest to the Lincolns, Gentryville, put in his way. David Turnham was the sheriff of the county, an able and kindly pioneer, in whom Lincoln had aroused a very genuine interest. It was in his home that Lincoln came across The Revised Statutes of Indiana.

The title does not sound hopeful, but as an introduction to the statutes, the book contained the Declaration of Independence, the Constitution of the United States, the Act of Virginia passed in 1783 by which the territory "northwestward of the River Ohio was conveyed to the United States," and the Articles of 1787 for governing this territory, containing the famous article reading:

"There shall be neither slavery nor involuntary servitude in the said territory, otherwise than in the punishment of crimes, whereof a party shall have been duly convicted; provided always that any person escaping into the same, from whom labor or service is lawfully claimed in any one of the original States, such fugitive may be lawfully reclaimed and conveyed to the person claiming him or her labor, as aforesaid."

That is, at eighteen, on top of the impressions derived from his study of Washington's life, Lincoln had put into his hands the documents on which this country has been built and shaped. They took a tremendous hold of him.

He followed the bit of autobiography quoted above a few days later with a second bit, drawn from him by the emotion which he felt at finding himself in the Hall of Independence in Philadelphia. "All the political sentiments I entertain," he said in confessing to his emotion, "have been drawn, so far as I have been able to draw them, from the sentiments which originated and were given to the world from this Hall. I never had a feeling politically that did not spring from the sentiments embodied in the Declaration of Independence."

It was in David Turnham's Statutes of Indiana that he first found these sentiments. He did not merely read the documents in the Revised Statutes, he studied them, pondered them, saturated himself with them. They were the strongest, most satisfying food his mind had yet found.

All of the discussion of contemporary politics which went on in the neighborhood, the weekly talks over the news that took place in Jones' grocery store in Gentryville after the newspaper had come in from Louisville—all of this gave him a chance to apply the principles and to check up the way they were working. He had his chance now to learn the fight that must be made before a fine article like No. 6 in the Ordinance of 1787 was assured of realization. An incessant struggle went on against that article in Illinois in these years, repeated petitions being sent to Congress asking its repeal. The struggle that Illinois was making for freedom was reflected in the Pigeon Church, the Baptists being sharply divided on the question of slavery. Indeed Lincoln must have known of the Baptist Church founded in Illinois in 1809 by a friend of Thomas Jefferson, the Rev. James Lemen, who early in the century had, at Jefferson's request, come to the territory for the express purpose of spreading anti-slavery notions, and who, at Jefferson's suggestion, finally organized a church on a strictly anti-slavery basis.

He must have heard often repeated, too, the story of Edward Coles of Virginia—high born, rich, cultivated, whose hatred of slavery was such that in 1819, after a preliminary

[147]

exploration trip in southern Illinois and the purchase there of a large tract of land, he had sold his Virginia home, gathered all his slaves together and turned westward. All up and down the Ohio Valley the story was told and retold of how Mr. Coles, after starting down the river on flatboats, had, for the first time, made known to his slaves his intention of freeing them. The scene that followed his announcement had moved the whole anti-slavery world. The black men and women had fallen on their knees and wept with gratitude, but they refused to leave their liberator until he was settled. In southern Illinois Coles deeded to each negro family 160 acres of land, and arranged to give them employment while they were settling and developing their holdings.

Every anti-slavery man in the country had at his tongue's end the preamble of the freedom papers Edward Coles issued on July 4, 1819, to these people:

"Not believing that man can have of right property in his fellow man, but that on the contrary all mankind are endowed by nature with equal rights, I do therefore by these presents restore to ........ ............ that inalienable liberty of which he (or she) has been deprived."

Do not imagine that young Abraham Lincoln was not familiar with this episode or could not quote this preamble, or that he was not familiar with the whole story of Edward Coles' splendid later fight which was so large a factor in making Illinois free.

There were many other things going on around him calculated to stir and enlarge his mind. The intellectual and moral resources of the section of the country in which Lincoln passed the years from seven to twenty-one were greater than the abundant reminiscences collected from his old neighbors in and around the Lincoln farm reveal. It was the intimate, daily thing they remembered about the boy and his life there;

it was not of the ideas that were stirring him, not of his inner mental life that Dennis Hanks and his kind could tell. In Lincoln we have a mind receptive to "things in the air" as well as indefatigable in the search for what he wanted most —that is, for men to talk with, books to read. There were more of both than I at least have until recently realized.

If we are to take literally what he once told a friend— that he had read every book within fifty miles of his home— he had read much more widely and generally than the meager list, so familiar to Lincoln students, indicates. That list includes, besides the Life of Washington and the Statutes of Indiana, mentioned above, the Bible, with which, of course, he was thoroughly familiar, Æsop's Fables, Bunyan's Pilgrim's Progress, Robinson Crusoe. These must have been only a small percentage of what he actually read. He drew on the resources of towns like Rockport, Booneville, Troy; he probably also drew on Princeton, Evansville, possibly New Harmony. He found ways to get to a book.

We must remember that from the time he was fifteen or sixteen, he was spending probably several months of every year away from home, at work, and that wherever he was, at home or abroad, he had the practice of joining the crowd when something unusual was going on—a murder trial, political gatherings, camp meetings—and that in these crowds he managed to make acquaintance with the most important men. The names of some of these men are familiar. There was Judge John Pitcher, of Rockport; there was Judge Breckinridge, of Booneville—men whose work in the development and upbuilding of their communities and their state have become part of the history of Indiana. Lincoln made his way to them, forced their attention, submitted his ideas —even his attempts at writing, to Judge Pitcher, whose comment on one of his compositions was that "the world couldn't beat it." Among others with whom he came in contact was a congressman of his district, Ratcliff Boone, and here there was more than a political connection—there was the long association of Boones and Lincolns, their inter-marriages, their pioneering together to give a background and a kind of intimacy. But that his association stopped with the three or four superior men whose names figure in all of the collections of reminiscences of Lincoln in southwestern Indiana is not likely.

There has been in the last few years a considerable amount of solid work done on the character of the men and women who settled this corner of the state; particularly important from the Lincoln standpoint, is that of Judge John E. Igle-hart, of Evansville, Indiana, president of the Southwestern Indiana Historical Society. Judge Iglehart's work gives us a better basis for judging of the caliber of the men under whose indirect influence at least Lincoln certainly came at this time, than we have ever had before. He has developed, with a wealth of detail, the character of the English settle-ment which started in 1817 north of Evansville and twenty-five or thirty miles west of where Lincoln lived—a settlement whose descendants are still among the leading people of the section.

These English settlers, as well as the Scotch and Scotch-Irish that came with or followed them, were intelligent, thoughtful people, many of them with property, who had left their homes because of the dark prospects in Europe. Their small properties, they complained, were "wearing to pauper-ism." Moreover, the interferences with their social and religious affairs were so constant and humiliating that they were willing to undergo any hardships to get a better chance and greater freedom in the world. The experiences of these men at home, the ideas that they brought with them, the way they went to work to build up communities—all of these things must have been matters of discussion at Jones' grocery in Gentryville and everywhere else that Lincoln met with men. The English settlers brought books, many of them, as Judge Iglehart shows, and it is his opinion that many of these books found their way into young Abraham Lincoln's hands.

Another stimulating and enlightening social experience that Lincoln had under his eye at this time was the brilliant though short-lived communistic undertaking which Robert Owen started in 1825 at New Harmony, Indiana, only fifty miles west of the Lincoln farm. Probably no communistic undertaking in the world ever began with better prospects, for Owen purchased outright a substantial town and thousands of acres of cultivated land which a religious communistic group known as the Rappites had brought to a fine degree of development. Owen not only had a town to start with, but he was able to gather about him many brilliant people, among them altogether the most distinguished group of scientists that the country had as yet seen. Owen and the best known of his followers came down the Ohio River in January, 1826, when Lincoln was running his ferryboat at the mouth of Anderson's Creek. The travelers were known up and down the river as the "boatload of knowledge," and we can well believe that their reputation stirred the curiosity and the ambition of the boy who, for all we know, may have watched them float by.

What was said and done at New Harmony was thoroughly reported in all the countryside, for the communists took pains to scatter not only their pamphlets, but copies of the weekly paper, The New Harmony Gazette, and also to send agents far and wide, trying to convert the settlers to their ideas. People of all sorts flocked to them; people of all sorts started

other communistic settlements in the surrounding country.
Groups of settlers, seeing the practical benefits of coöperation,
made their own little attempts at "the New Social Order,"
as Owen called his undertaking. For five years it ran like
a fever over the country, and then as quickly as it started,
as quickly it collapsed—too much of a strain on impatient
human nature, ready to take all the advantages of beautiful
dreams, but unwilling to make the sacrifice and give the effort
that realization demands.

From this, the most exciting episode in their part of the
world in his time, Lincoln must have learned many things.
The emphasis Owen and his friends placed on universal education at public expense took hold of him. The rightness of
larger religious as well as social and political freedom of
thought appealed to him; and the continual emphasis placed
on kindness, courtesy and sincerity by Owen found a response
in his nature. That is, the newcomers, whatever their practical limitations, filled the air with noble ideas, developed
with ardor and conviction—ideas which may have had much
more to do with the development of young Abraham Lincoln
than he himself realized.

It was here in southwestern Indiana, too, according to a
bit of autobiography which he once related to a friend, that
romance for him was born. This friend told me the story
years ago, and it still remains, so far as I know, the most
revealing thing that we have of this side of Lincoln's nature
in the Indiana period. The awakening started in an incident
common enough in that day. A passing wagon had broken
down near the Lincoln home. There were a woman and two
girls in the party, and, with pioneer hospitality, Mrs. Lincoln
had invited them to cook in her kitchen while repairs were
making. While waiting the woman read the children stories
from books she had with her, the first, Lincoln says, he ever

heard. One of the girls took his fancy; he could not forget her after the party moved on, and began to spin a romance: He would take his father's horse, follow the wagon and persuade the girl to elope. In imagination he did so, and they started off across the prairies. But the horse came back to camp. Three times they tried this, and every time the horse came back. And then they concluded they ought not to elope. But that was not the end; he stayed in the camp until he had won the father's consent to marry the girl! This, he told his friend, he believed to be "the beginning of love" with him.

It is safe to say, I think, that in these fourteen years that Lincoln spent in southwestern Indiana, hard as he labored, pinching as the times often may have been, meager as his apparent opportunities, his nature and his mind were awakened to noble ideas and emotions, and while he undoubtedly came in close contact with meanness, grossness, vulgarity of every sort, and while undoubtedly he shrank from no experience and no exhibit of human nature, he came through unscathed. It was a fine, big, manly, thoughtful boy that left Indiana in the spring of 1830, for in March of that year the Lincolns "moved out." Their determination had been taken the year before, preparations had been made through the winter, and in March they started.

# XIII

WHY did Tom Lincoln decide in 1829 to move his family from southwestern Indiana, after a residence there of some fourteen years? An easy way to dismiss the question has been to answer that he was shiftless and unstable. The more we know of him the more this judgment is unsatisfactory. As a matter of fact, he was preparing, when he decided to move, to build a new house on his Spencer County farm, part of the lumber having already been turned out. Why the sudden change?

There was a combination of reasons. Undoubtedly, there was the pull from Illinois. The tide of immigration at this period was all west to Illinois and Missouri or north to Michigan. Tom's brother Mordecai had already moved into Hancock County, Illinois, and his wife's relatives, William and Joseph Hanks and their families, were settled in the new state. Wonderful tales of fertility came back. Then, too, Spencer County was standing still. Looking over the records at Rockport recently, I found few land entries between 1818 and 1832. But undoubtedly the deciding factor was the panic that seized the Lincolns when, in 1829, there was another outbreak of the disease which had carried off Nancy Hanks and so many of their neighbors in the fall of 1818. They literally fled for safety, but they took their time preparing for it!

In September, Mr. and Mrs. Lincoln went back to Elizabethtown, where they owned a lot. This they sold for $123.

[154]

# STARTING OUT FOR HIMSELF

The deed in this sale disposes of the theory that Sarah never went back to her old home after her marriage to Thomas Lincoln, since the clerk, Samuel Haycraft, who made out the deed, declares that she "was examined by me privately and apart from her said husband" and did "freely and willingly subscribe" to the sale. In February of 1830 the Lincolns sold their Indiana farm of eighty acres to Charles Grigsby for $125, "paid before the signing"—an indication of the little value there was in Spencer County property at that moment.

In March a party of Lincolns, Hanks and Johnstons— thirteen in all—started for Macon County, Illinois. One who has been over the roads of southwestern Indiana even to-day and when they are dry—a hair-raising experience in some places for a car—cannot but wonder that even a group of pioneers would start at that time of year. However, they were probably better equipped for their undertaking than biographers have represented. That they started out with "one team of four oxen," as I once set down, is certainly incorrect. I was taken to task for this statement by a pioneer who had done business in the region in early days. My critic, Mr. John Davis of Junction City, Kansas, declared that old settlers would agree that it would have been difficult for four oxen to have drawn even an empty wagon through the deep mud of an Illinois March.

"I remember well," he wrote, "that in the forties it was impossible for four good horses to draw the usual mail coach in the muddy spring time on the mail route from Springfield to Terre Haute. So, in March and part of April the coach was usually abandoned, and the leather letter bags only were taken through on a two-wheeled cart, drawn by four good horses, with relays of fresh horses every twelve or fifteen miles. The sacks of newspapers and similar matter were stored up at the station until the roads got better.

"In the spring of 1851 I myself had occasion to send a load of nursery stock from a point in Macon County to several points in

[155]

Shelby and Coles Counties, southeastward from Decatur. I selected a very strong light wagon, usually known as a two-horse lumber wagon, and loaded it with about fifteen hundred pounds of plants. And it required seven yoke of oxen in the hands of two experienced drivers to make the trip. These are examples. I spent forty-seven years of my life (1825 to 1872) in Sangamon and Macon Counties, and it was no uncommon thing to see men 'stuck in the mud' with four horses attached to an empty wagon. Sometimes wheels were abandoned for weeks at a time, and traveling was done on foot or on horseback. The use of two tall wheels, surmounted by a light pine box, drawn by two horses, was not uncommon for several weeks during muddy weather.

"So, then, a team of 'four oxen' to that Lincoln wagon would have been a very helpless team indeed; and to have started it on a journey without any other team to help it through the worst places would not have been attempted by sensible people."

This is sound sense. Moreover, as Mr. Davis points out —something that I had overlooked—Lincoln himself says of their moving that their "mode of conveyance was wagons drawn by ox teams," he driving one of the teams.

Twenty-five years ago I went to some trouble to work out what seemed to me the probable route the party followed; but no sooner was my map published than I began to receive criticisms from points along the Wabash. The librarian at New Harmony was sure, for instance, that they had crossed there. His evidence was that a clerk of the Circuit Court, living three miles out in the country, told him once that the Lincolns stopped at his father's house on their way to Illinois. If the matter was to be decided by people who to-day feel sure that the Lincolns had spent the night with their fathers and grandfathers, we would have a route that zig-zagged up and down Indiana from New Harmony to Vincennes and criss-crossed some half a dozen different counties. The best that ever will be done in fixing the route has been done in Indiana by the Lincoln Highway Commission in its report to Governor

[156]

Ralston, made in December, 1916; and in Illinois by Charles M. Thompson's admirable and interesting "Investigation of the Lincoln Way" reported by the Illinois State Historical Library to the Illinois legislature in 1915. According to the first the Lincolns journeyed northwest into Indiana, through Jasper and Petersburg to Vincennes. "Official" though the decision, I heard no little grumbling over it around Booneville last fall. Somebody's grandfather had talked with them as they passed!

In Illinois Mr. Thompson decides on the following points:

"1, a point on the Illinois bank of the Wabash River opposite Vincennes, Indiana; 2, Lawrenceville; 3, Christian Settlement; 4, Russellville; 5, Palestine; 6, Hutsonville; 7, York; 8, Darwin; 9, Richwoods; 10, McCann's Ford; 11, Paradise; 12, Mattoon; 13, Dead Man's Grove; 14, Nelson; 15, Decatur; 16, 'Lincoln Farm,' Macon County."

One thing we do know from Lincoln himself, and that is that when finally, after a fortnight of the heaviest kind of travel, the caravan approached Decatur in Macon County, for which they were headed, they drove in from the south and, as near as Mr. Lincoln could estimate, along the main line of the Illinois Central Road.

When one is on a Lincoln pilgrimage, such as I am reporting here, he has the first sense of being in a living Lincoln country when he reaches Decatur. It is the first place where there are still people who really knew him, and is one of the four or five Illinois towns which treasure most sympathetically and intelligently its Lincoln contacts, which seem really not only to revere but love the man. This comes naturally not only from the fact that their recollections date from his first appearance in Illinois, but that they are continuous to his death. In 1918 at an Old Settlers' meeting in Decatur there were 150 persons present who had seen Lincoln and remembered something about him. Every spot connected with his life there is being properly marked, and the town has in its fine library one of the choicest small Lincoln collections in the country. When your interest in Lincoln is known people press to aid you.

The first thing of course is to follow the route which the Lincoln caravan probably took out of the town in 1830, to what is now known as "Lincoln's Riverside Home." This was the piece of land, some eight miles away, which John Hanks, who had preceded them into Illinois, had selected for them on the bluff above the Sangamon River. Here they "squatted," built a cabin, cleared and fenced ten acres of land, and put in a first crop of corn. Of this work Abraham did a full share, for though he was now past his twenty-first birthday, he seems to have been unwilling to abandon his father until he was settled.

The young man's life in the first year in Illinois has been generally neglected by his biographers. As a matter of fact, it was an interested and varied, if hard, year for him. The country into which they had come was sparsely settled and very poor. The taxes of Macon County in 1829 had amounted to only $109.32½. Decatur was only nine months old, and although plotted and officially the county seat, the first session of court was not held until May, 1830. The only building of any size was Uncle Jimmy Renshaw's general store. There were as yet no roads, only trails. The mail came in rarely, and only from the north. The vast prairies were regarded as unfit to till, and reasonably enough, for they were under water a good part of the year. The grass which covered them was like a jungle, growing six to eight feet high, while the sod was so tough that no plow then known could cut it. Yet these plains were rarely beautiful. Those who remember them tell you of acres upon acres of blue iris, so thick that one could scarcely pass through it—of strawberries so many and so big that the legs of the horses would be stained red to the knees.

Of game there was of course no end. One of the most interesting of Decatur's early settlers, Dr. Pasley, contends that if ever there was a country which God prepared especially for settlers, it was this Illinois land; that here wild hogs, wild turkeys, deer, game of every kind was to be had for the capture, and that this gave not only food for the family, but valuable meats for the St. Louis market. Then there were bees. It was a bee hunter's paradise, and honey was one of the best crops.

There was plenty of work for a sturdy young man like Lincoln, among the neighbors as well as at home. The family for which he probably worked most steadily and which has passed on the most interesting reminiscences of him, was that of Major Warnick, three or four miles away from where he lived. Here he helped with the plowing, the planting, the harvesting and clearing; and here, as he had done in Indiana, he searched the house for books and at the noon hour stretched himself out to read.

It was here at Warnick's, if we are to believe tradition, that Lincoln had his first serious love affair—serious enough for him to wish to marry the girl. Major Warnick had a daughter Mary, and the story goes that Lincoln paid her somewhat impassioned court. However, as she was married the summer after he came to Illinois, it must have been a short courtship. He is reported to have been attentive later to another young girl of the neighborhood, Miss Jemima Hill, and this story is not spoiled by Jemima's marrying the year Abraham was her neighbor. Just how seriously he was stirred it is impossible to say. Of course he was interested in girls at that time. Of course his mind was turning to a mate.

And equally of course many a family that would have looked askance upon him as a member in those days is glad now to boast that he wanted to marry one of their grandmothers. Mr. H. W. Fay, the custodian of the Lincoln Monument in Springfield, says that if all the different visitors who tell him that Lincoln once courted their grandmothers state the truth, the man must have been the busiest of philanderers! At all events, it is good to know that there were young women of fine families like the Warnicks and the Hills who were friendly enough to him to give even slight ground for the traditions. It shows that he was able to make a place for himself in the new neighborhood if not to win a wife!

Possibly, if it had not been for sickness and disastrous weather conditions which ended in driving Tom Lincoln away from the "Riverside Home," Lincoln might have been permanently associated with Decatur. But some six months after their arrival the whole family was stricken with fever and ague—the bane of the prairie countries in those days. The miasma which poured from the undrained lowlands, the fogs which shut them in like a black, wet blanket, all encouraged the disease. One gets a hint of how it was affecting Tom Lincoln from the accounts of James Renshaw's general store in Decatur, for in October of the year charges began to appear opposite Tom Lincoln's name for what was called "Barks"— a Peruvian bark and whisky tonic generally used by settlers for ague. Poor Tom and his family must have been badly afflicted, judging from the amount of "Barks" which they bought!

On top of this affliction there came the most terrible winter known in the written history of Illinois—"the winter of the deep snow." It began on the twenty-ninth of December —a fall of two and a half feet, all over the northern part of the state. A frost followed, and on top of this came

*August 16th 1830*    **11**

*Samuel Miller   Dr*
To 1 oz allos  — — — — — —   18½
   1 cake Soap  — — —  12½

*John Ingram   Cr*
By Cash  — — — — — —  1   00

*Thomas Lincoln D By Son*
Do ¼ lb Barks  —  @ 25    1   00

*Seth Sinet   Dr*
  To 3 lbs Shugr  —    50

*William Toren Dr By Star*
Do ¼ lb Nails  —  @ 16⅔    4½

*William King Dr By Frederick*
Do 1 lb Cotton    50

**14**    *August 28th 1830*

*Thomas Larner   Dr*
To 3 yds Shirting   @ 16⅔    50

*David Florey Senr Dr*
To ½ qire Paper    12½
To ½ lb Tobaco  — —  9½

*Jacob Cotton Barger Dr*
*Benj Slatters   Dr*
To Leather    **3 25**

*Thomas Lincoln Dr By Jansom*
To 1 oz Barks  — —  19¾

*Landa Darrall Dr By wife*
To 3 lbs Butter    25

FRAGMENTS FROM THE DAYBOOK OF JAMES RENSHAW, WHO KEPT A GENERAL
STORE IN DECATUR, ILLINOIS, AT WHICH THE LINCOLNS TRADED.

another deep fall. For over two months the country was under something like four feet of snow. Many of the settlers were so nearly entombed that it was only at the risk of their lives that they were able to get out to have their corn ground. Deer frequently joined the herds of cows, and the wolves, which were able to go about on the light crust, were more fierce and bold than ever. There is no doubt that the Lincoln family suffered terribly in this winter. In this period Abraham is said to have frozen his feet in trying to get to Major Warnick's, so that for a considerable period he had to be cared for at their home.

However hard the winter may have been, it did not prevent Abraham, John Hanks and John Johnston, his step-brother, from contracting to take a flatboat down the Illinois and the Mississippi to New Orleans as soon as the season opened.

It was the first of March before they could get out of Macon County, and even then there was no traveling over-land, so flooded were the prairies by the melting of the big snow. There was nothing to do but to buy a canoe and float down the Sangamon River. "This is the time," says Lincoln's autobiography, "and the manner of Abraham's first entrance into Sangamon County."

It was the time and the manner, too, of his first going on his own. Indeed, there was nothing for him to do but let the Lincolns, the Hanks and the Halls shift for themselves. Tom Lincoln never attempted to prove up his title to the land on which he had built his cabin and made improvements. Indeed, the first certificate of entry for the "Lincoln River-side Home" was in 1836 by one Percy Strickland. The land, as the chain of titles in the Decatur Lincoln collection shows, passed through many hands. Now it is under a trusteeship, set aside by its last owner to establish and maintain, after his wife's death, a home for orphan children under sixteen years of age. What better monument to Lincoln's year in Macon County could we have?

From the "Riverside Home" Tom Lincoln went into Coles County, some twelve miles from Charleston. There he entered land, and there, in 1851, he died. The disastrous year on the banks of the Sangamon seems to have broken him entirely. He was fifty years old when he moved out of Indiana—a serious age at which to be attacked by fever and ague. He never recovered entirely from it. It is a disease which saps energy, and for energy Tom had never been distinguished. Never again was he able to get hold, and indeed it was a very difficult thing in the neighborhood where he had gone for even a young and healthy man. He might raise good crops, but to dispose of those crops, cut off as he was from markets by the lack of any kind of reasonable transportation, was almost impossible. For him, shaken with chills and fever, discouraged by the loss incident to his last move, it was rather too much to be expected. Most of the party that had come with him into Illinois settled about him, but none of them ever did more than to grub out a meager existence. But, as we shall see, they never dropped out of Lincoln's life; to the end he was their counselor and their chief dependence.

The Sangamon River, down which Lincoln floated in March of 1831, is a powerful winding stream, cutting out high bluffs and leveling big plains, all the way from the northern part of what is now Champaign County, southwest to Decatur, then westward to within a few miles of Springfield, then northwestward to the Illinois River near Beardstown. It is wayward as it is winding, overflowing vast stretches of country at times of the year; its channel frequently blocked with driftwood; its moods as uncertain as those of the

Mississippi or the Missouri; its possibilities of use and of destruction only limited by its size.

To Lincoln the river from the start was the hope of the Illinois country. He saw, as every intelligent settler did, that unless there could be practical connections at once opened to markets, there was little chance of poor settlers, like his father and himself, being able to hold out long enough to establish themselves permanently. Roads meant time and money. Here was a river. His experience on the Ohio and the Mississippi, the reliance of southwestern Indiana upon them, made him feel strongly from his first coming into Macon County that their hope was in the Sangamon.

Indeed, his first public speech in Illinois, so far as tradition goes, was on this very theme. It was one of John Hanks' favorite stories about him. As Mr. Herndon tells it—and he had it first hand—it goes: "After Abe got to Decatur, or rather to Macon County, a man by the name of Posey came into our neighborhood and made a speech. It was a bad one, and I said Abe could beat it. I turned down a box and Abe made his speech. The other man was a candidate—Abe wasn't. Abe beat him to death, his speech being on navigation of the Sangamon River."

It is too late a date for the spot on which this speech was made to be fixed, but there is no early Illinois reminiscence of Lincoln of more real importance than this, the first political speech of which we have an account, and one on a theme so essential to the life and growth of the town and of Illinois —transportation. Decatur ought to find a possible spot and put up a marker!

He studied his subject as they paddled their way down the stream to meet the man to whom they had hired themselves out—a man who for a year or two was to have a considerable part in young Lincoln's life. This man, Denton

Offutt, had promised to have the flatboat which he had hired the boys to take down the Mississippi ready at Beardstown on the Illinois River. They were to meet him at Springfield; but when they reached Springfield they found the boat was not ready; and they hired themselves out to him at $12 a month each to get out lumber and build a boat.

This work was done at a settlement on the Sangamon River, seven miles northwest of Springfield, known as Old Sangamon. To-day nothing remains of the town, except possibly an occasional sunken foundation of a former cabin; and yet it is a spot to be remembered, for if it was in Macon County that Lincoln first comes into history as a political speechmaker, it is in Sangamon County that he first appears as a royal story teller.

Twenty-five years ago I knew in Springfield, Illinois, an interesting old gentleman, John Roll—a young man in Old Sangamon when Lincoln and his companions appeared there to build their flatboat. He was one of several who helped in the undertaking, and, according to Mr. Roll, no gang of workers ever had more amusement out of a companion than they did out of Abraham Lincoln.

It was at the noon hour especially that he made his hit with them. Seated on a long log, he would tell stories so irresistibly droll that at their end the whole gang would, according to Mr. Roll, "whoop and roll off." For a time after Lincoln had gone about his business "Abe's log" was a favorite resting place for the group at evening time and his stories their favorite entertainment. Abe's log deserves a tablet, not only because here he first displayed that accomplishment which was to play so important a part in the sway he came to exercise over men, but because here he first demonstrated in Illinois his characteristic courage and resourcefulness.

[165]

The swift current of the flooded river had overturned a log canoe in which a couple of men were paddling. They had taken refuge in a tree where they really were in danger of their lives. Lincoln improvised a rescue by attaching a long cable to a log. A daring chap straddled this and piloted it to the tree, but in his rashness fell into the water and had to find a perch with the others. It was Lincoln himself that then took charge of the log life boat, and in his cool fashion made his way to the refuge and gathered in the wet and half frozen captives. Nobody in that community forgot the episode, we can be sure.

It was along about the middle of April that Denton Offutt's flatboat was finally loaded and launched and started on its way for New Orleans. Only a few miles below Old Sangamon Lincoln met with an adventure which has played a large part in pictures and stories of his life. There used to hang in the capitol of Illinois in Springfield a crude but realistic painting of this episode. They have taken it away —mistakenly, I think. It may be "crude and inaccurate" as I myself once wrote in describing it, but it is amusing and interesting. Moreover, it has a real place in the development of the pictorial side of Lincoln legends. This picture shows —which was the fact—that just below a great bend in the Sangamon a mill dam and a mill had been built, and that when the Lincoln boat reached the spot, instead of going properly over, it caught, the cargo settling back and the boat filling with water.

The news of the accident brought all the inhabitants from a town on the top of the bluff near-by, New Salem, to the mill dam. There, as spectators, they had Sangamon County's second evidence that there was passing through it a young man of unusual cool-headedness and resourcefulness, for, while everybody shouted contradictory counsels, he, unmindful, unloaded his goods into a boat he had borrowed, bored a hole in the end of the craft which hung over the dam, tilted it until the water ran out, when over it slipped and soon went on its way. He had given New Salem something to talk about. They might not know his name or expect ever to see him again, but they rehearsed the tale in Rutledge's tavern on the bluff that night, as well as in more than one cabin.

It was the handling of these two difficulties, and others that we can well believe must have occurred in the long trip down the Mississippi and in the trading at New Orleans, that led Lincoln's employer, Denton Offutt, to feel that he had found just the man he wanted for a business enterprise he was undertaking at New Salem. He had started a store on the bluff above the mill dam and a mill on the river. He wanted a trustworthy manager for both. Lincoln was his man.

The trip down the river took three months, bringing him back to New Salem in July of 1831. A developing experience it had been. That is, the young man who walked across country from Beardstown, where the steamer would have left him in those days, to New Salem was something more of a man than the one who had gone down the river three months before. He had had a month in one of the most exciting and riotous cities on this continent at that time— a month rubbing elbows with flatboat men, river captains, would-be pirates and filibusters, and he had seen for the first time an institution of slavery unknown to the world in which he had lived—although it might recognize slavery, as Kentucky did, and hold on to a few slaves as southwestern Indiana and Illinois still did, in spite of ordinances and laws —this was the slave market.

I think the most we can say for this experience in the New Orleans slave market was that it aroused an emotion in regard to slavery which he had never before experienced. Up to this time Lincoln had had the moral and intellectual conviction that slavery was wrong, but that he had real feeling about it I doubt very much. That what he saw in New Orleans aroused a flare of hatred and revolt seems to be certain, and it is that experience which makes his trip down the river in 1831 of particular importance in his development —a thing not to be forgotten as we follow his life.

That he came back to New Salem with any other idea than that he had here a job which seemed a little advance on what he had had before and that possibly, too, it was a job which would give him an opportunity to read more than he had ever had a chance to do before, I doubt very much. All that New Salem could have seen in Abraham Lincoln when he joined the settlement was an unusually resourceful, diligent and cheerful jack-of-all-trades. The interesting thing is that they remembered him; he had done something in passing three months before that impressed them. They welcomed him back. Indeed, one of the most significant things about his first few months in Illinois is that he made a definite impression on everybody of intelligence whom he touched.

The cultivated and delightful gentleman in Decatur of whom I spoke above, Dr. Pasley, now eighty-five years of age, told me that his father, who first came to Macon County in 1826, knew Lincoln in the months that he labored near Decatur, and remembered specific things about him. Abraham Lincoln as a young man, he claimed to be one of those people that nobody forgot—the Warnicks, the Hills, the Pasleys, all remembered him—remembered him as diligent, kind, strong, and as "different"—somebody who knew and did and said things that you could not forget.

# XIV

## NEW SALEM ADOPTS LINCOLN

THE most unique, and I am inclined to believe the most popular, monument that ever will be erected to Abraham Lincoln, is the restoration of the town of New Salem on the Sangamon River, in Menard County, Illinois, the town to which Lincoln came back in July, 1831, to take a position as clerk in a grocery store. Here he spent the six years following his arrival—years of liveliest intellectual and social activity—here he discovered that he had a power over men which could be utilized to further his natural ambition for public life—here he definitely decided to make a profession of the law—here there came to him the deepest love and the greatest sorrow of his life.

It was a town of short life—this New Salem—short, but colorful. Founded in 1829, it thrived amazingly for seven or eight years; then, as quickly as it had sprung into life, it dropped out. In a dozen years it was a deserted village; one by one all but one or two of its cabins were carried away, and the little that was left crumbled to dust. For forty years New Salem was only a rough cow pasture.

But it was an unforgettable spot. Here Abraham Lincoln had lived for six years, and here was the scene of a hundred episodes of his life—grave and gay. In New Salem he had found himself—and men had found him. The memory of his life there had become the great romance of Menard County, and a few years ago descendants of the very people who had made New Salem began to talk of its restoration. Out of the gradually growing interest there arose what was called "The Old Salem Lincoln League," committed to rebuilding the village.

The idea captivated the imagination not only of Menard County but of the state. What a monument, not only to Abraham Lincoln, but to their own heroic pioneers! Fittingly enough, the leaders and backers in this undertaking were of the town of Petersburg, two miles up the Sangamon—a town born after New Salem, and really born to absorb it.

A more rewarding site than New Salem for such an undertaking as that of the league could not be imagined. It lies along the top of a bluff, a hundred feet or more high, a segment of the long chain of bluffs that in past centuries the Sangamon River has worn out of the soft Illinois soil. The land rises sharply from the river bank, a highway at its foot, and spreads back into wide prairies. From the top one looks to-day over a long winding stretch of the river, over broad plains, and north, south, and east upon segments of bluffs like that on which the town was set, all heavily timbered—white-limbed sycamores along the river, maples, locusts, beeches, oaks on the hillsides. Sixteen miles in a straight line to the east the dome of the capitol at Springfield is visible—a lovely picture, awakening an involuntary comparison to the scene from the height at Mt. Vernon.

As a first step toward the permanent remaking of New Salem which it dreamed, the league decided on a pageant as its contribution toward the Illinois centennial of 1918—a pageant rehearsing Lincoln's life in the town. It began its work in the rough field at the top of the bluff—a field now a tangled bed of prairie grass and underbrush. The first investigations were more rewarding than had been expected —a little cutting and digging revealed depressions, foundation stones, walls, the tracks of old roads, until soon—to the joy of the league—they had New Salem plotted more perfectly than most of them had dreamed it ever could be. The windings of the roads, the location of the tavern, of the stores and houses in which Lincoln had worked and lived, the position of the dam where he had made his first dramatic appearance—these things fixed upon, log cabins were quickly erected, and in September of 1918 the pageant was given.

It caught attention, stirred interest far and wide, doing not only what the devoted and enthusiastic group hoped it might do, but much more. The state itself was not slow in seeing that Menard County had a big and beautiful idea, and it has given since full backing to the plan of permanent restoration of the town, acquiring most, if not all, of the land needed for a complete piece of work. It has built, too, on the bluff overlooking the river, a small but most attractive and satisfactory museum in which a collection of Lincoln and pioneer relics is growing healthily. It is not going to be very long—possibly before the end of the present year—when the entire town will be reproduced in solid timber and according to carefully worked out specifications. It is hoped to furnish cabins, shops and mills as they were in 1831. Luckily, not a few original articles are to be had in Menard County itself.

When a New Salem stands again complete on its bluff overlooking the Sangamon River, the six happiest and most fruitful years Abraham Lincoln had spent up to this point in his life will lie before us more truthfully and vividly than pen or brush could ever reproduce them. One can see the town into which he walked that July day in 1831, see the store in which he was to work, the mill over which he was to preside, the homes of the friends he so readily made.

New Salem when Lincoln first found it was only two years old, but in those two years it had gathered a population of something like a hundred people and had, scattered up and down its one long street, between twenty and twenty-five cabins of varying size—from the big, two story, doubled-roomed tavern down to a tiny 8 ft. x 12 ft. bachelor quarters.

The group of people, taken as a whole, which Lincoln now joined, was altogether the most substantial, the widest awake and the most cultivated with which he had so far been associated. Take James Rutledge, the owner of the mill and also of the tavern on the hill. Here was a man of the famous Rutledge family, who, with his wife, had first come into the Illinois country from Kentucky a dozen years earlier, and had prospered there. He had a large family of fine children —ambitious, upright, generous people, the Rutledges. Take the Rev. John Cameron, James Rutledge's partner in the mill. He was a Cumberland Presbyterian minister, devout, courageous, and with an eye to sound business—the kind of man that everybody respected and listened to. Born in Kentucky, he and his wife had moved to Illinois in 1815, and in 1829, when he and Rutledge decided that they wanted a mill at a particular bend in the Sangamon River, he had taken land on the bluff above the spot and incorporated the town of New Salem, with the results we have seen. Then there was a young man of parts, around Lincoln's age, Samuel Hill, a storekeeper, an all-around good citizen. There was Dr. John Allen, who attended to spiritual as well as physical wants, running a Sunday school and temperance society. There was a school teacher, one Mentor Graham of good mind and acquirements, intent on seeing that the children of New Salem did not grow up ignorant, and fostering every spark of interest in knowledge that he found.

Already the little town was something of an industrial center. There was a blacksmith, a tinner, a cooper, a wheelwright, a weaver, a hatter—industries carried on on the premises where the craftsmen lived. They had a large, fairly prosperous section to serve, for, in the dozen years since the first settlers had come, some of them had already taken strong hold—men like Squire Coleman Smoot, who lived across the river, and in time built up a great fortune; men like Squire Bowling Green and James Short, successful farmers already.

But the New Salem into which Lincoln came in 1831 had not only its substantial, decent people, interested in building up an orderly community and educating its children—the ambition of its boys and girls was already stirring to get a year or more in the academy at Jacksonville, thirty miles away—it had, like every pioneer settlement, a boisterous, sporting element. A little way outside of the town, and using it as their market and trading place, there was a settlement called, from its founder, one of the first to come into the country, Clary's Grove. The young men of this neighborhood had banded themselves into what we would call to-day a gang, a group of as ingenious and reckless rowdies as ever enlivened and terrified a countryside. Mr. Herndon, who knew them first hand, declares that they were as generous as they were riotous; but it is not their generosity which figures in tradition.

One of the Clarys from the settlement had a grocery in New Salem, not on the main street, but, as the map in the new museum shows, around a bend in the road, bringing it directly above the dam and effectively concealing it from the town proper. Whisky was the chief stock in Clary's grocery, it is said. The place had come to be a rendezvous for all that was rough in the countryside—here horse races began and ended, and here regularly cock fights and gander pulling went on. To this store, night after night, after the day's work was done, the Clary Grove boys made their way, racing down the half-mile street of New Salem, whooping

[173]

and shouting, terrifying the children and making all good citizens shake their heads.

As chance had worked it, the store of which Lincoln was to take charge was not in the main part of the town, but directly above the mill dam, side by side with Clary's grocery, and across the street from the cock pit. The nearness was such that inevitably Lincoln was forced almost at the start of his life in the town to settle on his relations to the Clary Grove boys. He could join the gang; he could withdraw from them and become their butt; but he did neither. By his superior skill in their favorite game of wrestling, he defeated their champion, and, by his fierce indignation and severe punishment when that champion tried to trick him, he won their whole-hearted admiration as well as a half-awed respect. His popularity with them only grew as time went on. The episode is significant. It shows the kind of a man he had come to be—one that could live among rowdies, beat them at their own game, walk untouched by their excesses and meannesses and yet be an acceptable, unquestioned umpire of their sports, already a self-directing human being, understanding and sympathizing with weaknesses and able to discriminate between weaknesses and meannesses, good intentions and malice, a man who could put up with idle, rough, drinking and adventuring men so long as they neither lied nor tricked nor practiced cruelty. Let them do that and they found quickly how heavy his blow, how stern his temper.

If Lincoln established his ascendency at the start with the lower half of New Salem, he was no less successful with the upper half. The good citizens of the town discovered quickly that here was a young man who was as ready with words, and even with pen, as he was with his fists, who fitted in, took hold, wherever there was anything going on; thus it happened that the returns of the first election held in

New Salem after his coming to the town are in his hand. They found he had a deep interest in politics, was informed, read the newspapers, could debate the issues of the day, national as well as local, was not afraid of discussion, of challenging an opinion, a fact, or of accepting correction. More than politics interested him. There was religion, and they found that in the continuous debate on the evidences and doctrines and practices of Christianity that divided the evenings on the doorsteps or around the stove in the grocery store with local gossip and politics, Lincoln was sure to take a serious and thoughtful part.

He soon knew everybody, knew their intellectual resources, and availed himself of them. His headquarters, of course, were his grocery store and the mill on the stream below, which Denton Offutt had leased and put in his charge—wonderful centers for acquaintanceship when a man had the genius for companionship that this young man had. The traders that came in from the country round, men like Squire Smooth and Squire Bowling Green and James Short, the prosperous men, listened to him, sized him up, and went home to repeat what he had said and comment, as men had in Macon County and back in Indiana, that here was somebody "different," somebody that was worth keeping an eye on.

That is, in a very few months after his appearance in New Salem, this chance young man had built up a following, was everybody's friend and had made everybody his friend. His following was on a solid basis, too, born of their liking and respect. Somehow he had contrived to meet every man on his own ground, establish a point of contact and interest with him. He liked them all and liked them for what was decent and natural and interesting in them. He already was the man of the White House.

Lincoln sensed his popularity in New Salem, knew men

[175]

liked him, saw that they listened to his views, respected his integrity. Why not capitalize his popularity? He was ambitious to be a public man. Was there anybody in the neighborhood more fit than he for public office? Did he not understand the pith of the matters to be handled as well as those about him? He thought so. Did he not hold the public good above his own advancement, and was not that the heart of the matter, after all? If these people whom he had won so solidly would back him, why should he not venture? There you have the young pioneer American, confident that whatever there is to be done he can learn to do in the doing—the inevitable product of the Declaration of Independence and the Constitution!

By this time Lincoln had made his way with the school teacher, Mentor Graham, as he had with all the rest of the town, and he discussed with him going into public life. Probably he said to the school teacher about what later he wrote into his first political address: "Every man," he says there, "is said to have his peculiar ambition. Whether it be true or not, I can say for one that I have no other so great as that of being truly esteemed by my fellow men by rendering myself worthy of their esteem. How far I shall succeed in gratifying this ambition is yet to be developed."

Graham, having some sense of the limitations of the young man, particularly of the handicap his handling of English would be when he came to be placed side by side with men who had had the advantages of the schools, suggested grammar to him. We can read between the lines that Lincoln's verbs and nouns did not always agree, that he spoke of "that there grub-hoe" and "them fellers." The significant thing of the episode is his immediate response to the suggestion, his ability quickly to take a hint, and never to resent it; his willingness to make a supreme effort, to sacrifice, labor to the point of weariness, to add something to his equipment. And so he studied grammar, borrowing his book, the only one in the neighborhood. Kirkham's Grammar it was; and the fact that in the winter of 1831-1832, down in New Salem, Illinois, Abraham Lincoln put in weeks of day and night labor over this book, gives Kirkham's Grammar, which, in the natural course of things, would have passed out of history forever, a permanent place on its page!

It is consoling that it is so good a book. Twenty-five years ago J. McCan Davis of Springfield, Illinois, who was assisting me in gathering pictures and verifying data for a life of Lincoln on which I was working, ran down the very copy which Lincoln studied. At that time it was in Dakota, owned by a descendant of James Rutledge, coming to him by a course of events which belong to a later chapter in our story.

Recently Miss Jane Hamand, the donor of the Lincoln collection housed in the public library of Decatur, of which I have already spoken, has secured the book for exhibition. I hope it means a permanent place in the Decatur Lincoln room. Certainly it will never anywhere have better care or be shown with greater pride. It was in this collection that last year I first went over Lincoln's copy of Kirkham's Grammar—went over it page by page, with a lingering hope that I might find somewhere a line in Lincoln's hand, but never was a book, although studied by many different people, more respectfully treated. There is not a written word in Lincoln's or anybody else's hand, aside from those on the title page and cover.

I suspect that a modern teacher would laugh at Kirkham's Grammar, and the "systematic order of parsing" which its author presents as a proof that he has done what no previous grammarian had ever been able to do. Whether

[177]

that is so or not, I confess I found the book not only entertaining but highly stimulating. I really think Samuel Kirkham was justified in claiming that his grammar would "accelerate the march of the juvenile mind in its advance in the path of science by dispersing those clouds which so often bewilder it, removing those obstacles that ordinarily retard its progress," that it would "render interesting and delightful a study which has hitherto been considered tedious, dry and irksome." He does it by an extreme conciseness of definition, a wealth of easily understood illustration, plenty of exercises in false syntax, and every now and then a paragraph of good advice to the student, such as:

"You will now please read this lecture" (Kirkham's Grammar is divided into lectures instead of chapters) "four times over, and read closely and carefully. . . . Exercise a little sober thought, five minutes spent in reflection are worth whole days occupied in careless reading."

What could you have better? Kirkham's Grammar was an excellent self-teacher, just the kind of a book for a young man of Lincoln's meager schooling and desultory reading. He came out from it with an ability to make nouns and verbs agree—indeed, to handle his "parts of speech" with a high degree of success. But the great thing it did for him, I imagine, was to show him the value of systematized knowledge of a subject. He must have found a real intellectual satisfaction in the clearness, the logical sweep, the orderliness of the matter in the book. He had read widely, far more widely, I am convinced, than we can prove; he had reflected much; but his mind was full of unrelated information. And it was a mind with a necessity for having things in their places, of seeing relations—a necessity, too, for expressing those relations so that he could get over to others what he thought and felt about them. He had come to this point when he took up this simple, practical, serious discussion of

Samuel Kirkham's; and I think there is no doubt that it gave him a sense of the possibilities in study which he had never fully grasped before. It was a sense expressed in his comment when he had mastered the book: "Well, if that's what they call a science, I think I will try another." A great intellectual discovery, you see.

His resolve to capitalize his popularity and this preparation he had been making in study, crystallized in February of 1832 in his first public document—indeed, the first written thing that we have from his pen, announcing himself as a candidate for the Illinois Assembly. It is his thinking on public affairs and his manner of expression that are really important about this document, outside of the fact, of course, that "humble Abraham Lincoln," as he calls himself in the announcement, should have had the audacity to plunge into a world that was unknown to him and for which, as he himself realized, he had so little preparation.

He wasted no time in attacking the "issue," which, in his judgment, was the vital one at the moment: "Easier means of communication" for the County of Sangamon. Reluctantly he argued that railroads and canals were not for them. His objection was "paying for them, and the objection arose from the want of ability to pay." He rehearsed a project then under consideration for a railroad from Springfield to Jacksonville, and argued that the estimated cost, some $290,000, caused what he called a "heart-appalling shock." There was nothing for their "infant resources" but improvement of the Sangamon River. Here he was at home; here he argued from his personal adventures and observation on the stream, and came out with a plan which is practically the same that is being applied today, over ninety years after the appearance of his "announcement," in more than one of the Middle West states.

[179]

Briefly, what Lincoln proposed was that the channel of
the Sangamon between New Salem and Beardstown should
be straightened: by damming the river at the upper end
of the great bends and then cutting straight through the
sod of the prairie a shallow channel which the water itself
would in a short time, he believed, sufficiently deepen. One
of the great difficulties in the navigation of the Sangamon
was the enormous amount of drift timber which piled up
at every bend, damming the water and making a passage impossible. This drift, Lincoln believed, would be carried
swiftly down stream if once the channel was straightened.
Above New Salem there were numbers of short loops in the
river which he proposed also to cut off.

There was no doubt about the common sense of the plan,
that every one who saw his announcement agreed. Here was
a young man, they said, that based what he had to say on
serious observation; it was not merely political palaver; it
was good and practical suggestion.

As for the writing, taking the document as a whole, it
shows that Lincoln had already begun to sense the difference
between imitative and personal expression, that he was already
struggling to make words say what was in his mind; that
clearness, making others understand, was the aim he had in
writing. This document of his shows very little effort at
fine writing, has few phrases that would be called purely
conventional, things said in the way he had heard other people
say them. He is still a little awkward, not entirely free with
words. Probably he was considerably under the influence
of Mentor Graham, who no doubt labored with him over the
document, though I suspect that aside from verbal changes
that Graham may have suggested, there is very little in this
first piece of writing that we have of Lincoln's that is not
his own. We must admit that it is a fine showing for a

pioneer boy of twenty-three, whose schooling, all told, had been less than a year, and whose strong and willing hand had been busy almost daily since he was eight years old with the ax and the grub-hoe, not with the pen.

Outside of transportation, the main subject he considers at length in his announcement is the exorbitant interest rates which were common in those days. With that characteristic frankness which so often impelled him to do what in later years his friends called "giving his case away," he emphasized his advocacy of a law fixing the limits of usury by saying that in case of extreme necessity there could always be means found to cheat the law! There is significance in his frankness; if he is going to frame a law with a loophole in it, a place of escape, he is not going to pretend that there is no such opening there. He is going to tell you in advance exactly what is in his mind. That is, here is no political dissembler, hypocrite; on the contrary, a youthful politician, both canny and honest.

Confident and bold as the address is in the main, it is quite evident that he put it out with more or less misgivings; his humility, his constitutional sense of inferiority, comes out at the end. "I was born and have ever remained in the most humble walks of life," he said. "I have no wealthy or popular relations or friends to recommend me. . . . If the good people in their wisdom shall see fit to keep me in the background, I am too familiar with disappointment to be very much chagrined," a combination of humility and philosophy which attended him to the end of his days.

It was in March that his address went out to his fellow citizens; but before he had time to follow it up, all Illinois was plunged into the excitement of an Indian war. Instead of campaigning, as he had expected in the spring and summer of 1832, Lincoln joined the state militia that was preparing to chase the Indian chief, Black Hawk, and his followers, out of the Rock River country in the northwestern part of the state. According to the arrangement of Black Hawk and his people with the government of the United States, they had the right to hunt and raise corn in this district until it was surveyed and sold to settlers. Squatters had invaded the territory. Black Hawk felt that his rights were being disregarded, and decided to evict the trespassers. Hence the call to evict him.

Lincoln did not hesitate. He enlisted with all the young men of his neighborhood.

# XV

## FEELING HIS WAY

ONE who attempts to follow the footsteps of Abraham Lincoln through his three months of soldiering in the Black Hawk War has before him as pretty a historical pilgrimage as he can ask. Students have charted the roads, marked not a few of the important points and here and there a monument has gone up, particularly impressive being Lorado Taft's heroic Black Hawk on the bluffs of the Rock River.

Captivating as the pilgrimage is, however, Lincoln's experience in the Black Hawk War cannot be regarded as of great importance in his development. For him it was largely a frolic—a frolic with much real physical hardship and no great satisfactions either in service rendered or adventures encountered—nothing in it that in the future he could do more than laugh at—as he did once in Congress. He was ridiculing Lewis Cass' war record. "By the way, Mr. Speaker," he said, "do you know I am a military hero? In the days of the Black Hawk War I fought, bled and came away. I had a good many bloody struggles with the mosquitos, and although I never fainted from loss of blood, I can truly say I was often hungry. . . . If they should ever take me up as a candidate for the presidency, I protest they shall not make fun of me as they have of General Cass by attempting to write me into a military hero."

Yet, if there are no great pages in his three months' campaigning, if he himself laughed at them, there was abundant excitement and color. It must have been an animated morning

in New Salem when the Governor's handbills, calling for
volunteers, were scattered; and there must have been much
lively badinage as well as suppressed forebodings as the
volunteers cleaned their muskets and the women poured
bullets for them. The march to Beardstown, the place of
rendezvous, the quick organization, his own election as captain
of a company—all this was stirring. And the last something
more—deeply satisfying. If he was popular enough for these
men to take him as a leader, was it not a sign that he might
win out in the election for the assembly, for which, as we
have seen, he had already announced himself? It was a good
omen. Men did esteem him—that thing which he wanted
so much.

The Illinois Volunteers, of which Lincoln's company was
a part, made their way from Beardstown, up the old Indian
trail on the east bank of the Mississippi, to a point not far
from the present city of Rock Island. Here they were sworn
into the Federal service. To-day this gathering place of the
volunteers is known as Lincoln Camp. There were many men
in that motley group far more conspicuous at the time than
he—there were regular army lieutenants and colonels on the
ground, but it is not the name of any one of them which is
given to the place. And this is true from one end to the other
of the route he and his men took.

"That's the trail Lincoln followed on his way to fight
the Indians," old men told Mr. John Hauberg who personally
has traced all of the Indian trails spreading from Black
Hawk's village, and whose findings have been published by
the Illinois State Historical Society. A conspicuous tree marking the route they call Lincoln's Tree—the point on the Rock
River where he was nearly eaten by mosquitos, a point which
he himself fixed—is locally famous. "Lincoln camped here,"
"Lincoln marched by here," they tell you the length of the

march from the first camp, northwest to Dixon, north to the scene of Stillman's defeat (May 15), where he saw the only Indians of the whole campaign—dead Indians!—southeast to Ottawa to be mustered out (May 27), and reënlisted (May 29) as a mounted ranger, northwest to Galena, considerably over a hundred miles in a straight line, back to Ottawa again to be mustered out on June 16 and mustered in again on June 20, to Dixon, to Kellogg's Grove, back to Dixon, then north to Turtle Village, now Beloit, Wisconsin, and on to Lake Koshkonong; finally to be mustered out for good and all at Burnt Village on the eleventh of July. Left high and dry in southern Wisconsin, his horse stolen, he made his way at fast as he could, on foot and by canoe, back to New Salem.

It was experience, of course, stories and a setting for stories which he used as long as he lived, but particularly Lincoln carried out of this helter skelter Indian chasing an enlarged knowledge of the kinds of men there are, and the way they act under stress and strain. The entire youth of Illinois had rushed into the Black Hawk War, some of them to stay but a short time, many of them to see the thing through. Lincoln met many a man then with whom he was to have relations of more or less value in later days. Look over any one of the county histories of Illinois and you will find proudly displayed rosters of those who served in the Black Hawk War. A large number of these were men with whom Lincoln was later to be associated in the law or in politics. Not a few of them were to become distinguished public servants.

As Lincoln never forgot anybody, and had an artist's sensitiveness to the details of scenes, he used his contacts in the campaign, even the slightest, to excellent purpose in the future.

"Major, do you remember ever meeting me before?" he

asked Robert Anderson when, fresh from Fort Sumpter, he came to report at the White House.

"No, Mr. President," Anderson replied.

"My memory is better than yours," Mr. Lincoln said, "you mustered me into the service of the United States in 1832 in the Black Hawk War."

I don't know that he ever had a chance to tell Jefferson Davis, Colonel Zachariah Taylor or Albert Sidney Johnston that he once campaigned with them, but we may be sure that if he had he took it. He missed no tie of that kind.

It was July when he walked into New Salem. His return must have been a rare treat for his friends. The things that he would tell them! How he had to wear a wooden sword for a day because he had fired his gun within the confines of the camp, of the great men he had seen, of the tales he had heard. He could tell them, too, about the event of the war which stirred the whole country more than any other single incident—the carrying off by the Indians in May of Rachel and Silvia Hall, two girls fifteen and seventeen, who had seen fifteen of their relatives and friends killed at their side, but who had themselves been saved as brides for young chiefs. For ten days these two girls had been hurried westward, and then, through the efforts of the Indian agent and friendly Winnebagos, had been bought off at the price of forty horses. We can be sure the story lost nothing in Lincoln's telling.

Looking for traces of the war in the letters and speeches of his later life, it is interesting to find that the very first letter that we have of his, though not, of course, the first he wrote, came out of this war. It is an amusingly frank statement of an incident, showing how little real respect the volunteers—Lincoln included—had for military rule. He had been asked about the transfer and discharge of one David Rankin.

# FEELING HIS WAY

"The transfer of Rankin from my company occurred as follows—Rankin having lost his horse at Dixon's ferry, and having acquaintance in one of the foot companies who were going down the river was desirous to go with them, and one Galishen being an acquaintance of mine and belonging to the company in which Rankin wished to go wished to leave it and join mine, this being the case, it was agreed that they should exchange places and answer to each other's names—as it was expected we all *would* be discharged in *very* few days."

Lincoln's reason for hurrying back after his final mustering out was that the election came off on August 6, and at best it was going to give him scant time for campaigning. He did only a little, but that little shows better than his announcement that he stood squarely for the Whig doctrines of the period: "I am in favor of a national bank. I am in favor of the internal improvement system and a high protective tariff"—a "loose constructionist" at the start, you see.

He was defeated. However, "this was the only time Abraham was defeated on a direct vote of the people," he says rather boastingly in his third person autobiography. His vote was not bad, all things considered. And he knew it. He had 277 votes out of the 284 that were cast in his precinct!

But there was something more important than politics for him at the moment, and that was to find something to do. Offutt's store had failed. It looks as if soldiering and the political ambitions of his clerk had had something to do with the failure. There is no doubt that Lincoln realized that it was high time to find something he could stick to. For the first time in his life, so far as I know, he thought of a trade—blacksmithing. At the west end of the street there was a village smithy. The man who kept it had a brother-in-law living in the same house, one Jack Kelso, a crony of Lincoln's—a treasured crony, for Kelso, fisherman and idler that he was, had books, knew Shakespeare and Burns, and was always

[187]

ready to read and quote and discuss with Lincoln. The black-smith wanted an assistant. It might be a good thing to learn a trade and settle down—near Jack Kelso!

But a big ambition that he hardly dared entertain stood in the way of his committing himself. Just when he began to dream of the law, we do not know; but that it was earlier than this is certain. He was thinking seriously this fall and regretfully telling himself that it would never do for him to undertake it, that he had not enough education. Please note that the lack of education did not stand in the way of his offering himself as a legislator! But that was different, to his mind. In politics it was man to man; in the law there was something intervening between men of which he stood in awe—books, learning, standards for which he had reverence but of which he had little understanding. No, it was not for "humble Abraham Lincoln" to think of reading law.

While hesitating over the problem, taking any odd job that came his way, a chance to buy a New Salem store presented itself. He had no money, but he had something in which New Salem had come profoundly to believe, and that was almost quixotic honesty!

When the owners of a dying mercantile establishment found he was willing to take half of it off their hands, they jumped at the offer; and so, a few months after he came back from the war he found himself in a general store, a stock of old goods on his hands, and with him, as a partner, an ineffective chap by the name of Berry, of good family, the son of a local minister, but too fond of drink.

Very soon after the firm of Berry & Lincoln came into existence its field of effort was enlarged by the most rapid and amusing bit of high finance the town ever saw. Across from the Rutledge Tavern stood the store of Reuben Radford. Radford sold groceries, and, like everybody else, whisky.

The Clary Grove boys were among his customers, and one day, when he was away, enraged by his clerk's refusal to sell them more than the number of glasses to which the rule of the place limited each man, they shot up the establishment, smashed counters and barrels, broke in the windows and tore off the doors. When Radford came back and viewed the ruins he said in disgust that he would sell to the first bidder. William Greene, better known as "Bill," was in the crowd.

"Four hundred dollars," said Greene.

"Done," said Radford. "It's yours."

Greene had no money, but he gave his note. Lincoln, who was watching the performance, suggested to him that they take an inventory. This was quickly done. It showed a more valuable stock than Lincoln had supposed, and he and Berry on the spot offered to assume the note Greene had given and add $200 (at least, authorities differ!) in cash (Berry's cash) and a horse, saddle and bridle. Before night the exchange was made, and Berry and Lincoln promptly transferred the goods from their first store, and set up shop in altogether the most convenient location for merchandising in the town of New Salem.

The story goes that when, rather late that night, young Greene went home, his father, who had heard rumors of the young man's speculating, was waiting to give him a sound berating. The boy said nothing, but sitting down in front of the fire, waited until the verbal wrath of the old man was exhausted. Then he began slowly counting out from his coat pocket where he carried his $200 the coins, big and little, and letting them ring on the fireplace hearth. The elder Greene watched the growing pile in amazement, softening as he did so. Finally he called: "Mother! Mother! Get up and get Bill a good supper; he has had a hard day."

Berry and Lincoln had assumed a big debt. The store did

[189]

not prosper. How could it, with one man drinking and the other with his head forever in a book? They had a chance to sell, and did so. But soon the purchasers disappeared, leaving their debts to swell the previous pile. Berry died, and the accumulation became Lincoln's burden—a burden which he manfully assumed and finally discharged, though it took him years.

This experiment as a merchant, which took up most of Lincoln's time through the year 1833, played a part all out of proportion to its real importance in his later political life, for in 1858, at the first of the Lincoln-Douglas debates, Mr. Douglas dragged it in. He had first known Lincoln, he said, when he was a "flourishing grocery keeper in the town of Salem." "He could ruin more whisky," Douglas went on, "than all of the boys in the town together." Over the reply that Lincoln made to this political badinage a sharp discussion arose.

"The judge is woefully at fault about his tale over Lincoln being a grocery keeper," he said. "I do not know as it would be a great sin if I had been, but he is mistaken. Lincoln never kept a grocery anywhere in the world. It is true that Lincoln did work the latter part of one winter in a little still house up at the head of a hollow."

How do you explain it? Well, in the first place, Lincoln's store was not what, in the vernacular of the day, was called a grocery. A grocery was nearer what we call a saloon. Even if it had been, it certainly never was "flourishing," but I hardly think that he would have fallen back upon quibbles of that kind; rather that he was so irritated at Judge Douglas' forcing him to spend time in answering personal charges that he did not exercise his usual caution in reply. The debate was altogether too serious a matter to Lincoln for him to have patience with such a question as whether he did or did not once keep a grocery.

# FEELING HIS WAY

Out of this discussion came the question: If he kept a store and not a grocery, did he sell liquor? There is no doubt that he did. There was no store of the day that did not have, side by side with sugar and molasses barrels, a barrel of

FACSIMILE OF TAVERN LICENSE TAKEN OUT IN MARCH, 1833, BY BERRY AND LINCOLN.

whisky. One must remember the practice and the point of view in regard to whisky in those days, so utterly different from to-day, and, indeed, what it was already becoming in 1858. Nearly ten years after Lincoln had abandoned his mercantile venture, he admirably described in a temperance speech that he made in Springfield this practice and point of view:

"When all such of us as have now reached the years of maturity first opened our eyes upon the stage of existence we found intoxicating liquor recognized by everybody, used by everybody, repudiated by nobody. It commonly entered into the first draught of the infant and the last draught of the dying man. From the sideboard of the parson down to the ragged pocket of the houseless loafer, it was constantly found. Physicians prescribed it in this, that, and the other disease; government provided it for soldiers and sailors; and to have

[191]

a rolling or raising, a husking or 'hoedown,' anywhere about without it was positively insufferable. So, too, it was everywhere a respectable article of manufacture and merchandise. The making of it was regarded as an honorable livelihood, and he who could make most was the most enterprising and respectable. Large and small manufactories of it were everywhere erected, in which all the earthly goods of their owners were invested. Wagons drew it from town to town; boats bore it from clime to clime, and the winds wafted it from nation to nation; and merchants bought and sold it, by wholesale and retail, with precisely the same feeling on the part of the seller, buyer, and bystander as are felt at the selling and buying of ploughs, beef, bacon, or any other of the real necessaries of life. Universal public opinion not only tolerated but recognized and adopted its use."

This quoted paragraph shows clearly enough how and why Lincoln sold whisky in his store. But Mr. Douglas was unfair—must have known he was unfair when he taunted Lincoln with "ruining more liquor than all the boys of the town together." That was never true. Lincoln never drank. The traditions of New Salem are that he frequently remonstrated with boys and young men that he thought in danger of intemperate habits. The one temperance lecture of his that we have, that delivered in 1842, from which I have quoted above, gives up ample proof of his opinion of whisky drinking and whisky selling:

"Whether or not the world would be vastly benefited by a total and final banishment from it of all intoxicating drinks seems to me not now an open question. Three-fourths of mankind confess the affirmative with their tongues, and, I believe, all the rest acknowledge it in their hearts."

He regarded the banishing of liquor as a revolution—a beneficent revolution.

"If the relative grandeur of revolutions shall be estimated by the great amount of human misery they alleviate, and the small amount they inflict, then indeed will this be the grandest the world has ever seen.

[192]

"Of our political revolution of '76 we are all justly proud. It has given us a degree of political freedom far exceeding that of any other nation of the earth. In it the world has found a solution of the long mooted problem as to the capability of man to govern himself. In it was the germ which has vegetated, and still is to grow and expand into the universal liberty of mankind. But, with all these glorious results, past, present, and to come, it had its evils too. It breathed forth famine, swam in blood, and rode in fire; and long, long after the orphan's cry and the widow's wail continued to break the sad silence that ensued. These were the price, the inevitable price, paid for the blessings it brought.

"Turn now to the temperance revolution. In it we shall find a stronger bondage broken, a viler slavery manumitted, a greater tyrant deposed; in it, more of want supplied, more disease healed, more sorrow assuaged. By it no orphans starving, no widows weeping. By it none wounded in feeling, none injured in interest; even the dram-maker and dram-seller will have glided into other occupations so gradually as never to have felt the change, and will stand ready to join all others in the universal song of gladness."

This ought to be answer enough to the bickering that has gone on in recent years as to whether Lincoln himself ever advocated prohibition. The fact that he undoubtedly sold liquor in his general store in New Salem in 1833, that he and his partner Berry took out a license to sell, that he once worked in a distillery, may be used to confuse the discussion, but it cannot by any fair process of argument destroy his position as an out-and-out believer in the wisdom of destroying the liquor business.

Lincoln never used liquor, he never used tobacco. A few years ago I was appealed to by a Lincoln student who had been told by a woman reared in Illinois and whose father was a friend of Lincoln that she could never bear to hear his name, that when he came as a visitor to her father's house she always left the room because he was so filthy in his use of tobacco, his face and clothes being stained with it. Firmly convinced that the lady had confused visitors, I appealed to friends of Lincoln still living in Illinois, among them Mr. Roland W. Diller, the proprietor of a drug store on the Square at Springfield, where for years Mr. Lincoln used to drop in and sit for hours with friends and neighbors around the drug store stove, swapping stories and discussing public questions. "I would certainly have known it," Mr. Diller wrote me, "with my intimate association with him. The lady was surely mistaken." There were other letters, the most important of them from Mr. Robert Lincoln himself:

"My father never used tobacco in any form."

That is, the young man struggling in New Salem to find out what he could do, and also whether he dared try the thing that he wanted to do, was clean in his habits. We can be sure that in all New Salem at this time there were few like him, few who did not have their tobacco and their glass of something strong. Why, even the Rev. John Cameron kept a barrel of whisky in his cellar!

Something was coming out of the struggle, however. Gradually his dream of the law was taking body, materializing. He was getting nearer and nearer to it, though he hardly knew it. It was he to whom people came now for advice when they had legal documents to fill out, bills of sale to prepare, bonds to give. On anything that required a legal turn, he was consulted. He had become their postmaster, too, an office that he could fill admirably in connection with the work of his store, and which he was to hold as long as it continued in the town. (The New Salem postoffice was discontinued May 30, 1836, because of diminished receipts.) But, most important of all, he was reading—reading Blackstone!

The story of the coming of the volumes into his hands, gives one a vivid picture of the town, its location, its visitors. The road from Springfield came up over the hill from the south, joining the town's one long street directly in front of

[194]

Lincoln's store. From there it turned westward to the prairies. Over this road went migrating settlers. How often Lincoln must have gone out to lend a friendly hand to somebody who had broken down or was stuck in the spring or winter mud! His kindliness brought him great reward, for in a barrel of plunder which he had bought to relieve an overloaded settler's wagon he found a full set of Blackstone—the first he had ever seen.

From the day that he pulled the books out from the pile of odds and ends which had been dumped into the barrel he read them at every chance—read them when at leisure, moiled over them when at work. How to get his hands on something that would give him the few things he must have—food and a roof to shelter him while he studied! If he could find a steady half-time job, then perhaps——

It came his way as the store was "winking out" and he was looking for jobs of chopping wood or other labor. It was probably late in the fall of 1833 that John Calhoun the surveyor of Sangamon County sent him word that he would like to depute him to assist him in his work in and around New Salem. The chance was logical enough when one remembers his reputation among his friends, but stirred as a sympathic reader must be, by what seemed to be his almost hopeless ambition, it comes like a gift from the gods. What had happened was that friends of Lincoln who knew Calhoun and knew that he was seeking a young man that promised to have the makings of a surveyor in him, had told him of Lincoln, his trustworthiness, likableness, knowledge. Let him lay out their roads and towns and farms, and there would be no come back—they knew Abraham Lincoln. It was on the recommendation of his friends that Calhoun finally appointed him.

Lincoln knew nothing of surveying, other than what every

woodsman knows—and that is considerable among the really intelligent—but he accepted. And he also promptly made sure that he was going to be able to keep his job, by hunting up a copy of Flint & Gibson—the stand-by of surveyors in those days—and mastering it. That done, his instruments bought, and he was ready. It was like a fortune to him, work at $3 a day, which kept his brain active, gave him a chance to extend his acquaintance, to sound out public opinion—and to read.

He was launched.

# XVI

## SURVEYOR, LEGISLATOR, LAW STUDENT

THE traditional occupation of impecunious young Americans ambitious for an education and a profession in Abraham Lincoln's early day, as in ours, was teaching. Not a few of those who in the future were to be his political and legal rivals and colleagues were at a teacher's desk in the years he was doing manual labor and tinkering at storekeeping—the most important among them being Stephen A. Douglas. Lincoln, however, was too conscious of his own lack of schooling, too doubtful of his store of knowledge, to think of teaching. When it came to surveying, it was a different matter. He knew he could make good at that; and when the appointment as a deputy surveyor in Sangamon County came to him late in 1833, he took hold of the work with relish and energy.

The first certificate of a survey of his which I have seen is one bearing the date of January, 1834, published many years ago by Mr. Herndon. Here he laid out a piece of land for a neighbor—a kind of work of which he was to do much in years to come, work not paid for in money. Lincoln received for this first survey two buckskins—something he probably needed, for he had them foxed on his trousers to protect them from briers.

The territory assigned to him by the chief of the Land Office was that part of Sangamon County lying in and around New Salem. That is, he had work among people who knew him. The whole section is sprinkled with reminiscences of the corners he marked, the roads he ran, the towns he plotted.

[197]

# IN THE FOOTSTEPS OF THE LINCOLNS

It was he that surveyed the new road running from "Musick's Ferry on Salt Creek," through New Salem out toward Jacksonville. It was he who plotted Petersburg, the town which was shortly to absorb New Salem, root and branch. It was

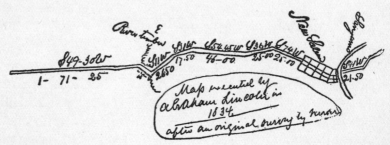

FACSIMILE OF A MAP AND REPORT OF A SURVEY MADE BY A. LINCOLN IN 1834.

he who fixed the corners of the land taken up by new settlers. Drive to-day in any direction from New Salem, and you will be told with pride, "Lincoln laid out this farm for my grandfather"—"There's a stake that Lincoln drove"—"There's a tree that Lincoln selected as a corner"—"This is Lincoln's road"—"This is one of Lincoln's towns."

Offhand one would say that surveying was a pursuit in

[198]

which there would be little chance for personality to express itself, but in Lincoln's case personality seems to have ruled even his compass and chain. Edgar Lee Masters, in his biting tale, "Mitch Miller," the scene of which is laid in Petersburg, introduces an incident, showing the triumph of his heart over his science. Mitch's chum is talking:

"Look at this house partly in the street and look at the street how it jigs. Well, Linkern did that. You see he surveyed this whole town of Petersburg. But as to this, this is how it happened. You see it was after the Black Hawk War in '36 and when Linkern came here to survey, he found that Jemina Elmore, which was a widow of Linkern's friend in the war, had a piece of land, and had built a house on it and was livin' here with her children. And Linkern saw if the street run straight north and south, a part of her house would be in the street. So to save Jemina's house, he set his compass to make the line run a little furder south. And so this is how the line got skewed and leans this strip kind of irregular clear through the town north and south. This is what I call makin' a mistake that is all right, bein' good and bad at the same time."

My first thought on reading this incident was that it was an invention of Mr. Masters; but in 1922 I looked up the original survey in Petersburg—a clean, careful and well drawn document. And there it was—a town veered a little out of plumb in order to save trouble and expense to the widow of a friend!

As a matter of fact, Lincoln found more opportunities in his new calling than he ever had before in any connection, to exercise a precious natural instinct very strong in him— the instinct to help one whom he saw to be in need. I take it that if we could have followed the young man from week to week in his surveying we would have a big collection of anecdotes of innate kindness. As it is, there are many. A favorite one along the lower Sangamon is that of the service he rendered a man who was to become one of the most prosperous and respected citizens of the county, Dr. Charles Chandler.

Dr. Chandler had come into Illinois from Kentucky in the spring of 1832, expecting to settle near Peoria. He arrived with the Black Hawk War, and could go no further at the moment than Beardstown. Looking about, he decided to take up a tract on the lower Sangamon. The claim was entered, a cabin built and cultivation begun. Busy with this work, Dr. Chandler put off going to Springfield to prove up his claim. Illinois at that time was alive with a pestiferous tribe of land sharks, and one of these gentry, ostensibly a new settler, had been befriended by Dr. Chandler. When he discovered that the full requirements of the tract which the doctor was developing had not been satisfied, he started for Springfield with the intention of grabbing the entire quarter section. When the news of this treachery came to the doctor, he saw there was but one way to save his property; and that was to head off the interloper. Hastily collecting the amount of "land office money"—gold or silver coin was required— he started on horseback for the county seat—a long and tedious ride over the unbroken roads. When he was some ten miles from the end of his journey, his horse began to show signs of giving out. Just then a young man rode up, commented on the condition of the animal, and asked why his hurry. The doctor explained the situation, and the young man, bounding down, said: "You take my horse; he's fresh. Get there before that rascal. I will follow and we will swap back when I get to town." The exchange was made, and Dr. Chandler hurried on, reaching the land office barely in time to save his claim.

Many months later the doctor asked that a survey of his land be made, and what was his surprise to find that the deputy sent him for the job—Abraham Lincoln by name—

was the very young man whose friendly act had saved his property.

Lincoln had never before made as much money as he did now, for while there might be a good many jobs for which he received produce—some of which he could use himself, as the two buckskins mentioned above, some of which he "traded in"—the county paid in cash $3 a day, with extras for maps and diagrams—not extravagant extras certainly— for road maps he received fifty cents! For a map of the town of Albany, $2.50. How surprised he would be if he knew that a day would come when many a collector would pay a hundred times $2.50 to own that map!

Surveying was an excellent occupation for Lincoln; it gave him a chance to exercise his passion for precision—and he was willing to take time to insure precision. He did not like to guess, to decide until he was confident he was right. It is said that no survey of his has ever been changed, though I do not know this to be true. We do know, however, that he steadily improved in map-making and in note-taking; that a comparison of his maps and plans shows clearly—also we know that his reputation for skill and accuracy became such that he was sometimes sent for in disputes outside of his territory. There was a corner in the northern part of Sangamon County locally famous in the Civil War because it had been fixed by Lincoln when called in as a referee. The care with which he did the work seems to have stuck in the minds of the neighborhood. He began by a resurvey of the whole section. Finally he drove in his staff: "Here's your corner." The disputants dug in and in a few minutes struck the original stake, its pointed end resting on the piece of charcoal which it was the custom of the early surveyors to use.

Nearly twenty-five years after Lincoln laid aside his surveying compass and chain, he was called upon by a convention

[201]

of surveyors who had gathered in Springfield to settle a mooted point in regard to the act passed by Congress in 1805 relating to surveys. Their selection was based not on the fact that he was an able lawyer, but that he had been a practical surveyor and had never lost his interest in the science. The opinion in Lincoln's own hand is in existence and was published in facsimile some twenty years ago in the writer's "Early Life of Lincoln."

It is quite unlikely that he had calls enough to keep him continuously busy at this time; if he had half a month's work he was probably doing well. But there is no doubt that as things were now turning for him, that was all that he cared for. His political ambition had revived. He sensed that the popularity which had encouraged him to offer himself for the assembly two years ago was stronger than ever. He had worn well—improved on acquaintance. Moreover, now he was "somebody." It was quite a different matter for a young man who had a right to walk into the land office at Springfield—one of the staff—to offer himself as a candidate, than it had been for the combined farm laborer, flatboatman and hired store-keeper of 1832. There was every reason why he should try it again.

Of course there were people to whom he seemed an unlikely candidate. A man who was to become one of his very good friends—Peter Wallace—later the Rev. Peter Wallace, D. D. of Chicago—told me once that in Springfield, where he was living in 1834, there was much hooting at Lincoln's ambitions. Wallace liked him, however, and voted for him; and there were many others in the town who did the same.

There is not a word in existence, as far as I know, of the platform on which he ran in 1834. None of his speeches have been preserved, no significant anecdotes. Two things are certain, however—he ran as a Whig, putting his emphasis on internal improvements, particularly on the improvement of the Sangamon River; and he was elected by a substantial majority.

The most important fruit of the campaign of 1834 was not his election. It was his final decision that he could and would

FACSIMILE OF LETTER WRITTEN BY A. LINCOLN, POSTMASTER OF NEW SALEM, ILLINOIS, FROM MAY, 1833, TO MAY, 1836, WHEN THE OFFICE WAS DISCONTINUED.

make a lawyer of himself. On the stump with him was a Springfield candidate, also a Whig, Major John T. Stuart. Lincoln already knew something of Stuart, for the company of which he had been captain in the first few weeks of the Black Hawk War had belonged to Stuart's command. The two men were thrown much together in the campaign and became friendly. They were about of an age, though their

[203]

experience in life had been totally different. Stuart had had "chances"—his father had been a Kentucky minister, a college professor; he himself was a college graduate who had studied law, comfortably and properly in a Kentucky firm. He had put out his shingle some time before in Springfield and was already well established. His birth, his associations, all his connections gave him a standing which Lincoln had never known. In spite of these things, the two men became good friends, and in their canvass Lincoln confided to Stuart his ambition to became a lawyer and his doubts of having sufficient education to justify him in undertaking the necessary study.

Stuart evidently realizing that Lincoln already had not only a fairly good start in the law, but excellent mental habits; offered him books, laid out a course for him—it was the turning point. He saw his way at last. He would do it. That is, he came out of the campaign of 1834 with his mind finally made up. Now there was nothing to do but work. He need no longer torment himself about his inability, his lack of preparation—he was going ahead; and just as he had done when he saw that a mastery of grammar was necessary to the handling of English requisite for political life—just as he had done when he saw that the mastery of Flint & Gibson was necessary to hold his surveyor's job, he began immediately the hard and systematic reading which must precede his admission to the bar.

He might have to ride twenty miles and back to get the books in Springfield—but he is not to be pitied for that! He had already developed habits of mind, methods of study which made him practically unconscious of his surroundings. He gathered up his material in moments of leisure, and on his journeys to and from Springfield, to and from his surveying jobs, he went over and over it, absorbing its meaning, saturating himself with it. No possible leisure, or association, no so-called advantage or opportunity could of itself have carried him so far as this habit of concentration and assimilation which he had worked out under the hard prod of necessity.

We can think of Abraham Lincoln by the fall of 1834, then, as a cheerful and satisfied young man. He was on his way, and he had the exciting experience before him of a first term in the Ninth Illinois Assembly.

It was December when he started for Vandalia, then the capital. The town lay some seventy-five miles to the south of Springfield, and then, as now, it was reached only by much zig-zagging. In all probability Lincoln went by stage coach. New Salem by this time was on a stage coach route. The line ran from Springfield northwest to the Mississippi through Monmouth. The trip took two full days and cost $9. By taking this route to Springfield, Lincoln could catch the coach south to Vandalia.

The state capital was not much to look at when Lincoln saw it for the first time in 1834. He had of course seen real cities—New Orleans, St. Louis, but Vandalia was the largest town in which he had ever lived—a town about fifteen years old, of probably not quite a thousand people—the court house a two-story brick building without any architectural pretension, its houses of worship still poor affairs, no great dwellings—but yet a town which, because of the men that had dominated it, had unmistakable distinction. Vandalia had known several superior men. There was Ninian Edwards, whom President Madison had sent to Illinois as its first territorial governor, who later had been a United States Senator, and after that Governor of the state. There was Edward Coles, a gentleman if there ever was one, Governor from 1823 to 1826—the man who because of his hatred of slavery had put fortune, position, comfort behind him, had brought his slaves to Illinois, freed them and established them there, and who had then put through the great fight to make the new state free. Then there was John Reynolds, as virile and picturesque a character as Illinois had known. The State assembly had always others of fine caliber—men of French descent and a touch of French cultivation—aspiring Kentuckians and Virginians, the best of timber.

As the terminus of the Cumberland Road, the only national highway westward, Vandalia had become a purchasing center for the surrounding country. Capp's store made the prices for all that part of the world, it was said, and had the reputation of keeping everything. Indeed, one of the favorite bets with a newcomer was that he could not mention anything that could not be found at Capp's. One newly elected assemblyman who had taken the bet asked for goose yokes. Mr. Capp promptly appeared with one, saying that they always kept them for legislators.

Vandalia had a sense of its dignity as capital of the state, and, on the whole, was an orderly town. There were bound to be fights, it said, philosophically, and provided for them an institution known as the Bull Pen, where every one was allowed to go and settle his difficulty without disturbing the streets!

To Lincoln, fresh from New Salem, and its little group of people, probably grown too familiar to be stimulating, Vandalia, with its senate of 26, its assembly of 55, with its Governor and official staff, with a crowd of lobbyists, with the animated social life incident to even a pioneer capital, was an exciting change. He came not as an outsider, but as a recognized insider, a representative of one of the important counties of the state, a county that everybody saw already must be reckoned with.

Lincoln was too modest by nature, too conscious of his

own limitations, to force himself on the assembly. His approach was different. He had to know his ground, understand his people, make up his mind, study the thing out before he would attempt to put himself forward. The result is that we have a young legislator who does what he does very quietly. No speech of his is reported—no signs of leadership show in the record. As a matter of fact, the two sessions of the Ninth Assembly—one in the winter of 1834-35 and an extra one called at the end of 1835—were given over almost entirely to Lincoln's favorite topic of internal improvements; and most of the time of the legislators was devoted to making and passing bills for railroads, canals, roads and bridges. There was little speech-making. The "heart appalling shock" which Lincoln confessed the cost of railroads gave him in 1832 seems to have entirely passed. The Whigs had gone over to the railroad, and they plunged into a scheme of development which takes one's breath away when we remember that the financing of their magnificent scheme must all be done on faith—faith largely in outside capital flowing in to take bonds.

Lincoln's solution of the problem of financing the improvements was that the Federal Government turn back to the states the proceeds of the sales of public lands. If this was done, Illinois could dig its canals and build its railroads, without borrowing money and paying interest on it. Although there was little hope of this, he was no more reluctant than his colleagues to go ahead with their schemes, without any sure means of paying for them. The map of the developments which they planned would be almost sufficient for Illinois to-day, though it has some lacks that look curious to us now. For instance, they ran a railroad straight north from Cairo, with a terminus at Galena. No road to Chicago! Chicago's western connection was a canal. The rivers were not neglected. They voted $50,000 for the improvement of the Kaskaskia River on which Vandalia lay, though, as one disgusted legislator declared, "Turtles have been known to have run aground on that stream."

It was not only for the improvement of rivers and the building of canals and railroads that this hopeful Ninth Assembly provided. It granted numbers of charters for private undertakings, among them many toll bridges, some of which possibly are still in operation. The second bill, indeed, that Lincoln introduced was for one of these toll bridges—Musick's bridge across Salt Creek, destined to be long known to Illinois travelers. It was to replace the ferry mentioned above in one of his surveys. And then there were schools, academies and colleges chartered, numbers of them. Transportation and education—these were the needs of Illinois, these were the things which the Ninth Assembly was encouraging, leaving it to luck, private initiative and the lure which the new land might have for investors for the money to pay for them.

If Lincoln's career as a legislator began modestly, it is certain he got his feet firmly on the ground in his first term. He learned the ways, he studied the men, he grew in confidence and directness—the last comes out interestingly in the hand bill he sent out in 1836, announcing his candidacy for a second term. Compare this document with the one he distributed in 1832, and you find him firmer in expression, more willing to present himself in few words, no longer feeling it necessary to apologize for himself as he did at the start.

The practical point in the little document is his reiteration of his idea of how money should be secured, in part at least, for all their fine undertakings—good Whig doctrine—the proceeds of the sales of public lands. There is one general proposition which smacks of buncombe, though I have no doubt Lincoln really meant it: "If elected I shall consider the whole people of Sangamon my constituents, as well those that oppose me as those that support me." One has heard the phrase repeated so regularly since Lincoln's day and has seen it so rarely applied that one instinctively revolts against putting the words into his mouth.

One short paragraph in this two hundred word announcement card has kept it alive and in the last few years has been constantly quoted in political campaigns, that is the one in which he lays down his notion of popular suffrage. So far as I know it is his only expression on the subject:

"I go for all sharing the privileges of the government, who assist in bearing its burdens. Consequently, I go for admitting all whites to the right of suffrage who pay taxes or bear arms" (by no means excluding females).

A suffrage only to those who pay or serve, is what it amounts to.

On the above platform Lincoln was elected in the summer of 1836 to his second term in the Illinois assembly.

He was not to go back to Vandalia, however, with the light and confident heart that he carried in 1834. True, he was further along in his public and professional ambitions, he had made great strides in his law reading, he had begun to see the end, to be sure that he would be admitted. He knew he was solid with his constituents, and probably could be reëlected as often as he might want, but his heart was heavy within him.

A singular feature of the frank and voluminous reminiscences we have of Lincoln's life in New Salem from 1831 to 1834 is that none of them recall any intimacy or even companionship with the young girls of the town and countryside. Back in Indiana his acquaintances remembered that he "liked" little Kate Roby. Down at Anderson's ferry on the Ohio they told how he gave a friend a scar "for life" in a quarrel over a girl to whom he had paid attention. In Macon County, Illinois, there are detailed traditions of his courting two young women in 1830 and '31 and wanting to marry both of them! Yet in New Salem, for nearly three years there seems to have been no one to whom he was so attracted that his sharp-eyed friends remarked it; and you may be sure they would have seen and remembered if there had been such a one.

It is not credible that through these years Lincoln was indifferent to women. I doubt if ever there was a time of his life when he was not keenly conscious of them, drawn to them. The truth undoubtedly is that on his coming to New Salem he was deeply stirred by a young woman of the town who he knew to be engaged to another man. It was not until 1834 that she was free and that he finally won her. There is no doubt that she was the first woman he had loved, the only one who ever brought him romance.

# XVII

## ANN RUTLEDGE

NO episode in Abraham Lincoln's life has been more maltreated than that of his love and loss of Ann Rutledge. It was his first romance—his only real romance. It was cut short by the death of the girl, and there is no doubt that he was shaken to the very core by his grief—no doubt that his whole life was affected by the blow. But as the story has grown in repeated tellings, it has become largely a study in morbidity. On one side it pictures a young girl who knew her heart so poorly that after accepting Lincoln she never gave him a full, free love, but so tormented herself with thoughts of one to whom she had earlier pledged herself, and who had not only deceived her as to his very name, but had apparently deserted her, that she brought on a brain fever from which she died. On the other side, we have a young man so poorly balanced mentally that for weeks after his loss he walks on the edge of insanity—unfit to care for himself, wandering at night about the country, muttering incoherent laments.

One cannot be too thankful that the work of recent Lincoln lovers has cleared this romance of the clouds of turgid sentiment that have enveloped it and brought out firmly and finally, I hope, its simple, touching lines.

Thanks to those who are restoring the town of New Salem and getting together there a pioneer museum of which Lincoln and Ann Rutledge are the center, thanks to Jane Hamand, of Iowa, who has made a specialty of Rutledge history in the choice Lincoln collection she has donated to

[211]

Decatur, Illinois, we have material for that authentic setting which always does so much to give reality and naturalness to any human drama.

I hold, however, as most important in clearing the story of its morbid streaks, the chapter on Ann Rutledge in Henry B. Rankin's "Personal Recollections of Abraham Lincoln," published in 1916. No one who has written of the two young people had a better opportunity to know the truth of their relationship than Mr. Rankin—no one by temperament, dignity of thought and feeling, carefulness of expression has been better prepared to tell what he knew. Mr. Rankin's mother, though some years older than Ann Rutledge, was not only her teacher and friend, but her confident at the time of her engagement to Mr. Lincoln. Henry Rankin, born in 1837, thus knew the story first hand from an intelligent, cultivated woman, of whose father's family, as later of her husband's family, Lincoln was a friend.

Mr. Rankin himself grew up in Petersburg, played as a boy around the fast disappearing cabins of deserted New Salem, went to the court house when Lincoln was there to see and hear him, and through all his youth heard his family and neighbors go over their recollections of the early days and Lincoln's part in them. When he was about twenty-one years of age he went into the office of Lincoln and Herndon in Springfield, and for four years was more or less constantly associated with the firm.

Among the treasured possessions in Mr. Rankin's carefully chosen Lincoln library is a worn book, inscribed on its front cover "Autographs." The very first of the collection is that of Abraham Lincoln.

"Today, Feb. 23, 1858, the owner honored me with the privilege of writing the first name in this book.

"A. LINCOLN."

# ANN RUTLEDGE

Mr. Herndon, Mr. Lincoln's partner, wrote at the same time the lines below. I do not know of any minor document which shows more clearly the difference in the two men:

"The struggles of this age and succeeding ages for God and man —Religion—Humanity and Liberty with all their complex and grand relations—may they triumph and conquer forever, is my ardent wish and most fervent soul-prayer.

"WM. H. HERNDON.

"Feb'y 23d, 1858."

Mr. Rankin later became a banker in Petersburg, and there, some forty years ago, was stricken with myalgia which has kept him on his back all the years since. Of a cheerful and courageous spirit, he accepted his physical handicap and has led a life not only of remarkable business activity —he has multiplied his estate by five and given a college education to his three children—but more important, of amazingly beautiful intellectual and spiritual quality. Always a lover and a student of Lincoln, he resolved a few years ago to set down his personal recollections of the man. In these is the chapter to which I referred above as contributing, to my mind, the most reliable, intelligent and sympathetic study that we have ever had of Ann Rutledge and Lincoln. With these materials adding to and clarifying what has been collected in other ways, chiefly by William H. Herndon, the story comes out clearly. The tragedy with which it ends is a natural tragedy, not one clouded by the introspection of a neurotic young girl or the abandonment of all control by an equally neurotic young man.

When Lincoln came to New Salem in the summer of 1831, as a clerk in a store, hidden from the main part of the town by a bend in the road, a section which with its gander pulling, cock fighting and drinking was outside the pale of the more respectable portion of the community, there was at least one girl of unusual attractiveness in the little settlement; she was the daughter of one of the leading citizens, a half owner in the mill and the owner of the tavern, James Rutledge by name.  The one thing upon which all of those who have left personal recollections of Ann Rutledge agree is that she was a healthy, natural girl, of an unusually happy disposition, well trained, industrious, ambitious.  And this we would expect, for the Rutledges were of a fine type, with traditions of orderly living, ambitious for their children.  Ann particularly had responded to their anxiety that all of their nine children should somehow get an education.  When Lincoln arrived in New Salem the girl was not only her mother's aid in the work of the four-room tavern, active at the spinning wheel and quilting frame, she was studying regularly under Mentor Graham, the schoolmaster.

Naturally enough, Lincoln would not be long in finding out that this charming girl had a lover.  Across the street from the Rutledge tavern—so near that one could call across —was the general store of Samuel Hill and John McNeill, both of whom had tried for Ann's favor.  The latter had won, but as she was eager for more schooling, so Lincoln would early learn, she had determined before she was married to spend one year at least in the academy at Jacksonville, some seventy-five miles away.

Now, one of the acquaintances that Lincoln made at the start in New Salem was the schoolmaster, Mentor Graham, and to him he went constantly for help in his studies.  The schoolhouse did not stand on the ridge with the little group of dwellings, but on a hillside to the south, not far from the road which led out to Springfield.  It was natural enough that the two young people should be drawn together over their books under Mentor Graham's tuition; that they should walk back and forth together to consult him.  The tradition is that when Lincoln was studying grammar, Ann Rutledge worked with him, and that it was to her he gave the book when he was through with it. The inscription on the flyleaf, "Ann Rutledge is now studying grammar," is believed to have been written by Lincoln's hand. At least the book went down in the family, and it was treasured for years by a nephew of Ann's, W. W. Rutledge, who again and again refused offers of large sums of money for the book, but finally placed it in the hands of Miss Hamand for the Decatur collection, only because he knew that there it would have the care that it deserved.

One cannot go through the streets of the little town and see the relation of the houses and shops in which the people were living and working without realizing how the two young people—grammar aside—would be thrown constantly into each other's company. There were all the local merry-makings—quiltings, corn-huskings, picnics—and there were long horseback rides (in the museum at New Salem Ann Rutledge's side saddle holds a place of honor). There were the nightly gatherings in cold and wet weather around the fireplace in the living room of the Rutledge Inn. It was a pleasant room, I have no doubt. The few possessions that we have dating back to that time show that there was refinement, interest in good things, in the family. There is a fine old pewter coffee pot in the New Salem museum, out of which Mrs. Rutledge poured coffee. There is the family Bible, with its carefully filled out lists of births and deaths. In Decatur there is the copy of the hymn and song books from which night after night they sang together—The Watt's Psalm Book, The Missouri Harmony. It was from the latter that Lincoln himself used to try to sing, it is said, though by all accounts he had little either of ear or voice. Legacy is a song in The Missouri Harmony with which he used to tease

[215]

Ann's little sister Nancy, who tells of having run out of the room blushing whenever he sang it to her—a modest little girl certainly, for the verses are harmless enough.

Another meeting place for Ann and Lincoln was in the home of Mr. Rankin's mother, the daughter of Col. Matthew Rogers, an early settler in the "Sangamon country," living some four miles to the east of New Salem. Lincoln had been first drawn to the Rogers home by the books the Colonel had brought from the East, books of which he became a borrower. Not only did the Rogers have books, they had newspapers that could not be found elsewhere. Then, too, there were in the family three or four young men near Lincoln's age, who had had excellent schooling, one or two of whom were carrying on medical studies. These were attractions enough, but it is not unfair to say that Lincoln may have found another in the fact that Ann Rutledge also went regularly to the Rogers home, where Mr. Rankin's mother, a teacher, was tutoring her for the Jacksonville Academy.

And so the acquaintance went on, quite naturally and intimately, based on mutual ambitions and the mutual activities necessary to realize those ambitions. There is not a hint, so far as I find in any of the recollections, that McNeill himself resented in any way this intimacy. He did disapprove, it is said, of Ann's spending a year in Jacksonville Academy. He wanted to be married. He was, for the time, a rich man, though one does not see it in the restoration of the little store of which he was part owner, across the street from the Rutledge tavern, but he had a farm outside, and was a clever trader—evidently a natural money-maker, though all agree a man of cold and reserved nature.

Lincoln's daring ventures into the mercantile field, described in a previous chapter, finally brought him from the riotous end of the settlement into a store side by side with that

[216]

of McNeill and directly facing the front door of Ann's home. There used to be a big tree in front of this store, the roots of which the New Salem restorers told me were recently unearthed. Under this tree Lincoln stretched with his books in idle hours, and when Ann sat at her spinning wheel in the shadow of the cabin in the afternoon, or sewed or studied there, he could call across to her, run across and visit, and no doubt did many a time.

The store petered out in 1833, but Lincoln stayed on. I have often wondered how much Ann Rutledge had to do with his holding on in New Salem in those months of uncertain occupation. Did he realize there might be a chance for him later? He was too keen eyed, too understanding of people, not to see that McNeill was moody and restless. He had decided that he must go East, so he told his friends. He was going to bring back his father and mother and put them on his farm. Finally he sold his interest in the store and, early in the spring of 1834, left. Lincoln, now postmaster of New Salem, must have noticed that weeks and weeks went on and no letter came back from McNeill. He must have realized Ann's anxiety almost as soon as her parents did; but he did not know that the girl, not hearing from her lover, had confided to them that just before saying good-by, McNeill had told her a strange story, that his real name was McNamar, that he had thought it best to change his name, because the family fortunes had been low in the East and that he had come West to redeem them. The girl could not but have doubted the explanation. Her family and friends, when they learned the truth, doubted it still more, and that, joined with his long silence—a silence later explained by the fact that he had been ill—led them to believe that the man was unworthy of her trust. Certain it is that as time went on and nothing was heard of McNeill the girl's feelings changed.

Lincoln was on the ground, and making his way fast. He was not only deputy surveyor of Sangamon County, but in 1834 he had been elected to the assembly. He had begun to study law. He was respected and backed by the best people in the vicinity. The whole community began to realize before he went to Vandalia for his first term in the assembly that he was thoroughly in love with Ann; but it was not until the spring of 1835, when McNeill, or McNamar, had now been gone over a year, that the two young people came together. There seems no doubt at all that Ann was as happy as Lincoln in this engagement. They were going to be very sensible; Ann was to have her year in Jacksonville, Lincoln was to finish his law studies and be admitted to the bar in 1836; then he would settle in Springfield and they would be married.

Mr. Rankin says that his mother told him that it was in the early summer of 1835 that Ann first confided to her that she had become engaged to Mr. Lincoln. She talked freely to Mrs. Rankin then of the absence and neglect of McNamar, acknowledging that her own judgment and heart at length approved the advice of both her own family and the few friends to whom she had confided the perplexities through which she had for months been passing. "My mother said," Mr. Rankin goes on, "that in the conversation with her she manifested no regret or wavering in the choice she had made. On the contrary, there was a decided spirit of offended maidenly dignity manifested in all the references she made to McNamar, such, my mother said, as could be expected of a well-bred Southern girl under circumstances showing such unaccountable neglect."

The year after Mr. Lincoln's death, in November of 1866, Mr. Herndon gave a lecture in Springfield, Illinois, which he called "Abraham Lincoln, Ann Rutledge, New Salem,

Pioneering, and the Poem"—the poem was "Why Should the Spirit of Mortal Be Proud." The story Mr. Herndon told in this lecture of Ann Rutledge's attitude of mind after her engagement to Mr. Lincoln is a direct contradiction to that of Mrs. Rankin.

✗"Her word of promise was out to two men at the same time, both of whom she loved, dearly loved; the consciousness of this and the conflict of duties, love's promises and womanly engagements made her think, grow sad, become restless and nervous. She suffered, pined, ate not and slept not. Time and struggle, as supposed and believed by many, caused her to have a raging fever, of which she died on the twenty-fifth of August, A. D. 1835."

So far as the actual personal recollections quoted by Mr. Herndon in this lecture go, they give only the flimsiest basis for this interpretation; and yet biographers generally, myself included, have accepted more or less at face value this morbid explanation. It is Mr. Rankin who has cleared the matter up, giving a natural reason for the girl's death.

It seems that the spring and summer of 1835 were hot and wet through all of the Sangamon country, and that after several months of this weather, there was an outbreak of what was called "bilious fever." There was hardly a household for miles around New Salem in which there was not some one ill. At the Rutledges there were several laid low, Ann being among the last. During this outbreak, as is the custom always in pioneer communities, those who had been spared became nurses. Lincoln was very active among his friends who were suffering, and, naturally, particularly attentive to the Rutledges. When Ann fell ill, he was already seriously worn out. Indeed, Mr. Rankin believes, from his mother's statement, that, for nearly a month before the girl's death he had himself been suffering from chills and fever, only keeping himself going by heroic doses of the favorite

[219]

remedies of the time. As long as there was a hope of saving Ann, he persisted in fighting his own illness, but when she finally died, he went completely to pieces.

✗ The girl's death came to him as a supreme tragedy—the failure of the most beautiful hopes that he had ever entertained. It is little wonder that, ill as he was in body, stricken as he was in mind and heart, he should have gone through a period of terrible despair. Fortunately for him there were understanding friends at hand to give him both the sympathy and the care he needed. One gets a high idea of the quality of neighborly kindness current in New Salem in 1835 from the way everybody rallied to Lincoln's help at this moment of distress. Among the strongest and wisest of the town's citizens was good Dr. John Allen—a physician of hearts and souls as well as bodies, all agree in calling him. Dr. Allen had cared for Ann Rutledge to the last, and now that she was gone he took charge of Lincoln, bringing him to the home of his old friends, the Bowling Greenes. Here Lincoln had long been like one of the family. Both Squire Greene and Aunt Nancy were of that kind we call the "salt of the earth," and they nursed Lincoln as if he had been a son.

It was not long before he had thrown off his fever and was at work—surveying, reading his law books, preparing for the extra session of the assembly called for December.

That he should have had during his illness and for weeks after he was about hours of uncontrollable grief seems to me to be expected. That he should have gone again and again to Ann's grave and wept over it is what any man so stricken would have done. To cry out that he could not bear the thought of rain and snow upon her grave was what those who have loved and lost through all time have done. It was the bitter grief of a man who had loved much and lost all.

But this was not insanity, as Mr. Herndon insinuates. It

[220]

was not even the "partial dethronement" he declares. I have gone over carefully the various interviews and letters from which Herndon quotes in his lecture and later in his "Life," and cannot find in them any substantial basis for the incoherent utterances which he puts into Lincoln's mouth, to give, as he says, "a fair idea" of his "mental state and condition" after Ann Rutledge's death:

"Who am I and what, 'mid nature's profoundest uncertainties, that come and go like chance, whither, no one knows. There, the cocks crow. Did I not read—but, stay, did I not read law beneath the shade of this tree, grinding 'round the sun? I love her. Oh! immensities above me, below me, and around me.

"The dogs, the very dogs bark at me. These limbs and legs, feet and hands, are mine; yet 'tis strange! and ah! thou mysterious state of things. Is't fate, chance, Providence, God—that so unwinds the worlds and all their life? Grief! What's that? I'm tired and weary. The clothes I've got on and wear, I know are mine, and yet they seem not to be. . . .

"What's that in the mill pond, going splash, splash? 'Twas a fish, I guess. Let's go and feed it, and make it joy, and be happy. I love her, and shall marry her on tomorrow's eve. So soul be content and endless joy shall come. Heart of mine be still, for remember sweet tomorrow eve. Oh! thou calmest, most boisterous, profoundest uncertainties of things, hold off, or take another path not coming here. What! did I dream? Think; what did I say? It cannot be. No, it cannot be. She's dead and gone—gone forever. Fare thee well, sweet girl! We'll meet again."

Mr. Herndon protests—over-protests—in setting out to write his story of Ann Rutledge and Abraham Lincoln that "truth in history" is his "sole and only motive," but this hysterical soliloquy in no way serves the truth—it obscures and distorts it.

But if we have no authority for saying that Lincoln "went insane" after Ann Rutledge's death, we have every reason to believe that he had received a blow which changed his outlook on life. Many and various interpretations have been given of the effect the death of the girl had on him. One of his legal associates in Illinois once declared that after he recovered enough to go about his business, he "leaped wildly" into public life. This, of course, is pure fiction; Lincoln was already in public life, serving his first term in the assembly when Ann Rutledge died. If he ever "leaped wildly" into politics, he did it in 1832 when, on as little backing as ever a young man had, he offered himself as a candidate. Another has told in great detail how in his last interviews with Ann Rutledge she obtained a promise from him to become a Christian, in her sense. There seems to be no basis at all for this statement. Others have seen in this the dawning of his devotion to freedom, to the nation.

Edgar Lee Masters has made the noblest contribution to these speculations in the sonnet which in recent years has been engraved on a bronze tablet and set into the great boulder which marks the grave of Ann in the cemetery of Petersburg:

Out of me unworthy and unknown
The vibrations of deathless music;
"With malice toward none, with charity for all."
Out of me the forgiveness of millions toward millions,
And the beneficent face of a nation
Shining with justice and truth.
I am Ann Rutledge who sleep beneath these weeds,
Beloved in life of Abraham Lincoln,
Wedded to him, not through union,
But through separation.
Bloom forever, O Republic,
From the dust of my bosom!

The death of Ann Rutledge opened wide the vein of melancholy in Abraham Lincoln's nature. His mind must have gone back again and again to the summer of 1818, when Pigeon Creek Valley of Indiana had been swept by a scourge

OUT OF ME UNWORTHY AND UNKNOWN
THE VIBRATIONS OF DEATHLESS MUSIC:
"WITH MALICE TOWARD NONE, WITH CHARITY FOR ALL."
OUT OF ME FORGIVENESS OF MILLIONS TOWARD MILLIONS,
AND THE BENEFICENT FACE OF A NATION
SHINING WITH JUSTICE AND TRUTH.
I AM ANN RUTLEDGE WHO SLEEP BENEATH THESE WEEDS,
BELOVED OF ABRAHAM LINCOLN,
WEDDED TO HIM, NOT THROUGH UNION,
BUT THROUGH SEPARATION.
BLOOM FOREVER, O REPUBLIC,
FROM THE DUST OF MY BOSOM!
JANUARY 7TH, 1813. ——— AUGUST 25TH, 1835.

ANN RUTLEDGE

GRAVE OF ANN RUTLEDGE IN OAKLAND CEMETERY, PETERSBURG, MENARD CO., ILLINOIS

of disease not unlike that from which the Sangamon country had just suffered. Then it was his mother who had been taken from him—now it was his love.

Was he always to lose those he loved best!

Mr. Herndon believes that it was in this period of desolation that Lincoln first came upon those verses on the tran-

---

**S. T. LOGAN & E. D. BAKER,**
ATTORNEYS AND COUNSELLORS AT LAW.
WILL practice, in conjunction, in the Circuit Courts of this Judicial District, and in the Circuit Courts of the Counties of Pike, Schuyler and Peoria.
Springfield, march, 1887.                     81-t

**J. T. STUART AND A. LINCOLN,**
ATTORNEYS and Counsellors at Law, will practice, conjointly, in the Courts of this Judicial Circuit.—
Office No. 4 Hoffman's Row, up stairs.
Springfield, april 12, 1837.                     4

THE partnership heretofore existing between the undersigned, has been dissolved by mutual consent.—
The business will be found in the hands of John T. Stuart.
                    JOHN T. STUART,
April 12, 1837.  84  HENRY E. DUMMER.

ABRAHAM LINCOLN'S FIRST PROFESSIONAL CARD FROM THE SANGAMO JOURNAL OF SPRINGFIELD, ILLINOIS, FOR APRIL 12, 1837.

---

sientness of life which men heard him quote at intervals as long as he lived:

> "Oh! why should the spirit of mortal be proud?
> Like a swift-fleeing meteor, a fast-flying cloud,
> A flash of the lightning, a break of the wave,
> He passeth from life to his rest in the grave."

Again and again in later life he repeated to friends the entire fourteen melancholy stanzas. Death was everywhere!

It seems probable that it was in this period, too, that Volney's Ruins took a deep hold on his imagination. I cannot but believe that Volney's picture of the passing away of civilizations, one people building on the tombs of another, one city growing on the ruins of another, became vastly more vivid in the light of the sweeping out of love and romance from his life.

But whatever he suffered, whatever light went out, he did not lose his grip on realities. On the contrary, he seems to have taken hold harder than ever, for the next four or five years' work fixed Lincoln permanently as a factor in the life of Illinois.

# XVIII

## 1837—LINCOLN'S FIRST BIG YEAR

THE first big year in Abraham Lincoln's life was 1837.
It was then that he first proved his skill as a political
leader, was admitted to the bar, began to make speeches that
were preserved, and, most important of all, demonstrated
that he had the moral courage to side openly with what he believed to be the right of an issue on which the whole country
was divided.

Active as he was, he was by no means free from melancholy. The shadow of Ann Rutledge's death still hung over
him. More than one of his friends in the assembly in the
sessions that followed her death in the summer of 1835 have
recalled how quiet he was, how many evenings he left the
group in the tavern to spend with some thoughtful friend.
The most interesting of the reminiscences of these winters in
Vandalia has come to us only recently in a series of letters
and fugitive memoranda from the Rev. James Lemen, a
minister well known in Illinois up to his death in 1870 at the
age of eighty-three.

Mr. Lemen was a son of that stalwart anti-slavery leader,
the Rev. James Lemen, Sr., who came to Illinois in 1786 as
a confidential agent of Thomas Jefferson, charged with building up anti-slavery sentiment in the northwestern territory.
During all the years after the ordinance of 1787 made this
territory free, James Lemen fought the strong factions in
Illinois and Indiana which repeatedly petitioned Congress to
repeal the anti-slavery articles of the ordinance. In 1809, at

[225]

Jefferson's request, he founded an anti-slavery branch of the Baptist Church and later the Illinois Anti-Slavery League—powerful influences in finally saving the state to freedom against an opposition whose strength it is very hard for us to realize to-day.

James Lemen, Sr., had six sons, all of whom, like their father, became Baptist preachers. It was one of these, his namesake, that Lincoln knew in Vandalia. Mr. Lemen wrote his recollections of this acquaintance years ago for his family, but, so far as I know, no part of it was published before 1915. In these notes he says:

"My period of public service in early and later Illinois, and my travels as a gospel minister, which covered a period of more than fifty years, gave me a more or less intimate acquaintance with nearly every public man in the state within that period, and none of them impressed me more favorably than Abraham Lincoln, from the first time I met him in Vandalia, in 1837, when he was a member of the Legislature. Generally, with strangers, Mr. Lincoln was secretive and shy, but, from some cause, we formed very strong attachments at our very first meeting, which steadily increased during his lifetime. My business at Vandalia that winter kept me there several weeks, and, both boarding at the same place, Mr. Lincoln and I were thrown together a great deal. Generally, for three nights every week, he was at my rooms until midnight, and certainly no one was more welcome. The members of the Legislature said they could not see why he made a companion of me as I was a preacher, and he cared but little for religion; but they were in error, as his conversations were chiefly on the Scriptures and related subjects, and I believe at every meeting I held on Sundays, in town or adjacent settlements while there, Mr. Lincoln was present.

"At later periods I was frequently at Springfield on business or duty, and there Lincoln spent three or four evenings, generally at my rooms, every week, and he certainly could not have enjoyed our meetings any more than I did. While there I generally preached every Sunday in town or country, and Lincoln was nearly always present, although, ordinarily, he was not a regular church attendant. There was a constitutional trait, or characteristic about Mr. Lincoln that colored nearly all of his life, and that was a settled form of melancholy, sometimes very marked, and sometimes very mild, but always sufficient to tinge his countenance with a shade of sadness unless a smile should dispel it, which frequently happened, as he enjoyed humor and often indulged in it. On matters spiritual, like the philosophical old apostle, Thomas, he was sometimes inclined to doubt, though to no greater extent than thousands of church-member Christians. But frequently he seemed to crave a stronger belief in the Bible truths, and on one occasion of that kind at Springfield he spent a whole night with me conversing on Scriptural matters, and at times we engaged in prayer, and finally he declared our meetings had restored his feelings to a better state of confidence, and that his doubts were subdued. At that stage he made a most beautiful prayer which so impressed me that after its conclusion I asked him if he could repeat it, which he did, and I wrote it down and preserved a copy of it. This was in 1856, and was our last meeting."

In reading these reminiscences, one must remember that they were written long after the event by an aged and fervently pious man who probably exaggerated his intimacy with Lincoln. I see little reason to doubt their genuineness. In a letter claimed to be from Mr. Lincoln to Mr. Lemen, first published in 1915, Mr. Lincoln says: "The memory of our many 'evening sittings' here and elsewhere, as we called them, suggests many a pleasant hour, both pleasant and helpful."

This letter, if authentic, corroborates Mr. Lemen's story in the main, but unfortunately it is only a copy. No original is known, and several serious historical students have challenged its genuineness as that of the reminiscences.

However deep in melancholy Lincoln may often have sunk in 1837, it did not interfere with either his political or his professional activities. And this is true of all those periods of gloom through which he went at different times and which have been interpreted by certain of his biographers as periods of practical insanity. A man who goes on with his work regularly and intelligently through a time of moral and mental abasement and despair is not a crazy man. And Lincoln always did this. At the time of Ann Rutledge's death, as we have already seen, it was only when he was absolutely prostrated by "chills and fever" that he gave up. As soon as that illness had abated he went about his business. It was so at this time. Quiet and brooding as he was, he was still able to conduct to a successful issue the most spirited bit of political work that the assembly of Illinois had seen in its twenty-seven years of life. This was the campaign by which the capital was taken away from Vandalia and transferred to the town to which Lincoln was to move—Springfield, the county seat of Sangamon County.

As one goes about Vandalia to-day and reviews its early history in company with the fine group of leaders there who are so eager to preserve everything of its early history, one cannot but sympathize with their loss of the capital, inevitable as it was. As a matter of fact, it was recognized in 1820 when Vandalia was chosen as the capital that it might soon prove to be too far south for the convenience of the state. Accordingly the legislature passed an act, saying that at the end of twenty years it might be changed, if it was so desired. In anticipation of the expiration of this period a vote was taken in 1833. There were six contestants at that time, the geographical center of the state, Jacksonville, Springfield, Alton, Vandalia and Peoria. Alton won.

They tell you in Vandalia to-day how stirred the town was when it realized its loss. "We will hold them," a few of the citizens said. "We will build a capitol ourselves, so fine they won't leave." And in the summer of 1837 two or three citizens, largely out of their own pockets, although aided by materials which could be filched from the stores the United States Government had collected in the vicinity for building bridges over the national highway, put up what was, at that time, the finest public building in Illinois, the building which is really the pride of Vandalia to-day, although, unhappily, it has been "improved" by later well-intentioned but mistaken groups of citizens.

In this building, now the County Court House, they show you the assembly room in which Lincoln sat, and where there went on the lively fight that he, as the head of the Sangamon County delegation, conducted in the effort to secure the capital for Springfield. Here he did his persuading, haranguing, "log rolling." Here is the window, they tell you, from which he once jumped to break up a quorum.

According to Mr. Herndon, it was four years later, and in the capitol at Springfield, that Mr. Lincoln executed this manœuver, though, I do not know why he should not have jumped from windows in two different capitols! If it would win a point, we may be sure he did! So let Vandalia stick to her tradition!

At all events, he won out as leader in this fight for removing the capital to Springfield. Vandalia's fine new capitol building proved to be a mausoleum for her hopes. To-day she contents herself with reminiscences, and although there is a long list of men of fine caliber and achievement connected with her early history, her chief pride is in the fact that here Abraham Lincoln spent five winters of his life.

At the close of this session in which Lincoln had distinguished himself as a political leader he moved to Springfield. It was less a wrench for him to leave New Salem after six years there because New Salem was moving out herself— moving root and branch to Petersburg, a mile or two down the Sangamon—a town which in 1836 Lincoln had surveyed and to which he had, in the course of his "log rolling" for the capital, secured the extension of the road from Springfield. Petersburg's absorption of New Salem was the victory of the

[229]

prairie over the bluff. The settlers had learned that the prairie could be made livable, that here was the wealth; they had learned, too, the difficulty of keeping up roads in towns situated as New Salem was—a difficulty obvious to visitors to-day.

There has always been a tendency to emphasize Lincoln's forlornness in making this move, but, as a matter of fact, he was stepping into a position superior to that which most young lawyers of twenty-eight have when they start in a new place, for Springfield, if a new home, was by no means a strange town to him. For three years now he had held a position in its land office. For three years he had been one of the representatives of the county at the state assembly. It is safe to venture that there were not many men in Springfield that he did not know. Moreover, most of these men were friendly to him, friendly because they had confidence in his integrity and in his ability. He came, too, fresh from the laurels that he had won at Vandalia. Springfield was grateful to him and to all the delegation, known in Illinois history as the "Long Nine," because no one of them was less than six feet in height; and all that summer barbecues and celebrations were given through the county to the delegation "as demonstrations of approbation for their course in the Legislature." I have before me a communication from Athens describing one of these affairs, with a list of twenty-six different toasts, one of them by "A. Lincoln" and at least three of them in his honor.

Lincoln was lucky in having a friend in Springfield with whom he could live, a friend who for several years now was to be the confidant of his always troubled heart, Joshua F. Speed. He was fortunate, too, in having a position in a law firm at once offered him. Major John T. Stuart, whom Lincoln himself credits with having encouraged him to study law, now took him in, and their card appears first in the Sangamon Journal for April 12, 1837.

That he was a real partner we have evidence from their fee book, facsimiles of extracts from which have been published at various times. In the entries for April of the year Lincoln went up to Springfield there is no fee higher than five dollars, though a little later we have one of fifty; it seems, however, to have been exceptional; but if fees were low, so were expenses. Mr. Charles W. Moores of Indianapolis, who under the title of "The Career of a Country Lawyer" has made one of the best studies of Lincoln's legal life which we have, unearthed a few years ago a number of interesting entries showing both the modesty of the fees and the modesty of the cost of living.

While unquestionably the connection with Stuart was a fine thing for Lincoln, he being a man of good breeding and education as well as of high standing in the community, Lincoln was a promising partner. Practically every one in Sangamon County was his friend and his reputation for honesty was such as to attract business.

The most significant thing in this big year, however, is by all odds the position Lincoln then took on the slavery question. To understand what he did we must recall the agitation at this particular moment, North and South. Anti-slavery sentiment was becoming more and more formidable through increased organization, and the multiplication of organs. The South was mightily stirred, and with reason. In the South, as well as in the North, anti-slavery sentiment was making its way; that is, more and more people were doing as Edward Cole, Governor of Illinois from 1823 to 1826, had done in 1819, leaving slave territory and freeing their slaves. The seepage from runaway slaves was increasing, and there was a disposition stirring in the North to protect the runaways. The South was determined that the agitation should

[231]

be stopped, and in this determination it had the backing of the conservative North. State after state passed resolutions at this time similar to those that the Illinois assembly passed in this year of 1837.

"Resolved, That we highly disapprove of the formation of abolition societies, and of the doctrine promulgated by them.

"That the right of property in slaves is sacred to the slave-holding States by the Federal Constitution, and that they cannot be deprived of that right without their consent.

"That the General Government cannot abolish slavery in the District of Columbia against the consent of the citizens of said District, without a manifest breach of good faith.

"That the Governor be requested to transmit to the States of Virginia, Alabama, Mississippi, New York and Connecticut a copy of the foregoing report and resolutions."

Lincoln refused to vote for these resolutions. He agreed that Congress had no power to interfere with the institution of slavery in the different states. He differed with the assembly, however, as to the power to abolish slavery in the District of Columbia, thought that it did have that, thought it should only be exercised if the people of the District requested it. His real objection to the resolutions was founded on his belief that no public expression on slavery should go out without a declaration that the thing was wrong. The protest on this point which he wrote then, and which he could find only one other member of the assembly to join him in signing, read:

"They believe that the institution of slavery is founded on both injustice and bad policy, but that the promulgation of abolition doctrines tends rather to increase than abate its evils."

Nine months after Lincoln turned in this protest there happened seventy-five miles or so from Springfield, in the town of Alton on the Mississippi River, a town which Lincoln undoubtedly knew well enough, a tragedy which tremendously stirred him. Alton was a lively town and in the main sympathized frankly with slavery—sympathized so much that when early in this year the Rev. Elijah P. Lovejoy, an active abolitionist editor, who had recently been driven out of St. Louis, set up his press there the citizens promptly threw it into the river. One after another three presses which Lovejoy brought on were destroyed, and then finally, in November, a mob, learning that he was starting a fourth press, raided the building, and before the riot was ended had killed Lovejoy.

In the letter to the Rev. James Lemen, to which I referred above, he says: "Lovejoy's tragic death for freedom in every sense marked his sad ending as the most important single event that ever happened in the new world."

This extraordinary statement, made by a man so careful in his use of words as Lincoln almost invariably was, if genuine, shows the depth of the effect the tragedy had had upon him. He goes on in this letter to draw a comparison between Lemen's and Lovejoy's work exceedingly interesting in itself and also because of the parallel he draws from the Scriptures:

"Both your father and Lovejoy were pioneer leaders in the cause for freedom, and it has always been difficult for me to see why your father, who was a resolute, uncompromising, and aggressive leader, who boldly proclaimed his purpose to make both the territory and the state free, never aroused nor encountered any of that mob violence which both in St. Louis and Alton confronted or pursued Lovejoy, and which finally doomed him to a felon's death and a martyr's crown. Perhaps the two cases are a little parallel with those of John and Peter. John was bold and fearless at the scene of the Crucifixion, standing near the cross receiving the Savior's request to care for his mother, but was not annoyed; while Peter, whose disposition to shrink from public view, seemed to catch the attention of members of the mob on every hand, until finally, to throw public attention off, he denied his master with an oath; though later the grand old apostle redeemed himself grandly, and, like Lovejoy, died a martyr to his faith. Of course, there was no similarity between Peter's treachery at the Temple and Lovejoy's splendid courage when the pitiless mob were closing around him. But in the cases of the two apostles at the scene mentioned, John was more prominent or loyal in his presence and attention to the Great Master than Peter was, but the latter seemed to catch the attention of the mob; and whereas Lovejoy, one of the most inoffensive of men, for merely printing a small paper, devoted to the freedom of the body and mind of man, was pursued to his death; his older comrade in the cause of freedom, Rev. James Lemen, Sr., who boldly and aggressively proclaimed his purpose to make both the territory and the state free, was never molested a moment by the minions of violence. The madness and pitiless determination with which the mob steadily pursued Lovejoy to his doom, marks it as one of the most unreasoning and unreasonable in all time, except that which doomed the Savior to the cross."

Some three months after Lovejoy's death Lincoln delivered his first formal lecture, so far as I know. This was for the Young Men's Lyceum of Springfield, a club which he had helped organize soon after he moved into the town. The lecture was published at the request of the club by the Sangamon Journal. It has the pretentious title of "The Perpetuation of Our Political Institutions." It is really an argument against violence as a political method. The Mississippi country had been rioting for a year or two. At Vicksburg only a short time before a group of professional gamblers had been hanged by a mob. This had been the first of a series of terrible deeds. As Lincoln reviews them, "negroes suspected of conspiring to raise an insurrection were caught up and hanged in all parts of the state; then white men supposed to be leagued with the negroes; and finally, strangers from neighboring states, going thither on business, were in many instances subjected to the same fate. Thus went on this process of hanging, from gamblers to negroes, from negroes to white citizens, and from these to strangers, till dead men were seen literally dangling from the boughs of trees upon every roadside. . . ."

Soon after this a negro had been burned in St. Louis. "This story is very short," Lincoln said, "and is perhaps the most highly tragic of anything of its length that has ever been witnessed in real life."

Then had come the affair at Alton. Lincoln's rehearsal of these crimes, of the danger they were to freedom, sounds very modern. Indeed, his argument might stand to-day if its illustrations were brought up to date. He declares that if this "mobocratic spirit" went on unchecked, it must inevitably end, in a government constituted like ours, in breaking down what, he declared, was its strongest bulwark, and that was the attachment of the people.

"I know the American people are much attached to their government," he said. "I know they would suffer much for its sake; I know they would endure evils long and patiently before they would ever think of exchanging it for another—yet, notwithstanding all this, if the laws be continually despised and disregarded, if their rights to be secure in their persons and property are held by no better tenure than the caprice of a mob, the alienation of their affections from the government is the natural consequence; and to that, sooner or later, it must come."

Here we have him, then at the beginning of his career, the first year in which he really had his feet on the ground as a politician and a lawyer, putting himself down boldly on the most difficult question the country has ever had to face. He went out of his way, both in the legislature and in a public lecture, to make clear his position, at a time when a protest, even of that character, might be almost fatal to his ambitions. It was to be ten years before events were to force him again to state his convictions; in the meantime life was to bring him many new experiences, the most important of these unquestionably being his marriage.

[235]

# XIX

## MARRIAGE OF LINCOLN

THE biographer who undertakes to correct what he believes to be a mistaken tradition in his subject's life must make up his mind that whatever his proofs, he will never be more than half successful. Twenty-five years ago I gathered and published what seemed to me to be convincing evidence of the falsehood of the widely accepted story that Mr. Lincoln failed to appear at his own wedding, set for January 1, 1841, in Springfield—a wedding for which elaborate preparations had been made. Whatever satisfaction I might have taken in shattering a story which I believed was the work of a morbid imagination building on flimsy, indirect evidence, was largely wiped out on the Lincoln pilgrimage here reported.

It was in Springfield itself where I had found the most substantial evidence of the untruth of the legend that I met its stoutest defenders. I should say that Springfield to-day is pretty evenly divided between those who believe that Mr. Lincoln ran away from the first wedding planned between him and Mary Todd, who later became his wife, and those who believe that he did not. It is one of several controversial points in his private life which readers will probably continue to settle according to temperament and mental habits. It is a fact that to-day there exists what you may call two "Lincoln wedding schools," just as there exists two schools of Hanks ancestry, two on the legitimacy of his birth, two on his condition of mind after Ann Rutledge's death. Frequently the followers of each spend more time in defending what they would like to think than in disinterested examination of evidence.

It was by accident that a doubt was first raised in my mind as to the truthfulness of the story of Mr. Lincoln's absenting himself from his wedding, published by Ward Lamon in 1872, from notes furnished him by William H. Herndon and later elaborated and published by Mr. Herndon in his life of Lincoln. I had been given a letter of introduction to Mrs. B. F. Edwards, the sister-in-law of Ninian Edwards, in whose family Mary Todd lived. Mrs. Edwards at this time was a woman of perhaps seventy, and of unusual distinction of manner and of speech. I had gone to her to ask what she remembered of Mr. Lincoln's place in the social life of Springfield in the late thirties and early forties.

Early in our conversation I mentioned the resentment they must have all felt over Mr. Lincoln's failure to appear at the wedding that had been arranged for January 1, 1841, between him and Miss Todd. I can still feel something of the chill which her look gave me when she said with indignation, "What do you mean?" Of course, I fell back upon Mr. Lamon and Mr. Herndon, quoting them nearly verbatim. Mrs. Edwards denied in every detail the truthfulness of the tale. Later she put her denial into a letter, which lies before me. "All that he says," she writes, "is a fabrication. He has drawn largely upon his imagination in describing something which never took place."

Such a lead as this was, of course, not to be neglected, and I immediately looked up several of the still living friends of Mr. and Mrs. Lincoln in a position to know about the matter. Important among them was one of the most delightful of the Springfield group to which the Lincolns belonged, a cousin of Mrs. Lincoln's, to whom both she and the President were devoted, and who later spent much time with them in Washington at the White House. "Cousin Lizzie Grimsley," as she was familiarly known, at this time, 1895, the wife of Dr. Brown of Springfield.

I put the question in writing to Mrs. Brown: "Did Mr. Lincoln fail to appear 'when the invitations were out, the guests invited and the supper ready for the wedding'?" This is Mr. Herndon's account.

"As to your question, I will say emphatically 'No,'" she replied. "There may have been a little shadow of foundation for Mr. Herndon's lively imagination to play upon, in that the year previous to the marriage, and when Mr. Lincoln and my Cousin Mary expected soon to be married, Mr. Lincoln was taken with one of those fearful, overwhelming periods of depression, which induced his friends to persuade him to leave Springfield. This he did for a time, but I am satisfied he was loyal and true to Mary, even though at times he may have doubted whether he was responding as fully as a manly, generous nature should to such affection as he knew my cousin was ready to bestow on him. And this because it did not have the overmastering depth of an early love. This everybody here knows, therefore I do not feel as if I were betraying dear friends."

Mrs. John Stuart, the wife of Major Stuart, who had taken Mr. Lincoln as his law partner when he moved into Springfield in 1837, was still living in 1895, and at Mrs. Brown's suggestion I saw her. At my request she set down her recollections:

"Mrs. Lincoln told me herself all the circumstances of her engagement to Mr. Lincoln, of his illness, and the breaking off of the engagement, of the renewal, and her marriage.

"So I say I do not believe one word of this dishonorable story about Mr. Lincoln. It is a sad thing for a man's character to be picked to pieces and defamed after his death."

Among others from whom I sought information was Mrs. Lincoln's sister, Mrs. Dr. Wallace, whose indignation at the story, with which she was familiar, almost choked her replies.

One remark she dropped I have always remembered as an illustration of how convincing as evidence a thing entirely trivial in itself may be. "Why," said Mrs. Wallace, "Mary Lincoln never had a silk dress in her life until she went to Washington!" This in answer to Mr. Herndon's description of the "bride bedecked in veil and silken gown, nervously toying with the flowers in her hair!"

One feature of my findings, particularly convincing to me, was that nobody had ever heard of this wedding before Lamon and Herndon published their books. It is impossible for me to believe that in a town of 2,500 people—Springfield's population in 1841—there could have been a wedding arranged between two of the members of its "fashionable set" and rudely broken by the non-appearance of the groom without the story becoming town property and being passed down for years as a part of its local history. But, as I say, nobody seems to have remembered hearing of the wedding.

After I had published the results of my investigation in 1896, I received from Mr. John Davis, of Junction City, Kansas, a letter in which he said:

"I spent the years 1846-7 in Springfield; saw Mr. Lincoln, the Edwards and others almost daily; and had frequent long talks with Mr. Herndon, but never heard a word of the horrible story which he afterwards published in his book. I do not believe it."

Wedding aside, however, the fact remains that Mr. Lincoln did not have the resolution to go through without a break with what undoubtedly had proved a tempestuous engagement. Given Miss Todd's temperament and his experience, it is understandable if regrettable. Four years before his one real romance had been ended by the death of the girl he loved. Heavy as was the blow he had pulled himself together. The next year he was even thinking of marriage with a young woman visiting in New Salem, the sister of one of his friends there. We have the letters he wrote at the time to this young woman, and they are almost comic in their disinterestedness and simple-mindedness. It seems that he had jokingly told a friend that he would marry her sister if she would bring her to New Salem. When the young lady appeared he jumped to the conclusion that there was a promise involved. He seems faithfully to have visited her, to have become her escort at New Salem festivities, and when in the winter of 1836-7 he went back to Vandalia, to have written her occasional amusingly conscientious and impersonal letters—letters headed "Friend Mary" and signed "Your Friend"!

After he moved to Springfield in the spring of 1837, he still had her on his mind. Did she or did she not expect him to marry her? He finally got up courage to bring the matter to issue:

"I want in all cases to do right," he wrote, "and most particularly so in all cases with women. If you feel yourself in any degree bound to me I am now willing to release you, provided you wish it, while on the other hand I am willing and anxious to bind you faster if I can be convinced that it will in any considerable degree add to your happiness. This indeed is the whole question with me. If it suits you best not to answer this, . . . a long life and a merry one attend you."

The young woman rightfully was unsatisfied with this kind of love-making and concluded that the affair had gone far enough.

There is an idea among many Lincoln students, I find, that when Mr. Lincoln came to Springfield he did not have what is called social position. That this is a mistake there is evidence enough. Springfield was a small town, of course, but it had a group of the finest sort of pioneers. There were the Edwardses, the Logans, the Stuarts, the Speeds, and from the start they were Lincoln's friends. A little document, such

as that published in this article, a facsimile of an invitation
to a cotillion party given in 1839, with its list of managers,
shows that he was already counted among social leaders!
And there is no question he was doing his part to keep up
the gaieties.

Only a few years ago (1917) there was published for the
first time in Gilbert Tracy's book of "Uncollected Letters
of Abraham Lincoln," the following amusing letter to his
friend, Mrs. C. H. Browning, written by him though signed
by a group:

(Probable date: Oct. 10 or 11, 1839.)
"To the Honorable Mrs. Browning:

"We, the undersigned, respectfully represent to your *Honoress*,
that we are in great need of your society in the town of Springfield
and therefore humbly pray that your Honoress will repair forthwith
to the seat of Government bringing in your train all ladies in general
who may be at your command and all Mrs. Browning's sisters in
particular (the above was written by A. L.), and as faithful and
dutiful petitioners we promise that if you grant this our request, we
will render unto your Honoress due attention and faithful obedience
to your orders in general and to Miss Brownings in particular.

"In tender consideration whereof we pray your Honoress to grant
your humble petitioners their above request and such other and further
relief in the premises as to your Honoress may seem right and proper;
and your petitioners as in duty bound will ever pray, etc.

(Signed) {
"A. Lincoln
O. B. Webb
J. J. Hardin
John Dawson"

Obviously it was the intention of the signers to bring
together for the first session of the legislature in Springfield
as many ladies as possible, and we can suppose that the
cotillion party was the first inaugural ball of the new social
capital of Illinois!

There was much gaiety in the town from that time on.
Young women came to visit not only from Illinois towns, but

[241]

## COTILLION PARTY.

*The pleasure of your Company is respectfully solicited at a Cotillion Party, to be given at the "American House," on to=morrow evening at 7 i'clock, P. M.*

December 16th, 1839

| | |
|---|---|
| N. H. RIDGELY, | 8. F. SPEED, |
| J. A. M'CLERNAND, | J. SHIELDS, |
| R. ALLEN, | E. D. TAYLOR, |
| H. H. WASH, | E. H. MERRYMAN, |
| F. W. TODD, | N. E. WHITESIDE, |
| B. A. DOUGLASS, | M. EASTHAM, |
| W. S. PRENTICE, | J. R. DILLER, |
| N. W. EDWARDS, | A. LINCOLN, |
| | Managers. |

FACSIMILE OF AN INVITATION TO A SPRINGFIELD COTILLION PARTY
OF WHICH A. LINCOLN WAS ONE OF THE MANAGERS.

[242]

from Kentucky itself, from which so large a contingent had moved into the new state. Mr. Lincoln seems to have done his share in entertaining these young women, and gossip says that he was the suitor of at least two of them before he became interested in Miss Todd. This happened in 1840.

Mary Todd was probably as spirited and accomplished as well as self-confident a young woman as Springfield had ever seen. She had come there in 1839 to live with her sister, Mrs. Elizabeth Todd Edwards, wife of Ninian Edwards, the son of a former governor of the state and himself a man of wealth and importance. Mary Todd naturally had many suitors, one of whom, it is said, was a man whom Mr. Lincoln had already picked as an antagonist, Stephen A. Douglas. Even if it be true that Mr. Douglas was the ardent suitor for Mary Todd's hand that many have believed, he left the field early, for before the end of her first year in Springfield she was engaged to Mr. Lincoln.

Things seem never to have gone very well. She was of ardent temperament, and I have always believed passionately in love with Mr. Lincoln. Mrs. Dr. Brown, the affectionate and intimate friend of them both, says in the letter from which I quoted above that in her judgment Mr. Lincoln always doubted whether he was "responding as fully as a manly, generous nature should to such affection as he knew my cousin was ready to bestow upon him. And this because it did not have the overmastering depth of an early love."

There of course was the real difficulty—Mr. Lincoln's inability to forget, his moody, brooding nature. Then, too, he was nine years older than Mary Todd, and came of humble people, though he himself underestimated the sturdiness of his origin. The Todds were "first families," aristocrats, priding themselves on a long line of dashing ancestors. I rather think Mary Todd was the kind who might at times have recalled Mr. Lincoln's attention to what she considered the superiority of her family over his. It is said that there were members of her family that did this, though I have a copy of a letter from her father, written in 1846, in which he rejoices that all his daughters had married gentlemen. This, of course, included Mr. Lincoln, whom Mr. Todd by this time knew very well.

The difference between him and the woman to whom he had become engaged, his doubt about his ability to make her happy, his consciousness that she did not arouse in him the depth of feeling of which he must have known himself capable, finally drove Mr. Lincoln to the breaking of the engagement. That done, he promptly fell into the very slough of self-abasement and humiliation.

There is much loose writing and talking about his having gone insane at this period, but a man who goes about his work through a period of depression is a man who has control of his mind and his actions. Through all this period of so-called insanity Mr. Lincoln was about his work. His vote is recorded on the roll call of the legislature on one of the very days when he was reported to have been wandering aimlessly about the country. On the very day on which he wrote one letter of great misery to his friend Stuart he made a speech in the legislature. Depression? Yes—ample proof of it. Insanity? No—ample proof against it. He was a humiliated and repentant man. Moreover, he found that though he might not care all he thought he ought to care for Miss Todd, he cared altogether too much for her to want to lose her.

The episode which brought about a reconciliation has been told many times, but there is one phase of it which I think has not had its full value, and this was the check it proved to the mischief that Mr. Lincoln was in danger of doing to himself and his friends by an unbridled use of his gift of satire.

Back in Indiana, where he easily dominated the youth of the community, one of the weapons he had used most effectively on his enemies was merciless lampooning. Long doggerels ridiculing the weak points of people who had displeased him, or, as he thought, done him an injury, have been preserved and portions of them published. After he left Indiana he seems not to have exercised this gift until 1837. In that year he fought a case in the newspapers, evidently enjoying himself hugely by exposing a politician who had tried to trick a widow out of property. A little later, in 1841, he attacked the Democrats then in power on their administration of state finances in a letter signed "Aunt Rebecca," coming from what he called the "Lost Township." This communication was particularly irritating to the auditor of the State, James Shields. In writing this letter, Mr. Lincoln, of course, was only following a practice of the day. James Russell Lowell was to do something of the same kind of thing in his "Bigelow Papers," so was D. R. Locke in the Nasby letters. That is, Mr. Lincoln in his "Aunt Rebecca" letter was a member of a distinguished company.

Trouble came, however, when Miss Todd and some of her friends, who thought they had reason to consider Mr. Shields over-gallant, sent a doggerel to the paper, ridiculing his philandering, signing the communication "Aunt Rebecca." Shields was a hot-tempered Irishman. He demanded from the editor of the paper the name of the author of the verses. The editor consulted Mr. Lincoln, who said, "Give my name and protect the ladies." The result was a challenge from Shields.

The documents in this case were gathered for my Life of Lincoln twenty-five years ago, when many of the actors were still living, by Mr. J. McCan Davis of Springfield, and all that seemed essential published. They show that Lincoln tried to get out of the duel; but when Shields pressed him so that it meant either give names or go ahead, he accepted. Being the one challenged, he had the right, of course, to select weapons, position, time and place.

I do not know anything funnier in Lincoln's life than his choice of weapons in this case, it being remembered that he was six feet four inches high and Shields so short that he could walk under his arm—"cavalry broadswords of the largest size." The place selected—and where the contestants and their seconds actually gathered—was a sandbar in the Mississippi River, opposite the town of Alton.

Visit Alton to-day and you will be sure to find some newspaper man with a bent for local history, or perhaps, better still, some old-timer who will take you out on the bluffs and show you where the duelists foregathered. They will tell you, too, how one of the spectators saw Mr. Lincoln just before the critical hour arrived pick up a broadsword, feel along the edge with his thumb as a barber feels the edge of his razor, and then stretching himself to his full height clip a twig above his head. "There was not another man of us," said this spectator, "who could reach anywhere near that twig, and the absurdity of that long-reaching fellow fighting with cavalry sabers a man who could walk under his arm came pretty near making me howl with laughter."

Luckily for both Shields and Lincoln, some of their level-headed friends back home heard of the affair and hastened to Alton, arriving on the scene just in time to prevent the actual use of the broadswords. Mr. Shields was made to understand that it was not Mr. Lincoln who had written the objectionable verses, the quarrel was patched up, and everybody went home in good humor.

# MARRIAGE OF LINCOLN

Mr. Lincoln's gallantry in being willing to fight a duel rather than to betray Miss Todd's name seems to have broken the ice that separated them. Through the manœuvering of friends they were soon thrown together, their misunderstanding settled, and a few weeks later, on November 2, 1842, they were rather hastily married at the Edwards home.

At last Mr. Lincoln's troubled heart was at rest. He had made his decision, and there was never any doubt that one of the chief businesses of his life henceforth would be to make the woman he had taken for his wife happy.

He had to suffer, however, for the manœuver which had brought them together. Dueling had ceased to be tolerated by the public. Alton and its citizens particularly resented the selection of a point near them as a dueling place. They could not and would not, they said, have there another "Bloody Island," as a spot in the Mississippi near St. Louis was called. The Alton Telegraph and Democratic Review published a scathing editorial:

"Our city was the theatre of an unusual scene of excitement during the last week, arising from a visit of two distinguished gentlemen of the city of Springfield, who, it was understood, had come here with a view of crossing the river to answer the 'requisitions of the code of honor' by brutally attempting to assassinate each other in cold blood. . . .

"We consider that these gentlemen have both violated the laws of the country, and insist that neither their influence, their respectability nor their private worth should save them from being made amenable to those laws they have violated. Both of them are lawyers —both have been to the legislature of this State, and aided in the construction of laws for the protection of society—both exercise no small influence in the community—all of which, in our estimation, aggravates instead of mitigates their offense. Why, therefore, they should be permitted to escape punishment, while a friendless, penniless and obscure person, for a much less offense, is hurried to the cells of our county jail, forced through a trial, with scarcely the forms of law, and finally immured within the dreary walls of a penitentiary, we are at a loss to conjecture. . . .

"The friends of Mr. Shields and Mr. Lincoln claim the affair to have been settled upon terms alike honorable to both, notwithstanding the hundred rumors—many of which border upon the ridiculous—that are in circulation. We are rejoiced that both were permitted to return to the bosom of their friends, and trust that they will now consider, if they did not do it before, that rushing unprepared upon the untried scenes of Eternity is a step too fearful in its consequences to be undertaken without preparation.

"We are astonished to hear that large numbers of our citizens crossed the river to witness a scene of cold-blooded assassination between two of their fellow-beings. It was no less disgraceful than the conduct of those who were to have been actors in the drama. Hereafter we hope the citizens of Springfield will select some other point to make public their intention of crossing the Mississippi to take each other's life than Alton. . . ."

Again and again in the next few years this duel obtruded itself into political campaigns where Mr. Lincoln was a candidate. Mrs. Lincoln may have been proud of it, but sober people saw nothing in it but a disgraceful performance—they would not vote for a man who had fought a duel!

He grew to be much ashamed of the whole affair—unwilling to talk about it. Frank Carpenter says that once when he was at work in the White House on a portrait of Mr. Lincoln, the affair was mentioned, and the President, with a real show of irritation, said: "I don't deny it, but if you desire my friendship, you will never mention the circumstance again"—a remark which hardly can be said to sound like Mr. Lincoln.

The important point, aside from the effect that it had upon his love affair, is that Mr. Lincoln learned at this time the danger of lampooning—never again, so far as I know, did he rush into print to lambast a political or legal enemy. He must many times have itched to do it, but his control of his capacity for satire, after the frequent use he had made

[248]

of it, is remarkable; and I have always believed that it came from the lesson he learned from the so-called Lincoln-Shields duel.

He was married, thirty-four years of age, a practicing lawyer, a member of the state legislature—well started, we

THE PEOPLE OF THE STATE OF ILLINOIS.

To any Minister of the Gospel, or other authorised Person—GREETING.,

THESE are to Licence and permit you to join in the holy bands of Matrimony *Abraham Lincoln* and *Mary Todd* of the County of Sangamon and State of Illinois, and for so doing, this shall be your sufficient warrant.

*Given under my hand and seal of office, at Springfield, in said County this 4th day of November 1842*

*N. W. Matheny* Clerk.

*Solemnized on the same 4th day of Nov. 1842*          *Charles Dresser*

FACSIMILE OF MARRIAGE LICENSE OF ABRAHAM LINCOLN AND MARY TODD.

should say, but a poor man still. And the question now seemed to be, Was he going to be able to support a wife— a wife who had come to him out of a distinguished family, and who had always been accustomed to a good degree of what the time called comfort?

# XX

## LINCOLN SETTLES DOWN

THE whole-hearted way in which Springfield, Illinois, has in recent years accepted the leadership of the Lincoln cult of the world is a genuine satisfaction to those of us who believe that there is where it belongs, and also who have felt in the past that the town was lukewarm towards its responsibility. The Springfield of 1923 is taking Lincoln to its heart and confidence in much the same way that the Springfield of 1837 did. He might be poor, uneducated, not familiar with, nor impressed by their social veneer; but, almost to a man, early Springfield believed in and honored Abraham Lincoln. He realized it. In 1861 when he left for his inauguration, he paid her an unforgettable tribute: "To this place and to the kindness of its people I owe everything."

It is not strange that the bitter dissensions of the War as well as the almost equally bitter periods before and after should have made Springfield as a whole reluctant to admit that Lincoln was its first citizen, much less the first American. They still were divided by political resentment—the slowest thing in the world to heal.

I recall that twenty-five years ago I met many men not only in Springfield but many other cities and towns of Illinois who seemed glad to belittle Mr. Lincoln. He was "ordinary" —"intellectually dull"—"without literary taste"—"always stole his stories." I find these trivial comments in my old note books. One gentleman of particular eminence bitterly resented Lincoln's remark after his re-nomination in 1864 that

[250]

the convention had probably concluded that it was best "not to swap horses while crossing the river." It wasn't "original" with Lincoln—he had heard it all his life!

Then Springfield was still too close to him. How are you going to accept offhand as the country's first citizen a man whom all your life you have seen carrying home beefsteaks for his supper!

There was a long period in which Springfield treated all Lincolniana with more or less indifference. The Lincoln monument in the town's beautiful cemetery and the Lincoln homestead, given in 1886 to the state by Robert Lincoln, with rather meager collections were all that was offered visitors. That period is closed. To-day not only are the collections at the monument and the homestead largely increased and admirably cared for, but the Illinois Historical Society has gathered at the capital what is probably for students the best Lincoln collection in the world. Recently the town has put up tablets marking sites formerly difficult to locate—Joshua Speed's store where Lincoln went to live in 1837; his different law offices and various other points of interest. To be sure, the taxi drivers and even some of Springfield's first citizens do not always know how to take you to them; but this will pass. The unbroken train of pilgrims coming to the town to honor Lincoln's memory will finally educate them.

It is because of these tablets that it is easy now to find the site of the Globe Tavern where Mr. and Mrs. Lincoln went to live after their marriage in November, 1842:

"On this site stood the Globe Tavern, the home of Abraham Lincoln and his wife from the time of their marriage on Nov. 4, 1842, until May 2, 1844. Here their first child was born."

It was an unpretentious enough place, but quite as good as the tavern in most of the Illinois towns at this date. And

[251]

it was cheap. Four dollars a week for room and board, so Mr. Lincoln wrote his friend Speed a few months after the marriage.

Was he happy here after his tempestuous courtship? One has a right to ask, since all the outpourings of his heart have been published and republished, and subjected to interpretations of varying degrees of understanding. And when I ask that I mean, Have we any written word to tell us? Not one—the only comment of his on his marriage I have ever seen was published only a few years ago—a brief word at the end of a business letter written a few days after the wedding:

"Nothing new here" (Springfield) "except my marrying which to me is a matter of profound wonder."

Not surprising that he should wonder. He had been through two years of self-torment; he had agonized over Mary Todd's supposed suffering; he had been through all the throes of a man stirred by passion and yet uncertain whether in the relation there could be permanent companionship and sympathy. And now his period of suffering had been ended by a farcical duel destined to torment him—and justly enough—as long as he lived! Not surprising that he was amazed finally to find himself with a wife.

Lincoln seems to have settled down at once in the Globe Tavern as a family man. A "coming event" soon contributed to his stability. In May he wrote to the Speeds, who had suggested a visit to Louisville, that they could not go, not only because of "poverty and the necessity of attending to business," but a "coming event." The "coming event" was Mr. Robert Lincoln, who was born at the Globe Tavern on August 1, 1843.

We have so many revelations of Mr. Lincoln's morbid-ness at this period that it is a great pity that there are no letters telling about Robert Lincoln's birth. A man never lived to whom the coming of a child would have brought more gladness than Abraham Lincoln; but we have nothing to tell us about it. Indeed, so far as I know, there is not a line in reference to his children published between this letter and one written also to Speed in October of 1846. It announced another boy—born on the 10th of March.

"Very much such a child as Bob was at his age," he writes, "rather of a longer order. Bob is short and low and I expect always will be. He talks very plainly" (he was now only a little over two years old)— "almost as plainly as anybody. He is quite smart enough. I sometimes fear he is one of the little rare-ripe sort that are smarter at about five than ever after. He has a great deal of that sort of mischief that is the offspring of such animal spirits. Since I began this letter a messenger came to tell me that Bob is lost, but by the time I reached the house his mother had found him and had whipped him, and by now, very likely, he has run away again."

That the Lincolns found life difficult at the Globe Tavern with a baby to care for was of course true, and by the end of the year Mr. Lincoln was looking for a home. In January he bought the house which, afterwards enlarged, he lived in until he left Springfield for the Presidency. He must have been getting on better in his profession than has been generally believed, to have been able to do this. Fees may have been small—they were—five dollars, ten, rarely fifty—often traded out; but he had been able to save enough to justify him in contracting on January 16, 1844, with the Rev. Charles Dresser—who had married him and Mary Todd—for a house and lot. He was to pay $1,200 for the place, plus a piece of property in what is now the heart of the town. He had part of the money, we know, from a curious document which went with the contract with Dresser—a contract by which Mr. Lincoln, in February, turned over to a probable creditor of

Dresser's, $750, with the stipulation that if he did not get
the house, the money was to be returned to him, with twelve
per cent interest! Twelve years before, when he first was a
candidate for the assembly of Illinois, he had proposed a law
regulating "exorbitant rates of interest"—but possibly in
1844 twelve per cent was not considered exorbitant!

The important point about the purchase is that Lincoln
was getting hold financially—his feet on the ground. It was
not easy, for he had not only his personal struggle, but he had
had a constant pull—and was to have through life—from
his family. His father and stepmother had been now for
about ten years in Coles County, to which they had moved
after the disastrous "winter of the deep snow" near Decatur,
but they had never been able to pay for their land. If Mr.
Lincoln had not come to their rescue the year before his
marriage they probably would have been homeless. He
helped them out of their difficulties by buying their land,
paying them $200, and giving them the right to its use as
long as either of them lived. That he was helping other
relatives is pretty certain. The Hankses and Johnstons and
Halls in Coles County, cut off as they were from transportation, were having a difficult time; it was natural enough that
they should think of Mr. Lincoln, who had risen to membership in the assembly and was now practicing law in the
capital of the state, as a rich man, their natural source of
support, and have made frequent demands on him. That is,
Mr. Lincoln when he married had within the state a group
of relatives, among them his own father and the stepmother
whom he so honored, that he could not entirely neglect, however much Mary Lincoln may at times have resented it.

It was natural that she should. Their income was small;
but that Mrs. Lincoln made it go a long way is certain. She
was a careful housekeeper. Those of her associates living in

Springfield in the late nineties with whom I talked, all spoke of her economies. "How is Cousin Mary getting on in the White House?" one of them told me of asking Mrs. Grimsley when she came back in 1862 from a long visit in Washington.

"Oh, Cousin Mary," Mrs. Grimsley said, throwing up her hands, "is locking up the sugar bowl in Washington as she used to in Springfield." But it was this locking up of the sugar bowl that, after all, helped lay the foundation of the $100,000 or thereabouts that Mr. Lincoln was to leave his family some twenty years later.

Mr. Lincoln did his part in the running of the house. He sawed the wood, chopped the kindling, kept his fires going, brought in the water, cleaned the walks. He naturally and unquestionably performed a multitude of little tasks to which his mother had trained him back in Kentucky and Indiana. He liked to do these familiar things—particularly to chop wood. He not only did it at home but at his office. Mr. Charles Moores of Indianapolis, whose interesting study of Lincoln as a lawyer I have already referred to, found in his researches the following entries in a record of expenses of the Stuart & Lincoln office:

> "Lincoln paid for wood............$ .50
> "       "        saw............ 2.25

A chance for an exercise he loved when the day was long and cold.

Springfield was a simple town, nevertheless an active social life went on, particularly in the winter when the assembly was in session; and the Lincolns were a part of everything. They went out to supper and invited people in, Mary Lincoln keeping up her end from the start—that is the general testimony, and although she might not have been cordial always to the variegated humanity that Mr. Lincoln

[255]

in his love of all the world would be inclined to pick up and bring home to supper, she probably put no greater restrictions upon him than most women would have been obliged to do in self-defense. The people she did like and received have left hearty appreciation of her hospitality. What better than this from Isaac Arnold's "Reminiscences of the Illinois Bar":

"I must not omit to mention the old-fashioned, generous hospitality of Springfield—hospitality proverbial to this day throughout the State. Among others, I recall the dinners and evening parties given by Mrs. Lincoln. In her modest and simple home, there was always, on the part of both host and hostess, a cordial and hearty western welcome, which put every guest perfectly at ease. Mrs. Lincoln's table was famed for the excellence of many rare Kentucky dishes, and in season, it was loaded with venison, wild turkeys, prairie chickens, quail, and other game which was then abundant. Yet it was her genial manners and ever kind welcome, and Mr. Lincoln's wit and humor, anecdote and unrivaled conversation, which formed the chief attraction."

He was working—working hard. Mr. Moores' studies show this, so does Jesse Weik's recent book, "The Real Lincoln," in which he has collected much fresh and interesting material on Lincoln's legal work. They show how his practice steadily increased in volume and range in these years. When he first was admitted, the circuit included but seven counties, but by 1845 these had been increased to fifteen, so that he had the chance, if the ability and will, to cover a large territory. Mr. Moores was impressed in his researches, as any student who goes over this ground even superficially must be, by the quantity of pleadings in Lincoln's hand which are still to be seen—which the thieves have left! It is true, as he says of them, that they are "as clear as if written yesterday. They cover so many sheets in the old Sangamon files, and in some other counties where the thief has not yet been that one wonders how Lincoln had time for anything else.

[256]

All are written with laborious care. The apt word is used; there are singularly few corrections, and the sand then used as a blotter still clings to the sheets. The spelling is reasonably correct—vastly more so, at any rate, than that of George Washington, in his autograph manuscripts."

There are few particularly interesting cases in his early practice. Possibly the most characteristic is that which Lincoln won by producing a murdered man alive and well. It came off in June of 1841. (The time when Mr. Lincoln is commonly reported to have been suffering from mental aberration in Kentucky under the care of his friends, the Speeds!) In a long letter to Speed, Lincoln tells the tale in graphic fashion: "We have had here for a week the highest state of excitement that our community has ever witnessed," he says. He can give only an outline because it would "require a quire of paper to give a full account." I suppose the reason Lincoln wrote so fully to Speed was because all of the persons in the case were known to him. These were three brothers, the Trailor boys, two of whom had accused the third of making away with a well-known Sangamon County loafer (I should judge he was a loafer from the side text) named Fisher. The two brothers were arrested and the country went crazy in an attempt to find the body, which they were supposed to have secreted. In the hunt a mill dam was destroyed, and then, says Mr. Lincoln, "the people swept like a herd of buffalo up and down the creek, fishing and raking and ducking and diving for two days, and after all, no dead body found." Lincoln went over the evidence brought in with gusto, and then came his defense—a witness proving to the satisfaction of the jury that Fisher, the man supposed to have been murdered, was ill at the moment at his (the witness's) house.

The effect of this testimony on the public which had been so sure that there had been a murder, amused Lincoln particularly. "Some looked quizzical, some melancholy, and some furiously angry. One man who had been very active in the search for the dead body swore that he always knew the man was not dead. Another who had cut down the mill dam and wanted to hang the owner for objecting, went away awfully woe-begone." He relished mightily the human comedy of the affair and probably took no little satisfaction in his own part in the proceedings. As a matter of fact, the case was one of the first to win him local fame, tickling the town's sense of humor and arousing admiration for his refusing to follow the mob and taking the obvious line of making sure at the start that the man was dead.

The most significant feature of this period of settling down was the repeated intrusion into his life of the slavery question, forcing him to take notice, to pronounce himself. It wormed its way into his law practice as it already had into his legislative practice, forcing study—decision. There were still legal remnants of slavery in Illinois—protected vestiges of the period before the state was made free, and there was a persistent effort on the part of believers in slavery to take advantage of these legal exceptions to freedom. In 1839 Lincoln had his first experience with such an attempt. A negro girl named Nance had been sold on condition that the man claiming to "own" her could produce evidence that she was his property. In spite of his failure to do this his heirs later sued the purchaser for her price. Lincoln proved that under the law Nance was actually free, and the court sustained his claim that since this was so she could not be sold or purchased. The case was frequently cited in future similar suits, both within and without the state, much to Mr. Lincoln's satisfaction.

A few years after this, however, we find him as counsel for a Kentucky slave owner, one Maston, who had brought into Coles County, Illinois, where he owned a farm, a negro woman Jane and her children. This woman's husband was a free man and already in the state. He and Jane believed that by her coming, she and her children were made free, and when her owner attempted, after two years, to take her back to Kentucky there was wild grief and appeals for protection to their church and their acquaintances. The church promptly refused to interfere, but a couple of prominent citizens took up Jane's case, and one of them, a tavern keeper, sheltered her and her family when they ran away. Coles County was mightily stirred by the situation. Probably half of it took the part of Jane's master and argued that he should be allowed to do what he would with her but the other half swore that she should never be taken from Illinois. Not only threats of violence, but preparations for it were made by both sides. There was much pulling and hauling in the courts, and Jane was kept for a long period in jail for safety. Finally the case came before the circuit court at Charleston, and this time U. F. Linder, Maston's lawyer and a friend of Lincoln's, invited him in.

We have practically no documents to show what was done, no records of speeches, but there were many which tradition declares to have been of unusual brilliance as well as violence. The history of the case was written some twenty-five years ago for the Coles County Bar Association by one of its members, D. T. McIntyre. From "all sources existing at the time."

Mr. McIntyre is severe with Mr. Lincoln for his part in the case. His argument was poor, he claims, and he gave the case away by admitting that if Maston (Jane's master) brought his slaves to this state to work on his farm, they were entitled to their freedom. The court thought so, too, and Jane was released. Her owner, sensing the severity of public opinion, promptly left Illinois and never returned.

Mr. Weik in his recent book, "The Real Lincoln," seems to think it strange that Mr. Lincoln did not at this, or at later periods, interest himself in defending runaway slaves. He could scarcely have gone out of his way to do that, consistently with his expressed views about the Fugitive Slave Law. He always condemned its violation. Laws, good or bad, were to be respected; but in urging that they be respected he made this qualification:

"When I so pressingly urge a strict observance of all the laws, let me not be understood as saying there are no bad laws, or that grievances may not arise for the redress of which no legal provisions have been made. I mean to say no such thing. But I do mean to say that although bad laws, if they exist, should be repealed as soon as possible, still, while they continue in force for the sake of example, they should be religiously observed. So also in unprovided cases. If such arise, let proper legal provisions be made for them with the least possible delay, but till then let them, if not too intolerable, be borne with."

It is practically certain that in at least one case of a runaway slave he acted for the defendant. This was a case which came into the Menard County circuit court in 1845. My attention was first called to this a few months ago by Mr. Henry E. Pond, the State's Attorney of Menard County.

Mr. Pond's grandfather, Samuel Sweezy Pond, was a Yankee, residing only ten miles northwest of New Salem. He was so staunch an anti-slavery man that he was called "Abolition" Pond, and proved his right to the title by operating a section of the Illinois Underground Railroad. Mr. Pond's practice was to pick up the runaways at Farmingdale in Sangamon County, cover them with tarpaulins and haul them to his home, from whence they were carried on to the next station which was to the north in Mason County.

# LINCOLN SETTLES DOWN

Mr. Henry Pond tells me that the community was so proslavery in those days that the life of his grandfather was frequently threatened. In 1845 they thought they had caught one of the family at last, his brother Marvin. Some of Mr. Lincoln's old friends, among them his schoolmaster, Mentor Graham, and Coleman Smoot, who had loaned him the money to outfit himself when he first went to the legislature, appeared as witnesses against Marvin Pond, charging that he had unlawfully harbored a negro slave. The grand jury found him guilty, but when the case came to trial he was acquitted. The truth, Mr. Pond says, is that the wrong brother was named in the indictment, Marvin B. being innocent, but Samuel Sweezy guilty.

Now, it seems that Lincoln and one Major Harris were the only lawyers defending criminal cases at that period in the Menard County court. Mr. Pond thinks that Lincoln must have defended in this case since Harris was a Democratic Congressman of strong pro-slavery views. His reason for not having positive proof of this is that "souvenir hunters have purloined from our court records every paper in the handwriting of Lincoln. The only pleading written by the counsel in the case against Pond is the motion to quash the indictment, and that is the only paper missing from the files." Mr. Pond is probably right in thinking that it is gone because Lincoln wrote it.

Another reason that Mr. Weik gives in his recent book for thinking Lincoln lukewarm on the slavery question at this period is that he finds no evidence that he supported the efforts in Springfield to found a colonization society for negroes. He fails to note, however, that Mr. Lincoln in his eulogy of Clay in 1852 gives emphatic approval to the society:

[261]

"This suggestion of the possible redemption of the African race and African continent was made twenty-five years ago. Every succeeding year has added strength to the hope of its realization. May it indeed be realized. Pharaoh's country was cursed with plagues, and his hosts were lost in the Red Sea, for striving to retain a captive people who had already served them more than four hundred years. May like disasters never befall us! If, as the friends of colonization hope, the present and coming generations of our countrymen shall by any means succeed in freeing our land from the dangerous presence of slavery, and at the same time in restoring a captive people to their long-lost fatherland with bright prospects for the future, and this too so gradually that neither races nor individuals shall have suffered by the change, it will indeed be a glorious consummation."

This doesn't sound lukewarm; and, as we shall see later, he followed up his opinion with repeated attempts to realize it when he was in a position of power.

No, convinced as Lincoln was at this time that all laws concerning slavery must be observed—in the very interest of its final extinction—he was not pussy-footing, publicly or privately. In his temperance address in 1842 from which I have already quoted he declared that the fall of slavery and the overthrow of intemperance would be the most powerful allies of the cause of political freedom. "And when the victory shall be complete," he exclaimed,—"when there shall be neither a slave nor a drunkard on the earth,—how proud the title of that land which may truly claim to be the birthplace and the cradle of both these revolutions that shall have ended in that victory."

That very day, Washington's Birthday, he repeated the idea in a letter written to his young friend, George E. Pickett —the Pickett of the famous charge at Gettysburg. I heard the story a number of years ago from Mrs. General Pickett, who for years lived in Washington, an employee of the Government. Her husband, who lived in Illinois in his youth, was appointed to a cadetship in West Point by Lincoln's partner, Major Stuart, who was at that time in Congress. Mr. Stuart made this appointment at Lincoln's request, and now the boy was off and Lincoln seems to have felt that it was his business to give him some parting advice.

"I have just told the folks here in Springfield on this 111th anniversary of the birth of him whose name, mightiest in the cause of civil liberty, still mightiest in the cause of moral reformation, we mention in solemn awe, in naked, deathless splendor, that the one victory we can ever call complete will be that one which proclaims that there is not one slave or one drunkard on the face of God's green earth. Recruit for this victory.

\* \* \* \* \* \* \*

"Now, boy, on your march, don't you go and forget the old maxim that 'one drop of honey catches more flies than a half-gallon of gall.' Load your musket with this maxim, and smoke it in your pipe."

Busy as Mr. Lincoln was with the law at this time, he was not forgetting his political fences. Indeed I get the impression from a reading of letters and speeches, augmented as they have been in recent years by pieces not found in his so-called complete works, that public life was what his heart was really set on, not the law. After serving four terms in the state assembly, in 1842 he refused reëlection. He wanted to go to Washington. Through the period of his stormy courtship, his marriage, his hustling to increase his practice that he might have money to support a family, that had been his serious ambition. These letters show how at this time he was building up a political technique, a code of political ethics, very essential to understand if we are to understand him and what he did later. Politics with Abraham Lincoln was no purely selfish matter. He had reasons for going into public life which were wrapped up with his political philosophy and his ambition to serve the world. He had his own notions of how to accomplish these ambitions, consistently with his moral code.

[263]

# XXI

## LINCOLN THE POLITICIAN

O NE of Abraham Lincoln's most engaging qualities as a
politician was his frankness. It first showed itself in
his openly expressed desire for public office. Every American
boy had the right to try for the presidency, why not he? His
devoted Indiana friend, Josiah Crawford, used to tell of
asking him one day as he watched him stretched along the
floor with a book, his lower lip "stuck out" as always in times
of concentration:

"Abe—what you goin' to be?"

"I'm going to be President, Uncle Jo," was his prompt
reply.

Wise and garrulous old-timers in more than one neighborhood of Illinois as well as Indiana, watching the boy, sensed
ambition in him and prophesied its fulfillment. It came early
to consciousness and though he might doubt his opportunity
and ability to realize it, he never denied nor concealed it.

Not a few students of his life, particularly in these latter
years, lean to the theory that his political ambitions needed
a prod, and that Mary Lincoln was the one that the Lord
provided. The records of his early life certainly shatter this
theory. He had been active in Illinois politics for seven
years, an officeholder for five years, and was planning for
Congress before he met Mary Lincoln.

Three months after his marriage he emphasized his plan
by writing to one of his political friends: "If you should
hear any one say that Lincoln don't want to go to Congress,

[264]

I wish you, as a personal friend of mine, would tell him you have reason to believe he is mistaken. The truth is I would like to go very much. . . . If there are any who would be my friends in such an enterprise what I want now is that they shall not throw me away just yet." (The letter in which this appears belongs to the fine collection of new letters first published six years ago by Gilbert Tracy.)

No doubt but that Mary Lincoln was interested in his going to Congress; he surely found satisfaction in their common ambition, but he needed none of her pushing at this time.

He was frank about it, and he also was practical—practical in a way that cost him something of a wrench at the start. He had held as sacred Americanism the then prevailing practice of self-nomination for office. You offered yourself to the voters in an address, and on this platform made your own campaign—everybody had a chance and the people decided. Then in 1835 the Democrats—wickedly, in the judgment of the Whigs—brought from the East a new political instrument—the convention. The Whigs fought it bitterly at the start; but it was not many years before they found that they were completely at their enemy's mercy— they must either organize or go out of business.

At the time of his marriage, Mr. Lincoln was mulling over the argument for the convention system, and four months later he presented it at a Whig meeting held in Springfield —an excellent piece of candid political logic. The time was past for discussing whether the system was right in itself or not. The simple fact was that "while our opponents use it, it is madness in us not to defend ourselves with it." It is interesting to find him using in this argument a maxim of practical philosophy which he was to employ in an unforgettable way a few years later. "That union is strength," he said, "is a truth that has been known in all ages of the world.

That great fabulist and philosopher Æsop illustrated it by his fable of the bundle of sticks; and He whose wisdom surpasses that of all philosophers has declared that 'a house divided against itself cannot stand!' "

The convention system was adopted by the Illinois Whigs on this argument of Lincoln's, and the machinery put in order. There were protests—plenty of them. He was obliged on the platform, by letter, in conversation, to fight for his decision. And he did it with spirit and candor—it was expediency, you might like it or not, but it was the thing that must be done if you were to meet the enemy.

Lincoln saw clearly enough that there might be difficulty in applying the convention system—"incidents temporarily painful," as he said; but I hardly think he could have foreseen that in the very first convention of his Congressional district he was to suffer from such an incident. He was a candidate as he had made clear he meant to be, but two of his friends were also candidates. One of these was as dear a friend as he ever had—an Englishman by birth—Edward D. Baker, the man for whom he named his second son, a Springfield neighbor, an assembly colleague for some six years now; the other was a friend of both his and Baker, General John J. Hardin, of Jacksonville, his colleague in the assembly since 1836.

Lincoln saw at once that he did not have a chance before the convention. Some of his chickens were coming home to roost. He had mightily offended a powerful element in the community by his duel, and he had chilled the ardor of some of his aggressively democratic friends in the county by his marriage—he had joined the aristocracy! The contest was between Baker and Hardin, and finally Baker, in an eloquent and magnanimous speech, withdrew. On the instant Lincoln executed one of those quick-witted political manœuvers for which he had a genius. Sensing the gratitude that Hardin's supporters felt toward Baker, he proposed, before it had time to cool, that the convention recommend Baker for the next term!

The Hardin men naturally did not like it, but, in Baker's debt as they were, they could not decently refuse and the recommendation was adopted. The inference from it was —certainly in the minds of Lincoln and Baker and their respective supporters—that in 1847, after Baker's term, Lincoln would be nominated. It was a quixotic effort to establish a principle of turn about when friends of equal ability were candidates—an impracticable and, on the whole, unwise idea—unwise because a single term in Congress amounts to little politically for either the man or his constituency. It takes one term to learn the ropes.

There was no trouble in 1845. Baker was nominated and elected, but by 1847 the ardor of the district for the principle of rotation had cooled a little. Baker withdrew in Lincoln's favor, but Hardin did not feel himself bound so to do. He announced his candidacy, and Lincoln had on his hands a problem which, for one of his temperament, was both ticklish and distasteful. He wanted to go to Congress—no doubt about that; he felt that under the plan of turnabout is fair play he should go. But at the same time he wanted to keep Hardin's friendship. How was such a situation to be handled?

He held tenaciously to his ambition and frankly let Hardin understand that he intended, under no circumstances, to withdraw. He also made it clear he would not quarrel. When Hardin proposed several novelties in the political practice of the district which Lincoln saw would put him at a disadvantage, as no doubt was the intention, he good-naturedly refused and frankly pointed out the inferences of the arrangement. He was candid but shrewd in his generosity almost to the point of cunning.

New flashes of light have been thrown in recent years upon this significant exhibit of the political technique Lincoln was building by the discovery of several letters. None of these are more characteristic than one which first appeared in Gilbert Tracy's collection. Among other things it shows his political pride. Lincoln was always jealous of his fitness for office. A supporting newspaper had argued that he should be nominated instead of Hardin because the principle of rotation in Congress for Whigs had been adopted in 1843; he protested warmly. He didn't care whether it had been or not, he wrote his correspondent. "If I am not in what I have done and am able to do for the party near enough the equal to General Hardin to entitle me to a nomination now that he had one, I scorn it on any and all other grounds."

Another characteristic point in this letter is the treatment of certain "mean insinuations" against him in the local press. He sends a friendly editor in the territory material to demolish them. "You may use it as you please," he writes. "I prefer, however, that you should show it to some of our friends, and not publish it, unless in your judgment it becomes rather urgently necessary. The reason I want to keep all points of controversy out of the papers, so far as possible, is that it will be just all we can do to keep out of a quarrel—and I am resolved to do my part to keep peace." That is, he would meet every accusation, but do it in a way which would not create more dissension—not "start anything"!

His tenacity, his at times almost plaintive frankness, his refusal to quarrel with Hardin or to let his friends quarrel with Hardin's friends—and they certainly did give some provocation, although, as Lincoln candidly said: "We have probably been just as much at fault"—his cleverness in strategy seem finally to have persuaded Hardin that there was no hope for him, and he rather begrudgingly withdrew. In May, 1846, Lincoln was nominated.

Mr. Lincoln was always a hearty campaigner—but he worked for himself now no better than he had worked for Hardin and Baker, though quite as well. He thought of everything, knew everything, neglected nothing. Looking over his published letters I find that he had a correspondent in almost every town of any size in his district. If he heard there was somebody disgruntled, he asked a friend to find out what the trouble was—arrange matters. He read the local papers and let no distorted story go unanswered. He was strong for parades and barbecues, speech-making, singing, "hollering." "Gather up the shrewd wild boys about town," organize them, "let every one play the part he can play best," was his counsel to his law partner, Herndon, when he was passing through a period of political depression.

He made so many speeches himself that he was known as the "talking Whig." The legal work which took him from county seat to county seat in his district attending sessions of the circuit court gave ample opportunity. The political leaders took advantage of the presence of the court to arrange for meetings at the noon recess as well as after adjournment at night. Usually these meetings were held in the court yard, a wide platform being put up for the campaign.

Henry B. Rankin in his "Recollections" describes a gathering of this kind at the fall session of the Menard County Circuit Court in which Lincoln was a central figure. Rankin was a boy of only ten then, acting as a court messenger, but the heat of debate, the lusty interest of the crowd, Lincoln's cordiality to his old neighbors, their pride in him, seem always to have remained fresh in his memory. His comment on Lincoln's appearance at this time is worth noting.

He says he was the "best looking lawyer attending the Petersburg Circuit Court"—his color fresh, his muscles well developed, a man overflowing with physical vigor and health. I am convinced that Mr. Rankin is much nearer the truth than are the score or more of Lincoln's contemporaries who vie with one another in drawing caricatures of him.

There is a serious misconception among many of the kind of speech that he was delivering at this time. "A string of stories," more than one biographer has said. He told stories, of course, but incidentally. For the most part the stories came in story-telling bouts, in conversation, in wayside speeches—very few of them in his serious discussions. If any one will take the trouble to examine the printed reports of all Lincoln's speeches, from the first one at Vandalia in 1837 up to his going to Congress ten years later, he will find in their many thousands of words but few stories.

His quick-witted political repartee was often more effective than his stories. One of the most telling retorts that Lincoln ever made belongs to this campaign. His Democratic opponent was Peter Cartwright, that violent, fighting, Western parson, one of the most picturesque characters of the time. He had a tremendous following. No matter where he went he was sure of an audience. Mr. A. L. Beall of Henderson County, Illinois, tells me of an old lady whom he once asked if she had heard Mr. Lincoln when he spoke in that county in the fall of '58. "No," she said, "we never took the trouble to go to hear him, but we always drove across the county to hear Peter Cartwright!" There were plenty of people who felt the same way. In the campaign of '46 Cartwright held a characteristic religious revival service in Springfield. Mr. Lincoln dropped in one night to hear him. When Cartwright was urging sinners to come to the mourners' bench he often appealed by name to persons in his audience, and this night, seeing Mr. Lincoln, he began to urge him forward, finally shouting: "If you are not going to repent and go to Heaven, Mr. Lincoln, where are you going?"

Lincoln slowly rose to his feet.

"I am going to Congress, Brother Cartwright."

Quick as was his wit, pointed as were his stories, it was not on them but on substantial argument that he depended— argument on the wisdom of a protective tariff, the necessity of a national bank, the division of the public moneys among the states, the improvement of rivers and harbors—that is, discussion of the practical, everyday problems of getting money to run the federal and state governments and to build up the country.

It is only now and then that one catches a glimmer in his political work of the question of human rights which was simmering beneath. The Abolitionists were increasing— increasing in Illinois—though it was only now and then as he went about that he ran upon them. It was one of these unexpected encounters that brought out the one statement which we have to show how he felt about the matter in the middle forties.

In sounding two of his old acquaintances, he had discovered to his surprise that they were "Liberty men," as one branch of the Abolitionists called themselves. They could not support the Whig platform: it neglected the slavery question. They were particularly violent about the annexation of Texas. In justice to himself, Lincoln wanted to get down on paper for them just how he felt. It was hard for him— a man of common sense—to understand why Liberty men, who looked on the annexation of Texas as a much greater evil than he ever had, had refused to join the Whigs to prevent it. The Whigs had opposed it. "Why then," he wrote his friends, "did you Liberty men not unite with us?

If you had, Mr. Clay would have been President, Texas would not have been annexed." Their retort was: "You must not do evil that good may come."

"This general proposition," wrote Lincoln, "is doubtless correct; but did it apply? If by your votes you could have prevented the extension, etc., of slavery, would it not have been good and not evil so to have used your votes, even though it involved the cast of them for a slaveholder? By the fruit the tree is to be known. An evil tree cannot bring forth good fruit. If the fruit of electing Mr. Clay would have been to prevent the extension of slavery, could the act of electing have been evil?"

Much more important than the argument of the practical get-what-you-can reformer was a definite statement in the letter as to what he believed to be the only legal and therefore right treatment of slavery:

"I hold it to be a paramount duty of us in the free States, due to the Union of the States, and perhaps to liberty itself (paradox though it may seem), to let the slavery of the other States alone; while, on the other hand, I hold it to be equally clear that we should never knowingly lend ourselves, directly or indirectly, to prevent that slavery from dying a natural death—to find new places for it to live in when it can no longer exist in the old."

A Fabian, you see, a step-by-step-take-what-you-can-get-within-the-law man—there lies liberty. If this is all the expression we have of the period, at least there is no mistaking his meaning or denying that he had thought seriously on the matter.

When the election came Lincoln defeated Cartwright, but somehow the flavor of success had gone. It did not please him as much as he had expected, he wrote Speed. What he had won another wanted—that other his friend. A man's life was built around his friends. Was a term in Congress worth the coolness he felt in Hardin and his supporters? This vague dissatisfaction could not but have been intensified in the February following when news came back to Illinois that Hardin had been killed in the battle of Buena Vista.

He had little time for brooding. As Congressman-elect he was now a personage, receiving calls which would not otherwise have come to him. Most important of these was his appointment as a delegate to the great River and Harbor Convention held in Chicago in July, 1847—the first national convention called to that city.

It is surprising but true that Lincoln biographers should all have overlooked his membership in that extraordinary gathering. For my part, I never heard of the River and Harbor Convention of 1847 until some three years ago Mr. James Shaw of the Aurora (Illinois) Public Library wrote me an accusing letter asking why I had not taken it into account in recording Mr. Lincoln's contacts with the larger world at this time. Mr. Shaw very rightly claimed that the convention must have influenced and enlightened him. As a matter of fact it was at this convention that Lincoln first met any large group of those "big men" about whom he was always so curious and with whom he never lost an opportunity to compare himself, check up on his limitations, appraise his values.

When I confessed ignorance Mr. Shaw generously wrote me an informal account of the convention which I quote below. He has since prepared a more elaborate paper, but the extract from his letter of three years ago serves better our purpose here, which is of course to emphasize the importance of the first national gathering of which Lincoln was a member.

"In August, 1846," writes Mr. Shaw, "President Polk sent to Congress a message vetoing a bill that made appropriations to the extent of $1,378,450 for the improvement of certain rivers and harbors. There were at that time two schools of political thought in the country. One school, called 'Strict Constructionists,' held that Congress had no power to do what the Constitution did not specifically authorize. Internal improvements were not, in so many words, authorized, and

[273]

therefore appropriations for that purpose were unconstitutional. The other school held to a more liberal construction of the powers granted to Congress by the Constitution. That instrument gave to Congress power 'to regulate commerce with foreign nations, and among the several States.' Under this power it was contended that appropriations for internal improvements were constitutional. President Polk was a strict constructionist, and his message was an argument along the lines held by that school of political thought.

"The veto aroused great opposition throughout the country, and particularly in the North and West. The people of the growing lake ports, Buffalo, Cleveland, Toledo, Detroit, Chicago, and the sections tributary to them, were especially angry. A movement was at once set on foot to voice the popular sentiment for internal improvements. A preliminary organization was effected, which called a convention to meet in Chicago, July 5, 6 and 7, 1847. In the way of reflecting popular interest in a subject, no convention ever held in the country was a greater success.

"Chicago at that time was a rather rough frontier town, with a population of about 16,000. Not a single line of railroad had yet reached the city. Entrance into and exit from it had to be made by sail or steam on the lake, or by carriage or horseback on land. That, under such circumstances, the question of internal improvements should have brought to the little city a crowd conservatively estimated at 20,000, nearly one-half of whom were certified delegates, is certainly marvellous. Chicago was quite unable to take care of the crowd. Its hospitality had the cordial character of a new, proud, ambitious and terribly self-conscious community. But it was simply overwhelmed. Thousands of visitors camped in the streets. Hundreds found accommodations in the lake vessels that brought them to the city. The convention held its meetings in a big tent, politely called a 'pavilion.'

"The convention was scarcely less remarkable for the character and position of many of its delegates than for the numbers in attendance. Its permanent president was Edward Bates, an eminent lawyer of St. Louis, a candidate for the Republican nomination for President in the convention of 1860, and Attorney General in the cabinet of President Lincoln. From New York came David Dudley Field, justly considered one of the country's leading lawyers, a member of a family famous for its achievements in many lines of endeavor. One of his brothers was the promoter of the first ocean telegraph cable; a third was the editor of a very successful religious paper.

"Other delegates from New York were Horace Greeley, then just rising into fame as the editor of the most influential journal the country has ever known; and Thurlow Weed, editor of the Albany Journal, one of our early political bosses, one of the best of his kind, and the guide, counsellor and friend of William H. Seward.

"The wonderfully eloquent Tom Corwin, Governor of Ohio, just elected United States Senator, was a delegate, and took an active part in the proceedings. Other delegates from Ohio were Governor Bebb and former Governors Warren and Morrow. Stanley Matthews, later a United States Senator, and Justice of the United States Supreme Court, came also from Ohio.

"There were present a score or more of future Congressmen, young men eager to represent a young and growing country, and perhaps not less than a dozen actual or potential governors of States.

"Illinois was represented by many of its ablest citizens. Several counties sent more than fifty delegates each. Farnsworth, future Congressman from the Kane County district, Washburne, destined to represent the Jo Daviess district, and Long John Wentworth, already in Congress from Chicago. These and many others then unknown to fame were there. From Sangamon County came Abraham Lincoln.

"One Illinoian was conspicuous by his absence—Stephen Arnold Douglas. The 'Little Giant' had a few months before been elected United States Senator from Illinois. He was possibly a strict constructionist. In any event, it is probable that he did not care to begin his Senatorial career by antagonizing the administration.

"Letters were received from some of the most distinguished men in the country. Daniel Webster wrote a 3,000-word letter, in which he argued with great power the constitutional right of Congress to appropriate money for internal improvements. Henry Clay wrote a cordial letter commending the purpose for which the convention was assembled. Letters were also received from ex-President Van Buren, from Senator Lewis Cass and Senator Thomas H. Benton.

"Abraham Lincoln took a modest but most effective part in that convention. It was his first visit to Chicago. The previous fall he had been elected to Congress, the only Whig representative from Illinois. By political affiliation he was an internal improvement man. He was therefore in hearty sympathy with the views which the convention had been called to express. It was the first opportunity that he had ever enjoyed to appear on what might be called a national stage. He there had the chance to measure himself with some of the big men of the country. David Dudley Field was there to hold the convention in check if possible.  He made an able speech, counseling conservative action and moderate statement.  But the convention was in no mood for moderation.  Lincoln was called to answer Field.  This he did, as Mr. Greeley said, 'briefly and happily.' "

In his formal article Mr. Shaw quotes Greeley's report in full:

"Abraham Lincoln, a tall specimen of an Illinoian, just elected to Congress from the only Whig district in the State was called out and spoke briefly and happily in reply to Mr. Field."

That is all, though Mr. Shaw says there is a tradition that Lincoln answered Mr. Field's objection to doing anything for the improvement of the Illinois River because it ran through a single state by asking through how many states the Hudson (a federally improved stream) ran!

More than one "great man" remembered not only his speech but other things about him—his greed for people, his skill in making acquaintances, arresting attention, not merely, as so many have slightingly said, by his stories, but by his interest in subjects, his remarkable skill in getting a man's ideas, sounding his information.  Men in Chicago at the River and Harbor Convention who ran up against Lincoln no more forgot him than those who knew him first in Decatur in 1831 or in Sangamon County in 1832.  He was somebody—you knew it at the start.

Of course Lincoln locally was very much of a political somebody at the moment.  The Whig newspaper, the Chicago Journal, emphasized this.

"Abraham Lincoln, the only Whig representative to Congress from this State, we are happy to see in attendance upon the convention. This is his first visit to the commercial emporium of the State.  We have no doubt his first visit will impress him more deeply, if possible, with the importance and inspire a higher zeal for the great interest of the River and Harbor improvements.

"We expect much from him as a representative in Congress, and we have no doubt our expectations will be more than realized, for never was reliance placed in a nobler heart and a sounder judgment. We know the banner he bears will never be soiled."

Abraham Lincoln had a great deal to think of as he jogged back the more than one hundred and fifty miles to Springfield on horseback, if that is the way he traveled! Three months more and he would be in Washington—a member of Congress. How did Congress look to him after this first experience with the kind of timber of which it was made? How did he feel about himself? Not less confident, I take it. The convention had probably only whetted his appetite for closer and longer contact with "great men."

Three months later and he and Mary Lincoln were on their way to Washington, going by Kentucky, giving them a chance of course to see the Speeds and the Todds.

# XXII

## THE FIRST TERM IN CONGRESS

WHEN Abraham Lincoln left Springfield, Illinois, in November, 1847, to take his seat as a member of the Thirtieth Congress, he must have felt much of that inner excitement and anticipation which goes with one's first deliberate journey abroad. Not since the years when, as a boat hand, he had traveled the Mississippi to New Orleans had he made a real journey—never had he made one under so happy and promising circumstances. He was like a hard-worked man who, tied by responsibilities all his life, has come to a point where he can break away, go to Europe, to the Orient—"see the world."

Things had been put into pretty good shape at home. His young law partner, Billy Herndon, now two years with him, if inexperienced and temperamental, was loyal to the core, proud of his chief, asking nothing better than to labor and to sacrifice for him. He had rented his house for ninety dollars for the year; he was taking Mary Lincoln and Bob and Ed—the one four years old, the other eighteen months. He was going to visit his Kentucky friends and relatives, and then, for the first time, to see Washington.

He would look forward to that. His patriotism was too pure and strong a sentiment for him not to feel that the capital of the country was a sacred place. He probably saw it more or less with the eyes of the engravers of the period, who certainly made it a beautiful thing—ignoring its defects, picturing it as it was hoped it one day would be. The town, when Mr. Lincoln first saw it, had its beautiful spots: the Capitol and its immediate surroundings, a few fine old homes, with their great gardens, the White House; but in reality it was a straggling and disorderly place. Pennsylvania Avenue, the heart of the town, was roughly cobbled, only partially built up, and many of its buildings low and mean. The Tiber (alias Goose Creek) rambled down from the northeast across the avenue into the Potomac, which thrust irregular, sluggish arms into what is now the Mall and the beautiful Potomac Drive. Animals fed and rooted in the fields below the Capitol and the White House, while in every direction were scattered squalid settlements of negroes—Crow Hill, Negro Hill, Swampdoodle. But these unpleasant sights did not interfere with a buoyant, dignified and even brilliant social life. Washington had some 36,000 inhabitants at this time, and most of them were in the streets on pleasant days. Robert Cruikshank's cartoon of the White House of the forties gives a notion of afternoons and evenings in the vicinity of the President's mansion. Here all the Washington world drove and promenaded, and in the throng you might meet anybody—Mr. Clay, Mr. Webster, Mr. Calhoun, even the President himself walked almost daily in the crowd.

Although everybody promenaded near the White House, members of Congress usually lived near the Capitol. There were probably seventy-five or a hundred boarding houses on Pennsylvania Avenue and Capitol Hill—Congressmen's messes. The Lincolns went to Capitol Hill.

It is a mistake to think of Lincoln in this first Washington experience as a strange or lonely man. Already he knew very well most of the members of the Illinois delegation—one of them very well, indeed, and for a long time had had his opinion of him—the most brilliant and successful man

[279]

that had come out of Illinois, Stephen A. Douglas, just elected to the United States Senate, and inclined to patronize his colleague of the thirties in the Illinois assembly. He remembered Mr. Lincoln, oh, yes. He had served with him in the legislature back in '36, but Mr. Lincoln had been "submerged," lost sight of as a public man since. As for himself, well, of course, he had always been in sight!

Lincoln knew the Illinois people, and he knew well the record of every man of importance in Congress—knew it from first-hand study of congressional documents—a political literature easy to obtain, and which he had always followed zealously. He knew fairly well the currents of opinion in the localities from which these men came—knew it from his wide reading of newspapers. Thus he had a substantial background of knowledge of men and opinions in the body of which he was to become a member.

One gets an impression from a reading of his letters and speeches and the recollections of him men have set down at this period, of a man taking hold with zest, making the most of every contact. His colleagues in the mess at Mrs. Sprigg's on Capitol Hill found at once and with delight that the tall Whig from Illinois was a wonderful table companion—modest, a good listener, gentle, full of fun, quick at repartee, a side-splitting story-teller—and, more still, a very serious and thoughtful fellow. In more than one established informal group—the kind of gathering inclined to be jealous of its personnel, slow to admit newcomers to intimacy, Lincoln, after a few days on the outskirts, was received into full fellowship. It was so at the bowling alley on the hill, at the group of choice story-tellers in the House postoffice, at Mr. Webster's breakfasts. In all these gatherings he came to be looked for, welcomed warmly, remembered after his term was over. More than one writer of his reminiscences of Washington in '48 and thereabouts has left a picture of Abraham Lincoln in these groups, something definite, characteristic.

He went to work at once—a little more freely, from a political point of view, perhaps, than if he had been a candidate for reëlection. He was not. He had repeatedly announced in his campaign that he still held to the principle of turnabout, which he had unwisely brought into being in the convention of 1843. He knew that his former law partner, Stephen A. Logan, was a candidate, and he felt that it was right that he should have the next term. Logan had worked faithfully for him—indeed, had made the speech nominating him. He did not intend to stand in his way, and when Billy Herndon and others wanted to go to work at once to make ready for his reëlection, he quite decidedly put his foot down. He was not a candidate—not if Logan was. This fact, however, had nothing to do with his energy and firmness in taking hold of congressional work.

Lincoln seems to have gone to Washington with the idea of making the tariff his principal interest—at least the tariff was the only issue, so far as we know, for which he had made special preparations. With Congressmen, however, as with men and women in most positions of responsibility, it is usually not the thing that you prepare to do that you do do. He never had a chance to make his tariff speech. He dropped it to accept the challenge President Polk threw down in his message. Polk was determined not only to get supplies for the Mexican War then in progress, but a vote declaring it a just and necessary war. He insisted that Mexico had made the war inevitable by "invading our territory" and "shedding the blood of our fellow citizens on our soil." This was too much for Lincoln, who had always contended that Polk had not only provoked the war, but begun it unconstitutionally. He took issue at once with the effort of the Administration to get a clean bill of health. "Where was the spot," he asked, "on which the blood of our citizens was shed?" "Was it in our territory or in Mexican territory?" His questions were so cleverly phrased, the arraignment of the President with which he followed up his "spot resolutions" so able, that the Whig side of the House was delighted. Here was a recruit worth cultivating. They saw in Lincoln at once certain important political qualities—that he was not afraid to speak his mind even in a body like Congress, which might naturally be expected to awe him into silence for a time. As a matter of fact, Lincoln found himself at once quite at home on the floor, "about as badly scared and no more as I am when I speak in court." The Whigs found him informed—with a genuine interest in facts, willing to work to get them, and surprisingly cunning in handling them. All this brought him at once into the inner confidential Whig circle, busy at the moment in selecting a candidate for the presidential election of 1848.

All of this Lincoln enjoyed. He was popular, trusted, listened to, admitted. But his success with the Whig circle in Washington had an offsetting feature at home. He probably had not foreseen that his fight on Polk would shock his district. The Sangamon country might be Whig in principle, but it would not stand for criticism of a war while the war was on. More than one of his good friends, Billy Herndon among them, protested. Herndon was thrown into a panic by the harm his course was doing to his political strength. There is nothing that shows Lincoln's capacity for clear thinking and expression at this period as well as his intellectual firmness when he had come to a conclusion which he believed sound, better than the letters that he wrote to his Illinois critics. There was one to a minister, the Rev. J. M. Peck, in his best controversial form, strongly suggestive of many a letter which he was to write in the last six years of his life. He drove the question of the war down to the facts. What were the facts? He reviewed them—the invasion of Americans into peaceful Mexican territory:

". . . What is the result of your reflections upon them?" he asked. "If you deny that they are facts, I think I can furnish proofs which shall convince you that you are mistaken. If you admit that they are facts, then I shall be obliged for a reference to any law of language, law of states, law of nations, law of morals, law of religions, any law, human or divine, in which an authority can be found for saying those facts constitute 'no aggression.'

"Possibly you consider those acts too small for notice. Would you venture to so consider them had they been committed by any nation on earth against the humblest of our people? I know you would not. Then I ask, is the precept 'Whatsoever ye would that men should do to you, do you even so to them' obsolete? Of no force? Of no application?"

Pretty spirited, clear-headed expression this—not at all a man, as some biographers have hinted, that did not know his own mind. Throughout the year there was no outward political wavering. He welcomed the nomination in June of General Zachariah Taylor—depending of course upon his war record, his freedom from any kind of political alliance, willing even to slide over the fact that he was a slave owner, and, so far as anybody knew, had no views of any sort on the slavery question. He went with alacrity into the campaign and kept it up to the election, going to New England in the fall, and then home to steady political speaking.

If we put together all that we have of his writing and speaking in the year we find hardly a hint of the fact that he had been following in the Thirtieth Congress a tremendous and prophetic discussion—a discussion in which there came out all those shades of opinion and of emotion on the question of slavery which later were to grow and harden until they drove all other opinions and emotions from men's minds, assuming finally such vigor and power that men no longer could control them, became their puppets, and fell back on war to settle that which mind and conscience had started, but were still too undeveloped to carry on to logical peaceful conclusion.

It was the acquisition and government of new territory that forced slavery to the front. There was Oregon—Texas—the land that we were compelling Mexico to sell us—should they all be free? Should Congress declare them free, as in 1787 it had declared the Northwest? David Wilmot of Pennsylvania had attached an amendment to the bill appropriating money for settling with Mexico, which made the funds conditional on slavery being excluded forever from any portion of the acquired territory. The South incensed, fought the proviso. Lincoln heard his friend Alexander H. Stephens of Georgia go so far as to threaten, if the combined vote of the North carried the Wilmot proviso, it would be for the South to take her own course—and he—why he would go with her—secession!

He listened to violent and noisy arraignments of the institution by men from free states—ridiculed by men from slave states. He heard attacks and defenses—constitutional—economic—social—religious. He heard the doctrine of "squatter sovereignty" announced and defended.

And at intervals he heard long protests from those who wanted to "do business," at the folly of allowing what Thomas Benton called the "pestiferous question" to absorb the whole thought of Congress. This "black question," he cried, "rises forever on the table. It is like the plague of frogs—everywhere." "I remember a time," Benton complained, "when no one would have thought of asking a public man what his opinion was on the extension of slavery any more than what was the length of his foot." Happy days—gone forever!

Forty-one different members of the House of Representatives and thirty-seven Senators spoke on one side or the other of the slavery question in this session—spoke long, sometimes wisely, often violently—but through it all Lincoln never raised his voice, save every time he had a chance to vote "yea" on the Wilmot proviso. That far he was clear—had always been clear: new territory must be free territory.

He might keep quiet in Congress—content himself with a vote; but when he came to campaigning, it was going to be different. He saw a crumbling of the old parties going on in the North—bolting Whigs, bolting Democrats—people who demanded louder, clearer, more unmistakable expressions on keeping the new territories free—people who not only wanted these expressions, but wanted denunciations of slavery as an evil, wanted to defy those who were supporting and profiting by it. And he saw rising, too, North and South in spots, something which looked like fighting blood, preparing to back demands.

While he sat franking documents in Washington after the adjournment of Congress, waiting for certain speaking engagements which had been arranged for him in the month of September in Massachusetts, more and more signs and sounds of the defection came to him. While he was still there in Washington, bolting Democrats and Free Soilers held a convention in Buffalo, New York, led by a man that he already looked on as one of the great men of the country, Salmon P. Chase of Ohio. There was no mistaking how this convention felt about slavery. Their slogan showed it: "Free Soil, Free Speech, Free Labor, Free Men." So, when he came to cast up the account of New England, to which he was going, he found the Whigs had lost there some of their best names—

and lost them because of the nomination of Taylor and his undefined position on the question of slavery.

Lincoln felt that it was not going to be possible for him to depend for speaking material in Massachusetts on the sins of the Polk Administration or the military record of General Taylor—he must meet the slavery issue.

His first engagement was to speak at a convention of the Whigs to be held in Worcester, and it was in this first speech that he set down that which shows clearly where he stood— imperfect as our report of the speech is—in the long scale of opinion on slavery. It shows, too, his temper.

"The people of Illinois," he told his great Worcester audience, "agreed entirely with the people of Massachusetts on this subject, except perhaps they did not keep so constantly thinking about it. All agreed that slavery was an evil, but that we were not responsible for it and cannot affect it in states of this Union where we do not live. But the question of the extension of slavery to new territories of this country is a part of our responsibility and care, and is under our control."

So much for his views and his temper. His real task, however, was to back up New England Whigs who were wavering because of their feeling that neither platform nor candidates were satisfactory on the subject of the extension of slavery. Lincoln's argument was one of expediency. They had a program, he declared; that program could only be interpreted as against the extension of slavery. And as for the "self-named Free Soil party," what had they to offer but opposition? You settled nothing by opposition. Your intelligence was given you to find a way, a plan, work out something. That was what the Whigs were trying to do. And as for the Democrats who had stood with the South, what could you expect of them? Was it not absurd to suppose the party that had annexed the territory against the protests of Whigs and Free Soilers could be depended upon to do anything toward keeping slavery out of it?

He made his impression—so strong an impression that invitations to speak poured in on him from all directions. He spoke at several points in the vicinity of Boston, and finally in Tremont Temple in Boston, on the same platform with Governor Seward. Seward in essence stood at this moment with Lincoln. The difference between them was the difference Lincoln had noted at Worcester between Illinois and Massachusetts. Seward was "constantly thinking about it" —Lincoln was not. Seward stirred him. Was it "irrepressible"—this struggle between free and slave? He was not the man to refuse to consider. If the forces of those who believed in slavery and its extension were becoming stronger, more aggressive, more determined than those who believed like him that it could be kept within certain bounds, and so kept must ultimately die, he must prepare to meet the new situation. He came out from Tremont Temple with Governor Seward, pondering, in his way: "I reckon you are right," he said; "we have got to deal with this slavery question, got to give much more attention to it hereafter than we have been doing." It was that thought that was to attend him for many, many of the following months. It lay incubating in his subconsciousness on his journey home. It was with him through the weeks he spent in Illinois before his return to Congress for the short term of the winter of 1848-49. The time was coming when he must be active, but how be active within the law? What could he do now—what tangible, lawful thing? There was one place in the country from which he believed that he had a legal right to work for the exclusion of slavery, and that was the District of Columbia. Twelve years before in the assembly of Illinois he had expressed this judgment. His months in Washington had put emotion into his conviction, for here he had seen, every time he went to the White House, Treasury, War Department, the signs of the city's slave market. It stood on the edge of the public grounds, near the Smithsonian Institution, and to and from it, along the avenue, gangs of negroes—often chained—were driven daily. To have this vivid picture of what slavery meant—a traffic in human life—always before their eyes stirred those who hated the institution mightily. "The 'slave pen' of the nation's capital—under the very walls of the building that housed the Declaration of Independence," appeared in more than one of the speeches that Lincoln listened to in 1848. He did not thunder. He prepared to do something.

On January 16, 1849, he brought in a carefully framed bill to abolish slavery in the District of Columbia. He brought it in, and he worked for it, soliciting votes, trying to get publicity. But the bill never came to the floor. He had done, however, all he could see to do, he had put himself on record.

And now his term was over. What had it amounted to? Men have called it a failure. It seems to me anything but that. He had proved himself an able and trustworthy national politician. He had shown, too, that, good politician as he was, he was not so good when it came to getting things for himself. The party had wanted to reward him, as they called it—keep him in Washington—give him a good office. The Land Office was suggested. He muddled it—not because he did not want it, but because there was a friend in the way who also wanted it. So long as he thought that possibly there was a chance for the friend he would not apply; when he found that there was not, he made his application—but he had waited too long. His sorrow, however, was not that he was too late, but that his friend felt that possibly he had been treacherous in applying at all.

There was one positive satisfaction from the experience. Then for the first time he learned something definite of the Lincoln family before it went into Kentucky. A fellow Congressman from the Shenandoah Valley told him of Lincolns in his district—gave him the name of one of them, a man prominent in Rockingham County, David Lincoln. He wrote at once. His father was born in Rockingham County, he told David Lincoln, his grandfather had migrated from there to Kentucky. "What of your family?" he asked. "Do you know anything of my grandfather? Do you know where my family came from when they settled in Virginia?"

The answer was gratifying. It told him that his grandfather was an uncle of the David to whom he had written, that the Virginia Lincolns had come from Berks County, Pennsylvania. He was pleased, but he wanted more. Particularly he wanted to know whether or not the Lincolns who came into Berks County were Quakers.

I found recently at Lacey Springs in the Shenandoah Valley, where David Lincoln's descendants still live, a tradition that Mr. Lincoln at this time actually spent a night with his kinsman, either in going or coming to Washington. There is no hint of it in his letters which these descendants still treasure. It is probably unfounded. But it is rather a pity that he could not have looked in on the prosperous settlement which this grandson of John Lincoln and his brothers had built up. At the time of the correspondence, David and his brothers had some 7,000 acres of land, kept an inn—famous in its day as the stopping place of all stage coaches along the highway—ran a mill, owned many slaves—prosperous Lincolns whom he would have been glad to know. He knew so few of that class!

[289]

It is a pity, too, that when he was in Worcester, Massachusetts, he could not have had the satisfaction of knowing that the mayor of the city, former Governor Levi Lincoln, was a kinsman. Governor Lincoln was of the sixth generation from the original Samuel Lincoln—Abraham of the seventh; but, although they met in Worcester, Lincoln dining in the stately Lincoln home, which still stands, one of the treasures of the town—it is a tradition that he said it was the finest dinner at which he had ever sat—they knew nothing of their common origin.

When he spoke in Tremont Temple in Boston, the secretary of the meeting was also a kinsman, Ezra Lincoln, Jr.— a prosperous printer and a leading Whig. But they knew nothing of their common ancestor. Nor did he know that one of the military heroes of the day, Captain George Lincoln, killed at the battle of Buena Vista, was of his family, and like himself of the seventh generation in America.

One gain of his congressional experience which he particularly prized was the extension of his acquaintance. His avidity for people had a chance. He sought them out, tapped them, often made lifelong friends with them. Wide as he and Alexander H. Stephens were apart, Stephens always prized his acquaintance with Lincoln, and it was at this time he learned to know him:

"I knew Mr. Lincoln well and intimately," he says, "and we were both ardent supporters of General Taylor for President in 1848. Mr. Lincoln, Toombs, Preston, myself and others formed the first Congressional Taylor Club, known as 'The Young Indians,' and organized the Taylor movement, which resulted in his nomination. . . . Mr. Lincoln was careful as to his manners, awkward in his speech, but was possessed of a very strong, clear, vigorous mind. . . . He always attracted and riveted the attention of the House when he spoke. His manner of speech, as well as thought, was original. He had no model. He was a man of strong convictions, and what Carlyle could have called an earnest man. He abounded in anecdote. He illustrated everything he was talking about by anecdote, always exceedingly apt and pointed, and socially he always kept his company in a roar of laughter."

Out of these contacts came a fresh, searching appraisal of himself. He was something, if not all that he wished. He had proved he could go with the best of them—sit at Daniel Webster's breakfasts, be listened to in Tremont Temple, walk the street with Governor Seward, sit at Governor Lincoln's dinner table—not so bad, when he remembered Indiana, his coming into Illinois, the flatboat, Offut's store, the odd jobs at rail-splitting—but still far below his thought. Knowledge was what he lacked. Here were men that knew things that he did not know. He was going back to the law. He had told Herndon at the beginning of his term, when the latter had urged reëlection upon him, that he had thought all along that the best thing for him was to return to the law after a second term. That held now, the law was all he had in mind. He must be a better lawyer.

## XXIII

### LINCOLN RETURNS TO THE LAW

THE Thirtieth Congress, of which Abraham Lincoln was a member, came to its close in March of 1849. After three or four unsatisfactory months given to office-seeking for Illinois Whigs, himself included, he went back to the law as, according to his own letters, he expected to do when he went to Washington. Does this retirement from public life—this return to his profession—spell failure? One recent Lincoln interpreter says that his congressional experience was not only a failure but a failure closed by an "ironic picture"—his presence at the inaugural ball of 1849! How about this "picture"?

Lincoln had gone to the ball with a party of friends, and they had stayed on until three or four o'clock in the morning. How like him! Interested in human beings and their ways— never tired of watching them—the last man to leave any gathering unless, indeed, he was overtaken by one of his frequent fits of despondency. I cannot see the least reason for describing Mr. Lincoln at this inaugural ball as this interpreter does, as a "worthy provincial, the last word for awkwardness" (the best answer to that is the daguerreotype made in Washington in this period), "socially as strange to such a scene as a little child, spending the whole night gazing intently at everything he could see, at the barbaric display of wealth, the sumptuous gowns, the brilliant uniforms, the distinguished foreigners, and the leaders of America, men like Webster and Clay, with their air of assured power—the men he had failed

[292]

to impress." As a matter of fact, in his two years he had done an extremely difficult thing for a newcomer in Congress, he had impressed men of "assured power."

Can it be supposed that men as clever as the leaders of the Whig party of that day would have considered sending the man of the above picture into Massachusetts—at that moment the most difficult point in the Union for the Whigs? But Mr. Lincoln had been sent—had been sent as the chief speaker at a pivotal point. He had been asked to speak on the same platform with Governor Seward in Tremont Temple in Boston. The impression that he had made had been so strong that there was a continued demand for his political services for some time after he left the state. That is not a political failure for a man in his first Congressional term.

And socially he had been popular—so popular that ten years later when as a disputant in one of the greatest debates, if not the greatest, which this country can boast, they began to hear his name, listen to his arguments, they said: "Why, yes, Lincoln, do you remember?" And they all remembered. No. Lincoln's term in Congress was not a failure, even socially.

The impression of failure is based on two things: First, that the appointment to the General Land Office for which he had applied went to a man whom all Illinois Whigs disliked; and, second, on the long period of silence that followed his return. Look over a collection of his letters for 1850, 1851 and 1852—you will find almost nothing. Until Gilbert Tracy published his little book in 1917 there had never been a letter of Lincoln's printed in any collection for the year 1850 or for that of 1852. Tracy found four of the first date, three of 1851. He spoke little more than he wrote, and when he spoke there was a strong note of sadness. This is unmistakable in a speech only recently come to light—one of the find-

[293]

ings of the indefatigable Rev. William E. Barton, who published it last year with notes. Lincoln was attending the United States district court at Chicago in July of 1850 when the news of President Taylor's death came. He was chosen to deliver the address at the memorial services. It is not much of a speech, to be honest. One significant thing there is in it, however: his characterization of Taylor's military talent as a combination of negatives—"absence of excitement and absence of fear." One can easily believe that it was upon these traits in Taylor that Lincoln had depended in advocating him. "I fear," he said at Chicago, "that the one great question of the day" (meaning slavery, of course) "is not so likely to be patiently acquiesced in as it would have been could General Taylor have been spared us." That is, at that moment, 1850, he felt that the safest temper for wise handling of the "one great question of the day" was "absence of excitement and absence of fear."

The close of this address drips with melancholy. Here for the first time, so far as I know, he quotes publicly his favorite verses beginning "O why should the spirit of mortal be proud?"—seven of the fourteen stanzas—an ending which must have left upon his audience an effect of a profoundly depressed man.

From a careful reading of the reminiscences of this period one carries away a similar impression of brooding melancholy. You even get something of it in his relations with his father and the group of relatives back in Coles County. They had never prospered. Lincoln had again and again given them small sums to help them out of tight places, and to his stepbrother, John D. Johnston, he was at this time giving advice which, accepted, was equal to a fortune. Early in 1851 letters from Coles County told him of his father's serious illness. He did not even answer the first ones—a neglect

unlike him and only to be explained by the hopelessness he
felt over the situation there.

"I have not answered them," he finally wrote, "not because I have
forgotten them, or been uninterested about them, but because it appeared
to me that I could write nothing which would do any good. You already know I desire that neither father nor mother shall be in want
of any comfort, either in health or sickness, while they live; and I feel
sure you have not failed to use my name, if necessary, to procure a
doctor, or anything else for father in his present sickness. My business
is such that I could hardly leave home now, if it was not as it is, that
my own wife is sick-a-bed. (It is a case of baby-sickness, and I suppose
is not dangerous.)"

What was back of this long, silent depression?

So far as politics had anything to do with his state of
mind, it was not his own failure to get the General Land
Office which was troubling him. At any time he could have
had that office, so the President himself said, if he had only
spoken. The cabinet had actually postponed the appointment
three weeks for his benefit; but one of his old and dear Illinois
friends, Cyrus Edwards, was an applicant. So long as Lincoln thought there was any chance at all for Edwards he refused to apply. When he finally saw that in no case would
the administration give the office to Edwards, he put in his
application; but it was too late. What overwhelmed him now
was that Edwards accused him of treachery, that in trying to
serve him both of them had lost the office and it had gone to
a man most unsatisfactory to the Whigs of his district.

It was these two things—his friend's feelings toward
him, and the resentment of his constituency at the appointment which had finally been made, that troubled him. "These
two things away and I should have no regrets—at least, I
think I would not."

This unpleasant mix-up and other unsatisfactory appointments in Washington brought a criticism upon President

[295]

Taylor, for whom he had been fighting so hard, that troubled him, too. The President was getting the reputation in Illinois of being a man of straw, unwilling to take the responsibility of appointments.

"This must be arrested," Lincoln wrote to the Secretary of State, John Clayton, "or it will damn us all inevitably. It is said General Taylor and his officers held a council of war at Palo Alto (I believe), and that he then fought the battle against unanimous opinion of those officers. This fact (no matter whether rightfully or wrongfully) gives him more popularity than ten thousand submissions, however really wise and magnanimous those submissions may be.

"The appointments need be no better than they have been, but the public must be brought to understand that they are the President's appointments. He must occasionally say, or seem to say, 'by the Eternal,' 'I take the responsibility.' Those phrases were the 'Samson's locks' of General Jackson, and we dare not disregard the lessons of experience."

The whole political situation was profoundly distasteful to Lincoln. He was one of those men that are only thoroughly happy where there is frankness, honesty of feeling, friendly coöperation. He was sensitive to concealed suspicions, to unspoken hostility, to critical silences. His own mind was so free, so candid, so without vanity of opinion, that the feeling that he now sensed in political circles disconcerted and saddened him.

But this political episode does not account for his continued sadness, I am convinced. A chief cause was another of those blows which had so staggered him in the past. Only a few months after his return from Washington, in February of 1850, his second child, now about three and a half years old, "Ed," as he always spoke of him in his letters, died.

For a man of his profound tenderness, with his passion for childhood, such a loss was overwhelming. The death of his mother had saddened his own childhood, the death of Ann

Rutledge had shaken the very moral foundations beneath him, and here was his little son dead! There is no doubt that he went through a period of terrible distress, and there is no doubt, too, that it was at this time that he first seriously sought to find if, in the Christian religion, there is a support for a man in periods of grief and distress. There is ample evidence of this. Possibly the most important is that of a Scotch clergyman, Dr. James Smith, the pastor of the Presbyterian Church in Springfield, a church of which Mr. and Mrs. Lincoln became attendants and Mrs. Lincoln a member soon after the death of their little son. With Dr. Smith Lincoln held many conversations on Christian evidences. The doctor was an able theologian, the author of a book called the "Christian Defense," which unquestionably Mr. Lincoln studied seriously, and which the doctor believed changed to faith his doubts on the fundamentals of the Christian religion.

Mr. Lincoln's friend, Jesse Fell, always believed that it was the putting of a certain sermon of William Ellery Channing's into Lincoln's hands at this period that wrought a great change in his thinking and that he came out with a profound belief in the goodness of God, and certainly in the efficacy of prayer. A brother of Jesse Fell's, Mr. V. Fell of Nashville, Tennessee, wrote me several years ago that he had often heard his brother say that Mr. Lincoln told him that he had never read anything that tallied more perfectly with his own views than Channing's works.

It is hardly believable that Mr. Lincoln would have sent such a message of conventional pious comfort to his father then in his last illness as we find in a letter written early in January of 1851 if he was the "atheist" and "scoffer" that Herndon and Lamon have made him out.

"I sincerely hope father may recover his health, but at all events tell him to remember to call upon and confide in our great and good and merciful Maker, who will not turn away from him in any extremity. He notes the fall of a sparrow, and numbers the hairs of our heads, and He will not forget the dying man who puts his trust in Him. Say to him that if we could meet now it is doubtful whether it would not be more painful than pleasant, but that if it be his lot to go now, he will soon have a joyous meeting with many loved ones gone before, and where the rest of us, through the help of God, hope ere long to join them."

It seems to me quite clear that a careful examination and weighing of the controversial literature on this subject—William E. Barton has assembled practically everything in his "Soul of Abraham Lincoln"—proves that while Mr. Lincoln could never bring himself to join any church, he believed sincerely in the essence of the Christian system; and that the impression he made on his friends at this time of a dissatisfied and unsettled man, was due, partially at least, to the spiritual struggle through which he was going. It seems to me clear, too, that it was at this period that he laid the foundations for a profound belief in the rightness of the judgments of God and for that deep and genuine humility which made him willing to accept and submit himself to those judgments, of which there is so continued and clear an expression through the period of the war.

But, as I have had occasion to reflect more than once, in these reports of my recent pilgrimage, you never find Lincoln's professional activities held up by his inner sufferings. He carried on, whatever his agony of spirit. He was carrying on now in the law with a clearer determination than ever to make a first-class lawyer of himself. He studied as he never had before, and he also attempted to work out his notion of the ethics of the profession. His well-known notes for a lecture on the law show this. The chief point in these notes is his Lincolnesque remark:

# LINCOLN RETURNS TO THE LAW

"As a peacemaker the lawyer has a superior opportunity of being a good man. There will still be business enough."

He laid it down as a rule that a lawyer should persuade his neighbors to compromise whenever it was possible, pointing out how a nominal winner is often a real loser—"in fees, expenses and waste of time." There could not be a worse man, he said, than one who stirred up litigation.

One can fairly ask how far he lived up to his preachings. Fortunately we have good evidence on the point, from members who traveled the old eighth circuit with him and who have left such an abundant crop of recollections. He practiced his preaching to a degree that some of them regarded as bad for business as his habit of scaling down his fees.

A rather amusing account of a settlement out of court which does not, so far as I know, appear in any of the excellent discussions of Mr. Lincoln as a lawyer, is told in a lecture on "Early Reminiscences of Alton," delivered in 1869 by Joseph Brown, a former mayor of both Alton and St. Louis. Incidentally, it was delivered for the benefit of the Lovejoy Memorial Association. It was put into my hands by Alton's chief historian, Mr. W. T. Norton. The incident happened, Mr. Brown says in his lecture, when he was mayor:

"A lady (by the name of Mrs. McReady) came to Alton on one of the Keokuk packets to give Shakespearian lectures, arriving at 2 o'clock in the morning, and, as luck would have it, she stepped on an old cellar door in front of 'Johnny Roe's' grocery and one leg went part way through the door so that it sprained her ankle and laid her up at the Franklin House for some time. The result was, she put in a claim against the city for damages, but the city refused to allow anything, and the result was, as she was permanently lamed, she sued for $5,000 in the United States Court at Springfield, Ill., and engaged Mr. Lincoln as her attorney; so when the time came for the case to be tried I went up to attend it, and on the day set I went to the United States Court and found Mr. Lincoln and his client inside the bar waiting for the court to open. I took my seat with my attorney inside

[299]

the bar, when Mr. Lincoln came over and said: 'Mr. Brown, I don't like to take this suit against your town; can't we compromise it in some way?' I said: 'I don't see how we can, as we don't think the city is liable for an injury done to the lady by a man having bad cellar doors.' 'Ah,' he said, 'but the city is liable for its sidewalks, and I feel sure we shall get judgment.' 'Well,' I said, 'if you do so she can come and help herself to the market house' (which at that time was an old dilapidated concern). 'Well,' he said, 'I think it is best to compromise if we can. How much will you give the lady? She is lamed for life with a stiff ankle.' I said: 'I can't make any offer; we have no money.' 'Well,' he said, 'will you give her $3,000?' 'No,' I said, 'there isn't that much money in the town.' Finally he got down to $1,500, and I felt that it was best to compromise at that, so I said: 'If we give the $1,500 are we to have the damaged limb?' Lincoln said: 'I will go over and ask,' and he did, and after talking with her a little while he came back and said: 'If you are an unmarried man, and as you are pretty good looking, you can have the entire woman!' So we compromised, but I did not accept the lady's marriage offer."

This is amusing, but not nearly so important as a letter—so far as I know, unpublished—that is to be found in the museum at New Salem:

"I understand," Mr. Lincoln writes to his client, "that Mr. Hickson will go or send to Petersburg tomorrow for the purpose of meeting you to settle the difficulty about the wheat. I sincerely hope you will settle it. I think you can if you will, for I have found Mr. Hickson a fair man in his dealings. If you settle I will charge nothing for what I have done and thank you to boot. By settling you will most likely get your money sooner and with much less trouble and expense."

He had his code of ethics, and, so far as I know, no student—even though unfriendly—of his legal career has been able to detect a practice in violation of that code.

He was a strong advocate of study—independent study—self-education in the law. To what we have already had on that point, his counsel of "work, work, work," to an inquiring student, has been added recently a letter to a young man who wanted to read law with him. It is a masterpiece of sensible counsel:

"I am from home too much of my time for a young man to read law with me advantageously. If you are resolutely determined to make a lawyer of yourself, the thing is more than half done already. It is but a small matter whether you read with anybody or not. I did not read with any one. Get the books, and read and study them till you understand them in their principal features; and that is the main thing. It is of no consequence to be in a large town while you are reading. I read at New Salem, which never had three hundred people living in it. The books, and your capacity for understanding them, are just the same in all places. Dr. Dummer is a very clever man and an excellent lawyer (much better than I, in law-learning), and I have no doubt he will cheerfully tell you what books to read, and also loan you the books.

"Always bear in mind that your own resolution to succeed is more important than any other one thing."

He worked, but his methods were original. Mr. Herndon remarks somewhere that he did not prepare many legal papers, but Mr. Charles W. Moore, who has made most careful research in the various court houses of the circuit on which Lincoln traveled, says that he found so many papers written by him that he marveled that he had time for anything else. Some of these papers that Mr. Moores turned up are most interesting exhibits of his unconventional but altogether effective methods of preparation for a suit.

One thing that Lincoln's term in Congress did for him was to increase his prestige and so his law practice. There was a wider demand for him undoubtedly because of his Washington experience. He had a large circuit, as the map on page 306 shows, and, as the documents in the various court houses prove, he made all of the points. It must have been long and tedious work. Mr. W. F. Hardy, the editor of the Decatur Herald, said at the time of the unveiling of the Lincoln circuit marker in his town that if the old circuit

George W. Albin
as
Thomas Baddin

In Slander—

1st. Albin stole Brady's horse out of my pasture last night— He is a horsethief, and that is what he came here for—

2nd. Albin stole that horse last night out of my pasture; and he is a horse thief, and I knew that was his business here—

3rd. He is a horse thief, and I always believed his business was horse stealing, and that is what brought him here——

4th. Albin stole Brady's horse out of my pasture last night; and it is not the first horse he has stolen— He is a horse thief and follows that business—

5th. You stole that horse out of my pasture, and it is not the first one you have stole—

6th. You know you stole that horse, and it is not the first horse you have stole; and I believe you follow the business—

7th. You are a horse thief and you came here for that business—and I believe you came here for nothing else— You are a horse thief—

8th. He is a damn'd little thief, his business is horse stealing, and I can prove it—

FACSIMILE OF BRIEF IN LINCOLN'S HAND USED IN A CASE TRIED IN 1850 IN EDGAR COUNTY, ILLINOIS.
From Charles W. Moore's *The Career of a Country Lawyer*

riders made ten miles an hour they did well, and "in fall and spring, when the roads were quagmires, progress was considerably slower. Fifty miles a day was enough travel for man and beast under the best conditions. A start from Decatur in the morning with Springfield as a destination probably meant that no court could be held that day. Members of the Macon County bar having legal business in Springfield, and leaving Decatur at 8:15 A. M., are now in the capital by 10, and home again at 5 P. M. after business day.

"Slowly indeed the miles must have been covered by the circuit riders, and wearisome enough must have been the landscape, most of it virgin prairie, for between 1847 and 1857, when Lincoln was a circuit rider, a vast number of sections were still unclaimed and uncultivated. Summer's heat was quite as intense and black soil dust quite as disfiguring as now. Insect pests were worse. The horses were terrible sufferers from the flies that bred in the tall prairie grass. Mosquitoes from the still undrained ponds that dotted the prairie added to the discomfort.

"As compensation for these magnificent spaces so tediously traversed, the lawyers fortunately had plenty of leisure. As they traveled with the court there was no danger of missing an appointment with a client or being late at a pleading. Time was the thing that most of the younger lawyers were rich in.

"Undoubtedly stories must have whiled away the time between county seats. But before that immense circuit had been covered the stories must have grown stale and the travelers must have tended to become weary and morose, as travelers do now when they are a little tired of each other's company.

"It is not at all certain that men were better conversationalists in a day when there was more time to talk, or that they became better thinkers in a period when one had to be

[303]

alone with himself. Much of the talk and thinking alike doubtless was trivial. The present age certainly does not read the 'Canterbury Tales' of Chaucer's pilgrims for their moral stimulation, but rather for their humor, much of it uncouth, judged by present-day standards.

"The Lincoln markers in the several county seats, of which Decatur is one, memorialize not the exploits of pioneers who effected great discoveries and faced great dangers, but the travels of men who accepted boredom, and physical discomfort all as a part of the day's work in a now all but forgotten period of Illinois history."

But even at this time Lincoln's practice was not confined to the eighth circuit. The reference to his funeral address in honor of President Taylor in Chicago in the summer of 1850 shows he was called on to give that address because he was in attendance at the circuit court. Among the new letters which Mr. Tracy published in 1917 is one showing that late in December, 1849, he was in Cincinnati on law business. That is, the demand for him was sufficient to encourage him to carry out his determination to "work, work, work," just as he counseled the young men that came to him.

# XXIV

## ON THE CIRCUIT

IT has always been a question with me whether Abraham Lincoln could ever have been made President of the United States if in the traveling he did for nearly twenty years before his nomination, week in and week out, over a tract of country one hundred by one hundred and fifty miles in extent, with many excursions to towns and cities outside the block, he had not won both the respect and the love of all sorts of people, particularly of the legal class, which, as everywhere in the United States, was the leading political class.

When it began to dawn upon these men in 1859 and '60 that Lincoln had earned a chance for the Presidency, by the character of his fight against the extension of slavery, their personal devotion put a fire into their efforts for him, which, in the final analysis, was perhaps the deciding element. What was there about the man that aroused such devotion?

The only answer is that he was naturally an extraordinarily lovable human being—one of the rare special kind that on the instant inspires affection and confidence, and that life never spoils. Such was the feeling for him in the '50's that his arrival in a circuit town was an event for many an admirer. "Lincoln's come," was welcome news not only in the court, but at the hotel and in many a household. Something of this welcome was certainly due to his quick falling in with whatever was going on—grave or gay—and this included sports of the young as well as the old. There was nothing that boys did in which he did not gladly take a hand, often ending up by treating a whole crowd with whom he had run a race or helped carry out a practical joke. He was excellent at games, playing them purely for fun and exercise, particularly the "game of fives"—a variety of handball popular in those days. It was excellent sport. A high dead

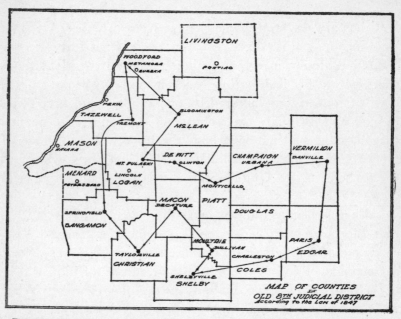

THE EIGHTH JUDICIAL CIRCUIT WHICH LINCOLN TRAVELLED INCLUDED FIFTEEN COUNTIES. LINCOLN MARKERS HAVE BEEN OR WILL SOON BE PLACED IN THE COURT HOUSE SQUARES OF ALL THE COUNTY SEATS.

wall was chosen, and horizontally across it two lines were drawn—one perhaps two feet, the other twenty feet from the ground. In front of this two ranks of five men each placed themselves, at agreed-upon distances. A man in the front rank threw the ball toward any point he chose between the black lines. As the ball rebounded, it was the business of the rear rank to knock it back against the wall. This operation was kept up until the ball fell to the ground or failed to strike the field. This was called a hand-out, and ten hand-outs on either side decided the game. Mr. Lincoln never missed a game of fives if he could help it, and I have heard men who saw him playing when he was fifty or more years old declare that there was no better player on the circuit than he.

His instinctive lending a hand where there was something to be done endeared him everywhere. A perfect illustration of this—and there are many of them—is found in the "Personal Recollections of Jane Martin Johns," published by the Decatur (Illinois) Chapter of the D. A. R. Mrs. Johns came to Decatur, the county seat of Macon County, in 1849, and first lived at the Macon House, which, she says, the court of the Eighth Judicial Circuit looked upon as an oasis in their itinerary, since there you found clean beds, good bread and a genial landlady. Mrs. Johns, in coming into Illinois, had evidently stipulated that certain things, rare in pioneer settlements, should follow her. One of these was a piano. After a long journey it arrived by wagon, but how were they to get it into the Macon House?

Now, it happened that this was court week in Decatur, and as the discussion of what to do with the piano was going on, the court adjourned and judge and lawyers began to join the crowd that had gathered around the wagon. There was a piano in the box, they were told. We want it unloaded. Who will lend a hand?

"A tall gentleman stepped forward," Mrs. Johns writes, "and throwing off a big gray Scotch shawl, exclaimed, 'Come on, Swett, you are the next biggest man.'

"That was my first meeting with Abraham Lincoln."

Mr. Lincoln took charge at once; bench and bar fell to, and amid great hilarity the instrument was unloaded, unpacked and finally set up. That night, after supper, the whole bar, Judge Davis included, asked Mrs. Johns for a concert. She gives in her captivating "Recollections" the program— a charming echo from the past:

"For show pieces, I played the 'Battle of Prague' and the 'Carnival of Venice,' then followed with 'Washington's March,' 'Come, Haste to the Wedding' and Woodup Quick Step,' to convince the audience that I 'did know a tune' or two. For tragedy I sang Henry Russel's 'Maniac,' and 'The Ship on Fire,' and then made 'their blood run cold' with the wild wail of the 'Irish Mother's Lament.' For comic, we sang 'The Widdy McGee' and 'I Won't Be a Nun,' topping off with 'Old Dan Tucker,' 'Lucy Long' and 'Jim Crow,' the crowd joining in the chorus. These were followed by more serious music. Mr. Brown and Mr. Swett joined me in the duet 'Moonlight Music, Love and Flowers,' 'Rocked in the Cradle of the Deep,' 'Pilgrim Fathers,' 'Bonaparte's Grave' and 'Kathleen Mavourneen.' Each and all met with applause.

"As a finale, I sang 'He Doeth All Things Well,' after which Mr. Lincoln, in a very grave manner, thanked me for the evening's entertainment, and said: 'Don't let us spoil that song by any other music tonight.' Many times afterwards I sang that song for Mr. Lincoln and for Governor Oglesby, with whom it was also a favorite."

There is another paragraph in Mrs. Johns' "Recollections" which should be quoted in this connection. It is a point which needs frequent emphasizing to counteract that caricaturing of Mr. Lincoln's personal appearance which has been going on ever since he became a candidate for the Presidency—a caricaturing which a multitude of photographs, from 1848 on, contradict:

"When I first knew Lincoln," Mrs. Johns says, "the ungainliness of the pioneer, if he ever had it, had worn off and his manner was that of a gentleman of the old school, unaffected, unostentatious, who 'arose at once when a lady entered the room, and whose courtly manners would put to shame the easy-going indifference to etiquette which marks the twentieth century gentleman.'

"His dress, like his manner, was suited to the occasion, but was evidently a subject to which he gave little thought. It was certainly unmarked by any notable peculiarity. It was the fashion of the day for men to wear large shawls, and Mr. Lincoln's shawl, very large, very soft, and very fine, is the only article of his dress that has left the faintest impression on my memory."

There is scarcely a town which Mr. Lincoln visited, either regularly or occasionally, on the Eighth Judicial Circuit that has not some such distinctive reminiscence of him; one particularly characteristic has within recent years come out of Albion. Early in the 40's, Lincoln went to the town to speak at a joint political meeting of Whigs and Democrats. The Democratic speaker was a former resident of Albion, a somewhat flowery and sentimental individual apparently, and Lincoln, knowing him fairly well, anticipated that he would start off by affecting references to the home and friends of his youth, so dear to his heart and whom he was so glad to be able to see again, which was exactly what he did. But Lincoln was ready. In the day he had borrowed a copy of Byron's poems, and he began his reply by declaiming "grandiloquently," according to the historian of the episode:

> "He, the unhoped but forgotten Lord,
> The long self-exiled chieftain is restored;
> There be bright faces in the hall,
> Bowls on the board and banners on the wall.
> He comes at last in sudden loneliness,
> And whence they know not, why they need not guess,
> They more might marvel when the greetings o'er,
> Not that he came, but came not long before."

This Albion story comes from a man who was a school boy there at the time, and who had been so stirred by a little talk Lincoln had given to the school children in the morning before the meeting, that he ran away in the afternoon to hear him again. All of the fresh reminiscences of the circuit that come to us in these days have a similar source; that is, they are from men who were boys when they first saw Lincoln. Often

[309]

this was in the court room, and not unfrequently at a murder trial. The boys of Illinois seem to have had the same kind of curiosity about murder trials that young Abraham Lincoln did when he lived in Indiana, and like him they would walk any distance, even run the risk of a thrashing, in order to get into court to "see how a murderer looked," as one of them once told me. And if Mr. Lincoln was in the case, they invariably remembered something of his defense. I say defense, for the impression seems to be, though I do not know that it can be sustained by documents, that he was always the defender and never the prosecutor of a murderer. A boy who had once heard him speak rarely forgot him, and was very apt later to watch for a chance to edge his way into any group where he knew Mr. Lincoln was talking or telling stories.

In many of the towns which Lincoln frequented there was a favorite rendezvous, like Diller's drug store in Springfield, chosen because the proprietor had that combination of human qualities which particularly delighted Lincoln—humor, shrewdness, frankness, unspoiled naturalness; and here he was almost sure to be found in his leisure hours. There was such a drug store in Knoxville, kept by a Dr. Duncan, who had been a friend of Lincoln's in New Salem times—one of the men who had predicted that he would one day be President!—and here Lincoln always made his way when he was in the county for court or a political speech. Among the boys in that town was one Henry H. Miller, who, true to his genus, ran away from school one day in the middle 50's and wormed his way into a crowded room where a murder trial was going on. "And it was here," he wrote me a few years ago, "that I first saw Lincoln, the tallest man in that court room." Such was the impression that Mr. Lincoln made on Mr. Miller that he never missed a chance after that to get a look at him, to listen to him. He discovered his habit of dropping into Dr. Duncan's drug store, and was always on hand to listen to the talk that was sure to go on when he was there. "Here," said Mr. Miller, "I heard a story-telling match between Lincoln and one we called 'Uncle Bill' Sanburn. It was a very even match. Dr. Duncan would not render a decision."

One could go on almost interminably with these recollections. One of the finest groups concerns itself with his friendliness and helpfulness to young men, particularly to youngsters starting in the law. He would go out of his way to help the shy, the confused, the ignorant. I doubt if there is a county seat on his circuit that has not made its contribution to this Lincoln trait. Senator Joe Blackburn of Kentucky used to tell a story, less familiar than many of the kind. He was very young, and for the first time was appearing in the United States Circuit Court in Chicago. The opposing counsel was Isaac N. Arnold, one of the most distinguished men of the Chicago bar and a friend of Mr. Lincoln. When the case was reached Blackburn was so nervous that he became bewildered and made only a very feeble effort.

"I was about to sit down," his story goes, "and let the case go by default, as it were, when a tall, homely, loose-jointed man sitting in the bar, whom I had noticed as giving close attention to the case, arose and addressed the court in behalf of the position I had assumed in my feeble argument, making the points so clear that when he closed the court at once sustained my demurrer. I didn't know who my volunteer friend was, but Mr. Arnold got up and attempted to rebuke him for interfering in the matter, when I for the first time heard that he was Abraham Lincoln, of Springfield. Mr. Lincoln, in his good-natured reply to Mr. Arnold's strictures on his interference, said that he claimed the privilege of giving a young lawyer a boost when struggling with his first case, especially if he was pitted against an experienced practitioner. Of course I thanked him and departed from the court as proud as a young field marshal. I never saw Mr. Lincoln

[311]

again, and he died without ever knowing who the young, struggling lawyer was he had so kindly assisted and rescued from defeat in his maiden effort before a United States tribunal."

Mr. Lincoln's ingratiating personal qualities had much more local recognition than has been popularly supposed. Men were pleased to honor him when they had a chance. Here is a little case in point: a town named after him as far back as 1853, the county seat of Logan County. It came about in this way. In 1839 he had been chairman of the state committee on counties that had cut Sangamon County into four parts; to one of these parts he gave the name Logan, in honor of one of his friends in the Assembly, the father of Gen. John Logan. As years went on, Mr. Lincoln built up a considerable practice among the leading settlers of Logan County. Early in the 50's three of the most energetic of these settlers, finding that a railroad had been routed across their county, quietly used their inside information to get control of a considerable tract of land which they believed could be made the future county seat. They secured title to the tract and proceeded to incorporate the town, Mr. Lincoln being asked to draw up the necessary documents. When it came to a point in the negotiations where the new town had to be named, the leader of the group in the speculation suggested that it be called Lincoln. "You better not do that," Mr. Lincoln said, "for I never knew anything named Lincoln that amounted to much." But Lincoln it was. And Lincoln it is to-day.

Judge Lawrence B. Stringer, in his admirable and interesting history of Logan County, says that when the day came for the sale of lots in the new town, Mr. Lincoln was present, and going to a temporary street stand where eatables were sold, bought two watermelons, and, one under each arm, presented himself to the incorporators. "Now," he said, "we will christen the new town."

One of the few pieces of property that Mr. Lincoln ever owned was located in this town of Lincoln. He did not get it in the original deal, as I have heard it cynically intimated, but several years later. The owner of the lot had borrowed money from him, giving it as security. As he never was able to pay the debt, Mr. Lincoln finally found himself with the property on his hands. His only relation to it seems to have been paying the taxes.

If Lincoln had been a mediocre, indolent, half-hearted lawyer, his personal lovableness would never have carried him far in the thoroughly able group of judges and lawyers on the Illinois circuit which he traveled. They were of the type that give confidence and loyalty only when they respect the intellect and character of a man. There is a big bulk of testimony from the best of them, correcting the early impression that Mr. Lincoln, after all, didn't amount to much as a lawyer. Such studies as Frederick Trevor Hill's "Lincoln, the Lawyer," Charles W. Moore's "Abraham Lincoln, Lawyer," and Jesse Weik's "The Real Lincoln," all challenge this earlier notion. Lincoln was an able if unconventional lawyer, and as the years went on he steadily grew in his profession by conscientiously following the two rules he had laid down for law students—rules born of experience: "Work, work, work," and "Your own resolution to succeed is more important than any other one thing."

There are several of his cases and not a few incidents in connection with different cases which are rapidly becoming fixed traditions, and it is of course desirable that these traditions should be as nearly accurate as possible, even if they may not be very important. For example, it is sometimes quoted against Mr. Lincoln that he took a pass on the railroad. It is not so many years ago that the best of us did—if we could get one. We had not yet seen the inevitable abuse of the practice. In Lincoln's day there never was any question of the propriety, at least of the counsel of the road, having a pass. There has long been a letter in circulation asking for a renewal of a pass!

"Springfield, Feb. 13, 1858.
"R. P. Morgan, Supt. C. & R. R. R.

"Dear Sir—Says Sam to John, 'Here's you old rotten wheelbarrow. I've broke it usin' on it. I wished you would take it and mend it case I shall want to borrow it this afternoon.' Acting on this as a precedent, here's your old 'chalked hat.' I wish you would take it and send me a new one, case I shall want to use it the first of March.
"Yours truly,
"A. Lincoln."

Several years ago I had this letter submitted to Mr. Morgan, then living in Dwight, Illinois, and I have before me his answer. The letter, which he believed to have been destroyed in the Chicago fire, was written, he says, in the spirit of a friend enclosing an expiring annual pass for renewal, which Mr. Lincoln was entitled to as counsel for the company.

"I remember the letter quite distinctly, and for such use as you may desire to make of it, give it as I believe it to have been worded and dated:

" 'Springfield, Dec. —, 1855.
" 'Richard P. Morgan, Jr.,
"Supt. Chicago and M. Rd.

" 'Dear Sir—Here's your darned old wheelbarrow broke; father wants you to mend it so he can borrow it again this afternoon.
" 'Yours truly,
" 'A. Lincoln.'

"I think I am safe in saying that the terseness of Mr. Lincoln's style will be better recognized by his personal friends in my recollection of the letter than in the publication you sent me.

[314]

"I am certain of three things:

"1st. That the letter was written and that it was received by me.

"2nd. That my wording of the letter as stated is substantially correct.

"3rd. That the date of the letter was in 1855 or 1856, most probably in 1855."

In spite of this letter to me, Mr. Morgan later went back to the original version quoted above. This was in an address that he gave at Pontiac on February 12, 1909. With the exception of the change in date, he quotes the form of the letter which he wrote me in 1895 he believed incorrect. He does not say that in the interval he had found the original, and I have been unable to get into communication with any one who could explain to me why he changed his mind.

There is no one of Mr. Lincoln's law cases which seems to me to show more clearly the kind of man he was or to illustrate better his lifelong habit of recognizing superiority when he met it, and trying to pull himself up to it, than that in which he was employed as counsel of Manny & Co., a firm of Rockford, Illinois, manufacturers of reaping machines, which had been sued early in the 50's by Cyrus H. McCormick for an infringement of patents. The best of counsel was employed by the Mannys. The greatest patent lawyer of his day, P. H. Watson, of Philadelphia, had charge of the case, and he had as assistant on the mechanical side a young lawyer, afterwards widely known, George Harding. Edwin M. Stanton was the leading forensic counsel.

Mr. Lincoln's coming into the case was due to the admiration and confidence of a young partner in Manny & Co., Mr. Ralph Emerson, of Rockford, who as a law student had been thrown into Lincoln's company. He wanted him because he believed in him. Mr. Lincoln seems to have been pleased and proud that he was retained; but it is doubtful

[315]

if he ever had had in his professional life as humiliating an experience. Two letters recently published in Gilbert Tracy's collection show that although he had met Mr. Watson in Illinois and discussed the case with him, Watson had considered him so negligible a quantity that he had not taken the trouble to send him copies of the printed documents as he had promised, and he evidently went to the trial, held in Cincinnati in September of 1855, without having heard from his principal. Nevertheless he had prepared his brief and expected to have a chance to argue the case. The story that he was not allowed to make his argument because of Mr. Stanton's contempt for his appearance is certainly, I think, exaggerated, if not entirely mistaken. It was for Mr. Watson not Mr. Stanton to decide who should make what was called the "forensic argument"; and when it was decided that there was to be but one speech of that nature, he properly enough chose Mr. Stanton in preference to Mr. Lincoln. The circumstances of this decision were such that Lincoln felt he had not been fairly treated. Moreover, there is no question that he was socially snubbed from first to last by his fellow counsel. Many years ago I discussed the case fully with Mr. Harding, the only one on either side then living, and published an account written by him. But there was a side light in his talk not in the published story. It is something of a confession:

"Twice in my life," he told me, "I have turned my back on men because of their appearance, and both of these men later became Presidents of the United States. The first was in Cincinnati in 1855, when I deliberately turned my back on Abraham Lincoln because he looked queer and provincial and held his umbrella in a way of which I did not approve. The second was at a little town in western New York State, where the hotel accommodations were crowded and I was asked to share my room with a strange lawyer, and refused because he was dusty and hot from travel. His name, I learned, was

Grover Cleveland. I think I have finally learned that you cannot always judge a man by his haberdashery and tailoring."

The big thing about Lincoln in this trial was that, disappointed bitterly as he was, neglected and possibly insulted as he felt himself, when the trial was thoroughly launched, and he realized that it was a contest between men of the highest technical knowledge, as well as the finest legal training and experience, he became utterly absorbed in the exhibit. His intellectual delight in the quality of the thing wiped out all personal feeling. It became a great professional experience. Emerson reports him as saying, as they walked the street after the close of the case, "Emerson, I am going home to study law. These big fellows are coming West soon, and I am going to be ready for them." He was ready a few years later to meet the biggest of them all, and to have him acknowledge him as his rightful master, though it was not exactly in the field he had expected that he met Edwin M. Stanton.

Without a doubt the law case which to-day has the strongest hold on most Lincoln readers and pilgrims is that in which Mr. Lincoln defended Duff Armstrong, the son of his old Salem friends, Jack and Hannah Armstrong, from the charge of killing a companion in a drunken brawl. In the first place, it has the fascination of being a murder case, something in which youth and natural human beings never lose interest; then the very incongruity of the setting—a camp meeting—catches the imagination. And yet, how typical it was! Orthodox Christians of Illinois had not learned in those days as later to protect their respectability from the contact of the wicked. The wicked formed a disreputable fringe around every camp meeting—drinking and quarreling and carousing. It was in such a fringe that the crime with which Duff Armstrong was charged was committed.

[317]

The case had the further appeal of sentiment. Here was one of Illinois' greatest lawyers and its second greatest man, who soon was to contest the Senatorship with her first greatest man, Senator Stephen A. Douglas, dropping important legal and political duties to come, at his own expense, to defend the wayward son of two simple, unimportant people who had been his friends when he was poor and unknown. It was a great man fighting to save a mother's tears.

This was enough to make it unforgettable. And on top of this came the charge that Mr. Lincoln saved Duff Armstrong from hanging by a trick. For years the case has been tossed back and forth between those who believe this true and those who deny it. There have been those who justified the trick, since it was successful; there have been those who, believing or half believing, have justified the trick because it saved a man's life; and there have been those, friendly and unfriendly to Mr. Lincoln, who decried it because it was a trick and proved him not always the honest man he was called.

The alleged deception came at a point in the trial when the charge against Duff Armstrong depended upon the truthfulness of the prosecution's chief witness, who had sworn he saw Duff strike the fatal blow.

"It was night, how could you see?"

And his answer had been that it was as light as day, the moon being full and about where the sun is at ten o'clock in the morning.

Mr. Lincoln, cross-examining the witness with gentleness, brought out repeatedly this point of the hour and the full light, until it was impressed upon the jury as the real crux of the case. And then at the proper moment he introduced an almanac—an almanac that showed that the moon at the hour of the murder, close to eleven o'clock, was in a position where, so he declared, it would not have given a light by which the witness could have seen the blow struck. The evidence of the almanac upset the testimony and in the end Duff was discharged.

Then came the accusation that to prove his point, Mr. Lincoln, discovering that the almanac of 1857 did not give him what he wanted, had caused the almanac of 1853, which did, to be falsified, the 3 changed to a 7 throughout. So far as I know the treated almanac was never put in evidence until thirty years after the trial. In 1888 an individual who claimed to have been at the trial said that he had discovered the very book, showing, under the glass, the obvious change of the figure. The story went the rounds, and the almanac finally found its way into the famous Lincoln collection of Gunther, the Chicago candy man. The August calendar of the falsified almanac sustained Lincoln. According to it, it is obvious that there was no moonshine at the time that the murder was committed that would enable any witness to see a blow.

But how about the true almanac of 1857? Would that be sufficient for Mr. Lincoln's purpose? Would it discredit the witness' contention that the moon was about where the sun was at ten o'clock in the morning? The almanac he used was the popular "Christian Family Almanac for 1857," a copy of which is on file in the New York Public Library. This shows that on August 29, 1857, the date of the murder, the moon was two days past the first quarter and set at three minutes before midnight, 11:57. That is, the moon at the hour of the murder was about an hour above the horizon, which is a good ways from where the summer sun is at ten o'clock a. m.

Then the question becomes, How much light would the moon, an hour above the horizon, give in the particular grove where Duff was said to have killed his comrade? One can hardly believe that it would have been enough to have seen distinctly the fatal act. I have always had a desire to settle this question by visiting the grove where the murder took place, if it still exists; or, if not, one near-by, about eleven o'clock on a night when the moon is to set at three minutes before midnight or thereabouts; but I have never had the opportunity, and I leave it to the Boy Scouts who, for a number of years now, have been making pilgrimages to the Armstrong home to carry out this particular piece of investigation. I am inclined to think that in a grove at that hour, and in that locality, and under these moon conditions, they could see but little. The point of which is that it was not necessary for Mr. Lincoln to forge an almanac in order to free his old friends' son, even if he had been a man given to trickery. It was not "like him" to do it. Moreover, he was certainly clever enough to understand that such a trick would be sooner or later detected and bring upon him the charge, which he of all others disliked, that he had done an unfair thing.

One could go on, far beyond the limits of this book, with these stories of Lincoln's relations to his fellows—of his wit, his ability, his unadulterated human nature—the kind of thing which stamped him as different from the ordinary man— more naturally kind, more naturally shrewd, less pretentious, less technical. It was the demonstration of the kind of person he was going on year in and year out, as he traveled the circuit, that finally made him the most generally loved and trusted man in Illinois. There is no question that the place that he held in the esteem and affection of men of superior as well as of humble parts was a powerful factor in finally carrying him into the Presidency. Still, that could never have happened if it had not been for what he did on the great question of the day from 1854 on.

# XXV

## LINCOLN BOLTS HIS PARTY

THE years of deep depression following Abraham Lincoln's first term in Congress were not only years of hard work at his profession. They were likewise years of profound reflection on the question of slavery extension. As a member of the Thirtieth Congress he had heard the tremendous discussion between those who insisted all new territory acquired by the country must be free, and those who insisted that since the South had shared in the cost of acquirement it was just she should have at least her half for slaves. The debate had gone on, finally heading in the compromises of 1850.

These compromises were not what Lincoln had hoped for —what forty times at least he claimed he had voted must be. To be sure, California was free, but it was left to the future citizens of New Mexico and Utah to decide whether or no they preferred freedom to slavery. He did not like the ferocious Fugitive Slave Bill. Returning runaway slaves he called "a dirty, disagreeable job," that as a rule "slaveholders would not perform for one another," but it was a law for which the South had paid with the abolition of the slave trade in the District of Columbia, and it must be obeyed.

It was not the compromises that made him sober, it was their failure to settle the matter. They were supposed to be "final." Why should they not be? Every inch of territory the United States owned was now under an agreement

[321]

as solemn as men could make. Why should there not be peace?

The chief immediate reason was that the North would not obey the Fugitive Slave Law—rejoiced in evading it. Nor would it keep silent about it. Among the papers for which Lincoln & Herndon subscribed was The National Era. Not long after both Whigs and Democrats had voted the compromises of 1850 a "finality" a woman began a serial in its pages—"Uncle Tom's Cabin"—a story of the workings of the hated law. With every instalment the wrath of the North rose higher and hotter—and with the agitation rose the wrath of the South.

Lincoln saw with growing alarm that out of the very measures intended to settle forever the conflict two dangerous classes were forming and expanding—in the South a group who, for the sake of perpetuating slavery, were beginning to assail and ridicule what he called "the white man's charter of freedom, the declaration that all men are created free and equal"; and in the North a group who, "rather than that slavery should continue a single hour, would shatter into fragments the union of these States, tear to tatters its now venerated Constitution, and even burn the last copy of the Bible."

Dangerous business, but so long as the settlements held, he for one held to his life-long belief that slavery confined must ultimately die.

And then there happened the one thing which could have made him change his mind as to the only practical and peaceful way of putting an end to it. In May, 1854, the Missouri Compromise, which he had always regarded as the most sacred of them all, forbidding slavery in any territory north of 36 deg. 30 min., was repealed; and the doctrine of "Squatter Sovereignty" installed. It was pulling his house down about his ears—shattering the one possible way, as he saw it, for the extinction of slavery.

What was the base of his belief that slavery quarantined must become extinct? Lincoln was counting on the nature of the human heart to bring about the end of slavery. He was convinced that the mass of mankind considered it a great moral wrong, that this feeling was "not evanescent but eternal." The men of the South in the past had shared this view. Had they not joined the North in ending the slave trade? Had they not agreed to the ordinance of 1787? Was it not a slave holder, Henry Clay, who had framed the Missouri Compromise? Had they not already actually freed nearly a half million of their negroes? Was it not true that Southerners were constantly coming North and becoming "tip-top" Abolitionists? Why, Illinois herself had been "brought in free" by the work of a former slave owner, Governor Coles! Keep slavery shut in and ultimately the human sympathies of the South, her sense of the wrong of slavery, would conquer.

But the crux of his faith was quarantine. And the quarantine was lifted. It must be restored; and he stiffened for the fight.

I find not a few people who believe that Lincoln's knowledge and feeling about slavery dates from the repeal of the Missouri Compromise, that up to this time he had given no thought to the subject, had no strong convictions upon it. Let such people study the speech with which he began his war on the Nebraska Bill, as the repeal now popularly came to be called. The author and backer of that bill, Senator Stephen A. Douglas, had come on to Illinois soon after it had been signed by the President to make peace with an outraged constituency. Lincoln was selected by general consent as the most fit to meet him. Their first encounter came early in

October, 1854, at the State Fair in Springfield, and a few days later at Peoria they repeated their debate. For vigor, compactness, logic, solid information one would have to go far to find the equal of this first speech of Lincoln's against the extension of slavery. It is packed with ideas, saturated with familiarity with the history and development of the thing. It is the kind of expression that comes only from long living with a subject. It demonstrates beyond question, it seems to me, that Lincoln from his boyhood had been, both consciously and unconsciously, observing and turning over the exhibits of what he regarded as a tremendous national wrong.

This speech of October, 1854, has in it, too, the seeds of all the arguments which he was afterwards to develop in the fight of which this was the first round. Here you have the first expression of that idea which afterwards was to play so large a part in his argument, that the repeal meant nothing else than the spread of slavery "over every part of the wide world where men could be found inclined to take it." Here, too, you find that he had no illusions about the terrible possibilities of standing out against the repeal. It meant "blows and bloodshed." "Could there be a more apt invention," he cried, "to bring about collision and violence on the slavery question than this Nebraska project is? If they had literally formed a ring and placed champions within to fight out the controversy, the fight could not be more likely to come off than it is." He saw more. Not only "blows and bloodshed," but that the first drop of blood shed might be the real death knell of the Union!

Nothing shows better how profound was his feeling on the subject than the way in which he immediately thrust aside all thought of party, except as it might serve the question. He was something more than a Whig now. The time had come when he would go with anybody that went right—with

Owen Lovejoy, the Abolitionist; with Lyman Trumbull, the Democrat; with his highly conservative Whig friend, O. W. Browning.

And what a great politician he was at the moment! How quickly he turned every effort to pulling all these scattered forces together! Rebuke them, was his cry. Show them they cannot do this kind of thing, that we will fight. We will get into office wherever we can the man that is against this thing, no matter what his party. He gave the most convincing evidence of his sincerity in this counsel when, in November, in the contest for the United States Senatorship—he had entered with a large following—rather than let the office go to a candidate whose anti-Nebraska sentiment he mistrusted (and who also had been intriguing in an underhanded way against him) he threw his own following to Lyman Trumbull, a Democrat, but an out-and-out anti-Nebraska Democrat.

I have always liked the way Lincoln reported this fight in the Legislature for the Senatorship in the fall of 1854 to his friend Washburne. "I could have headed off every combination and been elected had it not been for Matteson's" (his Whig rival) "double game, and his defeat now gives me more pleasure than my own gives me pain."

Here for the first time in several years we have something like the old buoyant political Lincoln. The Nebraska men were more disturbed by Trumbull's election than they would have been by his. ". . . hated it worse than anything that could have happened," he wrote Washburne. "It is a great consolation to see them worse whipped than I am." Here is a man who can keep his sense of humor in a tremendous moral fight!

He was in no way disturbed by the flocking of extremists to the anti-Nebraska crowd. When his anxious Whig friends said: "They are going to call us Abolitionists," he told them

[325]

they were silly, that the only thing at stake now was not what you were called but whether you were fighting the repeal. Douglas gibed him unmercifully for his willingness to attack wherever he saw a chance to gain an inch. He was not disturbed. "Remember," he replied, "you took us by surprise. We were thunderstruck, stunned, reeled and fell in utter confusion, but we rose, each fighter grasping whatever he could first reach—a scythe, a pitchfork, chopping ax or butcher's cleaver. We struck in the direction of the sound, and we are rapidly closing in on you. You must not think to divert us from our purpose by showing us that our apparel, our dress, our weapons are not entirely perfect and uniform."

Of course he was headed direct for a new party, that party which was slowly forming itself out of the bolting fragments of every other party and which was collecting to itself every variety of extremist and theorist scattered about the land. Twenty-five years ago I had the satisfaction of knowing in Illinois a number of the men who in the middle 50's had been leaders in gathering up these fragments. Among them was Paul Selby, in 1854 the editor of a paper in Jacksonville. Mr. Selby was a careful, scholarly, conservative person in 1896, but in 1854 you could not move fast enough for him. He was one of a few young men eager to bring together all of the righteous indignation which had been showing itself in spontaneous mass meetings in Illinois. It seemed to this group that a mass meeting at the State Fair of 1854 might crystallize the excitement. So it was called, but it had anything but a friendly reception at the capital. They would not allow them to hold a meeting in the State House as they had expected to do, and there was not a printing office in the town, Mr. Selby told me, that would set up their handbills, so he was obliged to print them himself in a job shop. It was during the session of this band of radicals that Lincoln first replied to Douglas. They took a recess to hear him. When they came back they appointed a state central committee and put Lincoln on it, as a representative of Sangamon. He refused to serve. He still had hopes of the Whigs, Mr. Selby told me, with a pitying little smile. And he did. But as the months went on the hopelessness of getting a fighting body from either of the old parties was more and more clearly demonstrated. The little anti-Nebraska nucleus that had been formed at Springfield and that Lincoln had refused to commit himself to grew. And how it was fed!

All through these months there were trailing across Illinois and down the Ohio groups of Eastern Abolitionists and Free Soilers, men, women and children, crusaders, determined that Squatter Sovereignty, cost what it might in hardship, should result in the freedom of Kansas. And Kansas' neighbor, Missouri, regarding these colonists as a direct attack on its prosperity and principles, had set up a retaliatory movement. The "blows and bloodshed" that Mr. Lincoln had prophesied at the State Fair in 1854 were beginning. The fighting blood of Illinois rose with the suffering in Kansas.

Early in 1856 Paul Selby called a second convention, this time of anti-Nebraska editors. They met in Decatur, and Lincoln found it convenient to be in town. He took no part in the day's public meetings, but when his help on the resolutions to be adopted was asked he gave it. He accepted an invitation for the banquet which was to be held in the evening, and spoke, thus openly going over to the bolters. He felt, he said, a sort of an interloper, and was reminded of an incident of a man not possessed of features the ladies would call handsome, who while riding through the woods met an equestrienne. (Mr. Lincoln hardly used that word. It certainly was put in his mouth by the editor who later told the story, Mr. B. F. Shaw of the Dixon Telegraph!) He reined his horse to one side of the bridle path and stopped, waiting for her to pass. She also checked her horse to a stop, and after looking him over in a curious sort of way finally broke out with:

"Well, for the land's sake, you are the homeliest man I ever saw."
"Yes, ma'am, but I cannot help that."
"No, I suppose not, but you might stay at home."

Mr. Lincoln suggested to the editors that he might have stayed at home on this occasion.

A state convention of anti-Nebraska forces was called for May 29, 1856, at Bloomington, and Lincoln this time accepted his appointment as a delegate from Sangamon. He was on hand for the meeting. That it was a great convention there is no doubt. One of the reports of a Chicago correspondent began with this paragraph:

"May 29, 9 a. m. The train arrived here an hour ago. The porches, halls and doorways of the Pike House are crowded with a dense mass of delegates. Men are here from all parts of the State. Egypt is in counsel with us. It is a spontaneous outpouring of the people."

All that followed at the Bloomington convention of 1856 justifies this correspondent's enthusiastic first paragraph. They organized. Men spoke. The thing went as well as a thing of that sort possibly could. It was left to Lincoln to make the speech which really crystallized the elements of the new party beyond any possibility of crumbling. The "lost speech" they have always called what he said that day—lost because under the emotion and sweep of it no reporter kept his head sufficiently to take a note.

# LINCOLN BOLTS HIS PARTY

Back in the 90's, when working on a Life of Lincoln in Illinois, one of my most tantalizing experiences was meeting men who had been present at this convention and who proceeded to give me glowing versions of this miraculous legendary speech. There was Thomas J. Henderson of Princeton, Joseph Medill and George Schneider of Chicago, J. B. Cunningham of Urbana, Judge Scott of Bloomington. The spell was still on them, but as for telling me what Lincoln said, there was not a man that could give me any idea. I have before me the yellowed notes made in Bloomington after a talk with Judge Scott. "Unless one heard that speech he cannot know what eloquence is," he had told me—and this from a man of controlled expression.

It was a challenge to one gathering up fragments to recreate an episode, and I went from place to place and man to man, trying from talk and newspaper files to collect enough little pieces to form at least the outline of a speech. It was while at this work I learned that Henry C. Whitney, a young lawyer who had been with Mr. Lincoln at Danville in the days before the convention, who had gone to Bloomington with him and who had heard the speech, was said to have made and preserved notes. Mr. Whitney was still living, a half invalid, at Beachmont, Massachusetts. And there I made my way, and found it to be a fact that he alone, of all that body gathered in the hall at Bloomington, had sufficiently kept his head to set down something of what Mr. Lincoln had said.

When I urged Mr. Whitney, in the name of McClure's Magazine, to write out his notes, he was reluctant. They were too imperfect, he said, and he showed me the yellowed sheets with their faded bits of writing—imperfect indeed, but still voluminous. I think he had long wanted to try to make something out of these savings but feared the result. When he finally yielded to my urging, he did his work with the utmost care, though with many misgivings. He knew well enough that whatever he produced would be severely criticized, and he went over and over his notes, carefully comparing them all with printed sources. When his work was finished he made no other claim for it than that it was the best he could do, after so long a time, with the material that he had.

The result seemed to the editors of McClure's Magazine worth publishing, but before this was done it was submitted to a number of the men with whom I had talked in Illinois. What did they think of it? Was it a fair report? The reaction was varied. Mr. Henderson thought little of it. "It has been so universally regarded as a masterly speech and the effect of it upon the convention was so wonderful," he wrote, "that I fear no report of it can be given to the public that would do justice to Mr. Lincoln or give a proper conception of the speech and of its remarkable power and eloquence."

There were others that felt like Mr. Henderson. McLean County, Illinois, held a commemoration of the Bloomington speech in 1900, and the gist of opinion there was so much against Mr. Whitney's version that when the County Historical Society published its report of the exercises it took pains to speak of Mr. Whitney's "alleged notes," and to add: "In this community, where many are now living who heard the great speech and where Mr. Lincoln was so well known and loved, all of his friends consider the speech still 'lost.' "

That may be true, but there were at least two persons, friends of Mr. Lincoln, and of importance in the movement, at the Bloomington convention, that felt differently in 1896. Among those to whom the magazine submitted the manuscript of Mr. Whitney's report before publishing it was

Mr. J. B. Cunningham of Urbana, whose honesty and fitness to judge of the speech I take it, no one, even in the McLean County Historical Society, would question. "After forty years," Mr. Cunningham writes, "I recognize very much in the utterances, manner and spirit of the speech, especially in the moderation which he counselled."

Mr. Whitney's report made the strongest impression on Mr. Joseph Medill, the editor of the Chicago Tribune. It stirred him to a spirited informal account of the convention and of Mr. Lincoln's part in it. It proves that at least one astute and qualified observer did not sniff at the Whitney report or question his good faith. Mr. Medill's letter also gives probably the best picture of the convention we have from an actual delegate.

"You invited my attention recently to H. C. Whitney's report of the great radical 'anti-Nebraska' speech of Mr. Lincoln, delivered in Bloomington May 29, 1856, before the first Republican State Convention of Illinois; and as I was present as a delegate and heard it you ask me to state how accurately, according to my best recollection, is it reproduced in his report.

"I have carefully and reflectively read it, and taking into account that Mr. Whitney did not take down the speech stenographically, but only took notes and afterwards wrote them out in full, he has reproduced with remarkable accuracy what Mr. Lincoln said, largely in his identical language and partly in synonymous terms. The report is close enough in thought and word to recall the wonderful speech delivered forty years ago with vivid freshness. No one was expecting a great speech at the time. We all knew that he could say something worthy of the occasion, but nobody anticipated such a Demosthenean outburst of oratory. There was great political excitement at the time in Illinois and all over the old

[331]

North West growing out of the efforts of the South to introduce slavery into Kansas and Nebraska. The free soil men
were highly wrought up in opposition, and Mr. Lincoln par-
took of their feelings.

"I am unable to point out those sentences and parts of the
reported speech which vary most in phraseology from the
precise language he used, because there is an approximation
of his words in every part of it. The ideas uttered are all
there. The sequence of argument is accurately given. The
invectives hurled at pro-slavery aggression are not exaggerated
in the report of the speech. Some portions of the argument
citing pro-slavery aggressions seem rather more elaborate than
he delivered; but he was speaking under a high degree of
excitement and the convention was in a responsive mood, and
it is impossible to be certain about it. The least that can be
said is that the Whitney report not being shorthand is yet
a remarkably good one and is the only one in existence that
reproduces the speech.

"During all the preceding year the public mind of the
West had been lashed into a high state of commotion over the
repeal of the Missouri Compromise the year before, which had
excluded the introduction of slavery into all territory north
of 36.30 degrees. Taking advantage of the repeal the slaveholders of Missouri and other slave states, aided by the Administration of Franklin Pierce, were striving to convert
Kansas and Nebraska into slave states. This bad work was
carried on actively in the spring of 1856. Many houses of
the free state men of the new City of Lawrence, including
their hotel, were burned. Printing offices were destroyed;
store goods were carried off; horses and cattle were stolen;
sharp fights were taking place; men were being killed, and
civil war was raging in 'bleeding Kansas.' In Washington,
Brooks of South Carolina entered the Senate chamber and

nearly clubbed to death Senator Sumner of Massachusetts."
(Mr. Medill might have added here that Paul Selby, who
had been working in Illinois for two years to secure this
convention, had, a few days before, been so badly beaten by
his political opponents in Jacksonville that he was at home
in bed instead of on the floor of Major's Hall in Bloomington.) "Judge Trumbull offered a resolution in the Senate
to prevent civil war in Kansas.

"While this state of things was going on the first State
Republican Convention ever held in Illinois, assembled in
Bloomington, May 29, 1856. It was composed of Abolitionists, Free Soil Whigs and 'Anti-Nebraska' Democrats. Owen
Lovejoy embodied the first named, Abraham Lincoln and
John M. Palmer the second and third elements. The whole
united made the new Republican party which has dominated
the State ever since, though Palmer, now Senator, returned
to the Democratic party, taking Trumbull with him, several
years ago.

"At this Bloomington Republican convention delegates
were appointed who voted to nominate Fremont for President.
Abraham Lincoln was placed at the head of the State electoral
ticket, and Colonel Bissell (of the Mexican War) was nominated for Governor, and free soil resolutions were passed.
Mr. John M. Palmer presided and made a stirring free soil
speech. Mr. Lincoln, who was a delegate, counselled every
step that was taken in his quiet, persuasive way. A sharp
dispute broke out in the platform committee between the
radicals, led by the Abolitionist Owen Lovejoy (afterwards
M. C.), and O. H. Browning (afterwards Senator and Secretary of Interior) leading the conservatives. Lincoln acted
as a peacemaker and counsellor. He advised the committee
to indorse 'the Declaration of Independence and the rights of
man, and to declare that in accordance with the opinions and

practices of the great statesmen of all parties for the past sixty years, Congress possessed full constitutional power to prohibit slavery in all territories and that such power should be exerted to prevent such extension,' which was done. Mr. Browning (Conservative) was allowed to add some high-sounding platitudes to the platform. He made the opening speech in the convention and delivered it in a courtly manner and orotund voice, advising great moderation, and invoking the convention 'to ever remember that slavery itself was one of the compromises of the Constitution and was sacredly protected by the Supreme Law.' He was followed by the radical, Owen Lovejoy, in a terrific declamation against slavery and all its works.

"Mr. Emery, a 'Free State' man, just from 'bleeding Kansas,' told of the 'border ruffian' raids from Missouri upon the Free State settlers in Kansas; the burnings, robberies and murders they were then committing, and asked for help to repeal them.

"When he finished Lincoln was vociferously called for from all parts of Major's large hall. He came forward and took the platform beside the presiding officer. At first his voice was shrill and hesitating. There was a curious introspective look in his eyes, which lasted for a few moments. Then his voice began to move steadily and smoothly forward. And the modulations were under perfect control from thenceforward to the finish. He warmed up as he went on and spoke more rapidly; he looked a foot taller as he straightened himself to his full height and his eyes flashed fire; his countenance became wrapped in intense emotion; he rushed along like a thunderstorm. He prophesied war as the outcome of these aggressions and poured forth hot denunciations upon the slave power. The convention was kept in an uproar applauding and cheering and stamping; and this reacted on the speaker and gave him a tongue of fire. The thrilling scene in that old Bloomington hall forty years ago arises in my mind as vividly as the day after its enactment.

"There stood Lincoln in the forefront, erect, tall and majestic in appearance, hurling thunderbolts at the foes of freedom, while the great convention roared its indorsement! I never witnessed such a scene before or since. As he described the aims and aggressions of the unappeasable slaveholders and the servility of their Northern allies as illustrated by the perfidious repeal of the Missouri Compromise two years previously, and their grasping after the rich prairies of Kansas and Nebraska to blight them with slavery and to deprive free labor of this rich inheritance, and exhorted the friends of freedom to resist them to the death—the convention went fairly wild. It paralleled or exceeded the scene in the revolutionary Virginia convention of eighty-one years before when Patrick Henry invoked death if liberty could not be preserved, and saying: 'After all we must fight.' Strange, too, that this same man received death a few years afterwards while conferring freedom on the slave race and preserving the American Union from dismemberment.

"While Mr. Lincoln did not write out even a memorandum of his Bloomington speech beforehand neither was it extemporary. He intended days before to make it, and coined it over in his mind in outline and gathered his facts and arranged his arguments in regular order and trusted to the inspiration of the occasion to furnish him the diction with which to clothe the skeleton of his great oration. It is difficult to name any speech by another orator delivered on the same subject about that time or subsequently that equaled it— not excepting those made by Sumner, Seward or Chase in strength of argument or dramatic power.

"It was my journalistic duty, though a delegate to the

convention, to make a 'long-hand' report of the speeches delivered for The Chicago Tribune. I did make a few paragraphs of report of what Lincoln said in the first 8 or 10 minutes, but I became so absorbed in his magnetic oratory that I forgot myself and ceased to take notes; and joined with the convention in cheering and stamping and clapping to the end of his speech.

"I well remember that after Lincoln had sat down and calm had succeeded the tempest, I waked out of a sort of hypnotic trance, and then thought of my report for The Tribune. There was nothing written but an abbreviated introduction.

"It was some sort of satisfaction to find that I had not been 'scooped,' as all the newspaper men present had been equally carried away by the excitement caused by the wonderful oration and had made no report or sketch of the speech.

"It was fortunate, however, that a cool-nerved young lawyer and ardent friend of Lincoln's who was present, with nimble fingers took down so much of the exact words as they fell from the great orator's lips that he was afterwards able to reproduce the speech almost identically as it was uttered, and has thus saved it to posterity.

"Mr. Lincoln was strongly urged by party friends to write out his speech to be used as a campaign document for the Fremont Presidential contest of that year; but he declared that 'it would be impossible for him to recall the language he used on that occasion, as he had spoken under some excitement.'

"My belief is, that after Mr. Lincoln cooled down he was rather pleased that his speech had not been reported, as it was too radical in expression on the slavery question for the digestion of Central and Southern Illinois at that time, and that he preferred to let it stand as a remembrance in the minds of his audience. But be that as it may, the effect of it was such on his hearers that he bounded to the leadership of the new Republican party of Illinois, and no man afterwards ever thought of disputing that position with him. On that occasion he planted the seed which germinated into a Presidential candidacy and that gave him the nomination over Seward at the Chicago convention of 1860, which placed him in the Presidential chair, there to complete his predestined work of destroying slavery and making freedom universal, but yielding his life as a sacrifice for the glorious deeds."

Mr. Medill is quite right in saying that the speech was too radical for the digestion of many parts of Illinois. Lincoln and Billy Herndon—and nobody rejoiced as Herndon did in what Lincoln had done—went back to Springfield, and, under the enthusiasm of the Bloomington success, called a ratification meeting at the court house. Three persons attended—Lincoln, Herndon and one whom Herndon describes in telling the story as "a courageous man named John Pain." Lincoln spoke. The meeting was larger, he said, than he "knew it would be"! He knew he and his partner would attend, he was not sure any one else would, and yet another man had been brave enough to come out. "While all seems dead," he exhorted Billy Herndon and John Pain, "the age itself is not dead. Be hopeful, and now let us adjourn and appeal to the people."

It was not only in Springfield so cold a shoulder was turned to him that he had need of all the faith within him to carry him through. He went to Shelbyville, a town between Springfield and Vandalia, to debate with his friend, Anthony Thornton. The county and the town were almost solidly against him. "I take some comfort," he told his audience, "from the fact that there are but sixteen Republicans in Shelby County, and therefore, however poorly I

[337]

may defend my cause, I can hardly harm it if I do it no good." But what he did by that one speech—the only Republican speech made in the county during the campaign of 1856—was to increase the sixteen Republicans to something over one hundred and fifty.

He went to Petersburg in October. Mr. Henry Rankin tells in his "Recollections" of the anger there. As Lincoln mounted the platform to present Fremont hurrahs for Buchanan filled the air. For a time it looked as if the meeting would be broken up. "No d—d Abolition speeches could be made in Menard County this campaign," the crowd declared. For a half hour cat-calls, whistles, tin horns filled the air, and through it all Lincoln stood with folded arms, surveying the scene. When the tumult grew less he began to talk. Little by little his hearers grew silent. In less than half an hour after he got his first hearing he was master, and for more than two hours he held the mastery. He enjoyed both the struggle and the conquest. "I never felt so full of just what a crowd ought to hear," Mr. Rankin heard him tell Herndon, "and never was a crowd more competent, from the common sense standpoint, than the Menard County one was to hear a fair and candid statement of facts, if I could just get them still for half an hour as an entering wedge. This I did, and I gave them my best. After I was well under way it was the most enjoyable of all the speeches I made through the entire campaign. The returns show I did a poor day's business down there for the State Committee so far as votes count. But I dropped some things among voters that day in Menard that will stay until the next election. I soaked that crowd full of political facts they can't get away from."

And so it went. I have heard a story of a Fremont procession in this campaign in which Mr. Lincoln and one fiery Abolitionist and his son were the only marchers. But two years later, in that same town, a thousand people marched behind him. It was they that had changed, not he.

Lincoln had no illusions about the nature of the conflict to which he had committed himself. It would be long. It might outlive him and the men of the Bloomington convention. It might mean war—would if there was an attempt at disunion. But he viewed the future with a resolution which seems never to have been shaken, though there is no doubt his soul was often torn with agony at the thought of the road to be traveled—its hates, its bitterness, its failures, its deceptions.

He knew what he was about, however, and was prepared to go where the road led.

People must be made to see what was at stake, that it was the very heart of the country at which the repeal struck. If he could help them to see that—he asked nothing more for himself.

At the end of the campaign which the Bloomington convention inaugurated, a campaign in which the new party, by this time frankly calling itself Republican, though it was only anti-Nebraska at the start—had wonderful success in Illinois, electing a governor and actually giving Frémont, the Presidential candidate nearly 100,000 votes—he summed up at a Republican banquet in Chicago his profound conviction that in the long run the thing they were after could be done.

'Public opinion on any subject,' he said in substance, "has always a central idea. That central idea in our political opinion is the equality of men. The late Presidential election was a struggle to discard that central idea and to substitute for it the opposite idea that slavery is right in the abstract. Let us reinaugurate the good old central idea. We can do it. The human heart is with us. God is with us.'

[339]

That is where he had come after the two years' fight against the repeal of the Missouri Compromise. The character of the fight he was making, his resolution and absorption in it, are the more interesting because at this very time he was carrying on the most important law work that he had ever had. As a matter of fact, all of Lincoln's big law cases were coincident with his fight against the extension of slavery.

# XXVI

## EDUCATING ILLINOIS

THESE United States have so far produced no finer model for would-be politicians than Abraham Lincoln. But they must be politicians more interested in upsetting wrong and strengthening decency and right than in perpetuating a party or in securing places for themselves. Lincoln is a hopeless model for the dyed-in-the-wool partisan, and his methods would keep a man out of office as often as they would put him in.

These years that we are now following, from 1850 to 1860, have several political "high spots," and the inclination has always been to see nothing in them but these spots—moments when Lincoln emerged from what we have regarded as obscurity and delivered a prophetic and soul-stirring message and then dropped out of sight. Now, the high spots are very high indeed, but heights were never reached by more persistent climbing, every step of which was carefully and considerately placed.

There was the first period of this decade, marked by the speech he made in 1854 on the Repeal of the Missouri Compromise—a speech at once profound and prophetic, which was the crystallization of years of conscious and unconscious reflection and study of the question of the extinction of slavery, of the wrong of which he had never had any doubts.

Then followed two years of experiment—the search of himself and those who felt as he did about the Repeal and had a need of something more than protest—to fuse the

[341]

revolting elements into a practical working unit. It ended
in his bolting the Whigs and joining the anti-Nebraska or
Republican party. His second "high spot" came at the first
formal convention of the new enterprise, in the speech which
has become one of Illinois' pet traditions—the "Lost Speech"
of May 29, 1856. It was a speech which, like that of 1854,
was born of living with the subject.

In this interval between 1854 and 1856, Lincoln gave
probably half of his time to political work—unpaid, of course
—a tremendous sacrifice. It no doubt caused domestic irritation, for it kept him poor, and yet he seems not to have
hesitated after the election of 1856 about going on. It is
the way he went on that matters. He was committed with
his fellows to educating Illinois to Republican principles—
the chief of which he declared was the Declaration of Independence. That was what was at stake, and that was what
people must be made to understand. But he realized as well
or better than any man in Illinois that political education
begins at home, and that if he was to teach he must learn.
One of the significant things about Lincoln at this time was
his incessant study of public opinion, his effort to understand
its fluctuations—its misconceptions and its progress. It was
the press on which he chiefly relied for this. I think it is
probably fair to say that there was not a paper in the state
that he did not know. He even got himself into domestic
trouble by the number to which he subscribed. One carrier at
least, attempting to deliver a copy of a new paper at the
house, was sent off by Mrs. Lincoln—curtly, we imagine,
from the note which Mr. Lincoln felt obliged to send to the
editor. "When the paper was brought to my house," he
wrote, "my wife said to me, 'Now, you are going to take
another worthless little paper.' I said to her, *evasively*, 'I
have not directed the paper to be left.' In my absence she

gave the message to the carrier—this is the whole story."
Considering the amount of time Mr. Lincoln had been giving
to public service, it is not at all surprising that Mary Lincoln
should feel grieved at further subscription to what she considered a "worthless little paper!"

It was not only the Illinois press that Lincoln followed.
The Lincoln and Herndon law office in Springfield was one
of the chief newspaper headquarters of the town. Mr. Henry
B. Rankin, who was a student in this office from 1856 to 1861,
gives an illuminating picture of the way the two men kept
themselves abreast of public opinion, North and South. Mr.
Herndon subscribed to the leading Abolitionist papers of the
North, and it was Lincoln who said, "Let us have both sides
on our table. Each is entitled to its day in court." The
result was that there came regularly to them the Charleston
Courier, the Richmond Enquirer, the Louisville Journal and
the Southern Literary Messenger. To this latter, Mr. Rankin
says, Mr. Lincoln was particularly devoted, preserving the
copies. When he was "redding up" in 1861 before leaving
for Washington, he turned the file of Messengers over to
Mr. Rankin, asking him to keep them for him as he wanted
to have them bound when he came back. These periodicals
Mr. Rankin has recently placed in the Illinois Historical
Library.

All of this periodical literature was thoughtfully read
and discussed.

"The most remarkable circumstance that now impresses me," says
Mr. Rankin, "as I look back over daily intimacies with this law firm
from 1856 to 1861, was the student-like ways in which they both
steadfastly kept the average political affairs of the whole nation under
attention; using all sources and, in their private conferences and
discussions with each other, reviewing and sifting all conflicting
opinions on national questions that came to their office table from
North and South, East and West. Had they foreseen the political

and executive battles before Lincoln, his preparation could not have been more thorough, exact and comprehensive to fit him for his duties as President in 1861-65."

Lincoln spent much time on party organization. In his judgment, you should be able to know the political opinion of every man in a district, and he believed this could be done by making what he called a map of the field. "From the poll books in the county clerk's office," he wrote in August, 1857, to a friend in Putnam County, "have made alphabetical lists of all the voters in each precinct or township. This will not be a heavy job, . . . and you see how like a map it lays the whole field before you and you know at once how and with whom to work."

And he adds this significant advice: "Let all be so quiet that the adversary shall not be notified."

One of his chief jobs was keeping the bolting Whigs and Democrats from bolting their new allegiance. The new party, as he said once, was "of strange discordant and even hostile elements, . . . gathered from the four winds." It was a difficult matter for lifelong conservatives to pull in the same harness with lifelong Abolitionists. Particularly did they doubt the wisdom of allowing them office in the new party. Here was Lovejoy seeking a place. It must not be. What wiser, fairer counsel could a man give in such a situation—a situation with which we are frequently confronted—than that which Lincoln gave? "If . . . upon a common platform which all are willing to stand upon, one who has been known as an Abolitionist, but who is now occupying none but common ground, can get the majority of votes for which all look for election, there is no safe way but to submit."

There is often amazement expressed at Lincoln's skill in handling men in the Civil War, he who is supposed to have had so little experience with men. Here was his school.

From 1854 to 1860 he was a leader in wielding conservatives, liberals and radicals of Illinois into a practical political organization.

He dealt with every variety of rashness, emotionalism, timidity, cowardice, trickery, as well as with all grades of nobility and unselfishness. There was not much left for him to learn about human beings when he graduated into the Presidency! That is, they could not fool him long. His success in the war was not divination. It was intensive experience.

Although we have but one published address of Lincoln's between the election of 1856 and his nomination for the senatorship in June of 1858, he did much talking. He felt so poor that he did not accept invitations to speak that would necessitate special journeys, but wherever his legal work carried him he talked. I spoke above of the Duff Armstrong trial in Beardstown in May of 1858—the case in which Lincoln has been accused of using a falsified almanac—a charge which all the documents as well as the kind of man he was seem to show to be untrue. The evening after the trial he spoke in the court house, not a political speech, rather a first attempt at a lecture on inventions on which he was then working.

One of his Beardstown audience remembered that he spoke about matches, recalling the first match that he ever saw, and commenting on what a misfortune it would be if they were wiped out. He talked on inventions, but dropped in more or less political gospel. A story he told that stuck long in the minds of his audience was of a man who appeared at a Democratic rally with a basket of pups for sale. He called them "Democratic pups"; a few days later, at a Republican meeting, he labeled them "Republican pups." Somebody recognized him and asked him how it was that one week they were Democratic and the next Republican. "Oh," said the man, "the pups have their eyes open now." There was more than one shrewd hearer in those times who, listening to Lincoln's sober and earnest talk, concluded, "That's what he's up to—'opening our eyes.'"

The pro-slavery party certainly gave him plenty of fresh material to use in opening their eyes. He seized it with avidity, turning it over and over, fitting it into what had gone before, using it to build up his argument—each thing was a part of a whole. There was the famous Dred Scott decision.

Only four months after the election of 1856, with its big demonstration of the strength of Republican feeling in the country, the Supreme Court declared that Congress had no power to keep slavery out of the territories. There was tremendous fury in Illinois, angry talk, angry threats. Lincoln kept so cool that he was irritating to many. His whole mind was centered on working out the logic of this new position and making others understand it. And what did it mean but that all the efforts of the past to prevent the spread of slavery were scrapped? No use now to talk about restoring the Missouri Compromise. The Compromise meant nothing—never had meant anything, was illegal. The very Ordinance of 1787 on which the freedom of Illinois itself was based was of no account. And where did it leave the negro? "Condemned to universal and eternal bondage. All the powers of the earth seem rapidly combining against him," Lincoln said. "Mammon is after him, ambition follows, philosophy follows, and the theology of the day is fast joining the crowd. They have him in his prison house. They have searched his person and left no prying instrument with him."

They must take a new tack—overrule the decision! Now,

the public has always been sensitive about criticism of the Supreme Court. Naturally enough it would like to believe it infallible—the one final authority which makes no mistakes. Mr. Douglas quickly seized on Mr. Lincoln's criticism of the court—his call for an overruling. He was severe in his denunciations of what he called Lincoln's resistance. "But who is resisting it?" said Lincoln. The overruling of a decision is no new thing in the history of the court. How about General Jackson and his resistance in the matter of a national bank? "I have heard Mr. Douglas denounce that decision and applaud General Jackson for disregarding it again and again. It would be interesting," he said, "for him to look over his recent speech and see how exactly his phillipics for resisting Supreme Court decisions fall upon his own head."

There is an admirable contemporary lesson in his carefully thought out and carefully worded explanation of his position:

"We believe as much as Judge Douglas (perhaps more) in obedience to, and respect for, the judicial department of government. We think its decisions on constitutional questions, when fully settled, should control not only the particular cases decided, but the general policy of the country, subject to be disturbed only by amendments to the Constitution as provided in that instrument itself. More than this would be revolution. But we think the Dred Scott decision is erroneous. We know the court that made it has often overruled its own decisions, and we shall do what we can to have it overrule this. We offer no resistance to it.

"Judicial decisions are of greater or less authority as precedents according to circumstances. That this should be so accords both with common sense and the customary understanding of the legal profession.

"If this important decision had been made by the unanimous concurrence of the judges, and without any apparent partisan bias, and in accordance with legal public expectation and with the steady practice of the departments throughout our history, and had been in no part based on assumed historical facts which are not really true! or, if wanting in some of these, it had been before the court more than once, and had there been affirmed and reaffirmed through a course of years, it then might be, perhaps would be, factious, nay, even revolutionary, not to acquiesce in it as a precedent.

"But when, as is true, we find it wanting in all these claims to the public confidence, it is not resistance, it is not factious, it is not even disrespectful to treat it as not having yet quite established a settled doctrine for the country."

As 1857 went on, it became increasingly difficult for Lincoln to adhere to his determination to keep his mind and the mind of his followers on the central issue of freedom. It became very difficult, indeed, when, in the fall of 1857, Douglas broke with Buchanan and a majority of his party over the constitution which the pro-slavery people had managed to force on Kansas, in spite of a clear anti-slavery majority in the new state. Nobody denied the majority, but trickery and violence had put over a pro-slavery constitution. And it was on this that Douglas broke with his associates, violently and eloquently. His doctrine of Squatter Sovereignty left it to the people to decide. It was not intended that that doctrine should be manipulated to defeat the majority rule. If the majority wanted slaves they had a right to have it so. He didn't care whether they voted slavery up or down, but he did care whether there was a free expression of public will, and that there had not been.

In a great fight the tendency is to think only of the manoeuver of the moment, that is all-important. Douglas was now on the side of a free Kansas, therefore Douglas was an asset for those who were fighting against the extension of slavery. Thousands of Democrats all over the North who had been pulling away from him flocked back. Many an Illinois Republican, a former Whig, whose mind had been so centered on the fight in Kansas that he had come to believe that the one issue was what happened to Kansas, turned with a certain relief to Douglas, who was, after all, the country's great man. Greeley and the Tribune were strong for winning him to the Republican party.

Lincoln's idea from the first had been that the Republicans should stand clear of what he called the "rumpus among the Democrats over the Kansas constitution." "In their view," he wrote, "both the President and Douglas were wrong, and they should not espouse the cause of either, because they may consider him either a little less or farther wrong of the two." But the espousing went on, so did the "eulogizing and admiring and magnifying" of Douglas!

Here was a new task—to show that Douglas' revolt had nothing to do with the heart of the matter. It was on a point over which he and the Republicans had never differed, Lincoln declared—the right of a people to make their own constitution. It did not touch the original Nebraska doctrine. Douglas was still educating people to care nothing about slavery—and slavery was wrong—contrary to the Declaration of Independence.

His insistence brought ridicule from Douglas, taking advantage, of course, of the revulsion of feeling that his revolt against Buchanan had brought him. Why this appeal to the Declaration of Independence from Lincoln? The Declaration had nothing to do with negroes. It referred to the white race alone, and to only a limited part of the white race. "The people who framed the Declaration of Independence," announced Mr. Douglas, "were speaking of British subjects on this continent being equal to British subjects born and raised in Great Britain." This insincere and contemptuous talk gave Lincoln a fine chance to arouse his serious and reflective hearers, and to set down, too, just what he thought the men who framed the Declaration of Independence did mean.

"They did not mean to say all were equal in color, size, moral developments, or social capacity. They defined with tolerable distinctness in what respect they did consider all men created equal—equal with 'certain inalienable rights, among which are life, liberty, and the pursuit of happiness.' This they said, and this they meant. They did not mean to assert the obvious untruth that all were then actually enjoying that equality, nor yet that they were about to confer it immediately upon them. In fact, they had no power to confer such a boon. They meant simply to declare the right, so that enforcement of it might follow as fast as circumstances should permit.

"They meant to set up a standard maxim for free society, which should be familiar to all, and revered by all; constantly looked to, constantly labored for, and even though never perfectly attained, constantly approximated, and thereby constantly spreading and deepening its influence and augmenting the happiness and value of life to all people of all colors everywhere. The assertion that 'all men are created equal' was of no practical use in effecting our separation from Great Britain; and it was placed in the Declaration not for that, but for future use. Its authors meant it to be—as, thank God, it is now proving itself—a stumbling-block to all those who, in after times, might seek to turn a free people back into the hateful paths of despotism. They knew the proneness of prosperity to breed tyrants, and they meant when such should reappear in this fair land and commence their vocation, they should find left for them at least one hard nut to crack."

It was to take Douglas some time to find that it was a nut too hard for him to crack!

This persistent appeal to fundamentals was disconcerting to Douglas. One gets the impression that he felt it was hardly fair play in politics to be so serious. One senses, too, constant irritation at Lincoln's persistent attack on his statement of facts—false through carelessness oftener, probably, than through malice or intent. Douglas was an orator. There was always a great deal of what Mr. Lincoln called "the roar of loose declamation" about his speeches. Lincoln knew—nobody better—the weakness of rotund periods, how they are the pitfalls of orators, trapping them into statements which when analyzed fall apart because they have little or no basis of fact. He was almost pitiless in his insistent pursuit of Douglas' reckless oratorical statements. John Bunn, one of the most interesting of the Springfield men of later years who knew Lincoln, used to tell a significant story illustrating this.

In October of 1854, the day after Douglas had made his first speech in Springfield, explaining his doctrine of Squatter Sovereignty, Lincoln met Bunn on the sidewalk.

"Did you hear the speech of Judge Douglas last night?" he asked.

"Yes," Mr. Bunn said.

"What did you think of it?"

"Mr. Lincoln, I think it was a very able speech, and you will have a great deal of trouble to answer it."

"I will answer that speech without any trouble," Mr. Lincoln replied, "because Mr. Douglas made two misstatements of fact, and upon these two misstatements he built his whole argument. I can show that his facts are not facts, and that will refute his speech."

"I was present," Mr. Bunn added, "and heard the reply which Mr. Lincoln made to Judge Douglas' speech, and to my mind he did disprove Douglas' facts, and, as I thought, completely answered his argument."

People were constantly having that experience—Lincoln was right, Douglas was wrong. It was said so often that it finally made him the unquestioned leader of the Republicans in Illinois. There were many able and devoted men in the party, but for nobody was there quite the same confidence and respect. When it came time, as it did in the spring of 1858, for the Republican party to nominate a candidate to contest the senatorship with Judge Douglas, there was little or no question that Lincoln would be the choice. So it turned out. He was nominated in Springfield in June—"the first and only choice of the convention." The

[351]

night after the nomination he struck another of the high spots, the highest yet—too high for his party's safety, many of his followers thought; yet in the speech that he made on the night of June 17, 1858, all that he said was but a freer and larger putting of the ideas which you find working like seeds in what he had been saying in the last four years. The speech is a splendid example of the natural growth and development of a man's mind when concentrated on a vital expanding theme. We know this speech as "the house divided against itself speech." So important is it in the history of the Republican party that they have put up a tablet in the court room in Springfield where it was delivered.

It put the issue so unequivocally that men shrank from it. "I believe this Government cannot endure permanently half slave and half free. I do not expect the house to fall, but I do expect it will cease to be divided. It will become all one thing or all the other." It was something nobody could get away from. Men might not be able to read, but they could still understand what these words meant. And he followed it by that extraordinary paragraph in which he pictured the campaign of pro-slavery advocates to make the house all their kind of thing. Nobody could doubt after that speech what the Republican party was facing. It left no haze in any mind that thought.

But, of course, few think. And, after all, few heard him or would read the Springfield speech. He must go on, educating, bringing more and more of that great Illinois mass to see what was at stake, to understand that here was an attack on freedom, and that the time had come when they were must face the fact that it was in danger, and decide whether they were willing or not to fight for it.

Douglas came into the field in June to stay until November. He sensed, better than anybody else, that he had a real fight on his hands. In those months he spoke fully one hundred fifty times, and Lincoln, usually trailing him, almost as many. But we forget the one hundred forty or so speeches and think only of the seven occasions on which the two men met on the same platform, answering each other, point by point. Lincoln's friends had been anxious for these meetings; the more thoughtful of them felt that this was the only way in which Lincoln could really overcome the fascination of Douglas' presence and oratory, his "greatness," the gain he had made by his fight against the bogus Kansas constitution. Pin him down, face to face, and you have got him. And Lincoln believed it, and so, after delays and hesitation on Douglas' part, it was arranged.

Lincoln went into the debates, held in October of 1858, saturated with his theme—his mind convinced of the soundness of his argument and his faith in the end unwavering. "The result is not doubtful," he told his followers. "We shall not fail; if we stand firm, we shall not fail. Wise counsels may accelerate or mistakes delay it, but sooner or later the victory is sure to come."

The sentences have the quality of those bits of English which we call his masterpieces, and they have, too, the tone of the prophet. It was a high spirit in which to undertake a great contest.

# XXVII

A PILGRIMAGE worth all the time and money it will cost the historically inclined American is a tour of the seven Illinois towns, in which in the fall of 1858 Abraham Lincoln and Stephen A. Douglas met in joint debate, rounding out a four months' campaign of stump speaking on the question of slavery extension.

Luckily for the pilgrim, the Illinois State Historical Society published a few years ago a volume on the debates which, if bulky, is the most comprehensive and illuminating guidebook a traveler could have, for this volume contains not only the texts of the debates but contemporary comments on both sides—recollections, specimens of the humor, descriptions of scenes; and it prints illustrations, the most of which have never before found their way into any volume. If you ever undertake this journey, beginning at Ottawa in the north of Illinois, thence to Freeport, Jonesboro, Charleston, Galesburg, Quincy and Alton—a full round of the state you will see if you look at the map—by all means take along a copy of the "Lincoln and Douglas Debates of 1858, edited, with Introduction and Notes, by Edwin Erle Sparks," and published in Springfield, Illinois, in 1908.

There are two things a serious traveler should have clearly in mind, and the first is that these seven debates were not an isolated incident; they were the climax of a long struggle. Remember, too, that Lincoln and Douglas both came to them with the backbone of their argument fully

[354]

developed, repeatedly reiterated. Douglas had from the start rung the changes on the theory by which he justified the repeal of the Missouri Compromise; that is, that it should be left to the inhabitants of each territory to decide whether or no they wanted slavery. At the same time he was defending the decision of the Supreme Court, handed down two years after the Repeal, declaring that Congress had no power to prevent the introduction of slavery into a territory.

Mr. Lincoln's effort was to destroy the position—destroy it historically, politically and morally—to show that these various doctrines lead to nothing less than the nationalization of slavery, that Douglas was willing to lend his strength to this result because he did not think slavery wrong—did not care whether it was extended or not. The joint debates set these positions forth more clearly, logically and forcefully because the two men faced each other and were forced to consider at the moment each other's statements and arguments.

Another thing that must be remembered in considering these debates is that it was not merely two men—it was a whole state discussing. It is doubtful if ever in the history of this country there has been at any time anywhere so general and long-extended popular discussion as that in Illinois between 1854 and 1858 on the extension of slavery. Everybody that could mount a rostrum and make a speech was doing it by this time. The work of Lincoln's partner, Billy Herndon, is an illustration. In Joseph Fort Newton's admirable study of Lincoln and Herndon, based on letters exchanged between Theodore Parker and Herndon in this period, you find constant reference to the work he was doing on the platform. Like Lincoln, he was neglecting business, going wherever he could get an audience, big or little, writing editorials, keeping the post busy with letters. And what Herndon was doing, at least half of the lawyers in Illinois were doing to a greater or less degree. Every schoolhouse, every pulpit, was a forum. At every country grocery, every post-office, every four corners groups had been going over and over the pros and cons of the matter for four years. The people of Illinois were saturated with the theme, so that when the debates were announced they flocked to hear their leaders, prepared and eager to listen.

Nothing but an interest which was almost an obsession could have induced people to leave their employments and travel, as they did, over long distances in heat and dust and wind, to the centers selected. Such was the interest, particularly of young men, that there were those who, like the late Clark Carr of Galesburg, trailed from place to place, as sport fans follow "events" to-day. The discomfort of it to one who looks at it from present standards seems intolerable. The best authentic picture of the crowds and their habits that I have come across appeared in the New York Evening Post. You'll find it in your guidebook.

"Over long, weary miles of hot and dusty prairie," it reads, "from Charleston on the procession of eager partisans came—on foot, on horse-back, in wagons drawn by horses or mules; men, women and children, old and young; the half sick, just out of the last 'shake'; children in arms, infants at the maternal fount, pushing on in clouds of dust and beneath a blazing sun; settling down at the town where the meeting is with hardly a chance for sitting, and even less opportunity for eating, waiting in anxious groups for hours at the places of speaking, talking, discussing, litigious, vociferous, while the roar of artillery, the music of bands, the waving of banners, the huzzas of the crowds, as delegation after delegation appears; the cry of peddlers, vending all sorts of wares, from an infallible cure of 'agur' to a monstrous watermelon in slices to suit purchasers—combining to render the occasion one scene of confusion and commotion. The hour of one arrives, and a perfect rush is made for the grounds; a column of dust rising to the heavens and fairly deluging those who are hurrying on through it. Then the speakers come, with flags, and banners, and music, surrounded by cheering partisans. Their arrival at the grounds and immediate approach to the

stand is the signal for shouts that rend the heavens. They are introduced to the audience amid prolonged and enthusiastic cheers; they are
interrupted by frequent applause, and they sit down finally amid the
same uproarious demonstrations. The audience sit or stand patiently
throughout, and as the last word is spoken, make a break for their
homes, first hunting up lost members of their families, gathering their
scattered wagon loads together, and as the daylight fades away, entering
again upon the broad prairies and slowly picking their way back 'to
the place of beginning.' "

This, with variations, is the scene which one must have
before his eyes as he visits every point of a Lincoln and
Douglas debate.

There was a dramatic contrast between the men themselves, their appearance, temper, career, that stirred and fascinated the crowd. It was the contrast between elegance and
ruggedness, elaboration and simplicity, a sophistication that
did not hesitate at misrepresentation and an honesty almost
childlike. It was particularly marked in their voice, platform
manners, approach to their audience. Douglas had a deep
bass voice, sonorous and tremendously effective; but he used
it recklessly, hurting it by too free drinking of water during
his speech, and by the time he had reached Alton, the last
debate, he could not make his audience hear. Mr. Lincoln's
voice had none of the appealing quality of Douglas'. It was
high and shrill but penetrating, and he must have known,
consciously or unconsciously, how to place it, for, in spite of
the terrific strain of the summer and fall's work, it never
failed him.

Douglas was a joy to the reporters, he was "strongly
regular" according to one of them; "he was distinct, he
paused between sentences, he used short sentences, he rarely
exceeded one hundred and twenty words a minute. It was
no trouble to report Douglas for he did not utter nearly
so many words as Lincoln in a given period."

"Lincoln was quite different, his voice was clear, almost shrill, every syllable was distinct but his delivery was puzzling to stenographers; he would speak several words with great rapidity, come to the word he wished to emphasize and let his voice linger and bear hard on that. To impress the idea on the minds of his hearers was his aim; not to charm the ear with flowing words. It was very easy to understand Lincoln; he spoke with great clearness but his delivery was very irregular."

There is another feature of the debates which those who use well the guidebook will notice and that is that Douglas had practically one speech, but that no two of Lincoln's speeches were alike. This was so nearly true that the stenographers would stop taking notes when Douglas reached certain points in his address, and taking their shears would cut out the paragraphs from some previously printed report and paste them into their copy. It led to a famous joke among them. The Chicago Times, Douglas' chief supporter, was accused of garbling Lincoln's speeches in a way that frequently made it appear that he was talking nonsense. "The Times," said one of the reporters, "mucilages Douglas and mutilates Lincoln."

If you linger long enough in the towns on this pilgrimage, you will be sure to run across somebody that remembers a particular episode of the discussion. It was here, he will tell you, that Lincoln, or Douglas, as the case may be, did so-and-so—said so-and-so. At Ottawa the story you are sure to hear is of Douglas' attempt to fix on Lincoln, by documentary proof, the charge of Abolitionism that he had been making for some time. He read a set of resolutions which he said had been adopted at the convention in Springfield in the fall of 1854, the convention which young Paul Selby and some of his earnest and enthusiastic friends had called and in which, after they had heard Lincoln's reply to Douglas, they had voted him to be of their stripe. Now, the resolutions adopted by Paul Selby's group were not more radical than Mr. Lincoln's speech of that date—they merely declared against any further extension of slavery. But the resolutions that Douglas read were, for the period, decidedly more objectionable; he called them "black Republican." All Mr. Lincoln could say was that he never subscribed to them, that he was not present, as Douglas declared that he had been, at the Springfield convention, and that, though he had been appointed a delegate, he had declined.

But it was a halting disavowal, with no proofs. It was left for a lively young man who was reporting the debates for the Chicago Press and Tribune, Robert Hitt, later to be for many years a member of Congress and an honored citizen of the country, to discover that, knowingly or not, Douglas had read a set of resolutions adopted at an entirely different meeting, held at a different place. "Forgery!" Lincoln's supporters cried; and many a man, a youth then, will tell you that that incident was the base of a growing doubt of Stephen Douglas. It justified a remark which Lincoln is said to have dropped about this time to a friend, and which was passed around the state, that Douglas was perfectly willing to lie to 10,000 people, even if he knew that it would be proved to 5,000 the next day that he had lied. This was considered good tactics. There were 5,000 that would not hear the proofs of the lie.

It worked that way in this charge of Abolitionism. It took hold. The late James Lowry of Minneapolis, a boy of fifteen at the time of the debates, living on a farm near Beardstown who with his father heard every speech that was made in a radius of a considerable number of miles, used to tell a story which illustrates the feeling. Young Lowry

[359]

was in a group following Mr. Lincoln up the street in Rushville. The whole population was out, among them many young women prominent in society, some of them, according to Mr. Lowry, "very dark complected." One of these girls, stepping in front of Lincoln, dangled a little negro doll baby in his face. He turned to her quietly and said, "Madam, are you the mother of that?" "It created quite a sensation in that small town," says Mr. Lowry!

The charge that Lincoln believed in "negro equality" finally became so serious an embarrassment to his supporters that one of them, Capt. J. N. Brown, of Berlin, Illinois, asked him for a clear statement which he could use in debates. Lincoln's answer is a fine illustration of the infinite pains the man was willing to take to make a position clear. He bought a little black-covered note book, and in it wrote what we may call the preface—the words reproduced on the next page. Following this he pasted in several newspaper clippings from his speeches, showing exactly his position, and each of these quotations he prefaced by a few written words telling their source. He followed the whole by a letter of 500 words in which he reiterates in brief what he regards as the substance of the extracts that he had given.

The only book by Abraham Lincoln which has ever been published is this little one prepared for Capt. Brown. The late J. McCan Davis of Springfield, Illinois, secured for McClure-Phillips Co., in 1903, the permission to publish it in facsimile, and prepared the introductory note which goes with the book. It is now a rare document, the edition having been exhausted.

At Freeport you will find, not only from your guidebook but from thoughtful inhabitants, if you are lucky enough to meet them, that the feature of the debate there was a question which Lincoln propounded to Douglas, forcing him to make

an answer showing the inconsistency of his position, his effort
to make the South believe that they could carry their slaves
into the territories, the North to believe that they could keep
them out, in spite of Repeal and Dred Scott decision—a

*The following extracts are taken from various speeches of mine delivered at various times and places, and I believe they contain the substance of all I have ever said about "Negro equality." The first three are from my answer to Judge Douglas, Oct. 16. 1854 at Peoria—*

FACSIMILE OF FOREWORD WRITTEN BY A. LINCOLN IN A CAMPAIGN BOOK
COMPILED BY HIM IN 1858 FOR A FRIEND.

position which Mr. Lincoln aptly characterized later as an
argument that a thing may be lawfully driven away from
where it has a lawful right to be!

And so it goes. At Quincy you will be sure to be told
the story which so delighted its hearers as well as those who
hear it for the first time to-day, of Lincoln's pulling off his

[361]

coat and saying to the boy to whom he handed it, "Here, you hold my coat while I stone Stephen."

"And he did do it, good and plenty," a fine old lady told me recently, who, a young girl then, was in his group of hearers.

As the debates went on the interest of the crowd was intensified and solemnized by a growing sense of certain inner differences between the two men which they had not at first realized.

Here was Douglas publicly confident, superior, treating Lincoln from the start with a smiling tolerance—he was a "kind, amiable gentleman" who had been "submerged" after a term in Congress, now breaking in where only the "great"— like himself—should be treading. That was Douglas' outward platform manner toward Lincoln, but privately he was more honest. More than one of those who have told their recollections of those days, intimates of Douglas, have recorded the reluctance which he confessed to have in meeting Lincoln. The "kind, amiable gentleman" of the platform became in these sober and honest moments a man of ability, a skillful debater whom he dreaded to meet. Mr. James Milliken, the founder of the Milliken University in Decatur, used to tell of a talk he had with Douglas in that town after the challenge had passed and been accepted. The people of the country, Douglas told Milliken, "expect me literally to eat Lincoln up, and I cannot do it—nor can any other man."

Douglas' followers did expect it. They showed it by their favorite headline:

## "THE LITTLE GIANT CHAWING UP OLD ABE"

Douglas' followers, so far as I know, never shared his doubt of the contest. They were completely under the sway of his dominating magnetic personality. His great swaying head, the deep roar of his voice, the eloquence of his words, his elegant presence, his years of success, gave them the feeling that he was indomitable. And he played up to their adoration.

David Locke (Petroleum V. Nasby), then an Ohio editor, attracted by the quality of the debates, went out to Illinois, to see and hear for himself. He records his impression of the difference between the two men in their opening words at Quincy: Lincoln "venturing to say" that both he and Douglas would perfectly agree that entire silence would be most welcome to them; Douglas announcing, "I desire to be heard rather than be applauded." "Lincoln claimed nothing for himself," says Locke; "Douglas spoke as if applause must follow his utterances." He characterized the incident as illustrative of "inborn modesty" on the one hand and "boundless vanity" on the other.

Slowly but surely the impression spread that Mr. Douglas' smiling patronage of Lincoln concealed anxiety, that though Lincoln admitted frankly that he had been a "flat failure," he was unafraid, could not be pushed off the track. The sense of his absolute faith that Douglas was wrong and he was right deepened. Little by little his boldness in the face of the great man, his refusal to be beaten down, diverted, humiliated, took strong hold on people.

As Douglas felt Lincoln's argument tightening around him, pinning him in, found that his attempts to stir up prejudice by charges of abolitionism and sectionalism, his efforts to divert attention by irrelevant personalities, were gaining him nothing, that he was failing in every effort to throw Lincoln into confusion, he began to lose his temper, to rage—exhibits that to those straight-minded people only too plainly showed that his confidence was breaking. It was on one of these occasions when Douglas had exploded in wrath that Lincoln told them, with cool, grim confidence: "I've got him."

It is not to be concluded that Lincoln himself never lost his even tenor. Read your guidebook carefully and you will find more than once irritation at irrelevances. At Charleston some one will be sure to tell you how, exasperated beyond control by Douglas' charges that he had refused to vote money for supplies in the Mexican War, he seized a Democratic colleague of those days and dragged him to the platform, angrily crying: "Here is a man who personally knows it to be a lie!" And the man had to admit it was. There are private remarks recorded, too, not only of irritation but of a certain contempt. "At least," he told some friends one day, "I don't have to drag my wife along with me as Judge Douglas does to see that I don't get drunk."

Now, people are serious. They resent being played with. They resent an assumption that they can be persuaded to carry water on both shoulders. They will rise to an appeal to their honesty, and more and more Lincoln's appeal to the integrity of their intellects as well as to the honesty of their belief in the wickedness of slavery grew upon them. Douglas was flippant. Lincoln never was. One lifelong Missouri Democrat, hearing the two men at Alton, went home to say he was done with Douglas, he was a "jumping-jack."

The deep sincerity of Lincoln's seriousness impressed people more and more. It was almost forbidding at the opening of some of his debates—that long, slow-lifting form, that sad furrowed face, that overwhelming sense of the gravity of the matter that he was discussing. This seriousness seems to have taken hold of youth particularly, and we must remember that the men now living who heard the Lincoln and Douglas debates were boys 12, 14 and 16 years of age at that time.

[364]

# A VICTORIOUS DEFEAT

Recently at Beardstown, Kentucky, I talked with Colonel Wickliffe, one of the few Kentucky Republicans of 1858. He told me that his interest in the debates was so great that when the two men reached the southern part of Illinois he went over to hear them. What impressed him about Lincoln, and what he talks of to-day, was the man's dignity and sincerity. "He knew and felt all that he said; he was simple and plain, but he moved you profoundly."

"And how about Douglas?" I asked.

"Oh, Douglas," said Colonel Wickliffe, "was an orator."

Judge Fifer of Bloomington records a similar impression of Lincoln. The first time that Judge Fifer heard Lincoln was in September, 1858, at Bloomington. Douglas had spoken there to such good purpose that Lincoln's backers—Leonard Swett, Jesse Fell and Judge David Davis—three as important men as he had behind him—urged him to make a reply. Judge Fifer describes how he and his brother wormed their way to the edge of the platform. After "a beautiful introduction" by Leonard Swett, Lincoln rose. "It seemed like he never would get through getting up," Fifer said. "It was hard for him to get started, and one of the boys near me said we ought to have nominated Swett. But when he once got hold of himself I never heard such a speech; it fairly raised the hair on my head and made my heart stop beating. The crowd was silent as death, their faces riveted upon him; he was the most earnest man I ever heard talk."

Again and again to-day one runs upon men who as boys record this impression of a profound, almost tragic seriousness.

These boys were important! Mr. W. T. Norton of Alton, Illinois, has recorded his impressions as a boy of the debate held in that town, the last of the series. One thing that he notes should never be forgotten in the history of these debates —it is safe to say that it is true of every town in which the two

[365]

᧧ ᧧ ᧧ ᧧ ᧧ ᧧ ᧧ ᧧ ᧧

## Last Great Discussion.

Let all take notice, that on Friday nex , Hon. S. A. Douglas and Hon. A. Lincoln, will hold the seventh and closing joint debate of the canvass at this place. We hope the country will turn out, to a man, to hear these gentlemen.

The following programme for the discussion has been decided upon by the Joint Committee appointed by the People's Party Club and the Democratic Club for that purpose.

Arrangements for the 15th inst.

The two Committees—one from each party—heretofore appointed to make arrangements for the public speaking on the 15th inst., met in joint Committee, and the following programme of proceedings was adopted, viz :

1st. The place for said speaking shall be on the east side of City Hall.

2d. The time shall be 1½ o'clock, P. M. on said day.

3d. That Messrs. C. Stiglman and W. T. Miller be a Committee to erect a platform; also, seats to accommodate ladies.

4th. That Messrs. B. F. Barry and William Post superintend music and salutes.

5th. Messrs. H. G. McPike and W. C. Quigley be a committee having charge of the platform, and reception of ladies, and have power to appoint assistants.

6th. That the reception of Messrs. Douglas and Lincoln shall be a quiet one, and no public display.

7th. That no banner or motto, except national colors, shall be allowed on the speakers' stand.

On motion, a committee, consisting of Messrs. W. C. Quigley and H. G. McPike, be appointed to publish this programme of proceedings.                  W. C. QUIGLEY,
                                          H. G. McPIKE.
Alton, Oct. 13, 1858.

To the above it should be added that the O. A. & St. Louis Railroad, will, on Friday, carry passengers to and from this city at half its usual rates. Persons can come in on the 10:40 a. m. train, and go out at 6:20 in the evening.

᧧ ᧧ ᧧ ᧧ ᧧ ᧧ ᧧ ᧧ ᧧

ANNOUNCEMENT FROM THE *Alton Daily Whig.*
Reproduced in Volume III. of the Illinois State Historical Library Collections, Lincoln Series.

men spoke—and that is that nine-tenths of the boys who in Alton cheered for Lincoln or Douglas three years later were cheering for the Union, and were soon carrying muskets or wearing shoulder straps in the Union army. The great debates were a school for boys. What they did from 1861 to 1865 shows something of the depth of the feeling the discussion aroused.

The debate at Alton on October 15 was the last of the series. Lincoln's supporters who heard him declared that it was the greatest speech he had yet made. In it he reviewed his entire argument, bringing it down to what he considered the crux of the whole matter. There are two memorable paragraphs in this speech:

"The real issue in this controversy —the one pressing upon every mind —is the sentiment on the part of one class that looks upon the institution of slavery as a wrong, and of another class that does not look upon it as a wrong. The sentiment that contemplates the institution of slavery in this country as a wrong is the sentiment of the Republican party. It is the sentiment around which all their actions, all their arguments, circle;

from which all their propositions radiate. They look upon it as being a moral, social, and political wrong; and while they contemplate it as such they nevertheless have due regard for its actual existence among us, and the difficulties of getting rid of it in any satisfactory way, and to all the constitutional obligations thrown about it. Yet having a due regard for these, they desire a policy in regard to it that looks to its not creating any more danger. They insist that it, as far as may be, be treated as a wrong, and one of the methods of treating it as a wrong is to make provision that it shall grow no larger."

"That is the real issue. That is the issue that will continue in this country when these poor tongues of Judge Douglas and myself shall be silent. It is the eternal struggle between these two principles—right and wrong—throughout the world. They are the two principles that have stood face to face from the beginning of time, and will ever continue to struggle. The one is the common right of humanity, and the other the divine right of kings. It is the same principle in whatever shape it develops itself. It is the same spirit that says: 'You toil and work and earn bread and I'll eat it.' No matter in what shape it comes, whether from the mouth of a king who seeks to bestride the people of his own nation and live by the fruit of their labor, or from one race of men as an apology for enslaving another race, it is the same tyrannical principle."

A few days after the close of the debates came the test of what they had done—the election of November, 1858— a majority of nearly 4,000 votes for Lincoln over Douglas. As between the two men a majority of the people of Illinois believed that Lincoln had it right. They were unwilling to admit that if one man chose to enslave another, no third man should be allowed to object.

Lincoln had won the people, but he had not won the Senatorship. It is the Legislature that elects, and there Douglas had a majority of eight.

"I suppose everybody but Billy Herndon will go back on me now," Lincoln was heard to say after the returns came in. But, though he may have felt his defeat enough to show it in private, you do not find a trace in his letters. His position was the same, almost regal one that it had been in 1854, in 1856. It was but another round in a long fight. Now, as always, it was a "durable" struggle they had on hand. Their victory was sure, but it would be one "of endurance born." "I have an abiding faith," he wrote to a friend, "that we shall beat them in the long run. Step by step the objects of the leaders will become too plain for the people to stand them. I write merely to let you know that I am neither dead nor dying." And to another: "You are feeling badly, but 'This too shall pass away,' never fear."

As for himself, his serenity was superb. "I think we have fairly entered upon a durable struggle as to whether this nation is to ultimately become all slave or all free, and although I fall early in the contest it is nothing if I shall have contributed in the least degree to the final rightful result.

There was no chance for him to "fall" now—East and West clammered to see and hear him.

# XXVIII

IF by any lucky chance there should turn up in Massachusetts, Wisconsin or California, somebody of Abraham Lincoln's caliber, to dispute the Senatorship with Mr. Lodge, Mr. La Follette, or Mr. Johnson, and these gentlemen should be forced, as Stephen A. Douglas was in 1858, to debate, day in and day out, for some four months, the principles underlying such a question as, let us say, the finding a peaceful substitute for war in the settling of international disputes, and the debate should take on something of the character of the Lincoln and Douglas debate, do you not suppose that after it was over, we, the people, would be very keen to see the stranger who had dared contest with the celebrated and long-established Mr. Lodge, Mr. La Follette or Mr. Johnson? We would. And from all over the country we would invite him to come and speak to us, wanting to judge for ourselves whether or no a leader who measured up to something like the democratic spirit within us had at last appeared.

That was the way people felt in many parts of the country after the Lincoln and Douglas debates. They wanted to see and hear Lincoln. But Lincoln was "broke," "hard up," and for the moment pushed off the advances the country was making. It was "bad to be poor," but if he neglected his business another year as he had the last, he would "go to the wall for bread and meat." When the chairman of the State Republican Committee, his friend Norman B. Judd, asked him to help out on the expenses of the campaign, he somewhat reluctantly consented that Judd put him down for $250, which was to be settled when they cleaned up "the private matter between us"—the private matter being a considerable loan which Lincoln had made to Judd—a note which seems not to have been paid until Lincoln's estate was settled in 1865, for in the list of his assets we find Judd's note for $3,000. It is one of several evidences that Lincoln loaned freely at this time, as at all times, to his friends—so freely that he was often cramped for money for current expenses.

The upkeep of his family was increasing for he had by this time three boys—Robert, old enough now to be in Phillips Exeter, preparing for Harvard, and a considerable expense of course, and at home, Willie, about eight years old, and Thomas, five. Mary Lincoln was hospitable—to those of whom she approved—and entertained as handsomely as other women in her Springfield circle. She reckoned more highly than Mr. Lincoln the political value of social life, and when the Legislature was in session in Springfield, or when there were important gatherings of any sort, she was sure to "give something." The cost of some of her parties seems rather surprising. For instance, the entertaining Mrs. Johns, of Decatur, tells of being snowbound on her way from Chicago to Springfield in January of 1855, along with a large number of legislators and politicians going to the capital for the election of Senator—the election in which Mr. Lincoln was a candidate but finally withdrew his vote in favor of Lyman Trumbull. The train was stalled for upwards of a week, and there would have been more actual suffering from hunger than there was if it had not been that two Chicago caterers were also on their way to Springfield—one with a supper for a reception to three hundred people that Mrs. Lincoln was giving, the other with supplies for a big dinner at the Governor's mansion. The hungry travelers bought out the caterers, but Mrs. Johns does not tell us whether or no Mrs. Lincoln ever held her reception!

Two years later, February, 1857, we find Mrs. Lincoln writing to a sister in Kentucky:

"I may surprise you when I mention that I am recovering from the slight fatigue of a very large and, I really believe, a very handsome and agreeable entertainment, at least our friends flatter us by saying so. About five hundred were invited, yet owing to an unlucky rain three hundred only favored us by their presence. And the same evening in Jacksonville, Colonel Warren gave a bridal party to his son, which occasion robbed us of some of our friends. You will think we have enlarged our borders since you were here."

This enlarging of her social borders went on steadily— and all that cost money! Lincoln's correspondence shows that he went immediately after the debates of 1858 hard at the law, and also that he had hopes of earning a little by lecturing. There are evidences that he long had had this possibility in mind. In 1839, we find a lecture of his given before the young men's lyceum of Springfield, printed at their request in one of the local papers. In his complete works, Nicolay and Hay, his secretaries, include several fragments—"notes for lectures"—which they found among his papers. Quick as he was to take a hint, that is, to ask himself whether this or that thing that somebody else was doing was not possible for him, it was natural that he should think of the platform. Population considered, there were probably as many speakers and readers, English and domestic, going up and down the Mississippi Valley in those days as there are now. Both Dickens and Thackeray had been West. Emerson was in Springfield in 1853, and gives a rather lugubrious picture of the town and of his quarters there, also of his fears that his time was not going to be paid any such rate as was promised him. It would be interesting to know whether Lincoln heard him. At all events, lecturing was one of the things that ambitious men of his type of mind tried out, and in the year following the Lincoln and Douglas debates he undertook a talk on "Discoveries and Inventions"—a subject which had always fascinated him and to which in one way or another his activities had contributed. When he was in Congress he had spent many an hour in the Patent Office at the time he sought a patent for his contrivance for getting boats over shoals—the model is still to be seen on the shelves of the Patent Office. He had a mind that no matter what interested it—a principle, a custom, a tool—went back to the start and traced the growth of the particular thing. Discoveries and inventions, their beginnings, their progress, their future —he never tired of studying them, speculating about them, and this lecture that he now tried, with the hope of earning a little extra money, was the outcome of long thinking and observation. He gave the paper only a few times, and without any particular success, in his judgment. He doubted whether it was worth the little sum he was paid; but there are observations in it which convince one that it was more of a lecture than he thought. For instance, "How could the 'gopher wood' for the ark have been gotten out without an axe? It seems to me an axe or a miracle was indispensable!"

His speculation about the use of wind as a motive power is interesting. He thought that possibly one of the greatest discoveries of the future would be the taming and harnessing of the wind. In line with his thinking in this lecture is the talk on the plow, whether or no it was possible to get some other force for running it than man's own muscular power, which is to be found in an address which he gave at the State Fair at Milwaukee late in 1859. It might be Henry Ford talking!

"I have thought a good deal in an abstract way about a steam plow. . . . To be successful, it must, all things considered, plow better than can be done with animal power. . . . That one which shall be so contrived as to apply the larger proportion of its power to the cutting and turning the soil, and the smallest to the moving itself over the field, will be the best one. . . . Railroad locomotives have their regular wood and water stations. But the steam plow is less fortunate. It does not live upon the water, and if it be once at a water station, it will work away from it, and when it gets away cannot return without leaving its work, at a great expense of time and strength. It will occur that a wagon-and-horse team might be employed to supply it with fuel and water; but this, too, is expensive; and the question recurs, 'Can the expense be borne?' When this is added to other expenses, will not plowing cost more than in the old way?"

How fascinated he would have been with the tractors of to-day!

The pressure on him from the outside was too great for him to find time to bring the lecture to anything like a satisfactory professional point, and he finally dropped it entirely. He was "in the public eye"—a harassing place! People sought his opinion on all sorts of public questions—the naturalization of foreigners, the tariff. The politicians would not let him alone—even sought to embroil him with Senator Trumbull and with Judd, the chairman of the Republican State Committee. The Republicans expected him to help them in carrying out the counsel he was continually giving, to hold together what they had built up, and, above all, to keep the principles on which they were working uncorrupted.

Lincoln had never had any doubt but what there was more work to be done, and that he would do his share. "Another blow-up is coming," he wrote Editor Ray of the Chicago Times after the election; "we shall have fun again. Douglas managed to be supported both as the best instrument to put down and uphold the slave power, but no ingenuity can long keep the antagonism in harmony." The "fun" began in a few months. There were powerful Republicans who now, as in the year before, were hankering after Douglas, believing that if he could be brought into the Republican party he would make its future secure. The most powerful of these was Horace Greeley, editor of the New York Tribune. He was doing his utmost to annex Douglas. Lincoln fought it. "The Republican principles can in nowise live with Douglas; and it is arrant folly now, as it was last spring, to waste time and scatter labor already performed in dallying with him," he told Senator Trumbull.

"Let the Republican party of Illinois dally with Judge Douglas," he told them, "let them fall in behind him and make him their candidate, and they do not absorb him— he absorbs them. They would come out at the end all Douglas men, all claimed by him as having endorsed every one of his doctrines upon the great subject with which the whole nation is engaged at this hour—that the question of negro slavery is simply a question of dollars and cents; that the Almighty has drawn a line across the continent, on one side of which labor—the cultivation of the soil—must always be performed by slaves."

There was no keeping out of the fray, and by the fall of 1859 Lincoln was in it again as hard as ever. Douglas had been in Ohio, and made an impression. In September Lincoln followed him, speaking in Columbus and in Cincinnati. At the end of the month he was in Milwaukee, in December in Kansas, where he spoke at least half a dozen times. On February 27, 1860, he delivered the Cooper Union speech, and followed it up by a tour in New England, the actual extent of which has never been recorded in the biographies. Only recently has there appeared a brochure on this trip by Percy Coe Eggleston, of New London, Connecticut, which shows it to be more extended than has been set down. Between February 28, when he spoke in Providence, Rhode Island, and March 10, when he spoke in Bridgeport,

Connecticut, he made nine speeches, nearly all of which were favorably and some of them enthusiastically reported in the New England press.

The significant features of this six months' work, coming as it did on the top of a very energetic effort to catch up financially, are its vigor and the extension of his range of thinking and of research. The work was fresh, not a rehash of the campaign with Douglas. To be sure, the backbone of his argument was that Douglas' doctrine of popular sovereignty meant the final nationalization of slavery, but he used fresh illustrations and fresh appeals, skillfully seizing every significant phrase or word that Douglas and others gave him. There was what he called "the Judge's moral climate line"—the idea developed by Douglas after election in a tour of the South, that the Almighty had drawn a line across the continent, on one side of which labor could only be done by slaves. "Once we come to acknowledge," answered Lincoln, "that it is the law of the Eternal Being for slavery to exist on one side of that line, have we any sure ground to object to slaves being held on the other side?"

He used Senator Hammond's "mud sill" theory of labor as pertinently. Cultivated society rested on an inferior or slave class, Hammond was arguing at this time, "as a house stood on mud sills." Lincoln picked up the expression and used it in his first talk on labor and capital—the first talk in which he shows that he had been wrestling with the economic theory under slavery. Here we have him attacking the idea that nobody labors unless somebody else owing capital induces him to do it by hiring or compelling him, and that the state of labor, hired or slave, is fixed—also that labor is incompatible with education or free individual progress. His treatment of this "mud sill" theory is keen, flexible, humorous—with many pointed, satirical comments, as that "a blind horse upon a treadmill is a perfect illustration of what a laborer should be—all the better for being blind, that he could not kick understandingly," or "a Yankee who could invent a strong-handed man without a head would receive the everlasting gratitude of the 'mud sill' advocates."

In Lincoln's work in this period, March, 1859, to March, 1860, a number of ideas come to the front which his previous speeches show had passed through his mind, but upon which he had not enlarged. There is his conviction of the injustice of bitter and vituperative attacks upon the Southern people. He never could forget that the people of the South had been born to slavery, that all their teachings and associations had led them to accept it as a matter of course, a part of the constitution of things, and that the North had had its part as well as the South in perpetuating the institution in the country. In his talk to the Cincinnati people in September of 1859 there was an effort to make them feel that while he thought slavery was wrong and must not be extended, and they felt it was right and should be extended, yet he did not hate or despise them, and he asked that they in turn should not hate or despise him.

Alongside with this effort at conciliation or better understanding was a vigorous expression in regard to disunion. His reply to the suggestion always had been certain, but never, perhaps, quite so emphatic as in one of his Kansas speeches of this time, where he used John Brown and his tragic fate as an illustration:

"Old John Brown thought slavery wrong, as we do; he attacked contrary to law, and it availed him nothing before the law that he thought himself right. He has just been hanged for treason against the State of Virginia; and we cannot object, though he agreed with us in calling slavery wrong. Now if you undertake to destroy the Union contrary to law, if you commit treason against the United States, our duty will be to deal with you as John Brown has been dealt with. We shall try to do our duty."

The speech at Cooper Union on February 27, 1860, shows best how hard Lincoln worked and how he grew in this period. The invitation to make the speech had come to him in the fall of 1859. He had been flattered and excited by it. He had consented to go, and had decided to make a political speech. Those who were with him in those days remembered well how many hours he spent that winter in the library of the state capitol and over Elliot's debates on the Federal Constitution, which he owned. The best proof of his labor is the lecture itself. The point which he set out to demonstrate in his opening was what the fathers who framed the government thought about slavery. He runs them down, one after another, the thirty-nine who signed the Constitution, and the result of his patient inquiry was proof that twenty-three out of the thirty-nine who framed the government under which we live were on record on the question, and that twenty-one, "a clear majority of the whole thirty-nine," were on record as believing that the Federal Government had the power to control slavery in the federal territories—the point at issue in the Dred Scott decision.

The point was so clearly and conclusively made, it was of such importance in the argument, that it won Lincoln immediate recognition in his audience of intelligent and superior people as a serious student. It gave a sound historical basis for the campaign against slavery extension that until then had been lacking. Here was proof that the Republicans were carrying on what the fathers had begun, that as Lincoln argued it was not the North but the South that was the revolutionist.

The reception of this speech certainly justified all the care that Lincoln had taken in preparing it. Four great New

[377]

York papers printed it in full, and there was a demand that it be put in pamphlet form for circulation. Charles C. Nott, whom in 1865 Lincoln appointed judge of the Court of Claims, wrote him about this. Nott had gone over the speech and suggested certain changes. Lincoln's comments on these changes are evidence of the care with which he had prepared the original speech, and of his sensitiveness to careless and unauthorized statements:

"So far as it is intended merely to improve in grammar and elegance of composition, I am quite agreed; but I do not wish the sense changed, or modified, to a hair's breadth. And you, not having studied the particular points so closely as I have, cannot be quite sure that you do not change the sense when you do not intend it. For instance, in a note at bottom of first page, you propose to substitute 'Democrats' for 'Douglas.' But what I am saying there is *true* of Douglas, but is not true of Democrats generally; so that the proposed substitution would be a very considerable blunder. The *impudently absurd* I stick to. The striking out 'he' and inserting 'we' turns the sense exactly wrong. The striking out 'upon it' leaves the sense too general and incomplete. The sense is 'act as they acted *upon that question,*' not as they acted generally."

Mr. Nott and those associated with him in editing the Cooper Union speech were anxious that there should be no questioning of the exactness of Mr. Lincoln's historical references. Accordingly, they asked him to give them a memoranda of his investigations. He wrote back that he had preserved no memoranda, and that to reëxamine and make notes for them would take more time than he could possibly spare. The result was that the editors undertook the investigation themselves, and with the speech published an appendix giving the exact references on which Mr. Lincoln based his statements. In order to do this they declared that they had to ransack all of the material available in the libraries of New York, and that they consulted as well the leading historians of the day—Bancroft, Hildreth, Goodell.

In their preface they said of this work that no one who had not actually attempted to verify the details of the speech could understand the patient research and historical labor which Mr. Lincoln had given to it.

"The history of our earlier politics," the editors went on, "is scattered through numerous journals, statutes, pamphlets, and letters; and these are defective in completeness and accuracy of statement, and in indices and tables of contents. Neither can any one who has not traveled over this precise ground appreciate the accuracy of every trivial detail, or the self-denying impartiality with which Mr. Lincoln has turned from the testimony of 'the Fathers,' on the general question of slavery, to present the single question which he discusses. From the first line to the last—from his premises to his conclusion, he travels with swift, unerring directness which no logician ever excelled—an argument complete and full, without the affectation of learning, and without the stiffness which usually accompanies dates and details. A single, easy, simple sentence of plain Anglo-Saxon words contains a chapter of history that, in some instances, has taken days of labor to verify, and which must have cost the author months of investigation to acquire. And though the public should justly estimate the labor bestowed on the facts which are stated, they cannot estimate the greater labor involved on those which are omitted—how many pages have been read, how many works examined, what numerous statutes, resolutions, speeches, letters and biographies have been looked through. Commencing with this address as a political pamphlet, the reader will leave it as an historical work—brief, complete, profound, impartial, truthful—which will survive the time and the occasion that called it forth, and be esteemed hereafter, no less for its intrinsic worth than its unpretending modesty."

There is no question but that the look the country had at Lincoln in the fall and winter of 1859 and 1860 more than satisfied those who were curious about him, that here was a leader. David Locke (Petroleum V. Nasby), whose admiration and respect for Lincoln was intensified by his talk with him in Quincy at the time of the debate in 1858, heard him at Columbus and was greatly impressed by the way that Lincoln had, as he said, pictured the future. He believed

[379]

that he already had a glimmering of what was to come. "Slavery," he told Locke in a talk they had after the speech, "is doomed, and that within a few years. In discussing it we have taught a great many thousand people to hate it who had never given it a thought before. What kills the skunk is the publicity it gives itself. What a skunk wants to do is to keep snug under the barn in the daytime, when men are around with shotguns."

Of course the impression made in New York was the most important, for here he was touching closely some of the chief springs of Republican action. There was William Cullen Bryant, the editor of the Evening Post, who introduced him, and of whom he said to one of the committee: "It is worth a visit from Springfield, Illinois, to New York to make the acquaintance of such a man as William Cullen Bryant." Then there was David Dudley Field, James W. Nye, Horace Greeley and James A. Briggs, all of whom spoke after the lecture, and the last of whom said, talking of whom the Republicans should nominate for President, "One of three gentlemen will be our standard-bearer in the presidential contest of this year—the distinguished Senator of New York, Mr. Seward; the late able and accomplished Governor of Ohio, Mr. Chase; or the 'Unknown Knight' who entered the political lists against the Bois Guilbert of Democracy on the prairies of Illinois in 1858, and unhorsed him—Abraham Lincoln."

That was a rash prophecy at the moment, and Mr. Briggs says that after the meeting some of his friends joked him as not being a good prophet. But that did not chill him. Two weeks later on his return from New England, Mr. Lincoln stopped over Sunday in New York and went to Brooklyn to hear Mr. Beecher speak. Mr. Briggs was with him, and called his attention to the postoffice, then a dark and dismal place. "I do this for a reason," he told him. "I think your chance for being the next President is equal to that of any man in the country. When you are President will you recommend an appropriation of a million dollars for a suitable location for a postoffice in this city?"

"I will make a note of that," Mr. Lincoln replied, and later he said to Mr. Briggs, "When I was East several gentlemen made about the same remark to me that you did to-day about the Presidency, they thought my chances were about equal to the best."

But he did not see much in it. He noted that it was not Greeley, or Bryant, or George William Curtis, or Thurlow Weed in New York City, nor Sumner, nor Wilson, nor Hamlin in New England that made these remarks to him. He was not fitted for the Presidency. He wrote it and said it to more than one. Any man that had made a dent, as he, of course, realized he had done in a great discussion, was bound to have his friends claiming him for the Presidency. It took more than one swallow to make a summer, and the last thing he proposed to do was to fool himself.

However, when he went back to Illinois he found that the Lincoln boom, which he had left behind him a healthy if not too large growth, had assumed state-wide proportions. It means a lot back home to have a favorite son go for the first time to New York City and make a speech, to be introduced by William Cullen Bryant, and to be reported verbatim in four metropolitan dailies. That is what had happened to Lincoln. And he had followed it up by speeches that papers in New England had declared the "most powerful, logical and compact" that they had ever listened to. It was a conquering hero who came back from the East to Illinois in March of 1860—a conquering hero who was most decidedly in the hands of his friends.

# XXIX

## IN THE HANDS OF HIS FRIENDS

SO far as I know, the first mention of Abraham Lincoln
as the Republican candidate for the Presidency in 1860
was made on November 6, 1858, the week of his defeat by
Douglas—a dispatch to the Sandusky Commercial Register
from Mansfield, Ohio, saying that an enthusiastic demonstration had just been made at a mass meeting there for Lincoln
as President. Who engineered this demonstration I do not
know, though I have always supposed it to have been David R.
Locke (Petroleum V. Nasby), who was the editor at or about
that time of the Mansfield Herald. Locke had just returned
from Illinois, where he had heard at least one of the debates,
that at Quincy. His impression of Mr. Lincoln I have already
quoted. He had come away deeply impressed that here was
a man of rare intellectual and moral vigor and integrity.

But it did not take an Ohioan to recognize Lincoln's
quality, as we know. One of the powerful and beautiful
effects of the honest, self-directed course which we have been
following was the impression it had made on youth. Young
men had been caught by the elevation of his thought, the lofti-
ness of his conception of our democratic scheme, and his faith
in its ultimate realization. He awakened the high-minded
youth of Illinois as no man in the State had ever done. The
distinguished Horace White, then a boy of twenty, first
heard Lincoln in 1854 when he made his great argument
against the repeal of the Missouri Compromise. He declared that the spell of that speech was upon him to the end

of his life. White had heard Webster's reply to Hayne, but he thought Lincoln greater in his English style, and that he excelled in "simplicity, directness and lucidity, which appeal both to the intellect and the heart." This is contrary to the judgment of those who find nothing distinguished in his style before he was President. After that speech Horace White had no doubt about who his leader in Illinois was to be.

## Commercial Register

**Published Daily, Tri-Weekly & Weekly**
BY HENRY D. COOKE AND C. C. BILL.

### SANDUSKY, OHIO,

SATURDAY MORNING, NOV. 6, 1858.

**Lincoln for President.**

We are indebted to a friend at Mansfield for the following special dispatch :

"MANSFIELD, Nov. 5th, 1858.

"EDITOR SANDUSKY REGISTER :—An enthusiastic meeting is in progress here to-night in favor of Lincoln for the next Republican candidate for President.          REPORTER."

FIRST ANNOUNCEMENT OF LINCOLN AS PRESIDENT
From Volume III of the Illinois State Historical
Library Collections, Lincoln Series.

Young men who, like Joseph Medill, had been swept off their feet by the "lost speech" at Bloomington in May, 1856, were from that hour wholly committed to Abraham Lincoln as a leader. Even more radical youths, like Paul Selby, who were engineering groups of protest before the Republican party had crystallized in the state, were so convinced of Lincoln's fundamental rightness that most of them were willing to merge their radical undertakings into any fusion of which he should be a leader. He had made the greatest of con-

[383]

quests, the conquest of youth—made it by virtue of the soundness of his thinking, the sincerity of his spirit and by the impression of superior wisdom that he made—made without any pretense, simply by power of the thing itself. When it came to the debates of 1858 this pull on young men increased.

The judgment of Lincoln's friends, those who had known him for years in Illinois as a politician, a lawyer, a companion, became increasingly serious as they watched him. Here was a big man. And with the close of the debates, far from dropping out of sight, the fate that Lincoln had intimated might happen to him, his name kept coming up among the Republicans—first as Governor, which he would not think of, and repeatedly as a possible Illinois candidate for the Presidency.

If the first mention of his name in the country was in Ohio, the first in Illinois was only a few days later in the Chicago Democrat, where a column-long editorial, headed "Abraham Lincoln," appeared, in which it was suggested that his name should be presented to the National Republican Convention, first for President, next for Vice-President. "We should then say to the United States at large that in our opinion the Great Man of Illinois is Abraham Lincoln, and none other than Abraham Lincoln."

So far as I know, there was no other mention of Mr. Lincoln's name at home or abroad until in May of 1859, when William O. Stoddard, the editor of the Central Illinois Gazette of Champagne, said in a discussion of "Who Shall Be the Next President?":

"As for Illinois, it is the firm and fixed belief of our citizens that for one or other of the offices in question (President or Vice President), no man will be so sure to consolidate the party vote of the State or will carry the great Mississippi Valley with a more irresistible rush of popular enthusiasm as our distinguished fellow citizen, Abraham Lincoln.

"We, in Illinois, know him well, in the best sense of the word, a true Democrat, a man of the people, whose strongest friends and supporters are the hard-handed and strong-limbed laboring men, who hail him as a brother and who look upon him as one of their real representative men. A true friend of freedom, having already done important service for the cause, and proved his abundant ability for still greater service; yet a staunch conservative, whose enlarged and liberal mind descends to no narrow view, but sees both sides of every great question, and of whom we need not fear that fanaticism on the one side, or servility on the other will lead him to the betrayal of any trust. We appeal to our brethren of the Republican press for the correctness of our assertions."

I have before me a letter from Mr. Stoddard written in 1896, in which he says:

"The 'Coming Out' leader was my own without suggestion from anybody. I sent copies to nearly every paper in the State and to a large number of journals all over the country. Hundreds of these reprinted the 'editorial' in whole or in part, and scores followed in the line of approval.

"The movement was not engineered in any way by anybody, it was altogether spontaneous."

It was not long, however, before what Mr. Stoddard had started became so impressive that a large group of Lincoln's friends in Illinois—chief among them being Jesse Fell, Judge David Davis and Leonard Swett—began seriously to discuss the possibility of nominating him. A strong leaning toward Lincoln began to appear in the Republican State Committee as well as in the Republican press. One skillful manœuver was the going of Joseph Medill, the editor of the Chicago Tribune, to Washington to tell everybody that he could collar there what a great man they had in Illinois—a man that could carry doubtful states. Medill carried on his work of talking up his candidate with energy, and finally in February of 1860

[385]

had it well enough in hand to bring out the Tribune for Lincoln.

By this time things had gone so far that Lincoln himself began to feel uncomfortable about what might happen to him in Illinois. He had, he knew, a solid and devoted following, but ever since the Republican party had been organized he and the majority of Republicans in the state had had in mind for the Presidency one man above all others, and that was William H. Seward of New York. And after Seward there was Salmon P. Chase of Ohio. These were men who had been in the front of the battle against the extension of slavery before Lincoln had been convinced that there must be a struggle. He had accepted them. They had been his leaders. Indeed, it was probably from Seward that he caught his first definite sense that a fight was inevitable. All the northern part of Illinois was committed to Seward he knew. What chance had he in his own state? Before he went to New York for his Cooper Union speech in February he was writing to the chairman of the Republican Committee that though he was not in a position where it would hurt much for him not to be named by the National Committee, it would hurt him not to get the Illinois delegates. That is, when Lincoln went East he was already a candidate for the Presidency of the United States.

That trip gave his friends more good ammunition than they had dreamed. Indeed, there were not a few that had doubted the advisability of his speaking in the East, fearing that he might undo the impression that he had made in his contest with Douglas. It was still hard for many to see in this man whom they had known from Vandalia days on— this man so simple in his habits, so unworldly in character and practice—anything that would impress the dignified Eastern group at the head of Republicanism. Lincoln better stay at home—let well enough alone—was their feeling. But Lincoln had gone, and he had come back with added glories. His enthusiastic supporters at home could now show to doubt-ers what the papers of New York and New England had said of him. He could have given no better campaign ma-terial to them than what he brought back. It was not only those who were familiar with him at home that realized that here were the points of a great man, it was those who heard him for the first time in the critical and cultivated East.

Lincoln's business took him at once to Chicago, for he was then engaged on the famous "sand-bar case," which meant so much to the city. And here he had plenty of evidence of the importance which was attached to his candidacy. They called for him right and left to talk, and he did yield far enough to go out to Evanston to spend a night, a trip every detail of which has been worked up by the Evanston Histori-cal Society and preserved in a memorial pamphlet. Here at Evanston, just as everywhere, he left behind a memory of his engaging personality. In an unpublished letter written me years ago by the great temperance advocate, Frances E. Willard, she says:

"When my brother was a theological student in the University at Evanston (1859-61), Abraham Lincoln, prominently before the country, came to Evanston as a guest of Gen. Julius White (the hero of Pea Ridge Battle). Gen. White brought Lincoln to the the-ological department, where he spoke briefly to the students, but what impressed them—and I heard my brother tell us of it in great glee when he came home at noon—Lincoln invited some of the students who were walking along with him in the campus to compete in jumping over a wall or fence, I don't remember which it was. This they did to the best of their ability, and at the close he vaulted over, as my brother said, 'profiting by his long legs,' and set them all into laughter and applause by his performance."

[387]

Candidate as he was, Mr. Lincoln was not reduced to a state where he was incapable of a clear judgment on what the chances of other men besides himself were in the state. There is a valuable letter to R. M. Corwine of Ohio, written early in April, just after he came back from Chicago, which shows this. Corwine wanted to know what Lincoln really thought about Illinois, and he answered:

"Remembering that when not a very great man begins to be mentioned for a very great position, his head is very likely to be a little turned, I concluded I am not the fittest person to answer the questions you ask. Making due allowance for this, I think Mr. Seward is the very best candidate we could have for the north of Illinois, and the very *worst* for the south of it. The estimate of Gov. Chase here is neither better nor worse than of Seward, except that he is a newer man. They are regarded as being almost the same, seniority giving Seward the inside track. Mr. Bates, I think, would be the best man for the south of our State, and the worst for the north of it. If Judge McLean was fifteen, or even ten, years younger, I think he would be stronger than either, in our State, taken as a whole; but his great age, and the recollection of the deaths of Harrison and Taylor have, so far, prevented his being much spoken of here.

"I really believe we can carry the State for either of them, or for any one who may be nominated, but doubtless it would be easier to do it with some than with others.

"I feel disqualified to speak of myself in this matter."

A little later he wrote to Senator Lyman Trumbull, who asked him to be entirely frank:

"As you request, I will be entirely frank. The taste is in my mouth a little, and this, no doubt, disqualifies me, to some extent, to form correct opinions. You may confidently rely, however, that by no advice or consent of mine shall my pretentions be pressed to the point of endangering our common cause.

"Now, as to my opinions about the chances of others in Illinois. I think neither Seward nor Bates can carry Illinois if Douglas shall be on the track; and that either of them can, if he shall not be. I rather think McLean could carry it with D. on or off; in other words, I think McLean is stronger in Illinois, taking all sections of it, than either S. or B.; and I think S. the weakest of the three. I hear no objection to Mr. McLean, except his age; but that objection seems to occur to every one, and it is possible it might leave him no stronger than the others."

These observations are entirely in line with our best opinion of Mr. Lincoln.

Unfortunately, there is a correspondence of this period that leaves a less pleasant feeling in the mind. It is with a Kansas politician, one Mark Delahay, who had written him saying evidently that he would like to go to the Chicago convention as a delegate, but that he did not have money enough, and probably intimating that if he did go he would support Mr. Lincoln. Delahay was not a stranger to Mr. Lincoln. He had known him when on the Circuit in earlier years— known him as a rather gay lawyer. Delahay later had settled in Kansas and had been active in the struggle against the introduction of slavery. He had urged Mr. Lincoln to come to Kansas to speak, and it was probably he that finally persuaded him to do so and arranged his itinerary. It is certain that he was Delahay's guest while there. Probably feeling that he was under obligations to the man, Lincoln wrote a letter in reply to his hint for money to go to the Chicago convention, which is the only one, I believe, of its kind in all his published correspondence. In it he tells Delahay that he cannot enter the ring on the money basis, first, because in the main it is wrong, and secondly, because he has not and cannot get the money. He goes on to say, however, that there are certain objects in a political contest for which money is both right and indispensable. Evidently he thinks paying the expenses of a delegate to a national convention may be one of them, for he says that he will furnish Delahay $100 to bear the expense of the trip.

In this same letter Delahay had asked his help in his ambition to be made one of the first senators from Kansas. Lincoln tells him there is nothing he can do for him as he is not personally acquainted with a single member of the legislature. As for his friendship for him, "that friendship," he says, "was abundantly manifest by me last December in Kansas." One of Lincoln's early appointments as President was Delahay as surveyor general of Kansas and Nebraska. Later he made him United States district judge for Kansas, where he seems to have made a scandalous record. It is hard to believe that at the time Lincoln was showing so many favors to the man he believed him to be a corrupt politician. He knew that he had been a staunch supporter of anti-slavery doctrines in Kansas; if charges of corruption came to him he probably set them down as largely due to political hostility. It was doubtless a case where he was favoring a man that he did not thoroughly know. The idea that he was purchasing a vote at the Chicago convention is of course absurd. As a matter of fact, the Kansas delegates were instructed for Seward, and Lincoln advised Delahay when he knew this: "Don't stir them up to anger, but come along to the convention and I will do as I said about expenses."

The Illinois Republicans did not get around to choose their candidate for President until the 10th of May, less than a fortnight before the National Convention was held. Why Decatur was chosen for that convention I do not know, but there is a certain satisfaction in having it so. Decatur, as we know, was where Lincoln had first landed when he came into Illinois, and two or three times a year at least, after he was admitted to the bar, he had spent more or less time in the town. In scores of ways he was bound to its people, so that when the convention met there in May, 1860, he knew that he was going among friends; but he knew well enough, too, that

[390]

he was not going to a unanimous convention. There was a strong group of Seward men in the body and a few supporters of Bates. For instance, one of his oldest friends, O. H. Browning, with whose family Lincoln had been intimate since the early days in Vandalia, was doubtful of the wisdom of nominating Lincoln, and much preferred that Bates should be the candidate. It is interesting to recall that when the delegates to the Chicago convention were being named at Decatur and Browning's name was up, Richard Oglesby urged Lincoln to disapprove of it. He refused. He knew all about Browning, he said, and it would be a good deal safer for him to be in Chicago with the delegation, where they could keep an eye on him, than working on the outside.

There is no doubt that Lincoln was distressed at the convention, as he had been from the start, by the thought of what seemed to him his unfitness as compared with that of Governor Seward. We have more than one proof of this feeling. It was in his mind as he watched the struggle between his own friends and those of Seward. At one point the debate grew hot to the point of an exchange of unpleasant epithets between the speakers. Lincoln sat crouching at one side, a picture of humiliation and despair.

There probably was no serious question in Lincoln's or his followers' minds but that the convention would select him, but no one could have foreseen the enthusiasm with which it was done. This was due to the vent that was given to pent-up emotions by the introduction of a banner mounted on two old fence rails, announcing Lincoln as

## THE RAIL CANDIDATE
## FOR PRESIDENT IN 1860.

The rails, so the legend below the headlines ran, were from "a lot of 3,000 split in 1830 by John Hanks"—he carried the banner—"and Abe Lincoln, whose father was the first pioneer of Macon County." (The legend was wrong in this statement—there were several settlers in Macon County ahead of Thomas Lincoln.)

Probably never in the political history of this country has there been anything picked up more quickly as a fitting campaign cry than those rails, unless perhaps the log cabin in the days of Harrison. Here was something typifying a stage in the development of the man, most precious to the great mass of self-made Americans. He knew what labor meant, for they all knew that cutting rails was real labor. There began that day at Decatur, when John Hanks marched into the hall with the rail that Abe made, an outburst of pioneer enthusiasm which has never been equalled in the country. Slogans, campaign signs, cartoons from now on used the rail as a party symbol.

What had happened at Decatur no doubt encouraged Mr. Lincoln that he had a chance at Chicago. One of the young men who was in his office at that time says that he had begun to build White House castles for Lincoln after the Cooper Union speech, but he would only laugh indulgently when he talked to him and say, "John, I haven't a chance in a hundred." But things moved fast now. John did not give up the idea, even prepared a speech which he expected to have a chance to deliver in case Mr. Lincoln was nominated. He asked Mr. Lincoln to hear it, but for a long time he declined. Then one afternoon, coming into the office, he said, "Well, John, I think I feel strong enough this afternoon to stand that speech."

One of the cleverest manœuvers of Lincoln's supporters was securing the convention for Chicago. It gave outsiders a chance to see what Illinois thought of her candidate, how they were willing to work for him. Held anywhere else it would have been practically impossible to have had on the ground a large group of men pledged to Lincoln's support, nor would it have been possible for them to have worked with the same self-assurance that they did in Chicago.

Simmered down, we can say that Lincoln's nomination for the Presidency in Chicago on May 19, 1860, was due, first, to William H. Seward's enemies, and, second, to his own friends. The honor of engineering the extraordinary effort necessary to convince a majority of the delegates, first that Seward could not be elected in Pennsylvania, Indiana, Illinois and New Jersey, and secondly, that Abraham Lincoln could, belongs to Judge David Davis, on whose circuit Lincoln had long traveled and whose personal devotion to the man exceeded even his political conviction that he was the best candidate. In a letter written me some years ago by Judge John M. Scott, of Bloomington, I find this judgment on Davis' Chicago work, and I think those who have studied the operations of the convention closest, will agree that it is a sound judgment:

"It is the belief of many that that which did more than any one thing else to force the nomination of Mr. Lincoln after the assembling of the convention was the personal power and influence of Judge David Davis, and without which it is not thought he would have received the nomination. Judge Davis possessed unusual power and ability to control a body of men by forming combinations and otherwise, but most of all by the force of his personal character. He was present with the coming of the first members of the convention, and from that time on he was among them—in the day and in the night—entreating and persuading delegates as few men had the ability to do. The cause of his friend was more to him than it would have been had it been personal to himself. He rested not in the great work from the time it commenced until the hour of triumph came. By nature he was vehement and forceful, but when aroused by an intense purpose he wielded an influence few men could withstand. This overcame when entreaty and persuasion failed."

# IN THE FOOTSTEPS OF THE LINCOLNS

To scores of the ablest men in the country Illinois' victory was a tragedy—a tragedy because it was Seward's defeat. In their judgment the nomination was due him not only because he had been so long the leader of the cause, but because of his experience, his training, his proved ability in public affairs. His rejection seemed a calamity to them. In the tremendous demonstration that followed Lincoln's selection the distress of Seward's supporters impressed even the boys in the crowd, as in the following story of the convention by W. T. Norton, of Alton, Illinois:

"I was then in school at Lake Forest. In company with my roommate, I came down to witness the great convention on the last day of its session. We got up at 5 o'clock in the morning, went down to the wigwam and planted ourselves against the main doorway. There we waited until the doors were opened at 9 o'clock. The rush of the crowd carried us down into the pit, clear to the delegates' platform. Boy-like, we climbed upon the edge of the platform, and no one had a better view of the proceedings than ourselves. I remember the roll call of states for the presidential nomination, and the response of the partisans of Lincoln, Seward, Chase, Cameron, Bates, as they were successively placed in nomination. It was at once noticeable, judging from the volume of the applause each candidate's name evoked, that, whatever the preference of the delegates, the spectators were overwhelmingly with Lincoln, with Seward's followers next in strength. Not only was the vast crowd inside for Lincoln, but the masses swarming outside were likewise cheering wildly for the man from Illinois. The clamor for Lincoln was not only enthusiastic, but insistent. Doubtless it had its effect on the delegates.

"Had the convention been held elsewhere than in Chicago, Seward, then the national leader of the new party, would doubtless have been nominated, but the crowd in the convention hall, and the supporters outside who echoed their shouts, were for Lincoln and would not be denied. Was this the prophetic instinct of 'coming events casting their shadows before'? The enthusiasm in the wigwam as the balloting progressed and the successive results were announced is indescribable, but the scene itself is indelibly inscribed on my memory. I have seen many great assemblies since, and varied national conventions, but never one like this, when the new party of freedom, in

[394]

its stalwart youth was choosing its leader with the foresight of those guided by inspiration. Of the speeches I recall but two which impressed me especially. One was that of Norman B. Judd, chairman of the Illinois delegation, in placing Lincoln in nomination. The other was that of William F. Evarts of the New York delegation who, after what seemed long delay, and in response to persistent calls of 'New York! New York!' rose to accede to the will of the majority as expressed on the third ballot. It was a bitter pill for Evarts and the entire New York delegation, whose idol had fallen. They were blindly devoted to Seward, and had moved their hosts to Chicago in full confidence of victory.

"I recall Evarts as he rose to speak—tall, straight, and spare of figure, with tears of disappointment coursing down his high-bred face. But he was a patriot and a statesman as well as a partisan, and made a wonderful speech in giving the adhesion of the Empire State to the new leader, who had come out of the West. I do not remember what he said, only the effect and the impression, and that he captured the crowd and the convention.

"After the last change of the vote of some state—I think Pennsylvania—on the final ballot had assured the nomination of Lincoln, pandemonium broke loose. The people had had their way. How they shouted and yelled and cheered, again and again, keeping up the din for a half hour! It seemed as if the roof of the building would be lifted up by the volume of cheers and the sides fall out to give them room. Outside a salute was being fired, but the boom of the cannon was drowned in the wild hurrahs of the people. I could see the smoke drift past the windows, but heard no report."

Mr. Norton's theory that noise nominated Lincoln is often met. It is not flattering to the convention. Carl Schurz, who was a delegate from Wisconsin and followed Seward to the end, has this to say:

"Much has been said about the superior volume and fierceness of the shouting for Lincoln in the packed galleries and its effect upon the minds of the delegates. But that is mere reporters' talk. The historic fact is that as the convention would not take the risks involved in the nomination of Seward, it had no other alternative than to select Lincoln as the man who satisfied the demands of the earnest anti-slavery men without subjecting the party to the risks thought to be inseparable from the nomination of Seward. That the popular demonstrations for Lincoln in and around the convention were indeed well planned and organized is true, but they were by no means a decisive factor, without them the result would have been the same."

Everything that happened at the Chicago convention was told and retold to Lincoln of course by the jubilant group of friends that had fought for him. Nobody would have enjoyed more the episodes of that strenuous week than he. And nothing could have given him a better idea of what they had gone through for him than the condition in which one of the most dignified of the delegates returned to Springfield. This was Judge Stephen T. Logan. (It might have been anybody else!) Mr. Henry T. Rankin describes the judge's appearance before and after the convention.

"He had gone there," says Mr. Rankin, "to head the Illinois delegation, clad in the finest new suit he had ever worn, and his head crowned with a tall new shining silk hat, the best that our Springfield 'Adams, Hatter,' had ever made. He came back with his suit a sight to behold, dusty, and wrinkled beyond all recognition, for he had not been out of it since he had left Springfield. He came back wearing a little Scotch cap, the glossy tall silk hat having been left somewhere in the debris of the wigwam, near Lake Michigan, after Logan had beaten it into shapeless ruin over the heads and shoulders of his fellow-delegates upon announcement of the third ballot. No one would credit this report at first, but everybody who had been there said it was true—except the judge. And he was silent."

Mr. Rankin further tells of the meeting between his own father and Judge Logan. ' "Rankin" '—he said it in a whisper for he had shouted away all the voice he had in Chicago— ' "I am even with Lincoln now. He made me drop him and vote for Trumbull for United States Senator in 1856, to keep Matteson out. I cried then like a baby with vexation and wrath. Now I've had my revenge. He will be President," and the two gray Kentuckians—old Whig veterans of the

Henry Clay campaigns—clasped each other, crying for joy like children."

In that picture we have the second biggest factor in the first nomination of Abraham Lincoln to the Presidency—the first being the opposition to Seward.

# XXX

## AWAITING THE VERDICT

A TALKING Presidential nominee is often his own worst enemy. The more excited the public, the sharper the division of opinion, the more damage he does himself and his party every time he opens his mouth or writes a letter. To be sure, we have candidates who must talk, never having said anything before nomination. Abraham Lincoln was not in this class. He had something to show—the soundest thinking, the most complete as well as the clearest statement of the subject that divided the country—the extension of slavery—made by any man in the long conflict. For six years he had given at least half of his conscious and probably all of his unconscious mind to developing his arguments. No national campaign committee ever had a more dignified and convincing body of material to send out than that which Lincoln provided the Republicans. And they made the most of it. Editions of his speeches, particularly of the seven debates with Douglas and the Cooper Union speech, were published in New York, Ohio and Chicago by different agencies, and spread liberally over the country.

Lincoln now took the position that he had said repeatedly all he had to say on the subject. He may have had some idea that everybody knew what he thought, but he must have been soon dissuaded, for after his nomination there descended upon him from North and South crowds of visitors and floods of letters, asking his opinions, begging him to come and tell them what his policy would be if elected, or to put it down in a letter so that they might show it to their friends. It was the discouraging experience that every public man suffers when, after having spent himself for years in expounding his views, he suddenly faces the fact that, after all, only a handful of people have listened to him and only a few of them understand what he has been saying.

Lincoln was lucky, however, in having these books and pamphlets at hand to turn over to those of his correspondents and visitors who seemed to him serious enough to really absorb the content of his argument. Copy after copy of the thin, black-covered book containing the debates with Douglas, published in 1860 in Columbus, Ohio, has been turning up from that day to this, bearing the inscription, "A—B— From A. Lincoln," on its title page. But there were not books and pamphlets enough to give to everybody, nor did everybody seem worthy of them, so that Mr. Lincoln finally instructed his new secretary, John G. Nicolay, to prepare a circular letter to fit the case. It is entirely Lincolnesque in terms. He had received many letters asking for his opinions, he said, but he had also received a greater number beseeching him to say nothing whatever on any point of political doctrine. His position, this second class of letters declared, was well known when he was nominated, and he must not embarrass the canvass by undertaking to shift or modify it, and that was his judgment and decision. Hundreds of copies of this letter probably went out.

All this did not prevent his answering many correspondents, particularly those from the South, with painstaking personal letters. Would he not write something disclaiming all intention to interfere with slavery in the states? they asked him. "It would do no good," he would answer. "I have already done this many, many times, and it is in print and open to all who will read. Those who will not read or heed what I have already publicly said would not read or heed a repetition of it. 'If they hear not Moses and the prophets neither will they be persuaded though one rose from the dead.' "

*As I would not be a slave, so I would not be a master. This expresses my idea of democracy — Whatever differs from this, to the extent of the difference, is no democracy —*

*A. Lincoln —*

FACSIMILE OF A DEFINITION OF DEMOCRACY WRITTEN AND SIGNED BY LINCOLN FOR MRS. BRADWELL, WIFE OF HIS FRIEND JUDGE J. B. BRADWELL.

They wanted his "conservative views."

"If I were to labor a month," he answered, "I could not express my conservative views and intentions more clearly and strongly than they are expressed in our platform and in my many speeches already printed and before the public, . . . yet . . . I have not decided that I will not do substantially what you suggest. I will not forbear from doing so merely on punctilio and pluck. If I do finally abstain, it will be because of apprehension that it would do harm. For the good men of the South—and I regard the majority of them as such—I have no objection to repeat seventy and seven times. But I have bad men to deal with, both North and South; men who are eager for something new upon which to base new misrepresentations; men who would like to frighten me, or at least fix upon me the character of timidity and cowardice. They would seize upon almost any letter I could write as being an 'awful coming down.' I intend keeping my eye upon these gentlemen, and to not unnecessarily put any weapons in their hands."

Of course he was right in thinking that any expression that came from him now would be maliciously twisted and turned. Misrepresentation, ridicule, willful lying are recognized tools in politican campaigns. The more acute the division of opinion the more freely they are employed. Good men go yearly into office in these United States hampered by suspicion and false judgments born of the reckless indifference to the truth which so often characterizes our political campaigns. They are handicapped from the start in their best efforts. We have it always with us, but our history affords no more flagrant example than what happened now to Abraham Lincoln. We are far enough away from his nomination —public opinion upon the man's worth is too well grounded for us not to read with shocked indignation the characterizations that were freely circulated and freely accepted by those who opposed his doctrines.

"He was a vulgar village politician," one great metropolitan daily declared; "a fourth-rate lawyer." The Cooper Union speech, which Horace Greeley, who heard it and who at the moment was not too friendly to Lincoln, declared to be the very best political address to which he had ever listened, and he added, "I have heard some of Webster's greatest," his opponents now sneered at as "hackneyed," "illiterate," "unmitigated trash interlarded with coarse clumsy jokes." This, of course, was angry, uncontrolled partisan expression, intended to besmirch and belittle Lincoln. It had no relation to fact nor was it intended to have.

Mischievous and misleading accusations began to spread —he had belonged to the Know Nothing or American party —had been seen going into Know Nothing lodges. So widespread and serious was the charge that he had to deny it to individuals. "I suppose," he wrote one gentleman, "that as good or even better men than I may have been in Know

Nothing lodges, but, in point of fact, I never was in one. . . .
And now a word of caution. Our adversaries think they can
gain a point if they can force me to openly deny the charge
by which some degree of offense would be given to the
Americans. For this reason it must not publicly appear that
I am paying any attention to the charge."

They tried to stir up trouble for him in Kentucky. Samuel
Haycraft, of Elizabethtown, Kentucky—we met this gentleman in an earlier chapter—wrote asking if it would not be a
pleasure for him to visit his old home. "Indeed it would be,"
Lincoln replied, "but would it be safe? Would not the
people lynch me?" He meant it to be jocular, and told the
story to friends. It was not long before it was spread over
the country that Mr. Lincoln said that a trap had been set
to inveigle him into Kentucky in order to do violence to him.
He was distressed, particularly on Mr. Haycraft's account.
It took much explaining to be sure he was set right in his
old neighbor's mind, as well as cautioning to see that he did
not make matters worse by his explaining.

Forged extracts, pretending to be from old speeches of
his were circulated. An outrageous one which particularly
incensed him characterized Jefferson as a man of "repulsive
character, continually puling about liberty, equality and the
degrading curse of slavery, yet he brought his own children
to the hammer and made money by his debaucheries. Even
at his death he did not manumit his numerous offspring, but
left them still a prey to degradation and the cart whip." A
nasty bit for a man as decent in thought and as careful of his
facts as Mr. Lincoln to see passed from newspaper to newspaper. He could do nothing more than to tell those who sent
the clippings to him, asking an explanation, that he never
said anything like it at any time or place.

A forgery of this sort, once it is set on its lawless round

of the press, however out of character with the man to whom it is credited, is hard to kill. This dishonest practice of putting into Lincoln's mouth for political purposes words that he never spoke still goes on. In the present year there was spread through the press of the country an alleged quotation from Lincoln, beginning, "I see a dark cloud on the horizon, and that dark cloud is coming from Rome," followed by a prophecy of a disastrous struggle with "Rome and her allies." The quotation was a clumsy fabrication.

For many years there has cropped up at intervals a forged quotation pretending to give his views on prohibition. It is often backed up with what looks like documentary evidence. Mr. Lincoln, it is claimed, said in a speech in the Illinois House of Representatives in December, 1840, when an act to regulate tavern and grocery licenses was under discussion:

"Prohibition will work great injury to the cause of temperance. It is a species of intemperance within itself, for it goes beyond the bounds of reason, in that it attempts to control a man's appetite by legislation and makes a crime out of things that are not crimes. A prohibition law strikes a blow at the very principles upon which our government was founded."

But the Journal of the House shows no such remarks. The only recorded connection of Lincoln with the bill was moving that the following amendment be laid on the table:

"That after the passage of this act no person shall be licensed to sell vinous or spirituous liquors in this state, and that any person who violates this act by selling such liquors shall be fined the sum of $1,000, to be recovered before any court having competent jurisdiction."

This was done by a vote of 75 to 8.

Years ago I had a careful search made in the House Journal and in the Springfield newspapers of the period for this quotation, but without result. When it cropped up again this year with a cunning use of documentary references, I wrote to the Illinois State Historical Library, asking if any proof of the authenticity of the quotation had been recently discovered; this was my reply:

"We have had hundreds of letters in regard to this from all over the United States, and also from England. This statement cannot be found in any of the public writings or speeches of Lincoln, and I herewith enclose to you the extract from the House Journal of December 19, 1840-41, page 136, entitled 'An Act to amend an Act,' etc.

"There were no speeches made on the subject. The files of the Springfield newspapers covering that period have been gone over very carefully time and time again by both the people in favor of prohibition and those against it, and they have failed to find that Mr. Lincoln ever made such a statement, so I do not know where they could go to verify it. . . ."

Throughout this period that we are now following, from Lincoln's nomination in May to his election in November, he lived in an atmosphere of caricaturing, misrepresentation, intriguing and lying, which became darker and thicker as public feeling on the slavery question became more intense and angry. One of the tests of a man's fitness for public office is the control, the humor, and the discretion with which he meets this deplorable but inevitable feature of public life. Lincoln had had experience enough with the meanness of men to know something of what he was in for, and the general good temper, quiet and cleverness with which he handled these partisan attacks augured well for the future; he must have realized that what was happening to him now was but an insignificant sample of what would come in the near future unless the public excitement could be allayed.

This unpleasant side of his experience as a nominee was, after all, but an episode. He was too busy from morning until night receiving in the Governor's room at the state capitol, which had been hospitably turned over to him as a reception office, men and women from one end of the country to the other, hordes of them merely friendly and curious, but numbers politically significant.

Judge David Davis and Leonard Swett, who had been his most important backers in Chicago, went East soon after the nomination urging men important in the Republican organization—most of them men who had been bitterly disappointed by the result at Chicago, who knew little of Lincoln other than his opinions, and who doubted his political wisdom and executive ability—to come to Springfield. Conspicuous among the visitors thus secured was Thurlow Weed, the editor of the Albany Argus, the friend and backer of Seward, the enemy of Horace Greeley—an enmity returned with interest. Weed had been so overwhelmed by the defeat that all he wanted was to get far away and forget the whole campaign, but Davis and Swett persuaded him to visit Lincoln in Springfield, and he finally came—to go away, as many another man was doing now, with the conviction that here was a sagacious, frank, self-directed man that would have to be dealt with intelligently and honestly.

Practically everybody of understanding and good will that came went away reconciled. One of the finest of recent contributions to this getting acquainted with Mr. Lincoln after the nomination, comes in a letter of Carl Schurz to his wife, for here you find another Seward man, of very different type of mind and training from Weed, well satisfied. His letter gives the best picture that we have, I think, of the simplicity and naturalness of Mr. Lincoln's home and public life at this period:

"I was with Lincoln yesterday," Mr. Schurz writes Mrs. Schurz under date of July 25, 1860. "He is the same kindly old fellow, quite as unpretentious and ingenuous as ever. The reception committee had reserved quarters for me at the hotel, and Lincoln was one of the first to knock at my door. He wears a linen sackcoat and a hat of doubtful age, but his appearance is neat and cleanly. We talked in my room nearly two hours. I was lying on my bed resting, when he came, and he insisted on my remaining so. He talked of the presidential election with as much placid, cheerful frankness as if we were discussing the potato crop. . . . In the evening I took supper with Lincoln. The Madam was very nicely dressed up, and is already quite skillful in handling her fan. She chats fairly well, and will adapt herself to the White House cleverly enough. Lincoln's boys are typical Western youngsters. One of them insisted on going about barefooted. After supper, to which a number of 'leading men' had been invited, we lit our cigars and chatted. At eight o'clock the Wideawakes came to escort me to my mass meeting in the capitol. I have never seen so large a torchlight procession. Lincoln insisted on accompanying us, although he had not appeared in public since his nomination. He declared that he must once hear 'that tremendous speaker.' And so the Wideawakes surrounded 'Old Abe' and me; thus arm in arm we marched to the capitol."

Such a visit as Schurz's must have been a great delight to Mr. Lincoln. And then in scores of ways he was receiving proofs of personal friendship, always so dear to him. Among the recently published letters of this period is one from a boyhood friend, Nathaniel N. Grigsby, whose brother Aaron had married Lincoln's sister. Grigsby was now living in Missouri, and he evidently had announced to Lincoln his intention of voting for him. Lincoln's reply shows him more interested in giving the news of his own family than he is in the possibility of a vote, for, after telling him various bits of family history, he adds that Grigsby can vote for him if his neighbors will let him, but he would advise him not to get into trouble about it.

Other friends from southwestern Indiana as well as from Kentucky wrote him. Lincolns from different parts of the country tried to discover if there was any relationship between them. All this personal side he enjoyed. Then, too, he took real satisfaction in the way the elections were going. He watched every state, almost every precinct, like a hawk, and

PORTRAIT OF ABRAHAM LINCOLN MADE JUST BEFORE HE LEFT SPRINGFIELD, ILL., FOR HIS INAUGURATION AS PRESIDENT OF THE UNITED STATES

This is one of the first pictures showing Lincoln with a beard. The original negative is owned by H. W. Fay, custodian of the Lincoln Tomb

in this period vastly extended his knowledge of the personnel of the Republican party. He learned not merely the names, but something of the abilities and character of state, as well as of local leaders. This, of course, was an extending into the nation his old political practice of mapping out the area in which a political struggle was on and learning the actors to the last man.

We have had evidence enough already of the way in which Lincoln went through the minds of men with whom he talked. He put his habit to good use now. These scores upon scores of politicians who wrote him or visited him in person, underwent a more or less unconscious scrutiny and appraisement of which they could have had no knowledge. He found out whom they hated or suspected, and balanced it by more or less knowledge of those who hated or suspected them, for it was not only misrepresentation of himself that he was obliged to meet, it was misrepresentation of the factions in the party. He had a busy time trying to pull together these divisions. When it was known, for instance, that Thurlow Weed had visited him, he was bombarded with warnings against Weed. It was taken as a certainty that Weed was intriguing, and he had to write and say to more than one that he "saw no signs whatever of the intriguing, that he had asked for nothing." His general attitude toward those who gave him what he called "historical details of local troubles" was that he had not heard so much upon the subject as they had supposed, that he was slow to listen to incriminations among friends, and that "his sincere wish was that both sides and everybody would let bygones be bygones and look to the present and future only."

Fortunately for Lincoln and for the Republican interest there were great bodies of men in all the northern states who sensed as deeply as he did this necessity of letting bygones be bygones. It was a question now not of men, but of the very fundamentals of human liberty. Happily enough he had evidence in his own circle of the working of this superior sense. For more than ten years now he had been estranged from a friend to whom he had once been deeply attached, Cyrus Edwards, who felt that in 1849 Lincoln had not played fair in regard to the General Land Office. No explanation of Mr. Lincoln's had ever softened Edwards' feeling of injustice; but now, with the future of the country at stake, he put his old grievance behind him and wrote to Joseph Gillespie —the friend of them both—that he pledged "a word which has never failed that he would bury the hatchet with Lincoln."

The political strength of the Republicans in the campaign of 1860 lay in the division of the Democrats. There were three tickets in the field, and so long as these three tickets or any two of them could be kept from fusing, Republican success was a practical certainty. Lincoln watched, catlike, every move on the part of Douglas to manage his competitors to his own advantage. He warned on all sides when he saw a sign of weakness, but there are no evidences in his letters that he ever had serious anxiety about the result. The Republicans grew not only in numbers, but in determination and in enthusiasm as the weeks went on. Lincoln's name was on their lips, but the fervor of a great idea was stirring their souls. They were swept by something of the same depth of feeling, the same largeness of view that had been driving Lincoln himself. Sitting there in Springfield through these weeks waiting for the election, Lincoln must have felt at times almost dismay at the tremendous thing which was sweeping through the North and West, of which he in all probability soon would be the leader, which he must hold together, put to use. It was at the moment so much greater than any man, and yet it was something a man might wreck by stupidity, vanity, obstinacy. At the same time it must have been heartening to see his long faith in the fundamental unsoundness of the thing which he had been fighting, demonstrated as it was. The opposition was crumbling daily. But there was tragedy in the disunion. Numbers of his opponents, feeling defeat in the air, did not hesitate to declare that they would shake the dust of the Union off their feet if the Republicans were victorious. The threat came to Lincoln often and more often as the election approached. He dismissed it in words which sound strangely to-day—sound as if he had never up to that time seriously considered the idea of secession. One visitor who came to him reports him as saying that there was no real disunionism in the country, and to a correspondent he wrote, "The people of the South have too much good sense and good temper to attempt the ruin of the government, at least so I hope and believe." It was treating as impossible a fearful possibility which he had more than once recognized in the past years and resolutely declared would be met by resistance if it eventuated. "We won't get out of the Union, and you shan't," he had said in 1856. Again and again similar declarations are found in his speeches.

A very good idea of the seriousness of the attention he had already given to the threat is found in a letter to Alexander Stephens, of Atlanta, Georgia, written four months before his nomination—a remarkable letter, only in the last few years given to the public, the longest letter that he ever wrote, he declared. In it he gives the historical basis for his belief that there was no legal way for a state to withdraw from the Union, that secession was revolution, and must be treated as revolution. It is probable that the material for this document was collected at the time he was ransacking the records to discover what the fathers of the country thought about the right of Congress to keep slavery out of the territories—the investigation which gave weight and importance to the Cooper Union speech.

Lightly as Lincoln tried to treat the threat of disunion in this period, there is evidence enough that he had sensed the possibility of the attempt ever since 1854, and that he was clear in his mind how it should be met. But now he must quiet alarms—ignore dangers. This was the policy of the Republicans—Seward, Schurz and Bryant were all characterizing the threats of disunion as largely political—an attempt of the opposing parties to persuade the public that Lincoln's selection was bound to drive the South into secession. And Lincoln sitting idle in Springfield must not embarrass those who were fighting the battle in the field.

His judgment of the result of the campaign was justified in November—victory, but a victory that had its sting. One million, eight hundred sixty-six thousand, four hundred and fifty-two men had cast their votes for him, but over two and three-quarter millions had cast their votes for others. The weakness of this majority was that it was divided between three candidates, the most popular of whom was Stephen A. Douglas. Lincoln had nearly half a million votes more than Douglas. The startling feature in his election was the sectional division of the country it showed. In ten adjoining states Lincoln had not a single vote, and in fifteen states he had no electoral vote. The Union was politically if not physically divided.

But Lincoln was not thinking overmuch of future perils as, alone with the operators, he received the returns of the election in the Springfield telegraph office, the night of November 6, 1860. His mind was busy with his future work —first of all his Cabinet.

The great-great-great-great-grandson of Samuel Lincoln who, two hundred and twenty-three years before had come from old England to settle on the coast of Massachusetts, had his mind on his task, in this moment of triumph and power even as all the long line of toilers who had preceded him, at every crisis of their lives. It was their daring and their endurance that were in his veins and had brought him where he was and now in victory he did as they would have done, kept his hand on his plough.

THE END

# INDEX

# INDEX

# INDEX

# INDEX

Lincoln & Herndon, 322, 343
Lincoln Farm Association, 95
"Lincoln Louisville Loop," 106
Lincoln, Robert, 194, 251, 252, 253
"Lincoln the Lawyer," 313
Linder, U. F., 259
"Little Giant,"—*See* Douglas, Stephen A.
Locke, D. R., 245, 363, 379, 380, 382
Logan, Gen. John, 312
Logan, Stephen A., 281
Logan, Stephen T., 396
"Lost Speech."—*See* Speech, "Anti-Nebraska"
Louis XIV, 31
Lovejoy, Rev. Elijah P., 233, 234
Lovejoy Memorial Association, 299
Lovejoy, Owen, 333, 334, 344
Lowell, James Russell, 245

## M

Massachusetts Colony, 3, 17
Massachusetts Historical Society, 10
Masters, Edgar Lee, 199, 222
Matthews, Stanley, 275
McCormick, Cyrus H., 315
McIntyre, D. T., 259
McLean County Historical Society, 330, 331
McNeill, John, 214, 216, 217, 218
Medill, Joseph, 329, 331, 333, 337, 383, 385
Mexican War, 281-282, 283, 363
Milliken, James, 362
Missouri Compromise, 322, 332, 335, 340, 341, 346, 355, 361, 382
Monthly Meeting, Philadelphia, 78
Moores, Charles W., 231, 252, 256, 301, 313
Moravians, 44
Morgan, R. P., 314-315
Morrow, Governor, 275
"Mud sill" theory, 375

## N

Nall, J. L., 129
Nasby, Petroleum V.—*See* Locke, David
Nebraska Bill, 323
New Jersey, call of, 30-43

"New Harmony Gazette, The," 151
Newton, Joseph Fort, 355
Nicolay, John G., 371, 399
Norton, W. T., 299, 365, 394
Nott, Charles C., 378
Nutt, Samuel, 35
Nye, James W., 380

## O

Offutt, Denton, 164-167, 175, 187, 291
Oglesby, Richard, 391
"Old Salem Lincoln League, The," 170
Oregon, acquisition of, 284
Owen, Robert, 135, 151-152
Owen, William, 135

## P

Palmer, John M., 333
Parker, Theodore, 355
Peck, Rev. J. M., 282
Peck, Robert, 5, 6
Penn, William, 37
"Personal Recollections of Abraham Lincoln," 212
"Personal Recollections of Jane Martin Johns," 307-309
Pickett, George E., 262
Pierce, Franklin, 332
Pigeon Church, 141-145, 147
Pitcher, John, 149
Plymouth Colony, 19
Polk, President, 273, 281, 282
Pond, Henry E., 260, 261
Pond, Marvin B., 261
Pond, Samuel Sweezy, 260, 261
Pope, John, 91
Puritan Plantation, 39
Puritans, 5, 11, 18, 25, 26, 44, 69
Pusey, Dr. W. A., 131

## Q

Quakers, 26, 31, 39, 44, 69

## R

Ralston, Governor, 157
Rankin, Henry B., 212, 269-270, 343, 396

[416]

# INDEX

# INDEX